Visions of the Heart

Issues Involving Indigenous Peoples in Canada

Visions of the Heart

Issues Involving Indigenous Peoples in Canada

Gina Starblanket & David Long

with Olive Patricia Dickason

FIFTH EDITION

OXFORD

UNIVERSITY PRESS

OXFORD
UNIVERSITY PRESS

Oxford University Press is a department of the University of Oxford.
It furthers the University's objective of excellence in research, scholarship,
and education by publishing worldwide. Oxford is a registered trade mark of
Oxford University Press in the UK and in certain other countries.

Published in Canada by
Oxford University Press
8 Sampson Mews, Suite 204,
Don Mills, Ontario M3C 0H5 Canada

www.oupcanada.com

Library and Archives Canada Cataloguing in Publication
Title: Visions of the heart : issues involving Indigenous Peoples in Canada / edited by Gina
Starblanket and David Long with Olive Patricia Dickason.
Names: Starblanket, Gina, editor. | Long, David Alan, 1958- editor. | Dickason, Olive Patricia,
1920-2011, editor.
Description: Fifth edition. | Includes bibliographical references and index.
Identifiers: Canadiana (print) 20190117117 | Canadiana (ebook) 2019011715X | ISBN 9780199033447
(softcover) | ISBN 9780199033461 (EPUB)
Subjects: CSH: Native peoples—Canada—Textbooks. | LCGFT: Textbooks.
Classification: LCC E78.C2 V58 2019 | DDC 971.004/97—dc2

Cover and interior design: Sherill Chapman

Oxford University Press is committed to our environment.
This book is printed on Forest Stewardship Council® certified paper
and comes from responsible sources.

Printed and bound in Canada

4 5 6 - 23 22 21

Contents

13 ● Moosehide Tanning and Wellness in the North   220

Mandee McDonald

14 ● Enacting Reconciliation   237

Joyce Green

Imagining New Futures: A Concluding Dialogue   252

Acknowledgements

It has been an absolute pleasure putting together this fifth edition of *Visions of the Heart*. David and I particularly appreciate the contributions and support received from a couple of people at Oxford University Press, including Richard Tallman, who provided thoughtful, challenging, and detailed copy editing. Thank you, Richard, for helping each chapter in this collection to become better and for advancing the collection as a whole. We are also especially thankful to Mariah Fleetham, the Assistant Editor for this edition of *Visions*. Her patience, encouragement, thoughtfulness, and good humour helped all of us bring this project to fruition in a good way. We have never met face to face, Mariah, but thank you for being so good at your job and so wonderfully supportive of us as well as our collaborators. We would also like to extend our thanks to Amy Gordon, the Associate Editor on this project, who offered important support and direction at the outset of this edition.

David and I both believe strongly that projects such as this volume are gifts that have been passed on to those who are mindful of their importance and who are willing to receive and then carry them out with gratitude. When David first approached me about this project in 2017, I initially declined the invitation. After coming to know him better and reflecting on the reasons why I set out to be an educator, namely, to try to cultivate awareness of and critical inquiry into matters of concern to Indigenous people, I ultimately agreed to take on this project. As the senior co-editor, David has taken great care to ensure that each of my expectations are realized, proving to be a tireless support, advocate, and friend in the face of surprises, challenges, and life changes that arose along the way, and for this I thank him.

It was over 20 years ago when David first approached the late Olive Dickason to ask if she had the time and inclination to work with him on putting together a book of readings that would engage current issues involving Indigenous peoples in Canada. He told Olive that he was aware that a few books on the market at the time addressed "contemporary Native issues in Canada," though he felt strongly that a better understanding of relations between Indigenous peoples and the rest of Canada would benefit not only from more voices, but more importantly from the voices of those who were committed to working across differences in the name of a better future. David was elated as well as humbled when Olive phoned him to say that she would be delighted to work with him on this "rather interesting looking collection."

David often talks about what a great privilege it was to edit the first three editions of *Visions of the Heart* with Olive; he speaks of her with great fondness and respect, having clearly learned a great deal from her over the many years they worked together. For the knowledge and experience she generously passed on to him and that has continued to guide this volume, we are both incredibly grateful. Just as he and Olive befriended each other in their own ways over the years, David and I have in turn developed a strong and unique friendship, one that defies our distinct locations and experiences.

The fourth edition of *Visions of the Heart* did not benefit from Olive's editorial acumen for she passed away peacefully on 12 March 2011 after 91 very full and incredibly interesting years. It is our hope that this fifth edition continues to carry Olive's ever hopeful spirit within it, and we trust that readers will learn to be thankful for all of her gifts and for her generosity of spirit in sharing them with us in a good way.

This edition is therefore not dedicated to Olive, but to all who seek to follow and continue to build upon her good and wise path. She has become one of those ancestors from whom many will continue to draw wisdom, laughter, and inspiration, as her legacy dances on into the future. It is our hope that this volume carries forward the importance of Olive's teachings: that careful, respectful listening to other people's voices and stories invites us to enjoy the gifts of all our relations.

Additionally, David and I gratefully acknowledge the many insights and comments provided by our friends and colleagues, many of whom are contributors to this volume. I especially want to acknowledge the feedback and support that I received from Mandee McDonald, Dallas Hunt, Daniel Voth, Heidi Kiiwetinepinesiik Stark, and Corey Snelgrove.

Finally, we acknowledge the patience, support, love, and encouragement of our families, including David's partner Karen and their children Jennica, Bethany, Sarah, and Kathryn Long, as well as my mother Danette Starblanket, my partner Jonah, and our children Anna-Marie and Aden Rankin.

Gina Starblanket
April 2019

Contributors

Kim Anderson
University of Guelph, Department of Family Relations and Applied Tradition

Jessica Ball
University of Victoria, School of Child and Youth Care

Yale D. Belanger
University of Lethbridge, Political Science Department

Lianne Marie Leda Charlie
Yukon College, School of Liberal Arts

Sara Florence Davidson
University of the Fraser Valley, Teacher Education Department

Joyce Green
University of Regina, Department of Political Science

Jan Hare
University of British Columbia, Department of Indigenous Education

Dallas Hunt
University of British Columbia, Department of English Language and Literatures

Robert Alexander Innes
University of Saskatchewan, Department of Indigenous Studies

David Long
The King's University, Department of Sociology

Jessie Loyer
Mount Royal University, Librarian

Olga Marques
University of Ontario Institute of Technology, Faculty of Social Science and Humanities

Mandee McDonald
Dene Nahjo, Managing Director; PhD student at the University of Alberta

Deborah McGregor
York University, Indigenous Environmental Justice

Lisa Monchalin
Kwantlen Polytechnic University, Department of Criminology

David Newhouse
Trent University, Department of Indigenous Studies

Leanne Betasamosake Simpson
Independent scholar, writer, and artist

Gina Starblanket
University of Calgary, Department of Political Science

Heidi Kiiwetinepinesiik Stark
University of Victoria, Department of Political Science

Daniel Voth
University of Calgary, Department of Political Science

Renae Watchman
Mount Royal University, Departments of English and Indigenous Studies

Introduction

Gina Starblanket and David Long

Like previous iterations, the fifth edition of *Visions of the Heart* is both a reflection of the current social, economic, and political climate in Canada and a critical engagement with that climate by a diverse collection of scholars. Moreover, the editors and contributors continue to acknowledge the importance of being personally and politically connected to the matters we are theorizing and writing about, and also are committed to working towards change. Unlike previous editions, however, this collection brings together representative voices from a growing assortment of Indigenous scholars, activists, artists, and non-Indigenous allies who are aware and unapologetically critical of the limitations in the predominant ways that "Indigenous issues" have been addressed, not only in literary and scholarly works but also in popular writings and a wide variety of mass media and social media contexts. The current edition of *Visions of the Heart* thus features many of these emergent voices alongside the voices of those who have revised and updated their contributions from previous editions.

While a number of common themes and shared perspectives run through the first four editions of *Visions of the Heart*, the uniqueness of each edition reflected the ways their contributors engaged with the emerging issues and perspectives of their times. The fifth edition continues this practice, and readers familiar with the fourth edition will recognize a significant shift in focus from reconciliation to questions of relationship and responsibility. Consequently, contributors to this edition engage Indigenous people's constructions and understandings of the various relationships they inhabit (with the land, waterways, other living beings, and the spirit world), specific relationships between Indigenous and non-Indigenous peoples (kinship, settler-colonial relations, and various forms of coexistence, treaties, and alliances), and the responsibilities these many relationships entail. As discussed in more detail below, this edition of *Visions of the Heart* reflects a fundamental shift that has been occurring over the past two decades in scholarly attention to "Indigenous resurgence." While broadly employed with varying meanings, the term generally encompasses scholarship, forms of activism, nation-building, and theorizing grounded in Indigenous philosophies, intellectual traditions, laws, and relations with creation. Importantly, the ideas, ethics, and values that these sources give rise to are embodied in the everyday; thus, resurgence is not an end goal but a practice or way of life in which the ends and means are not distinct from one another but are one and the same.

What follows, then, is a collection of writings grounded in the belief that Indigenous visions of the future cannot be achieved merely through reconciling Indigenous imperatives and aspirations with those of Canadian society, but by working towards the structural change required for implementation of the forms of relationship that Indigenous peoples want to be part of. Further, while previous editions had as their central concern the need to cultivate understanding and more positive relationships between Indigenous and non-Indigenous peoples in Canada, the editors of this current volume did not want to presume this to be the most crucial aspiration of Indigenous people today, nor did we want to pre-empt other initiatives and processes that Indigenous people might see as necessary in working towards their visions of the future. Rather, our hope was to create "open spaces" for contributors to make these determinations themselves. While this results in a collection that reads very differently from previous editions, the editors of this edition once again invited contributors to engage three rather basic questions in their issue-areas and in their own ways: What are Indigenous individuals, families, communities, and/or nations' hopes for the future? What hindrances stand in the way of these visions? And what do "good ways forward" look like in the lives and communities of Indigenous people and in relations between Indigenous peoples and other peoples in Canada?

Readers of this collection may note that the chapters do not fit within the traditional disciplinary boundaries or classifications through which Indigenous life has often been examined by scholars, and this is because contributors were encouraged to avoid mere descriptions or surveys of an issue and to engage the politics and power relations surrounding their specific topics. As exemplified in Watchman and Innes's examination of Indigenous masculinities (Chapter 8), Hunt's analysis of urban Indigeneity (Chapter 6), and Stark's analysis of the deep relationship between colonialism and gendered violence (Chapter 4), contributors were also urged to challenge simplistic assertions, generalizations, or representations of Indigeneity that often serve to essentialize Indigenous concerns, perspectives, and experiences. Our purpose in challenging totalizing representations of Indigenous life reflects our conviction that nuances, distinctions, and conflicts at times can provide the most important and representative insights into admittedly complicated issues. Many of the authors therefore explore several interrelated themes, and some advance arguments that may seem inconsistent or contradictory. As a result, the representations and analyses of Indigenous and colonial realities that follow are far from uniform and conventional.

Although the diversity of perspectives and ways of engaging issues in the following contributions may unsettle some readers, a degree of diversity in perspective and focus has been a strength of each edition of *Visions of the Heart*. In this edition, for example, while authors such as Watchman and Innes, Simpson (Chapter 3), and Hunt are less concerned, at least for the time being, with the need for dialogue and engagement with non-Indigenous people, others, such as Anderson and Ball (Chapter 9), McDonald (Chapter 13), and Newhouse and Belanger (Chapter 2), are committed to improving the day-to-day struggles experienced by Indigenous people within colonial contexts by strengthening relationships between Indigenous and non-Indigenous peoples. Despite these and other differences, all contributors fundamentally agree that addressing ongoing structures of settler colonialism requires that existing settler populations and newly arrived immigrants accept responsibility to work towards new kinds of relationships, and that all parties in these relationships be committed to engaging in broad, open, honest, and critical dialogue, awareness, and self-reflection. These conversations will undoubtedly raise degrees of discomfort for different audiences, and as in previous editions, readers are encouraged to revisit their own stories, the mythologies they perpetuate, and the assumptions underlying them as they engage with each chapter in this collection.

Understanding the Crises in the Current Relations between Indigenous and Non-Indigenous Peoples in Canada

Fifty years ago, Harold Cardinal (1969, 138) proclaimed in *The Unjust Society* that "the Buckskin Curtain is coming down." While Cardinal's proclamation can be interpreted in a number of ways, this phrase is generally recognized as referring to the metaphorical curtain of ignorance, neglect, and bigotry plaguing Indigenous–non-Indigenous relationships in Canada. By proclaiming a commitment to dismantling the Buckskin Curtain, Cardinal was signalling that Indigenous peoples would henceforth actively combat the myriad forms of oppression they faced and the ongoing denial of their distinct legal and political status. The chapters that follow express commitment on the part of its authors to doing just that. Along with identifying many of the ways that Indigenous peoples are no longer allowing Canada to deny their fundamental and distinct rights, they clearly challenge the perpetuation of Canada's mythological image as a nation committed to cultivating peaceful, honourable relations with Indigenous peoples. In doing so, they support Cardinal's assertion that as the Buckskin Curtain comes down, the historical and ongoing operations of settler colonialism will be exposed.

Cardinal was particularly keen to reveal the hypocrisy and injustice in Pierre Elliott Trudeau's proposal to achieve a "just society" through the social, economic, and political assimilation of Indigenous peoples into the Canadian nation and through the recognition of Indigenous "cultural contributions" to Canada's multicultural tapestry. In Chapter 2, "The 'Canada Problem' in Indian Politics," Newhouse and Belanger provide a sense of key historical developments that culminated in the Trudeau government's 1969 White Paper, a document outlining the government's plan to address issues facing Indigenous people with a vision to bring about political equality and economic parity with non-Indigenous people in Canada. Their analysis of events preceding the release of the White Paper clarifies in what respects, in the words of Cardinal, the White Paper was little more than "a thinly disguised program of extermination through assimilation" (Cardinal 1969, 1). And Stark's troubling analysis in Chapter 4 of the symbiotic relationship between colonialism and gendered violence reveals how and why the government's thinly disguised program of extermination has continued unabated as it has managed to "construct Indigenous bodies and lands into categories that naturalize gender violence."

Despite the efforts of political leaders, scholars, and community activists to bring about the kind of change envisioned and hoped for by Cardinal, it remains unclear after 50 years to what extent the Buckskin Curtain and that which it has tried to conceal have been dismantled, if at all. At an institutional level, observers might cite recent judicial developments such as the declaration of title in *Tsilhqot'in Nation v. British Columbia* (2014) or the negotiation of self-government agreements, land claims, and impact benefit agreements as evidence of the willingness of multiple governments to come to the table and honour the interests of Indigenous people. However, as discussed by Starblanket (Chapter 1), Charlie (Chapter 5), Simpson, and Green (Chapter 14), such claims can easily be complicated by critical analyses of the ways in which these and other signs of progress and reconciliation in fact extend colonial and capitalist power relations deeper into the lives of Indigenous people. Despite the constitutional protections afforded to Aboriginal and treaty rights under section 35 of the Constitution Act, 1982, and despite the evolving governmental and institutional rhetoric expressing a commitment to honouring Indigenous treaties, nationhood, and rights, Cardinal's call for fundamental changes in attitudes towards and treatment of Indigenous people in Canada have clearly gone unheeded. And as is evident in many of the chapters that follow, most notable of these is the opposition by many Canadians, including political leaders, to the fundamental right of Indigenous peoples to advance solutions to improve the various relationships they inhabit *on their own terms* rather than on terms imposed by the Canadian state.

In regard to the relationship between Indigenous and non-Indigenous people in Canada, the Buckskin Curtain certainly appears to have remained firmly in place. According to John Borrows (2013), we have also long-since passed the tipping point in the relationship between Indigenous people and others in Canada: "We are in crisis mode, and there is no politically driven prospect of salvaging the relationship. It is already broken and lies in ruins all around us." In contextualizing the crisis-ridden state of Indigenous and non-Indigenous relationships in Canada, Borrows cites the shorter life expectancies of Indigenous people in Canada and the disproportionately high rates of Indigenous suffering indicated in higher levels of poverty, injury, and incarceration and significantly lower levels of education, income, and health. As Stark, Anderson and Ball, Monchalin and Marques (Chapter 10), and Hare and Davidson (Chapter 12) all observe, changes in these indicators of injustice and Indigenous suffering have been at times gradual and at other times not, though they have always occurred along a spectrum as settler colonialism has evolved in accordance with varying social, economic, and political conditions.

McGregor (Chapter 11), Simpson, Charlie, McDonald, and Starblanket also note that the current socio-political landscape speaks to the urgent need to theorize and implement ways of improving the configurations of violent and unsustainable relationships between humans, and between humans and the living earth. Each of these authors highlights that it is not only human relations that have reached a crisis level; as we have known for decades, human relations with the living earth have also reached a point of unsustainability and require urgent attention. Moreover, they explain why questions surrounding land and the responsibilities that Indigenous people hold towards the land should not be abstracted from conversations surrounding Indigenous–settler relations.

In shifting the focus of this volume to transforming relations of colonial oppression through Indigenous forms of resurgence, our aim is to centre Indigenous visions of freedom and the "good life" within discussions on how to improve all our relations. Certainly, this has not always been the case—European settlers have traditionally imposed visions of what Indigenous peoples' proper interests and priorities should be. As Olive Dickason (1997) notes, the colonial vision of European newcomers was in part legitimized by their perspective that the Indigenous inhabitants of the lands they sought to steal were *l'homme sauvage*. Consequently, whether the colonizers viewed the "savages" they sought to assimilate or exterminate as noble or hopelessly inferior, their "New World" vision had little if any room for Indigenous ways of being, thinking, and acting. As the chapters in this collection attest, the spirit and imprint of this colonial vision and its attendant racist beliefs and attitudes remain evident in virtually every spiritual, physical, cultural, relational, and structural area of life for Indigenous people in Canada.

For example, a 2016 poll on Canadian public opinion towards Indigenous people indicated that while awareness of some of the challenges and disparities that Indigenous people face seems to have grown among non-Indigenous people over the past decade, negative attitudes towards Indigenous people continue to abound (Environics Institute 2016). A majority of respondents to this survey rejected the notion that the rights and political status of Indigenous peoples are distinct from other cultural or ethnic groups in this country. In line with their belief that Indigenous people do not experience systemic institutional discrimination or that settler Canadians benefit from such ongoing discrimination, most respondents also believe that Indigenous people have a sense of entitlement about receiving special treatment from governments and taxpayers. Although awareness of Indigenous issues therefore seems to be increasing, many non-Indigenous people continue to have a distorted understanding of Indigenous people's unique legal and political position vis-à-vis the Canadian state. They also fail to recognize the profound harm that colonial systems, legislation, and policies continue to have on the lives of Indigenous individuals, families, and communities throughout the country.

Many of the authors in this collection examine some of the taken-for-granted ways in which the racist attitudes and distorted understandings of non-Indigenous people in Canada are maintained and disseminated. Notable here is the contribution by Hunt, who begins his analysis of the experiences of Indigenous people in an urban context by critiquing the damage-centred and depoliticized narratives propagated by well-meaning settler scholars. Hunt asserts that denial of their complicity in the colonial enterprise enables these scholars, and presumably others who help to perpetuate the story of "the traumatized Indian," to disregard Indigenous-led decolonization efforts and remain blind to genuine expressions of Indigenous existence and modes of Indigenous political and social life. As Monchalin and Marques, Stark, Anderson and Ball, Hare and Davidson, and Watchman and Innes also note in their chapters, Indigenous people are often told in their interactions with representatives of non-Indigenous judicial, social service, educational, literary, and media agencies and institutions to leave "history" or "race"—and thus colonialism—out of the picture and to deny the many ongoing ways in which settler colonialism has shaped and continues to shape Indigenous experiences. The result, they argue, is the perpetuation of genocidal experiences, broken and unhealthy relations, and deeply embedded and thoroughly oppressive cultural attitudes and institutional structures.

The editors and contributors of this collection acknowledge Canada as an evolving colonial structure and share a fundamental concern that the issues impacting Indigenous peoples in Canada cannot be divorced from historical *and* contemporary colonialism. Nonetheless, most contributors to this fifth edition of *Visions of the Heart* do not focus on making the case that contemporary Canada is a settler-colonial political formation; rather, they agree that Indigenous people have had to make this case for too long and that it has occupied enough intellectual and emotional resources. In a similar vein, the editors and contributors are not interested in reciting mythologies of post-colonialism or focusing attention on describing positive indicators of reconciliation that have been cause, at least for some, to celebrate.

While we agree there are many indications of change in Canada, we ask the reader to reflect carefully and critically on what, and whose, metrics are being used to measure change. We are cautious of how these measures of success have been used for a variety of reasons, not least of which has been to maintain the legitimacy of colonial institutions in response to Indigenous people's evolving critiques and assertions of our rights. Two of the most obvious reasons for questioning how far we have come are: (1) clear evidence that suggests colonizing experiences, relations, processes, and structures continue to abound in Canada and that Indigenous individuals, communities, and nations have to fight each day for the right to have control over practically every area of their lives; and (2) government actions that show little evidence that official representatives of the Canadian state are sincere in their commitment to "achieving reconciliation with Indigenous peoples through a renewed, nation-to-nation, government-to-government" relationship based on "recognition of rights, respect, co-operation, and partnership as the foundation for transformative change" (Canada 2018). Decades of hindsight now allow us to engage in a well-evidenced critique of the problem with understanding success as the integration or incorporation of Indigenous people, world views, and ways of being within colonial structures and power relations. While a number of contributors, including Newhouse and Belanger, Hare and Davidson, and Anderson and Ball, do attend to some of the positive changes that have taken place, they nonetheless acknowledge that such changes do not mitigate the ongoing experiences of violence, oppression, injustice, and suffering faced by many Indigenous people. As a result, they are careful not to presume that recent transformations have been liberating or empowering for all.

All contributors to this edition of *Visions of the Heart* therefore fundamentally agree with Green, who notes in Chapter 14 that decolonizing dialogue and action requires imagination, collaboration, and a commitment to replace the colonial status quo with a concrete set of acceptable, liberating alternatives. Such imagination and commitment are evident in Charlie's discussion of Indigenous collage theory, and in McDonald's and Hunt's respective discussions of emergent forms and iterations of land-based, resurgent practices. Similarly, in Chapter 7 Voth and Loyer's analysis of the Métis "ethic of reciprocal visiting" exemplifies Simpson's insight that Indigenous people have rich bodies of theory, tradition, and laws that are more than simply cultural practices, and that their theory is a way of shaping how we can engage respectfully and sustainably with other living beings as we move through the world.

Honouring Diverse Indigenous Knowledge

One of the most challenging aspects of putting together a collection of writings about matters of importance to Indigenous peoples is ensuring that it reflects and honours the diversity of Indigenous identities, knowledge, and experiences. Although they recognize that generalizations can be useful and visions of the past, present, and future can be shared, contributors to this volume have all attempted to offer nuance and insight into the range of opinions and perspectives on any given issue. This is a particularly difficult task when speaking to a broad audience from a range of backgrounds with varying degrees of foundational knowledge and experience. Given the differences in our perspectives, circumstances, and approaches, it should come as little surprise to readers that the chapters in this collection do not flow in a smooth and uniform manner from beginning to end.

Another challenge is that the quantity of Indigenous content has grown exponentially across disciplines over the past decade, and the increase in scholarship, creative works, and multimedia on matters of concern to Indigenous people has given rise to considerable variation and nuance in Indigenous methodologies, theoretical approaches, schools of thought, and critical analyses. Moreover, this variation is amplified by generational differences in Indigenous intellectual and creative productions, as new generations build upon the foundations developed by early Indigenous scholars and construct new and innovative approaches. Contributors to this collection respect and honour the important contributions made by early scholars in the field, and we recognize the particularly isolating and difficult challenges they faced in navigating Western institutions and their often blatant hostility to Indigenous ways of knowing and being. We think it important to acknowledge that their efforts were not in vain, and that their contributions to dismantling the Buckskin Curtain made possible the emergence and growth of critical Indigenous scholarship. While each of the contributions in this edition builds upon the work of many Indigenous scholars, artists, and activists, the array of issues, perspectives, methodologies, angles of inquiry, and voices in this current collection illustrates the necessity of continually pushing our discourse beyond questions of decolonization and/ or Indigenization. The analyses and discussions that follow thus highlight the importance as well as the benefits of creating spaces for Indigenous peoples to thrive without having to tailor our theoretical approaches, methodologies, and analyses to Western requirements for knowledge production. As Charlie notes in Chapter 5, bringing together many disparate, deconstructed, and apparently inconsistent fragments can prompt us to engage in imaginative ways with seemingly incommensurable pieces of an issue in order to make sense of them.

Just as the contributions to this collection do not simply represent the idiosyncratic concerns and perspectives of their authors, neither are they merely summative or simplistic descriptions that impart an objective "truth" about any given issue. In acknowledging that Indigenous issues are diverse, complex, and messy, contributors to this volume offer their own accounts while prompting readers to draw their own conclusions. Consequently, the chapters do not offer "objective" or detached descriptions; rather, they challenge the framing of issues involving Indigenous people and explore the politics of dominant approaches to engaging with them. Furthermore, they challenge the very notion of objectivity, demonstrating that we are all situated in relation to issues impacting Indigenous peoples in Canada and that from these different locations arise various privileges, disadvantages, rights, and responsibilities.

While many audiences are in search of a generalized, fundamental truth or an objective, neutral discussion of issues, contributors to this edition of *Visions of the Heart* are very aware of competing versions of "the truth" about relations between Indigenous peoples and the rest of Canada and that there are many ways to tell Indigenous stories about "the truth." The diverse formats and methodologies of each chapter offer various windows into the issues faced by Indigenous people that are at times broad and sweeping and at other times detailed and precise. For example, quantitative data used by Monchalin and Marques (Chapter 10), Hare and Davidson (Chapter 12), and Anderson and Ball come from a wide variety of sources, including their own research, government-sponsored national, provincial, and territorial task forces and surveys, various federal and provincial ministries, other academic and non-government studies, and numerous reports and discussion papers. Although their analyses provide important insight into trends and issues, they caution readers about the dangers of generalizing from data that have been drawn from regions, cities, reserves, settlements, and towns with vastly different geographical, historical, and social characteristics.

As an important alternative to storied accounts about statistical patterns and trends, most contributors discuss how and why the foregrounding of Indigenous knowledge and theory in qualitative research enables us to flesh out our understanding of human experiences and relationships. The contributions of Starblanket, Stark, Watchman and Innes, Simpson, Voth and Loyer, and McDonald elucidate how stories can honour the diverse expressions of Indigenous philosophy, law, and politics, as well as challenge readers to reflect critically on the power and validity of different kinds of stories and storytellers. Further to this, Hunt reminds us that this is fundamental to all transformative discourse since it highlights not only that social analysis is a highly interpretive act, but also that the narratives created and disseminated by academics and others can all too easily do more damage than simply clouding our understanding.

In their own ways, each contributor to this volume challenges the essentializing of Indigenous peoples and is mindful of the diversity in Indigenous identity as well as the factors that can shape and affect it. While Stark, Watchman and Innes, Anderson and Ball, and McDonald invite readers to reflect on the everyday grassroots experiences and perspectives of Indigenous people, their chapters focus, respectively, on some of the gendered dilemmas facing Indigenous women and girls, Indigenous boys and men, traditionally based educational initiatives, and ancestral cultural and language revitalization efforts in Indigenous communities in the North. Hunt explores the complex questions surrounding Indigenous identity and resurgence in urban areas, while in a different realm Monchalin and Marques discuss Indigenous people's experience of (in)justice vis-à-vis the criminal justice system and suggest how the identity of individuals can be profoundly harmed by the environment that shapes them. McDonald looks at the importance of land-based, culturally and relationally grounded practice in bringing forward the empowerment and resurgence of Indigenous peoples. McGregor offers insights into the importance of Indigenous visions of environmental care in a time and place where resource development, regardless of the harm to creation, has become politically and economically prioritized by mainstream Canadian society. All of these authors demonstrate that, despite the violence that has plagued nearly every facet of Indigenous life, diverse engagements in a range of contexts can deepen our appreciation of the creative visions and determination at the heart of the identities and aspirations of Indigenous peoples.

Interrogating the Ways, Means, and Framings of Colonialism

Prior to the early 1960s, those who supported the dominant social scientific perspectives of the time assumed that political resistance, social inequality, and intercultural conflict between minority groups and dominant society reflected their inability and/or unwillingness to adjust to rapid social and cultural change. The assumption underlying the perspectives of mainstream social scientists, who were apparently blind to their own ethnocentrism, was in many respects the same as that held by those whose vision it had been to colonize the "New World." Theirs was a taken-for-granted superiority since they viewed it as their right and even destiny to dominate whatever individuals, groups, and societies they deemed inferior. Consequently, in much early writing about Indigenous peoples in Canada, First Nations were blamed for having inadequate skills, for lacking understanding of European ways, and for an apparent unwillingness to do anything to alleviate their personal and social problems. Scholars, government officials, and others perpetuated notions of dependency and this "blaming the victim" mentality through their interpretations of the data they had gathered on everything from Indigenous people's rates of physical and mental illness, family violence, suicide, homicide, and incarceration to unemployment and standards of living. Moreover, many academic and government representatives assumed that change could only occur through assimilation, since along with blaming Indigenous people for their own problems, they also saw them as lacking adequate technical and interpersonal skills—as well as the commitment needed—to address their own problems in constructive ways.

A different set of theoretical assumptions began to take hold during the 1960s in relation to the social and political matters faced by Indigenous people in Canada. According to those writing out of this post-colonial perspective (which was inspired in part by such diverse writers and movements as Frantz Fanon, Malcolm X, Paulo Freire, Vine Deloria Jr, Harold Cardinal, the US civil rights movement, the American Indian Movement, and even Quebec separatism), colonizing social structures and processes needed to be examined in light of the experiences and perspectives of those who had been oppressed and disadvantaged by colonization. In their analysis of issues affecting Indigenous people in Canada, Indigenous and non-Indigenous scholars described and examined the many ways that the colonizing project of Europeans had formally (re) organized all aspects of Indigenous life through policies and legislation that primarily served the economic, political, legal, and cultural interests of the colonizers. In doing so, they drew attention to the fact that colonialism represents a "totalizing" phenomenon since it leaves no area of life unscathed, including how academics and others give account of the experiences and circumstances of Indigenous people as well as their relations with the rest of Canada.

Over time, scholars began to criticize the increasingly popularized use of the term "post-colonial," particularly in relation to contexts where the permanency of colonial settlements and concentration of power in the hands of colonial governments rendered it impossible to ever achieve a truly post-colonial state. Scholarship on colonialism increasingly began to distinguish between the inner workings of various colonial contexts, exploring the particular logics and configurations of oppression in settler-colonial states (as opposed to contexts of colonialism where permanent settlements are not established). As Veracini (2011, 2) notes, attending to analytical distinctions and dissimilarities between colonial formations enables scholars to account for the fact that different conditions cultivated in various colonial contexts could lead to different patterns of relationships and consequences for those involved. One outcome of distinguishing between different forms of colonization is that it can serve a clarifying function for the question of decolonization in settler societies. However, this should not be interpreted as implying that decolonization is a formula to be applied *above* the diverse struggles of Indigenous peoples for freedom. Thus, while settler-colonial scholarship has gradually gained some traction, it has increasingly been subject to sympathetic critique by Indigenous studies scholars and others for not adequately attending to Indigenous peoples' epistemologies, understandings of Indigenous–settler relations, political framings and formations, and diverse aspirations (Snelgrove, Dhamoon, and Corntassel 2014; see also Vimalassery, Pegues, and Goldstein 2016, with responses by Young 2017).

To varying degrees, then, resurgence scholarship has increasingly sought to problematize not just the theory of settler colonialism but also the multi-faceted ways that colonialism intersects with structures of racism, capitalism, classism, ableism, sexism, and heteropatriarchy to produce the everyday struggles facing Indigenous people. As is evident throughout this collection, there are important consequences to emphasizing Indigenous peoples' efforts to not only respond to these struggles, but more importantly to reframe them in the everyday contexts of our own lives and on our own terms. Most significantly, doing so acknowledges that Indigenous articulations and aspirations are distinct from those of non-Indigenous peoples; that is, Indigenous laws, political orders, economic systems, social structures, and so on are important not just because of what they might offer non-Indigenous peoples or relations, but because they are vital in and of themselves. Diverse engagements with this perspective are evident throughout this collection, including in the chapters by Simpson, McDonald, Hunt, and McGregor. These authors highlight the fundamental importance of ancestral relations with the land, waterways, and other living beings, and they stress that the ongoing ability to embody this relationality is central to Indigenous visions of freedom and liberty. Conversely, Voth and Loyer, Charlie, and Starblanket explore the forms of damage to Indigenous political traditions and aspirations that can occur when the significance of these relationships is overlooked or only accounted for in a partial or limited way.

The relatively recent growth in the scholarship on Indigenous resurgence helps us understand why many of our contributors seek to centre Indigenous voices and visions in a non-apologetic way while also drawing attention to the many ways that the attitudes and actions of individual settlers often help maintain colonial relations and structures. Starblanket, Charlie, Hunt, Stark, Green, and others all examine the "improvements" in Indigenous–non-Indigenous relationships by interrogating whether such developments and ways of representing and talking about them are actually positive or whether they further legitimatize, consolidate, and extend the power of the settler state. They consider, for instance, the ways in which concepts such as "Indigenous consent" or "self-government" can represent either an explicitly anti-colonial stance or contemporary processes of assimilation depending on how they are invoked and the contexts in which they are applied. These and other contributors are keenly aware of the political implications of these distinctions and are eager to detect and explore both the underlying assumptions and possible consequences of claims to progress in the lives of Indigenous people in Canada. This is another reason that readers may find their writing to be unsettling, since it seeks to hold scholars across the disciplines accountable for intentionally or unintentionally reproducing colonial power dynamics by failing to engage respectfully with and foreground Indigenous philosophies and epistemologies in their writings about Indigenous peoples.

While some contributors to this collection highlight the strengthening of relationships between Indigenous and non-Indigenous peoples in Canada rather than Indigenous resurgence, we all agree that in this somewhat tumultuous age of de/reconstruction, academic writers and readers must take seriously our role in storytelling. We share the view that open, constructive dialogue depends on everyone involved having a sense of how and why we view the relationship between scholarly research and storytelling in the way we do. This does not necessarily require everyone telling their own personal story every time they speak or write, but it does invite us to reflect honestly on certain fundamental philosophical, methodological, and theoretical issues in our research and writing. The result, as in previous editions of *Visions of the Heart*, is a collection of writings that reflect the unique experiences, perspectives, styles of writing, and approaches of its contributors to engaging issues involving Indigenous peoples in Canada.

Concluding Remarks

Having recognized that colonialism continues to structure all of the issues examined in this volume, contributors to the fifth edition of *Visions of the Heart* question what comes next, what can be done to attend to the day-to-day struggles faced by Indigenous people, and, most importantly, what sort of work is currently being undertaken to renew and animate Indigenous knowledges and ways of being. This collection of writings highlights that many of these efforts are being expressed in wonderfully resourceful, creative, and visionary ways that prompt us all to think outside of disciplinary or conventional categories. Each chapter draws our attention to diverse ways and contexts in which the revitalization of traditional knowledge, pedagogies, cultural practices, and social and political systems are occurring, and all contributors make it abundantly clear that the raison d'être of these various approaches is the continuity of Indigenous people's many relations and their ability to carry out their rights and responsibilities within them.

The contributors to this volume recognize that Indigenous people's sense of responsibility to bring forward healthy and sustainable relationships with creation and with other living beings has long animated their drive to negotiate coexistence across difference. Our shared hope is that this collection will contribute to a visionary dialogue and to positive, transformational change in at least two ways: by offering a critical examination of past and present sources of oppression and injustice in the lives of Indigenous people in Canada, and by challenging/enabling readers to see the many ways that Indigenous people, in the face of these experiences, have continually worked towards the creation of worlds where they can honour and implement their ancestral ways of being in the present *and* their visions for what will be in the future.

This edition of *Visions of the Heart* thus invites readers to reflect critically on how and why they and others make sense of relations between Indigenous peoples and the rest of Canada in the ways they do. We regard this as one of the most transformative possibilities of education, for it helps us to recognize diverse and sometimes competing versions of individual and collective experiences, circumstances, and events. To encourage dialogue beyond this book, questions specific to each contribution are included at the end of each chapter. Beyond these specific questions, we encourage readers to reflect on the more general questions of who should be responsible to initiate change and how they should go about their tasks. As the many initiatives involving the collaboration of Indigenous and non-Indigenous people indicate, openness to learning about ourselves and our differences is also essential to positive and lasting transformational change in all our relations.

1 Crises of Relationship

The Role of Treaties in Contemporary Indigenous–Settler Relations

Gina Starblanket

The Treaties were not meant to be the last word on the relationship. Renewal of the relationship was necessary to ensure that both parties could continue to thrive in changing environments.

—*Restoule v. Canada [Attorney General]*, 2018 ONSC 7701 at 422

Introduction

This chapter is about treaty relations; not treaty people, but treaty-based modes of relating. I have chosen this focus deliberately as it allows for more multi-faceted engagement with the challenges and possibilities of coexisting across difference in shared spaces. In treaty territories, Indigenous and non-Indigenous people are indeed "all treaty people," yet treaties do not merely implicate humans; they are about relationships with and between all elements of creation. Moreover, the rights and responsibilities that different groups of people hold under the treaties are not uniform; Indigenous and non-Indigenous people have distinct rights and responsibilities that we inherit from our ancestors and the commitments that they respectively made in entering into treaty relations.

A focus on relationship allows us to reflect on the diversity of roles, contributions, and responsibilities that all living beings hold. It creates room to consider the perspectives, world views, histories, interpretations, and visions of multiple parties to treaty, avoiding narrow examinations that arise from a one-dimensional lens. Further, it widens the conversation beyond questions of treaty rights, exploring the process of living through treaties as political frameworks rather than engaging with them as one-time transactions that give rise to a fixed set of terms.

In focusing on treaty relations, then, this chapter is not limited to the interactions of human communities but takes up the need for healthy and regenerative relationships between all treaty partners. It considers the transformative possibilities of treaties when they are conceptualized as frameworks for creating and renewing broad and interconnected networks of relationship. These include relations between humans, with other living beings, and with the rest of creation. Yet I'm also interested in the dual potential of treaty

Idle No More protestors participate in a march in January 2013 from Victoria Island in the Ottawa River to Parliament Hill to remind the Canadian government of its responsibility to maintain its treaty relationships with Indigenous leaders.

relationships, namely, how they can represent relations of erasure, violence, and oppression (both towards human communities and the living earth) when they are narrowly interpreted or selectively invoked, and how they can represent relations of generative, non-hierarchical, dialogical coexistence when they are inhabited in accordance with the laws and intentions of all the parties who signed them. In discussing the various configurations of relationship, it is important to note that I do not intend to reproduce a binary way of thinking about good/bad or generative/violent relations, as these can and often do coexist at the same time.

The overarching objective of this chapter is thus to explore how treaty discourses can function either to challenge or to sustain relations of settler colonialism, depending on how they are interpreted and the contexts in which they are applied. I aim to demonstrate how this dual potential relies on processes of storytelling and meaning-making, which can lead to substantially different understandings of what treaty relationships are and what their contemporary implications could be.

Specifically, colonial mythologies surrounding treaties can minimize and detract from their contemporary legal and political implications. For instance, such mythologies include one-sided representations of treaties as static, fixed-term land transactions through which Indigenous peoples ceded and surrendered their rights to the land and to political jurisdiction. Such mythologies include one-sided representations of treaties as static, fixed-term land transactions through which Indigenous peoples ceded and surrendered our rights to the land and to political jurisdiction. I demonstrate that these narratives have direct material consequences, including the repression of Indigenous political agency and erasure of our jurisdiction and rights to land. Then, I describe the transformative possibilities of understanding treaties as they are understood by Indigenous people—as agreements about how to relate with one another and with creation. I reflect on what we might learn about healthy modes of coexistence through greater understanding of the spirit and intent of treaties as understood by Indigenous people, as well as through critical engagement with the ways in which treaties have been misinhabited, that is, how they have not always been properly inhabited by those who are party to them.

This chapter proposes that the prerequisite to the resurgence of treaty-based modes of relating in contemporary contexts is the crucial need to confront and deconstruct how treaty mythologies have been proliferated in popular culture, as well as how they are continually reproduced in Canada's social, educational, legal, and political institutions. Moving beyond a transactional approach towards a more relational interpretation of treaties gives rise to a much broader range of possible ways of maintaining respectful relationships among and between living beings. It also employs a cyclical conception of time, showing that the possibilities of relationships in the present are always already configured by that which came before us, and by our intentions for a future that has yet to come. The point is to encourage reflection on human experiences not as independent from other living beings, but as existing in shared worlds and thus contributing to the creation of the positive and negative experiences of others in those worlds. With treaties as a central focus, I demonstrate how the act of privileging one set of stories, desires, and priorities (i.e., the Crown's written record) minimizes the capacity for Indigenous treaty partners to have a significant voice and role in the relationship, thus perpetuating their marginalization and exclusion.

While practices of treaty-making with settlers have a lengthy history in eastern Canada, in the context of this chapter I am generally referring to the numbered treaties negotiated between Indigenous peoples and Canadian government authorities from 1871 to 1921. Yet, I should clarify at the outset that when I refer to "treaty relationships" or "treaty-based modes of relating," I mean the diplomatic practices intended to govern relationships that Indigenous peoples have practised with other living beings since time immemorial. Here I am referring not exclusively to the numbered treaties but rather to the long-standing practices of treaty-making that Indigenous peoples have engaged in to inform our relationships with animals, plants, places, and other living beings.

Reviewing the Contested Terrain of Relationship

I was born and raised in Treaty 4 territory. I spent my formative years becoming acquainted with the contrasting relationships that characterize prairie geographies. On the one hand, my homeland embodies deeply rooted memories and experiences of engaging in generative, creative relationships with other people and the living earth. The people and other living beings with whom I shared the majority of my early life exist in Treaty 4 territory. It is a very powerful place, home to medicines, animals, and waterways that provide for our nourishment, well-being, and knowledge, as it did for my ancestors. This land houses my family's stories, names, memories, and connections to one another and the Creator. Following Mishuana Goeman's (2017) discussion of the body "as a meeting place," I understand Treaty 4 to be far more than a physical location; rather, it is a hub where multiple overlapping relationships of time and place intersect and regenerate.

Relationships between human bodies and bodies of land and water from the past and present are layered in these places, alongside relationships between our ancestral ways of knowing and being and the future possibilities they might offer my children. Even though I now reside at a distance, I recognize the foundational impact of these relations in my life and I strive to continually learn and grow from them. These are the relationships that gave me life, that I try to give back to, and that are maintained through an ongoing cycle of reciprocity and renewal. On the other hand, these lands have also borne witness to many violent, crisis-ridden, and unsustainable relationships between human communities, and between humans and the living earth.

While I deeply appreciate and have much to learn from the rich and meaningful relationships that exist in Treaty 4, I am also intimately aware of the racist, colonial, and gendered hierarchies, attitudes, words, and actions that have become so deeply naturalized in these geographies. These simultaneous and contradictory experiences give rise to the problematic of how to address violent relations and cultivate healthier modes of coexistence between living beings in contexts of colonialism. I am constantly asking what I might learn from this push-and-pull dynamic and from the tensions of coexistence at play in these spaces. What modes of relating are inspiring and potentially transformative? Conversely, what stands in the way of achieving healthier relations of coexistence in these spaces? I should clarify that by coexistence I don't mean the basic survival of multiple entities, which can be sustained even in the harshest contexts. Instead, I am referring to the ability for multiple entities to live and thrive in accordance with their own world views and the rights and responsibilities that they give rise to, even across differences.

Having grown up learning about the importance of treaties to past and future generations, I've always been inclined to look to the resources we already have to deal with the disputes and challenges of coexistence. Treaty-based modes of relating, when understood as legal and political frameworks between nations, can offer important alternatives to violent, destructive, and asymmetrical models of coexistence between individuals, communities, and the worlds we share. Unlike in non-treaty regions, those who inhabit treaty relations don't have to invent protocols to govern their interactions from scratch: we already have frameworks in place that can and should inform the relationship. Unfortunately, treaty relations between Indigenous peoples and settlers have for the most part been misinhabited, and as a result they have not involved healthy, generative experiences for Indigenous populations or for the environments we share. Thus, bringing forward change is certainly not as simple as garnering greater understanding surrounding the spirit and intent of treaties. We must also have realistic assessments of the structural issues surrounding implementation, that is, the asymmetries in power, authority, and jurisdiction that are not only part of this country's foundation, but that have functioned to prevent the implementation of treaty relationships since their signing. As I will explain throughout this chapter, an important place to begin addressing these structures is by deconstructing and correcting the discourses that inform and uphold them.

Processes of storytelling and mythmaking can have significant material implications, particularly in terms of the everyday ways in which Indigenous and non-Indigenous peoples understand their responsibilities and relationships to one another and to the living earth. Dominant narratives of peaceful social, cultural, and economic hybridization between Indigenous and settler populations necessarily obscure the very real experiences of violence and marginalization, as well as attempts at the erasure of Indigenous peoples that were an integral part of settlement in these spaces. For one story to exist as the "real," dominant, or authoritative version of Canadian history, other versions of events that contradict it must continually be absented from the record. Consequently, the genocide of Indigenous peoples gets subsumed within dominant cultural narratives that have ranged from racist and evolutionary justifications, to multicultural rhetoric, to discourses on reconciliation that frame colonial violence as a past and temporary phenomenon that Canadian society has since departed from.

However, colonialism cannot be neatly defined as a mere gaffe in the historical record. As Patrick Wolfe (2006) and other scholars have argued, settler colonialism is an ongoing structure and not a historical event. Engaging with colonialism as a continually expanding and evolving structure can enable us to make sense of the supposedly historical events such as treaty-making that are so deeply embedded in Canada's national identity and discourse. Thus, this chapter is driven by a number of related questions: How does understanding settler colonialism as a continuous, ongoing process help elucidate the role of treaties (as they have been selectively interpreted in Canadian institutions) in continually producing relations of political domination and dispossession? How might all treaty partners work to disrupt the narratives that are elemental to the inner workings and future of settler colonialism, and that serve to perpetuate current crises of relationship between living beings?

To engage and revisit these narratives, and to create space for mutually respectful dialogue, all parties must demonstrate a commitment to recognize and challenge their own biases and assumptions. Thus, this chapter and many other chapters of this volume invite readers to critically consider their own stories and what sort of world view informs that which they believe to be true. What do our own normative ideas prohibit or blind us from, and how might this preclude possible ways of addressing contemporary crises of relationship? The discussion raised in this chapter extends beyond the realm of treaty relations, for treaty-based modes of relating can offer important insight into many different types of interactions, from interpersonal to intergroup interactions.

Demythologizing Treaties

Between 1871 and 1921, Indigenous nations negotiated 11 treaties with the Dominion of Canada in order to identify the terms and conditions upon which they would share the land with newcomers (see Figure 1.1). Often referred to as "the numbered treaties," these agreements encompass the regions between the Lake of the Woods to the Rocky Mountains (including territory across present-day northwest Ontario, Manitoba, Saskatchewan, Alberta, the Northwest Territories, and northeast British Columbia and southeast Yukon). In settler historical records, the numbered treaties are represented as some of the largest land transactions in the world. Collectively, they represent a foundational element of the narration underlying what scholars such as Joyce Green refer to as "Project Canada" (Green 2004). As Green writes, the configurations of the colonial relationship between Indigenous peoples and Canada "are perpetuated by a mythologized history and by judicial and political institutions that proclaim and defend this mythology-cloaked, unhyphenated colonialism" (Green 1995). Significant events such as treaties are drawn together to form mythologies that distort our collective consciousness, centring Western interpretations while making others invisible.

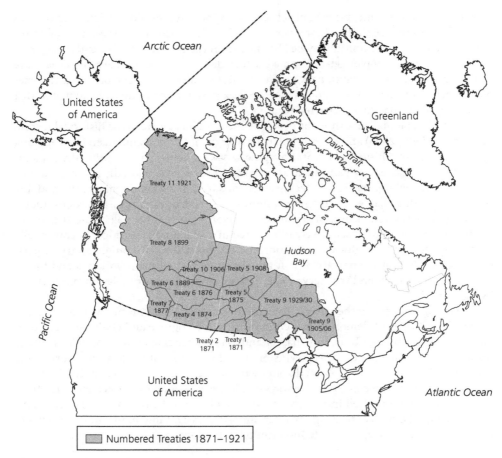

Figure 1.1 The numbered treaties, 1871–1921
Source: Indigenous and Northern Affairs Canada.

Canadian narratives of settlement and development often depict a story of European newcomers navigating harsh environments and negotiating forms of consensual trade and coexistence with Indigenous populations. The negotiation of the numbered treaties plays a central role in this story, as the treaties supposedly facilitated the extinguishment of Indigenous claims to the land and brought Indigenous peoples and their territories under the legal and political jurisdiction of the newly confederated Canadian nation-state. The main characters of this story are the skilled negotiators such as Alexander Morris, David Laird, and other Crown officials, glorified for their ability to surmount vast intellectual and cultural chasms, to survey seemingly infinite horizons, to provide for the extension of imperial rule, and to break uncultivated ground in order to realize its unfulfilled potential. Notably absent from the story is Indigenous agency in negotiating treaties. Rather, the metanarrative surrounding the historic treaties depicts the Indigenous nations and their leaders as being saved from famine and a disease-stricken existence; eager to be offered the gift of civilization; tricked, manipulated, conquered, or simply lacking the intellectual capacity to understand the treaties they were entering into. In each configuration, the political agency of Indigenous people, and especially that of Indigenous women, is absent. And while these stories find their roots in a historic past, they are retold over time in such a way that weaves them into Canada's national origin story.

It is through the story of historic treaties as land transactions that the Canadian government legitimates its presence on and claim to title over local lands and waterways. Yet despite the centrality of treaties to Canadian narratives of settlement and development, they play a relatively insignificant role in informing the direction of Canadian law and policy. When they are mentioned, they are most often framed as historical events or as a form of legal contract that surrendered Indigenous title in exchange for a fixed set of rights and benefits. The legal and political configurations of the Indigenous–state relationship are informed by these narratives, eclipsing Indigenous understandings of treaties as relationship agreements. The concept of "treaty mythologies," that is, the selective construction of treaties as fixed-term transactions, therefore provides a useful lens to understand and challenge the one-sided narratives surrounding the formation and ongoing configurations of Indigenous–settler relations in Canada.

The transactional understanding suggests that Indigenous populations ceded and surrendered title to the land to the Crown in exchange for a fixed spectrum of rights and entitlements. This interpretation is reflected in the description of treaties offered by Canada's Department of Indigenous and Northern Affairs (INAC), which suggests:

> At their base, the treaties were land surrenders on a huge scale . . . in the eyes of the Federal Government, the act of signing treaty brought Aboriginal people of the Northwest under the jurisdiction of the Dominion of Canada and its laws. The early numbered treaties—Treaties 1 through 7—became the vehicle by which the Department of Indian Affairs implemented existing and future assimilation policies in the Northwest while the latter treaties allowed for the opening of the North and access to valuable natural resources. (Canada 2013)

Of significance here is how the intent of the treaties is framed as the integration of Indigenous people into the broader Canadian legal and political system. Note, too, that the treaties are said to have facilitated both settlement ("the opening of the North") and capitalist pursuits ("access to valuable natural resources"). Treaties are commonly represented by the Crown as instruments of colonial expansion and settlement, a story that in turn gives the impression of the peaceful absorption of Indigenous peoples into the fledgling Canadian state. In the process, various forms of violence, dispossession, and social, cultural, and political repression—such as the reserve system, the pass system, the residential school system, vagrancy laws, and other policies and legislation both within and outside of the Indian Act (some of which had no basis in law)—are removed from the narrative.

The perspective that the numbered treaties represent surrenders of land and of political authority is not exclusively held by the federal government, but is proliferated in the hallways of Canada's educational, cultural, and political institutions. Even some contemporary post-secondary textbooks designed to provide balanced perspectives and comprehensive information into processes of colonialism continue to position treaties as land transactions (Dickason and Newbigging 2010, ix). In its final report, the Royal Commission on Aboriginal Peoples (RCAP) commented on the role of historical mythmaking in informing the public perception regarding treaties, writing that the commonly held perceptions regarding treaties are "the direct result of schoolboys having been misled or at least deprived of the truth about the treaties and about the peoples that made them" (RCAP 1996, II, 15). Mythologies of the numbered treaties as mechanisms through which Indigenous people surrendered land and political authority proliferate misinformation, half-truths, and uncertainty that cloud their contemporary political implications.

The transactional interpretation of treaties stands in direct contrast to the meaning and intent of treaties described by treaty Elders (Cardinal and Hildebrandt 2000; Hildebrandt, Rider, and Carter 1996) and documented by Indigenous academics (Borrows 2002; Cardinal 1969; Craft 2016; Ladner 2003; Little Bear 1986; Simpson 2008; Stark 2010; Venne 1998; Williams 1999; Henderson 2002), as well as by settler historians and anthropologists (Asch 2014; Carter 1999; Miller 2009; Milloy 2009; Tobias 1986; Tully 2000), all of whom recognize that treaties represent the establishment of a legal and political framework intended to govern the coexistence of various communities in a shared space. One of the most highly contested issues resulting from these varying interpretations is the question of whether treaties extinguished Indigenous peoples' rights to the land. As the RCAP (1996, vol. 2, 43) explains, "notwithstanding clear words calling for extinguishment in many historical treaties, it is highly probable that no consent was ever given by [Indigenous] parties to that result. [Indigenous] people, who believe that the Creator set them on their traditional territories and gave them the responsibility of stewardship of the land and of everything on it, are not likely to have surrendered that land knowingly and willingly to strangers." Far from a "sale" of land, treaties are regarded by Indigenous peoples as land-use frameworks, which generally involve the establishment of separate governments and jurisdictions in distinct spaces, and dual governance and jurisdiction in shared spaces and matters of mutual concern.

By and large, the Crown's understanding of treaties as land transactions is regarded in Canadian discourse and institutions as the neutral, unbiased record of events, regardless of the now widespread consensus that it is an inaccurate representation of what occurred during treaty-making. As both the Crown's own written records of negotiations and Indigenous records dispute the notion that a transaction of land ever took place, the "land-cession" view of treaties can be characterized as a mythology rather than merely one of many interpretations of what transpired. Nevertheless, Indigenous accounts of treaties are often deemed less viable by non-Indigenous individuals and institutions because they find their source in Indigenous oral histories and world views (Hunt 2016). The privileging of selective understandings of treaty-making is not a new phenomenon, but dates back to early colonial interactions.

From the outset, the Crown regarded treaties as the mechanisms through which it might secure a sense of finality and permanence over the land question. With treaties negotiated, the Crown could develop the territories—by establishing a police force and British-based rule of law and by building a transcontinental railway—and open them up to settlement. Under the Royal Proclamation of 1763,[1] settlement of lands by non-Indigenous people was prohibited until the negotiation of treaties covering the region in question. The Proclamation offered theoretical affirmations of Indigenous rights and of a nation-to-nation relationship between Indigenous peoples and the Crown, reserving un-ceded land for Indigenous populations while also delineating an understanding of treaties that presumed their purpose to be the facilitation of land transactions.

In a similar vein, while the Crown assumed dominion over Indigenous lands in the West with the transfer of Rupert's Land and the North-Western Territory from the Hudson's Bay Company (HBC) to Canada in 1870, it could not open the land to settlement and development until it negotiated "surrenders" of Indian lands through treaty-making or other means. To achieve these ends, the story of treaties that the Crown proliferated in early colonial policy reduced Indigenous peoples' pre-existing relationships with the land to a mere "interest" that could be cleared through treaty-making. Treaties were not regarded by the Crown as agreements between political equals but as the mechanisms through which the claims of Indigenous peoples would be reconciled with the overarching sovereignty and jurisdiction asserted by the Crown (Taylor 1985).

Following from this understanding of treaty-making, the Crown's written records of the numbered treaties focus heavily on land acquisition, despite the subject of land being consciously avoided by the Crown during many treaty negotiations. For instance, according to the transcripts of the negotiation of Treaty 4 at Qu'Appelle, the question of land was only discussed in reference to the location on which negotiations were to occur and in relation to Indigenous peoples' concerns surrounding the purported "sale" of land from the HBC to Canada (Morris 1880). While Treaty Commissioner Alexander Morris stated at the outset of Treaty 4 negotiations that he was there to talk to the people about the land, the transcripts of negotiations include no mention of an exchange, surrender, or cession of land.

In his research report on Treaty 4, John Taylor notes that while land surrender was a prominent written term of every treaty and the primary purpose for which the Crown made them, the subject of land was not usually raised at all by treaty commissioners. Taylor explains that the question of land took a unique turn at the Treaty 4 negotiations as Indigenous spokespersons focused four of the six days of discussion around their own concerns about the purported "sale of land" from the HBC to the Crown. Thus, even when given the opportunity to clarify the distinctions between Western and Indigenous under-standings of land tenure, Crown treaty negotiators neglected to do so. As Taylor (1985) notes, while [Morris] "might have used the occasion to explain what he meant about Indian title and its extinguishment by treaty . . . he did not." The Crown's avoidance of the land question during treaty negotiations was not a mere oversight but a conscious omission intended to sidestep Indigenous challenges to Crown claims to ownership or jurisdiction over the land. For instance, in describing the context leading up to colonial expansion westward, Treaty 3 Commissioner Simon Dawson (1868, 28) cautioned against raising the topic of land at treaty negotiations, writing that:

> I think a treaty with [the Indians] should, in the first instance, be confined to this one point, namely, RIGHT OF WAY. This they expressed their willingness to accord many years ago, but the question of relinquishing land for settlement was always taken by them *en delibere*. [emphasis original] . . . The first great point is to get the communication opened, and the first treaty should be confined, as I have said, simply to right of way. By combining it with the land question, surveys of townships for settlement, reserves for the Indians, and so forth, complications might arise which would prove embarrassing.

Dawson further noted that Indigenous populations were "extremely jealous as to their right of soil and authority over the country which they occupy" and had previously expressed displeasure at parties that traversed into their territories "without their consent being first asked and obtained" (Dawson 1868, 27). The haste to secure consent resulted in little opportunity to discuss the notion of land and the nature of the relationship that was being entered into between Indigenous people and newcomers. The Crown inaccurately assumed that treaties had effectively extinguished Indigenous peoples' title to the land in accordance with its own legal systems, instituting the mythology of land cession through treaty into Canadian law and policy. Yet, establishing clear and plain intent to extinguish Indigenous rights to the land would have required significant dialogue surrounding the land question in order to translate European concepts into terms that were understood within Indigenous world views, as well as extensive discussion regarding which tracts of land were to be surrendered.[2]

Such a significant disconnect highlights how colonial mythologies such as those related to the nature of treaties both emerge from and are also continually reproduced by colonial institutions. Such mythologies function to privilege Western legal principles but also restrict and confine the legal practices and philosophies of Indigenous peoples who are party to the treaties. While the Crown has sought to integrate "Indigenous perspectives on the spirit and intent of treaties," it has continually failed to take into account the significance of treaties under Indigenous legal and political orders. As Kent McNeil observes, "Although Canadian law allows for the surrender of Aboriginal title to the Crown, this does not mean that it is surrenderable under Aboriginal law" (McNeil 2001). Indeed, treaty Elders and Indigenous legal scholars have repeatedly stated that in Indigenous legal systems, land is not a property that can be transferred or sold.

Indigenous legal scholar and knowledge keeper Leroy Little Bear has written that Indigenous law would not have permitted the notion of transferring land to the Crown: "the standard or norm of the aboriginal peoples' law is that land is not transferable and therefore is inalienable. Land and benefits therefrom may be shared with others, and when Indian nations entered into treaties with European nations, the subject of the treaty, from the Indians' viewpoint, was not the alienation of the land but the sharing of the land" (Little Bear 1986, 243). In neglecting to engage fully with Indigenous legal traditions, Canada's historical narratives, social and cultural assumptions, and judicial and political decisions continue to rely on the notion that title to the land was surrendered through treaty-making.

Relational Understanding

This is hopefully the start of an on-going process so that this relationship, the treaty relationship can be discussed openly on a continuous basis and not revisited only once every 125 years which is obviously quite wrong.

—Arnot 1997, 27

As the previous section has demonstrated, treaty mythologies of land cession and surrender function to sustain the status quo by depicting treaties as the end point for Indigenous legal and political authority and to contain alternate political arrangements that would be made possible under a more relational approach. It has always been my understanding that treaties are sacred undertakings, and that to understand treaty relationships you need to understand the world view and spirituality of those who enter into treaties. The Indigenous people who entered into treaties with European newcomers sought to create a relationship framework to share the land; we sought assurances that our traditional ways would not be interfered with while also wanting to learn from each other, understand more about one another, and use that knowledge to create a sustainable future for generations to come (Cardinal and Hildebrandt 2000). By and large, this desire has not been reciprocated by settler populations.

For hundreds of years, Indigenous people have had the values, lifestyle, and religion of settlers forced upon us. Settlers who arrived in Canada looked to treaties as a way of clearing the land of Indigenous people and our outstanding "claims" against Crown assertions of jurisdiction so they could make their homes here. But it was not just Indigenous bodies that needed to be erased; it was our laws, political orders, social values, spirituality, economic systems, languages, and cultural practices (Simpson 2017). Newcomers have not been required to learn about Indigenous ways of living, as Indigeneity has alternately been treated by the Canadian state as something that should be voluntarily relinquished, outlawed, assimilated, legislated away, reduced to the status of a cultural minority, appropriated, or otherwise vacated of meaning. But the most damaging attack of all has been on our relations, not just in the present, but our ways of existing in all our relations. This includes an assault upon our relations with the past, manifesting through the continual marginalization and repression of our ancestral knowledge and practices. It also includes an assault upon our relations with the future, through efforts to freeze Indigeneity in the past, which would, in turn, delimit our ability to create new ways of being Indigenous into the future. Further, the asymmetry in understanding has meant that treaty relations have primarily been theorized and inhabited through Western interpretations of what treaties, and what Indigenous and non-Indigenous relations, can and should look like.

Within and outside of Indigenous communities, many efforts have been made and resources dedicated by knowledge holders, scholars, and policy-makers towards arriving at "a common understanding" of what was agreed upon through treaty-making. Yet all too often, such efforts fail to focus on the nature of the relationship framework that was to be established through treaty-making. They presume that treaties represented contracts or transactions with a fixed set of terms, and that the project of treaty implementation must be geared towards ascertaining and bridging Indigenous and non-Indigenous understandings of specific terms. Yet treaties were not intended to establish a static set of terms that would be fixed in time, but to provide a framework that is dynamic, relational, and contextual and that could guide the interactions of treaty partners over time.

For Indigenous peoples, the negotiation of treaties with settler newcomers followed a long tradition of treaty-making with other living beings and human populations. Practices of treaty-making predated the arrival of Europeans, helping to mediate the relationships between various Indigenous populations and other living beings in shared spaces. Elder Danny Musqua explains:

> We had peace and friendship treaties between our brothers, the Cree, our relationship to the Cree over 500 years. Into that relationship came the Assiniboine Indian people for almost 300 years. We had land use agreements between

ourselves and we respected those terms and agreements along that use of territory and that land. And so when we came to the table in 1874 and 1876 and beyond, we came with that kind of understanding that the use is what we want to convey to the Crown. (Musqua 1997, 10)

Elder Musqua describes the nature of land-use agreements that existed between Indigenous populations prior to contact in greater detail:

When I say the use of that land, we had agreements between one another, hunting territories that we shared, trapping lands that we shared, gathering lands that we shared, medicinal lands that we shared, co-opted peace territorial lands that we designated for shelter and safety for our people. That's how they set out things between one another. They understood use, they understood the means by which land was used. (Musqua 1997, 6)

His insights demonstrate that agreements were traditionally used to manage shared or separate jurisdictions over various spaces and geographies by delineating their intended use. Yet these frameworks of coexistence were not exclusively concerned with the nature of human interactions, but also with the ways in which humans would coexist *in relation to creation.*

In contemporary contexts, treaties are commonly understood as agreements that have been entered into by human communities. However, Indigenous origin stories and philosophies of relationality do not position humans as distinct from creation but as an embedded part of a complex network of rights and responsibilities with other living beings. The premise of shared land use emerges from a world view that sees Indigenous peoples as inhabiting relationships of interdependence with the land, animals, and waterways, rather than as holding authority or ownership over these. Humans are not the only beings with whom we have to coexist successfully, and Indigenous peoples also have lengthy histories of negotiating and maintaining relationships with animal nations in order to navigate the complexities of coexistence. The creation of such understandings follows from a world view that regards all living beings in a non-hierarchical way. It requires a commitment to listen and work together across differences, in order to comprehend the needs of those who do not speak the same language or employ the same legal or political concepts.

Treaties provide important inspiration for how human communities might govern our interactions based on the ways in which Indigenous peoples have historically worked to sustain healthy and generative relations within the natural world. By gaining an awareness of the complex systems of interdependence, symbiosis, and reciprocity that are inherent in the rest of creation, humans are able to observe how the various parts of the natural world play different roles while working together to nourish and sustain one another. Indeed, as John Borrows (2010, 28) writes, one of the many sources of Indigenous law is natural law; that is, we identify and learn about law through observation of the physical world around us. From contemplating the interactions of the natural world, we can gain direction for how to approach human interactions in a non-interfering, sustainable way. As Glen Coulthard (2010, 82) writes, Indigenous peoples' senses of place situate us as an "inseparable part of an expansive system of interdependent relations covering the land and animals, past and future generations, as well as other people and communities" from which a number of ethical-political norms follow. In other words, by observing the living earth we can gain a greater sense of responsibility and accountability in relation to humans and all other living beings.

For instance, in *Recovering Canada*, Borrows looks to a treaty between the Anishinaabe and the Deer nation to identify the resource laws intended to inform the relationship between humans and animals. In the Nanabush/Deer story, Borrows describes how Nanabush broke the law through trickery and disrespect in killing the deer and in failing to follow proper protocol, which caused an imbalance in the relationship between humans and animals. This represented a violation of the laws outlined in the treaty between the Anishinaabe and the Deer nation, which required humans to exercise honour, dignity, and respect towards other living beings and their environments. Note how in this story, the treaty represents a way of living well in relation to others; just as Elder Musqua indicated, the intent of the treaty is to determine use and its purpose is to delineate how the Anishinaabe agreed to live in a sustainable and balanced way with other living beings and their environments.

In a similar yet distinct story, "The Woman Who Married a Beaver," Heidi Stark demonstrates how treaties elucidate the values and proper behaviour necessary for two or more groups of living beings to create and maintain alliances with one another (Stark 2010, 147). This story outlines a treaty relationship established between the Anishinaabe and beavers as one founded on respect, responsibility, and renewal. In this story, the treaty is similarly prescriptive and procedural in nature, as it outlines the values and behaviours necessary to create and uphold good relations over time. The key to both of these stories is that the treaty represents a way of agreeing to live together rather than an exchange of objects or terms. These broader understandings of relationality can help unsettle dominant understandings of who we see as political actors with a stake and voice in treaty agreements. Here, governance is the business of all living beings, not merely that of elected leadership. The responsibilities and rights that are affirmed in treaties are shared by all living beings, and implicate the animals, birds, waterways, lands, ancestors, spirits, and Creator as political actors. Understood in this way, treaty-based modes of relating give rise to an understanding of a political community as something far greater than a collective of individual humans, but rather as something comprised of the relationships between people and places interacting in the present and in different time periods. Further, such relational understandings of treaties can bring forward greater awareness of women's political agency by demonstrating that Indigenous women did in fact play important roles in Indigenous practices of treaty-making, even if these roles have a tendency to be obscured or intentionally minimized by colonial records.[3]

As a relationship framework, treaty implementation is a continuous process with no end point—it is intended to live on in perpetuity through ongoing engagement, maintenance, and renewal. Treaties are made possible through the interaction of parties. As Margaret Kovach writes, treaties are not "things" that exist independently of ongoing and equal involvement of parties that agree to them; rather, the word *treaty* "describes an active relational process that includes seeking continuous counsel and dialogue on matters that have bearing on the parties it involves" (Kovach 2013, 112). It is for this reason that treaty Elders often describe treaties as international or nation-to-nation frameworks (Cardinal and Hildebrandt 2000, 42). They exist in the relationship between political entities, and are intended to ensure that Indigenous peoples will continue to engage with newcomers over matters that impact us and our territories as nations engage with other nations, that is, within a relationship of political non-subordination. Importantly, this also means that Indigenous peoples reserved our rights not just to govern ourselves but to continue to carry out our responsibilities to the land and waterways.

All too often, treaties are seen merely as agreements that give rise to rights for Indigenous peoples within the overarching Canadian legal system. Aimee Craft (2013, 6) has written of Treaty 1 that since there was no body of inter-societal laws when treaties were negotiated, Indigenous people relied on their own laws to inform their understanding of the treaties. It follows, then, that contemporary understandings of treaties should be informed by both Indigenous and non-Indigenous laws in contemporary discussions of treaty implementation. As Borrows (2010, 28) has argued, treaties can and should represent an important source of inter-societal law, yet this requires Indigenous legal traditions to be taken seriously by non-Indigenous treaty partners and for these laws to be implemented in a substantive way.

This means acknowledging that Indigenous peoples' ongoing ability to carry out our responsibilities to the land is an integral part of our laws and governance that we sought to affirm in entering into treaties. Indigenous understandings of treaties are not based on ownership of the land, past or present, as land is not something that can be owned by a human being. For this reason, it could never have been sold or transferred to the Crown through treaty-making. Rather, use of the land was of paramount importance to Indigenous people entering into treaties, not just in terms of identifying limits on settler actions in treaty territories, but in terms of guaranteeing Indigenous peoples' ongoing use of the land while also ensuring that settler use of the land would not interfere with the existing relationships between other living beings and the environment.

One of the central priorities for Indigenous people in determining use of the land was to ensure that our traditional ways of life would not be interfered with, that the relations inherent in that way of life would remain intact. However, the phrase "way of life" is rarely interpreted by the Crown as including protection for our legal and political systems. At the minimum, "way of life" is interpreted as our ability to hunt, gather, and harvest, and at a maximum it has been understood to embody a limited spectrum of self-government responsibilities, akin to those of a municipality. Discussions surrounding way of life cannot be divorced from questions of governance and jurisdiction relative to the living earth, as central to the maintenance of our way of life is the need to maintain a vibrant and healthy land base in order to sustain our relations with plants, animals, and other living beings into the future.

When implemented as a framework for a non-hierarchical relationship, treaties can situate multiple parties as having equivalent moral but also political standing, creating new laws to govern the relationship while also affirming the continuity of the pre-existing forms of governance of involved parties. Thus, they have the potential to inspire a framework that allows multiple self-determining parties to engage in mutually beneficial forms of coexistence with one another while remaining autonomous. Yet all too often, contemporary discussions of treaty implementation are taken up in ways that are geared towards the continued integration of Indigenous peoples into Canadian political culture. Here I am thinking of depictions of contemporary treaty implementation (the so-called modern treaties dating from the James Bay and Northern Quebec Agreement of

1975) as primarily involving economic development and resource revenue-sharing with Indigenous communities. Such representations selectively emphasize areas where treaty implementation can serve the broader "national interest" rather than thinking about treaty implementation in a way that disrupts Canada's existing political and economic landscape. The mythology that gets reproduced in such narratives is that Indigenous peoples consciously decided to give up our rights to the land in exchange for a new means of livelihood, which equates to socio-economic parity achieved through inclusion in the Canadian economy. While treaty Elders certainly describe the motivations of Indigenous parties to treaty as including the desire to learn new skills and technologies from one another, translating Indigenous understandings of livelihood to participation in the "modern economy" drastically narrows the scope of dialogue surrounding treaty implementation to questions of financial well-being. Also, in the "Indigenous development" framework, the imperative to "learn from each other" is depicted as a unidirectional, one-way learning process in which Indigenous people are those who must learn from the advancements of Western society. However, as Stark (2017) makes clear, treaty-making also entailed a process for teaching newcomers about their responsibilities to creation; in other words, treaties are also intended to provide frameworks to facilitate multidirectional learning processes.

Neo-liberal imperatives of economic participation and restructuring not only eclipse the nature of the treaty relationship, they detract from the fundamental goal of treaties, which has been the preservation of Indigenous ways of living with each other and the world around us. While the retention of Indigenous livelihood and wellness are certainly imperatives of treaty-making, of primary importance is the maintenance of the relationships that make that livelihood possible. As Leanne Simpson writes, Indigenous political mobilization will be inherently limited if our goal is the proletarianization of our people: "This is not the new buffalo. The massive shift of Indigenous peoples into the urban wage economy and the middle class cannot be the solution to dispossession, because this consolidates dispossession" (Simpson 2017, 82). Here Simpson repurposes the often-cited metaphor that education represents "the new buffalo." This phrase is frequently invoked by Indigenous people to suggest that knowledge, both of traditional and of new ways, is key to our survival. It flows from the metaphorical notion that the buffalo represented the original source of Indigenous freedom and autonomy on the prairies. Indeed, the late Elder Gordon Oakes (1997, 76) explained that Indigenous peoples "had self-government before the coming of the white man. The buffalo provided every need that a nation would require and that was our self-government flowing from there. Today we have no land base to sustain ourselves." In invoking this metaphor, then, Simpson confronts the suggestion that the accumulation of capital can replace the ways in which Indigenous relationships with creation have been impacted through colonialism, as the primary impulse of colonialism has been the drive to possess and exploit resources such as the land. The economic development approach to treaty implementation reduces the political significance of treaties to the reconciliation of Indigenous interests with Canadian nation-building, a reality that has not departed significantly from the initial phase of treaty-making with settlers. In so doing, it reproduces a transactional understanding of treaties by privileging a notion of economic reciprocity whereby all parties gain—resource revenues, land for development, compensation packages—while the broader political implications of the treaty relationship get lost in the process.

Are Treaties Relevant, and to Whom?

While members of Indigenous and non-Indigenous populations living in areas that are not covered by treaties often interrogate their relevance and applicability to contemporary contexts, I argue that treaties are relevant to all who make their home in contemporary Canada. They remain relevant for the possibilities of coexistence that they offer when understood in accordance with the legal traditions of all who signed them, but also because of the violence they stand to reproduce if they continue to be misunderstood and misinhabited.

It is certainly important to recognize that not all Indigenous peoples understand their relationships through treaties. However, I am of the perspective that how Indigenous peoples understand their relationships with other living beings and how they have sought to protect those relationships through treaties hold many parallels with the ways in which many non-treaty Indigenous peoples understand their spiritual, familial, political, and legal relationships with Creation. It is also important to acknowledge, as Charlie and Green do in Chapters 5 and 14 of this volume, that many Indigenous people have critiqued the use of the term "treaty" to describe modern land negotiations and agreements, for they depart from Indigenous peoples' long-standing practices of treaty-making in process, content, and form. Yet, this also suggests that the ideal of treaty as expressed in the numbered treaties remains an important reference point to ground contemporary critiques of Indigenous–state engagements such as modern treaty or land claim negotiations.

At the same time, Indigenous peoples who reside outside of treaty territories can often be heard characterizing their ancestral territories as "unceded." This serves an important function as it makes clear both the rights of those Indigenous peoples who have lived on and governed those territories for centuries and delineates limits upon the actions of those peoples and of non-Indigenous peoples seeking to enter into the territory. Yet, this language can also have the effect of reproducing the assumption that treaties represent cessions or surrenders of land.

Descriptions of the numbered treaties as land-cession treaties are ultimately grounded in the assumption that the Indigenous people who signed these treaties sold our land and assented to legal and political domination, and therefore that we have no legitimate claim in perpetuity to title, jurisdiction, or sovereignty over our own affairs. Similarly, descriptions of the "peace and friendship" treaties entered into prior to Confederation often define their purpose and intent by way of contrast with the numbered treaties. It is true that pre-Confederation treaties were negotiated in different legal, political, and cultural climates than were the numbered treaties, the 1850s Douglas treaties on Vancouver Island, and the Robinson Huron and Robinson Superior treaties of 1850 in Ontario. These are relevant contexts and factors, but it is important to understand that the political, diplomatic, or "peace and friendship" character of the earlier pre-Confederation treaties should not be invoked so as to minimize the diplomatic character of the numbered treaties by way of contrast.

Such period-specific understandings of treaty-making can be useful when trying to understand the particular form and implications of Indigenous peoples' interactions with the Canadian state across different times and places. However, they may also reinforce Canadian narratives and categorizations of the history of Indigenous–state relations in a way that clouds the potential similarities in Indigenous world views and philosophies of relationality. While we must be careful not to collapse diverse Indigenous polities into a pan-Indigenous body, it is important to acknowledge that we might have something to learn from engaging with the ways that other communities have sought to negotiate sustainable and generative forms of coexistence in shared spaces, rather than dismissing them as irrelevant. Such determinations highlight the ways in which many Indigenous peoples have allowed the Canadian courts' interpretations to inform their own understandings of the numbered treaties. Additionally, the view that practices of treaty-making aren't relevant to those who did not sign the numbered treaties discounts the practices of treaty-making that occurred prior to contact with settlers and that many Indigenous communities engaged in. All communities have their own practices of how to coexist with others, and many have engaged in some form of treaty-making or other means of negotiating coexistence in shared spaces in past times. The questions of relationship that emerge from discussions surrounding the numbered treaties are directly relevant to these practices and traditions.

Moreover, treaties are relevant and important to engage with because of the violence they stand to perpetuate when they are improperly or selectively inhabited. The negotiation of the numbered treaties did not occur in isolation, but was part of a broader web of colonial policies intended to facilitate settlement across the country. The Canadian government's interpretation of the responsibilities it holds and does not hold under treaties has undoubtedly informed the policies and positions implemented through the Indian Act, various pieces of legislation, the courts, and other legal and political instruments. For instance, the treaty promise of providing education that would supplement traditional forms of education with Western teachings was implemented by the Crown in the form of the assimilationist and ultimately genocidal residential school system (Carr-Stewart 2001, 126). Claims that treaties are irrelevant to non-treaty Indigenous people overlook how all Indigenous people have been impacted by gender discrimination, the reserve and pass system, residential schools, bans on Indian spiritual and cultural practice, band systems of governance, and other legislation imposed by a state that used (and continues to use) treaties to bolster its claims to authority and jurisdiction over Indigenous peoples. All Indigenous peoples, treaty or not, have been impacted by the policies and processes that have arisen from narrow, transactional understandings of treaties. Further, these narrow understandings continue to delineate the scope of how "treaties" are approached in the modern era.

Moreover, all Indigenous peoples are impacted by the ways in which treaty mythologies inform racist, gendered, and colonial stereotypes and assumptions. At the level of interpersonal societal relations, the depiction of treaties as land surrenders impacts how non-Indigenous people may interpret the contemporary rights of all Indigenous people. It informs non-Indigenous perceptions of Indigenous "entitlement," or of getting "special rights" or "handouts" from the government. Certainly, the myth that all Indigenous people get their post-secondary education paid for, or get free comprehensive health and dental care, arises in part from misinterpretations of the relevant treaty clauses. These are incorrect perceptions, as neither of these is acknowledged by the government as a treaty right, despite various iterations of written and oral promises across the numbered treaties indicating that the Crown and Indigenous people would provide assistance and care to one another in times of need and starvation.

And at the same time as treaty mythologies can operate to fuel racist stereotypes about Indigenous peoples, they can also operate to mask or soften the forms of colonial violence committed against all Indigenous people. For instance, the understanding of treaties as land transactions does a whole host of things that distort their nature, such as limiting them to their written substance, locating them in the past, and minimizing the political authority of Indigenous peoples from the moment of treaty negotiations. But most relevant to the current discussion is the way in which treaty mythologies legitim-ate Canada's otherwise unjust and illegal appropriation of Indigenous lands, permitting its claim to title and the extension of its legal and political jurisdiction. Put simply, this position perpetuates the dispossession of Indigenous peoples and territories and the en-trenchment of a colonial relationship characterized by political hierarchy and domina-tion. The contemporary configurations of the relationship between Indigenous people and non-Indigenous people in Canada are informed by these narratives, as are the societal and governmental responses to present-day crises in Indigenous communities. Thus, the term "treaty mythologies" does not merely refer to incorrect interpretations of treaties as an isolated event in our historical consciousness. Rather, it refers to how ongoing interpret-ations of treaties as fixed-term transactions function to continually reproduce structures of settler colonialism.

Challenging treaty mythologies, then, does not just involve a process of correcting our historical understanding. It also means critically interrogating the active and ongoing role that misrepresentations of treaties play in sustaining structures of settler colonialism in the present. Demythologizing treaty relationships involves much more than correcting a singular inaccuracy in the historical record; rather, it involves critical inquiry into the ongoing and long-term dangers of the static and transactional view. Instead of taking up treaties as historical agreements that were entered into but have long since been violated by the Canadian state, it is important to confront the ways they are selectively and stra-tegically invoked in dominant institutions and systems to continually produce Canada's claims to sovereignty in response to shifting socio-political climates. Breaking down treaty myths not only helps illustrate how treaties have functioned to subjugate Indigen-ous peoples, but it allows us all to begin to open our horizons to new ways of animating treaty-based modes of relating in the everyday.

Throughout this chapter, I have argued that settler-colonial mythologies do not just shape how we understand historic events, but also how we approach relations in the present and future. Sometimes, these mythologies are subtle and insidious, shaping the tone, connotation, or implication of contemporary narratives, such as in school hist-ory lessons, media stories, or the narratives surrounding the Truth and Reconciliation Commission and the National Inquiry into Missing and Murdered Indigenous Women and Girls. Other times, they are explicit and direct, invoked as justification for racist and derogatory views about Indigenous peoples expressed in the comments sections of social media or online communities. And yet other times they serve to form part of Canada's national narratives, shaping the ways Canada depicts its engagements and interactions with Indigenous peoples today. Consider, for instance, the stories of the numbered treaties as having extinguished Indigenous title to treaty territories or our rights to prior, free, and informed consent on proposed economic development projects. Canada's support for the Trans Mountain pipeline without the consent of Indigenous peoples of treaty territories and the nationalization of such projects represent direct violations of treaty relationships. Treaty implementation does not equate to minimal powers of self-government that do not interfere with the overarching jurisdiction of federal and provincial governments. In fact, the proliferation of the notion that treaty relationships are being implemented, when in fact they very clearly are not, is perhaps even more damaging than if they were outright denied. Awareness of how treaty mythologies can be invoked to reproduce systems of settler colonialism can help make visible the systems of power and privilege that shape the configurations of all of our lives today and into the future.

For a Better Future

In my understanding, treaties are meant to represent both the continuity of the respective relations that parties bring with them and the beginning of something new. They affirm the continuity of different ways of being in shared spaces and provide a framework to help navigate the tensions and inconsistencies that arise across difference over time. Not intended to exist in a fixed and immobile state, treaties are to be continually renewed in relation to the conditions of the time as a way of ensuring the continuity of each treaty partner's ways of life. Thinking about treaties in this way requires a much more flexible conception of what a political arrangement can look like, and it necessitates a willingness to revisit the foundational assumptions that many people have surrounding the nature of Indigenous–settler relations.

   In this chapter, I have argued that revisiting dominant myths and assumptions is an absolutely necessary part of bringing forward healthier relationships; if we fail to do so, our imaginations become constrained by static ways of thinking, by that which we already adhere to and cannot see beyond. I have further argued that treaty-based modes of relating provide excellent inspiration for moving beyond the ways of thinking that all too often limit our ability to conceptualize new possibilities in the world. Throughout, I have asked readers to be mindful of their own stories and the ways in which we all consciously or unconsciously reproduce the world views and assumptions inherent in them. These include the normalization of Western historical records, claims to truth, and the legal and political principles embedded within them. However, they also include ways of thinking of humans as separate from or above the living earth, as well as binary conceptions of time that create a divide between our past, present, and future. Treaties transcend each of these divisions as they represent a means of affirming pre-existing ways and applying them to the birth of new relationships, of seeing one's existence defined by multiple sources, including relationships with the land, with one's family, with broader communities, and with newcomers.

   While Indigenous peoples' relationships with settlers will undoubtedly continue to change in response to social and environmental factors, the values and precepts underlying treaty relationships are intended to be applicable to multiple contexts. Similar to the daily and seasonal cycles of the sun, the grass, and the rivers, treaties are intended to undergo cycles of renewal and rebirth that exist when treaties are conceptualized as something that is embodied, practised, and lived. Thus, treaties transcend notions of a divided past, present, and future by showing that future-oriented political arrangements do not require us to relinquish our past relations, but that these can and should inform the creation of new relations with the worlds we live within.

In thinking about what generative, healthy relationships might look like, treaty-based modes of relating can direct our attention beyond "the present," as treaties themselves are defined by multiple states of being; for instance, we inherit responsibilities to carry forward the knowledge of our ancestors, to learn from it, grow, and pass it on to our children. We inherit stewardship responsibilities towards other living beings and to the spirits that care for the living earth, and know that we must honour those to sustain life into the future. These ways of understanding relationship can help remind us of the limits of only thinking in terms of "the present," as our existence emerges from the relations that have come before us and has a direct impact on those who have yet to come. Indeed, the point of treaty-making has always been to affirm the continuity of past ways while also thinking about the sort of future that was desired for future generations. As Menno Boldt (1993, 40) writes, the chiefs who negotiated the treaties "strained to peer over the horizon of their time to see what their future needs for survival and well-being as Indians would be in the emerging world." Rather than remaining cemented in pre-existing ways of thinking, Indigenous treaty negotiators demonstrated a form of intellectual mobility that allowed them to make decisions based on that which they could not yet see, attempting to envision new relations that had yet to come about.

There are so many entrenched ways of thinking that preclude/prohibit our ability to imagine new social and political arrangements in the world. What I hope to have made clear in this chapter is that treaty-based modes of relating can provide inspiration to think beyond such intellectual forms of containment. Working towards the decolonization of Indigenous–settler relations means a lot more than making space for the recognition of Indigenous interpretations of treaties within Canadian institutions. It involves a commitment by all who make their home in Canada to work towards the implementation of new configurations of relationship that are informed by Indigenous laws and understandings of responsibility and accountability. Otherwise, ongoing neglect for the laws and governance of all treaty partners will keep us deeply enmeshed in the very crises of relationship that our ancestors sought to protect against.

Discussion Questions

1. What are some of the assumptions or mythologies you hold regarding the relationship between Indigenous and non-Indigenous peoples in Canada?

2. Have you ever been in a relationship where you felt silenced, or that was narrated entirely by the other party? How did it feel? What was the resolution?

3. What are the implications and limitations of representing treaties as "historical events"?

4. What does it mean to inherit relationships from our ancestors?

5. What are some of the ways that the "spirit and intent" of treaties can be activated on an everyday level?

6. What are some of the contemporary rights and responsibilities of treaty partners in Canada?

Recommended Reading

Asch, Michael. 2014. *On Being Here to Stay: Treaties and Aboriginal Rights in Canada*. Toronto: University of Toronto Press.

Cardinal, Harold, and W. Hildebrandt. 2000. *Treaty Elders of Saskatchewan: Our Dream Is That Our Peoples Will One Day Be Clearly Recognized as Nations*. Calgary: University of Calgary Press.

Innes, Robert. 2013. *Elder Brother and the Law of the People: Contemporary Kinship and Cowessess First Nation*. Winnipeg: University of Manitoba Press.

Simpson, Leanne. 2008. "Looking after Gdoo-Naaganinaa: Precolonial Nishnaabeg Diplomatic and Treaty Relationships," *Wicazo Sa Review* 23, no. 2: 29–42.

Stark, Heidi. (2010). "Respect, Responsibility, and Renewal: The Foundations of Anishinaabe Treaty-Making with the United States and Canada," *American Indian Culture and Research Journal*, 34, no. 2: 145–64.

Notes

1. Royal Proclamation, 1763, R.S.C., 1985, App. II, No. 1.
2. See Justice Morrow's rationale in *Re Paulette et al. and Registrar of Titles (No. 2)*, 1973 Can LII 1298 (NWT SC), p. 33.
3. For an overview of Indigenous women's roles in treaty-making, see Venne (1998).

2 The "Canada Problem" in Indigenous Politics

David Newhouse and Yale Belanger

Introduction

It has been more than two decades since the Royal Commission on Aboriginal[1] Peoples (RCAP) presented its final report in 1996, outlining principles for a renewed relationship between Aboriginal peoples and Canada and proposing recommendations to implement this new relationship. Grounded in the belief that Aboriginal peoples are full and equal partners in Confederation, the RCAP report presented a vision of a Canada as encompassing 10 provinces, three territories, 40 to 60 Aboriginal Nations, and a parliamentary-embedded First Nations House, all confirmed and given expression by treaties (1996). The vision was seen by many as unworkable and costly, although, to be fair, the cost was mainly viewed in relation to addressing the colonial legacy—i.e., cleaning up the past. The Canadian government's lukewarm response to the RCAP's recommendations suggests that the conversation about Canada remains framed and dominated by the English and French, two ancient rivals whose transplanted-from-Europe rivalry eclipses other voices (Canada 1997).

Since the establishment of Canada in 1867, Canadian government officials have largely been unable—or have refused—to consider Indigenous peoples as political equals. Ongoing opposition to Canada's efforts to see Indigenous peoples abandon their historic social, economic, and political ideals and their ideal of a nation-to-nation relationship has been framed as the "Indian problem." Indigenous leaders, on the other hand, have acknowledged what they could define as the "Canada problem"—that is, those of French and British ancestry remaining loyal to Canada's European roots to the exclusion of Indigenous voices as equal political actors informing its ongoing evolution.

These differences notwithstanding, Indigenous and Canadian leaders agree that the politics surrounding Indigenous peoples have yet to resolve the many contemporary issues that bear the mark of our country's long colonial history, most recently reiterated in the final report of the Truth and Reconciliation Commission (TRC 2015). Established in response to an RCAP recommendation for a public inquiry, the TRC was tasked in 2008 "to investigate and document the origins, purposes and effects of residential school policies and practices as they relate to all Aboriginal peoples, with particular attention to the manner and extent of their impact on individuals and families across several generations, on communities, and on Aboriginal society as a whole" (RCAP 1996, 383). It is with this brief overview in mind that this chapter examines Indigenous politics through the lenses of the "Indian problem" and the "Canada problem."

Indigenous Peoples and Canada

In a country where the century-old legacy of residential schools has only recently been discussed and examined, the general lack of public knowledge about the presence of Indigenous people on Turtle Island for thousands of years prior to European contact and the continuing role they have played in Canada's evolution is disappointing, though not surprising. Take Aboriginal constitutional recognition as an example. The British North America (BNA) Act of 1867 (now renamed the Constitution Act, 1867) assigned to the federal government the responsibility for Indians and lands reserved for the Indians, thereby creating a guaranteed constitutional presence. Few people in Canada know about this, and those who are aware frequently interpret the word "responsibility" in much the same way as the early Europeans, which was that Canada needed to transform Indians into Europeans—more particularly, into either British or French people—and to ensure their absorption and assimilation into the body politic.

That Indians have continually resisted efforts to be colonized has been an enduring challenge for Canada, for eradicating the "Indian problem" has been the foundation of Canada's Indian policy since before Confederation (Dyck 1991). Resolving this perceived problem was based on assimilating Indigenous people into the dominant social, economic, and political culture of Canada. Indeed, the government championed its assimilationist policy until 1971, when it withdrew its last formal attempt at assimilation, the *Statement of the Government of Canada on Indian Policy* (the notorious White Paper of 1969). Self-government policies gradually replaced the official policy of assimilation during the next three decades, even if many Indigenous people contend that assimilationist and racist attitudes continue to inform policy development.[2] In this disruptive milieu Indigenous peoples have nevertheless stood firm to their own social, political, and economic principles. They are now recognized as constituting distinct cultural and political communities grounded by Supreme Court–acknowledged rights that have been slowly evolving and expanding since the 1970s. This is a remarkable turn of events for those who for so long have been seen by Canada's government through the lens of the "Indian problem."

For Indigenous peoples, the "Canada problem" in Indigenous politics is about the ongoing colonial project that involves both the denial of their political sovereignty and the theft of their lands. Canada has not transformed into a territory that: (1) respects and doesn't interfere with Indigenous peoples' ability to live as sovereign nations, (2) recognizes their inherent rights and jurisdictions as Indigenous peoples, and (3) lives up to its many historic and contemporary treaty promises. Some Indigenous leaders have framed their work in ways that honour both their peoples' political distinctiveness and their rightful inclusion in Confederation's great unfinished project. Upon Nunavut being established as part of Confederation, for example, some Inuit leaders referred to themselves as "Mothers and Fathers of Confederation." Chief Joseph Gosnell of the Nisga'a Nation remarked on the ratification of the Nisga'a treaty in April 2000: "Today, the Nisga'a people become full-fledged Canadians as we step out from under the Indian Act" (http://social studies.nelson.com/history/teachweblinks_15.html). The framing of these efforts as part of the continuing process of Confederation is controversial. Some scholars see negotiation of self-government as a form of negotiated inferiority and not resulting in Indigenous peoples as proper partners in Confederation as RCAP states (Ladner 2001). This view is echoed by community leaders such as Russ Diabo, who argues that the long-term goal is to "foist municipal style governance on First Nations" (Smith 2018). Some chiefs have also expressed concern about this approach. Onion Lake Cree Okimaw Henry Lewis states: "We will not stand by and allow Canada to turn us into a fourth level of government when we are the Original Governments" (Murray 2018). Over the last few decades, Indigenous leaders have adopted the terminology of "nation-to-nation" as the political objective to be achieved. This terminology is based on the wording of the Royal Proclamation of 1763 in which the British Crown recognized Indian polities as nations.[3] What they are working for is for Canada to recognize Indigenous peoples as nations and to forge a new political community that recognizes this important political goal.

There have nonetheless been some signs that the relationship between Canada and Indigenous peoples has been changing for the better as governments have started to recognize not only the historical Indigenous presence in Canada, but more significantly that the land Europeans settled on and claimed as their own had been already occupied by Indigenous peoples for thousands of years. For example, the British Columbia Speech from the Throne in February 2003 began by acknowledging the failure of provincial institutions to respond to Indigenous peoples' needs (Belanger 2017, 74). Similarly, in July 2014, the Ontario Throne Speech recognized Indigenous peoples' contributions to the province's development and the location of the provincial legislature at Queen's Park in Toronto within Mississauga traditional territory. On 15 December 2017 Prime Minister Justin Trudeau committed Canada to reconciling with Indigenous peoples, based on the belief that Canada can accommodate Indigenous peoples as charter members of Canadian society.

In terms of the latter, it appears as though Trudeau's idea of reconciliation is drawn from the 1966 Hawthorn Report, specifically its conclusion, which contends that, in addition to being charter members of Canadian society, Indigenous peoples possessed more rights than ordinary citizens (Hawthorne 1966, vol. 1). Hawthorn devised the language of "citizens plus" to describe a situation in which Indigenous peoples were considered to be Canadian citizens who enjoy additional though limited self-government rights, as delegated to them by Canada.[4] Prime Minister Trudeau has stated that the "constitutionally guaranteed rights of First Nations in Canada are not an inconvenience but a sacred obligation," and that the relationship between Canada and Indigenous peoples was to be guided by the spirit and intent of the original treaty relationships on a nation-to-nation basis (CBC 2017).

However, honouring the spirit and intent of the original treaty relationships and obeying Supreme Court rulings have proven to be challenging for Canadian governments. One of these rights is the right to be consulted and accommodated on any project that affects Indigenous lands, as confirmed by several Supreme Court of Canada decisions.[5] This right has been recently tested in the consultations over the Trans Mountain pipeline in 2016–18 when the Federal Court of Appeal concluded in 2018 that consultations must be more than simple note-taking exercises—they must result in accommodation of the concerns identified.[6] The fragility of this duty to consult was highlighted following the 7 June 2018 Ontario election when new premier Rob Ford chose to ignore Indigenous issues while transferring the Ministry of Indigenous Relations and Reconciliation to the Ministry of

The Kwekwecnewtxw Protect The Inlet March against the expansion of the Trans Mountain pipeline, just days prior to the Trudeau government's purchase of the pipeline project from Kinder Morgan.

Energy, Northern Development and Mines. More significantly, the federal government's $4.5 billion purchase during the summer of 2018 of the Trans Mountain pipeline project from Kinder Morgan will test Canada's commitment to consultation and accommodation on projects involving Indigenous lands.

Such actions mimic the Confederation debates, which were characterized by Canada's exclusion of Indigenous leaders from the discussions (Ajzenstat et al. 2003). Consequently, Indigenous relationships with the British and the French were framed without their involvement, which resulted in their being portrayed as dependent wards to the Canadian government's guardianship (Milloy 1992). Indigenous political objectives since that time have revolved around asserting their sovereignty, and in recent years Indigenous peoples have found levels of support for this objective. The most recent advocate for this right has been the Supreme Court of Canada, which in *Tsilhqot'in Nation v. British Columbia* (2014 SCC 44) ruled that the doctrine of *terra nullius* (i.e., unoccupied or vacant land) never applied in Canada, thus signalling another milestone in Indigenous attempts at correcting the historical record. In 2016, the Supreme Court in *Daniels v Canada* (2017 SCC 12) ruled that the Métis people were to be considered Indians under section 91(24) of the Constitution Act, 1867, and that they could legitimately negotiate with the federal government to develop policies that address their issues.

While Canada has followed a consistent and often blatantly colonial Indigenous policy until recent decades, Indigenous peoples have likewise been unwavering in their assertion that their sovereignty applies to historic political relationships as well as new ones, and that their way of relating to other nations has always been based on a political philosophy rooted in the ideals of respect, co-operation, sharing, and harmonious relationships. Robert Williams (1997) contends that the early treaties between Indigenous peoples and Europeans are an excellent primary source for examining Indigenous political thought. He notes that successful relationships between peoples were based on a foundation of mutual reliance that required visible signs of trust. Signs of linking arms and creating a circle of security, peace, and happiness included sharing a peace pipe, exchanging hostages, and presenting one another with valuable gifts such as land and hunting grounds. These and similar processes informed both the pre- and the post-Confederation political organizing of Canada's Indigenous peoples (see, e.g., Mercredi and Turpel 2003; Belanger 2006). The RCAP report likewise proposed an Indigenous political vision of Canada based on ideas of mutual respect, mutual responsibility, and sharing, ideas further elaborated by the First Nations Leadership Council of British Columbia in 2006 and again by the Truth and Reconciliation Commission. There is general agreement that the political vision of Indigenous peoples since the early 1960s has increasingly focused on self-determination and self-government, which for most Indigenous leaders means a return to the nation-to-nation relationships as originally articulated in the Royal Proclamation of 1763. As the following discussion indicates, this is a daunting challenge given Canada's ongoing commitment to its colonial agenda.

The Colonial Legacy

Since the European arrival to Turtle Island and especially after 1763, European governing officials have struggled with how to engage the original inhabitants of this land. In their own ways, the French and English had a particular understanding of the "Indian problem." The problem would variously be framed by questions concerning the humanity of Indigenous people and whether they had souls; what was needed to turn them into good, civilized Christians; how to coexist alongside their communities while inducing them into military alliances; how to tear apart their families and destroy their communities; how to eliminate their languages and eradicate their cultures; how to assimilate them or, more recently, how to promote their transformation into an ethnic group as part of Canada's self-proclaimed multicultural mosaic (see, e.g., Williams 1992; Henderson 1997). Each of these views of the "Indian problem" has led to a range of proposed policy solutions by government officials, whose actions have been informed by the colonial denial of Indigenous sovereignty, their belief in Indian inferiority, and their attitude that the government needed to protect Indians from being exploited. Underlying this protectionist and special status view was a civilizing ideology that sought to convert "the Indians" to Christianity and teach them to live and work in the manner of Europeans (Tobias 1976). If they were to become civilized, it was believed, Indians would be able to leave their traditional ways of life and assimilate into Canadian society. There is general consensus that this was the core government policy until the retraction of the White Paper in 1971.

Canada's approach to developing Indian policy was (and arguably remains) ideologically and practically grounded in the Indian Act, which was originally adopted in 1876 as a consolidation of previous legislation and the policy ideas underlying it (Goikas 1995). While the Act has been amended from time to time, its underlying premises have not changed. John Tobias, a historian of Indigenous people writing in 1976, identified a consistency to Canada's Indian policy over the previous 100 years or so—which we contend has changed little in the last four decades. He argued that the three policy pillars of protection, civilization, and assimilation in place by Confederation have always been the goals of Canada's Indian policy (Tobias 1976; see also Milloy 1992). What has changed over time has been the relative emphasis placed on each.

Addressing the "Indian Problem" in the Second Half of the Twentieth Century

The Hawthorn-Tremblay Commission Report of 1966

There was a growing feeling during the 1950s that the integration of Indian people into greater Canadian society was progressing too slowly (Leslie 1978). Granting the franchise originally was considered a primary method for accelerating the assimilation process, and despite minimal success generating support for it at the community level, in 1960 the federal government unilaterally extended the franchise and full citizenship to all Indian people nationally without abolishing Indian status. These steps at the time appeared to be a progressive shift towards the type of Indian political/societal participation Canadian politicians had long envisioned for Indigenous peoples—Indians absorbed as citizens practising Euro-Canadian norms even if a joint parliamentary report asserted in 1961 that: (1) most Canadians considered Indians to be a racial minority, and (2) the time had come for them to "assume the responsibility and accept the benefit of full participation as Canadian citizens" (Canada 1961, 605).

Growing concern about the poor social and economic situation of these new citizens led the federal government to launch a number of studies, with Harry Hawthorn and Marc Tremblay preparing the most influential report. Appointed in 1963, Hawthorn and Tremblay presented their report to Parliament in two volumes: Part I in 1966 and Part II in 1967. The Hawthorn Report in many ways laid the foundation for modern Indian policy, provocatively suggesting that Indians ought to be "citizens plus" while rejecting the idea of assimilation. Instead, the report suggested that Indians had more rights than other citizens "by virtue of promises made to them, from expectations they were encouraged to hold, and from the simple fact that they once occupied and used a country to which others came to gain enormous wealth in which the Indians have shared little" (Hawthorn 1966, vol. 1, 6). Further, the commissioners stressed "a common citizenship as well as the reinforcement of difference" (Hawthorn 1966). The notion of "citizens plus" would prove exceptionally powerful, so much so that the Indian Chiefs of Alberta (1970) chose the term as the title to its response to the government's now infamous 1969 White Paper.

Hawthorn and Tremblay recognized the need for Indians to govern themselves and for Canada to accommodate those governments. Recommendations 67 and 68 of the Hawthorn Report state: "Continuing encouragement should be given to the development of Indian local government" and "The problem of developing Indian local government should not be treated in the either/or terms of the Indian Act or the provincial framework of local government. A partial blending of the two frameworks within the context of an experimental approach which will provide an opportunity for knowledge to be gained by experience is desirable" (Hawthorn 1966, 18). Further, according to recommendation 72, "The partial ad hoc integration of Indian communities into the provincial municipal framework should be deliberately and aggressively pursued while leaving the organizational, legal and political structure of Indian communities rooted in the Indian Act" (Hawthorn 1966, 18). In other words, the aim was to create a federal–provincial–Indian hybrid.

The White Paper of 1969

Just as Indigenous leaders were acquainting themselves with the Hawthorn Report's progressive recommendations the federal government in 1969 tabled its *Statement on Indian Policy*, which rejected the Hawthorn–Tremblay "citizens plus" formulation. The White Paper,[7] guided by Pierre Trudeau's concept of a "just society," envisioned Indians as ordinary citizens with neither special status nor any entitlement to different administrative arrangements or legal relationships. The central ideas of the proposed policy were the liberal notions of "equality" and "equity" for all individual citizens, expressed in the overall goal of enabling Indian people "to be free to develop Indian cultures in an environment of legal, social and economic equality with other Canadians" (Canada 1969). The White Paper went so far as to propose the transfer of programs and service delivery to provincial jurisdiction, thus finalizing the transfer of "Indians, and lands reserved for the Indians" to provincial jurisdiction first proposed in the early 1950s (Abele and Graham 2011). It also recommended that Indians should receive government services from the same agencies as other Canadians.

   Trudeau's government argued that the policy of a separate legal status for Indians "kept the Indian people apart from and behind other Canadians," and that this "separate road could not lead to full participation, to better equality in practice as well as theory" (Newhouse and Belanger 2010). The White Paper sought to repeal the Indian Act of 1876 and end separate Indian legal status. It also proposed to dismantle the Department of Indian Affairs over a five-year period and appoint a commissioner to establish an Indian land claims policy to deal with grievances resulting from discrepancies in treaty interpretation. Yet the treaties were described as "historic documents" and thus they were to be interpreted as containing only "limited and minimal promises" that had in most cases been fulfilled (Canada 1969). Indian reserve lands would be turned over in fee simple to Indian bands, which could then determine ownership among their members. In other words, the White Paper proposed that Indians would assume mainstream citizenship responsibilities by being accorded the same legal status and rights afforded all Canadian citizens, and that relations between the government and Indian people would move away from the policy regime of protection and special rights. In short, the solution to the Indian problem was to do away with Indian status and the unique constitutional relationship established through treaties.

Addressing the "Canada Problem"

The Red Paper of 1970

Most Indian leaders immediately opposed the White Paper. They argued that the government's proposals ignored or minimized treaties, dismissed separate Indian legal status, and pointed to a future that envisioned Indians as a part of an emerging multicultural society, that is, as non-self-governing ethnic groups. Reflecting on the Hawthorn Report's position and the recent White Paper discussions, the Indian Chiefs of Alberta (ICA) presented their position in 1970 in a paper entitled *Citizens Plus*. Known as the "Red Paper," the ICA presented a political vision of the nature of the Indian–Canada relationship grounded by the belief in special status. The Red Paper expanded the Hawthorn Report's interpretation to infer that "citizens plus" was rooted in the treaties: "To us who are Treaty Indians there is nothing more important than our Treaties, our lands and the well being of our future generation" (Indian Chiefs of Alberta 1970). The continuation of Indian status was presented as essential for justice: "The only way to maintain our culture is for us to remain as Indians. To preserve our culture, it is necessary to preserve our status, rights, lands and traditions. Our treaties are the bases of our rights. . . . The intent and spirit of the treaties must be our guide, not the precise letter of a foreign language."[8]

Regarding Indian lands, "The Indians are the beneficial (actual) owners of the lands. The legal title has been held for us by the Crown to prevent the sale and breaking up of our land. We are opposed to any system of allotment that would give individuals ownership with rights to sell" (Indian Chiefs of Alberta 1970). On services, the Red Paper concludes that "the Federal Government is bound by the British North America Act . . . to accept legislative responsibility for 'Indians and Indian lands.'" In exchange for the surrendered lands, the Indian Chiefs assert, the treaties guaranteed certain benefits to the Indians:

a. To have and to hold certain lands called "reserves" for the sole use and benefit of the Indian people forever and assistance in the social, economic, and cultural development of the reserves.
b. The provision of health services . . . at the expense of the Federal government . . . .
c. The provision of education of all types and levels to all Indian people.
d. The right of the Indian people to hunt, trap and fish for their livelihood free of governmental interference and regulation and subject only to the proviso that the exercise of this right must not interfere with the use and enjoyment of private property. (Indian Chiefs of Alberta 1970)

Based on Indigenous notions of reciprocity and respect—"we share these lands in return for guaranteed rights and services"—the Red Paper grounded the basic political philosophy used to guide Indigenous leaders for the next three decades, during which time numerous reports and declarations expressed opposition to the White Paper philosophy of elimination. Perhaps more importantly, however, these various reports and manifestos articulated unique visions regarding the place of Indigenous peoples in Canadian society and the steps that needed to be taken to improve Indigenous–Canada relations.

While the Red Paper effectively revealed Indian misgivings about the federal government's White Paper proposal, *Wahbung: Our Tomorrows*, released in 1971 by the Manitoba Indian Brotherhood (MIB), best captured the emerging Indigenous political vision. The preamble of the paper stated:

The Indian Tribes of Manitoba are committed to the belief that our rights, both aboriginal and treaty, emanate from our sovereignty as a nation of people. Our relationships with the state have their roots in negotiation between two sovereign peoples. . . . The Indian people enjoy special status conferred by recognition of our historic title that cannot be impaired, altered or compromised by federal–provincial collusion or consent.

Wahbung suggested an inclusive approach to the development of Indian communities, both economically and as central to Indian life. It asserted that development should not proceed piecemeal but rather according to a comprehensive plan focusing on several specific outcomes. There were three elements to this plan: (1) helping individuals and communities recover from the pathological consequences of poverty and powerlessness; (2) protection of Indian interests in lands and resources; and (3) improved and sustained support for human resource and cultural development. The MIB plan rested on the idea that development and change needed to be directed by Indian people themselves so that they would have control over changes that addressed both their individual and communal interests.

The growing Indigenous vision articulating the return to the original nation-to-nation relationship was given a boost in 1973, following the Supreme Court of Canada's *Calder* decision, which ruled that Aboriginal rights were in fact pre-existing, albeit relegated to a lesser position in Canadian society.[9] This judgement entrenched Aboriginal rights within the country's political legal landscape and laid the foundation for the renewal of the treaty process and the contemporary land claims policy (Dockstator 1993). It forced the government to consider the beliefs expressed in the Red Paper and *Wahbung*—that Aboriginal rights in certain cases entailed self-government. *Calder* pointed out that prior to the encroachment of settlers onto Native territories, "Indians were there, organized in societies occupying the land as their forefathers had for centuries." A new way of looking at the history of Indigenous–settler relations had now been established.

The *Calder* case represented a turning point in how Indigenous peoples could address the "Canada problem": the judiciary and the law were now formally drawn into the politics surrounding Indigenous peoples. Increasingly, Indigenous people used the courts to pursue land claims, redress past mistreatments, and further define their legal rights. This shift led Canadian officials to increasingly rely on the courts to guide them when modifying Indigenous policy and law. And while the Supreme Court justices proved in some respects to be good allies during the next two decades, with landmark decisions handed down on Aboriginal fishing rights in *R. v. Sparrow* (1990) and *R. v. Marshall* (1999) and on land title and the validity of oral historical evidence in *Delgamuukw v. British Columbia* (1997), these decisions included elements that have extended provincial jurisdiction, minimized constitutional protections, and created greater mechanisms to infringe upon Aboriginal and treaty rights. For example, while the 2014 *Tsilhqot'in* decision acknowledged the inherent rights of Aboriginal people in relation to their lands, it also allowed room for the provinces to infringe on these rights depending on the nature of proposed developments and the interests of the provinces (Borrows 2017).

Shortly before the *Calder* decision, the Council for Yukon Indians (CYI) presented its plan, *Together Today for Our Children Tomorrow*, for regaining control over lands and resources that included a comprehensive approach to development in its land claims statement to Prime Minister Trudeau. The CYI argued to "obtain a settlement in place of a treaty that will help us and our children learn to live in a changing world. We want to take part in the development of the Yukon and Canada, not stop it. But we can only participate as Indians. We will not sell our heritage for a quick buck or a temporary job" (CYI 1973, 18).

The CYI paper also promoted the importance of retaining a land base: "Without land Indian people have no soul—no life—no identity—no purpose. Control of our own land is necessary for our cultural and economic survival. For Yukon Indian People to join in the social and economic life of Yukon we must have specific rights to lands and natural resources that will be enough for both our present and future needs" (CYI 1973, 18). In contrast to the colonial view, land is seen not as a repository of resources awaiting exploitation but rather as fundamental to Indian identity and essential to any form of Aboriginal self-government.

The Push for Indigenous Self-Government

Momentous social and political shifts characterized the immediate post–White Paper period. Substantial political resistance to the White Paper led to a resurgence in national and provincial Indigenous political organizing, and mounting pressure led Prime Minister Trudeau to both retract the White Paper proposal and initiate a policy of program devolution to band councils. Greater consultation with groups such as the National Indian Brotherhood resulted. The Canadian courts sided with what were now being identified as historic Indigenous claims to pre-contact territorial occupancy, which forced government officials to reflect on the nature of their relationships with Indigenous peoples. Notably, for the first time since Confederation in 1867, government officials were being forced to consider the idea of Indigenous self-determination, specifically within the context of Indian self-government. Was it, as Indigenous leaders proposed, an inherent right, as opposed to a municipal model delegated through federal legislation? Many Indigenous groups nationally began to openly challenge Canada's understanding of what self-government meant, but arguably none were as articulate as the Federation of Saskatchewan Indians (FSI, now the Federation of Sovereign Indigenous Nations or FSIN). In particular, its paper entitled *Indian Government* (1977) sought to solve the "Canada problem" by advancing principles of Aboriginal self-government that quickly became and remain familiar to public policy-makers throughout Canada.

Indian Government starts by articulating a foundational and immutable set of beliefs that its authors argued cannot be refuted: "No one can change the Indian belief. We are Nations; we have Governments. Within the spirit and meaning of the Treaties, all Indians across Canada have the same fundamental and basic principles upon which to continue to build their Governments ever stronger." It sets out eight fundamental principles: (1) Indian nations historically are self-governing; (2) section 91(24) of the BNA Act gives the federal government the authority to regulate relations with Indian nations but it does not authorize regulation of their internal affairs; (3) Indian government powers have been suppressed and eroded by legislative and administrative actions of Canada: Indian government is greater than what is recognized or now exercised and cannot be delegated; (4) treaties reserve a complete set of rights, including the right to be self-governing and to control Indian lands and resources without federal interference; (5) treaties take precedence over provincial and federal laws; (6) the trust relationship imposes fiduciary obligations on the trustee; (7) the federal government has mismanaged this relationship; and (8) Indians have inalienable rights, including the "inherent sovereignty of Indian Nations, the right to self-government, jurisdiction over their lands and citizens and the power to enforce the terms of the Treaties."

Drawing on the language of sovereignty, the FSI considered the right to self-government to be inherited, of the people, and as both "inherent and absolute." Sovereign self-government in this setting was something the Indians had neither surrendered nor been stripped of in a military conquest. Indian governments furthermore had traditionally exercised the powers of sovereign nations, the most fundamental right of which is the right to govern their people and territory under their own laws and customs. Possessing the inherent right to self-government meant that Parliament or any other branch of any foreign government could not grant that right, a position the FSI concluded was reinforced by the treaties. Returning to this issue in a second paper published in 1979, *Indian Treaty Rights: The Spirit and Intent of Treaty*, the FSIN further argued that between 1817 and 1929 more than 20 major international treaties were signed between the Crown and the Indian nations. In return for these treaty rights, the Indian nations agreed to cede certain lands for shared use and settlement (Henderson 1994). The FSIN advanced an understanding that treaties recognized the powers of Indian nations and established sovereign relationships between Indian nations and Canada.

Discussions surrounding self-government broadened over the ensuing years to include Métis, non-status Indian bands, Inuit, and Indigenous peoples in urban contexts as talks about repatriating Canada's Constitution began. Not only did the terminology shift from that of Indian to Aboriginal self-government, but the FSIN view of Aboriginal self-government came to dominate the subsequent discussion, specifically its conclusion that Aboriginal peoples were self-governing nations with a broad and entrenched treaty right to self-government. This view resonated throughout the country and captured the political imagination of Indigenous peoples far beyond those with treaties as they openly and categorically rejected the White Paper's idea of a universal citizenship.[10] Most Indigenous leaders had taken the Dene's lead, who in 1975 began to press the government for recognition of their claims to nation status (Second Joint General Assembly 1975).

The dialogue developed into the early 1980s, and, in 1982, after considerable debate, the Constitution Act, 1982, formally recognized Aboriginal peoples as including[11] Indian, Inuit (formerly Eskimo), and Métis peoples. It also affirmed existing Aboriginal and treaty rights (although it left them indeterminate). Looking to clarify the substance of Aboriginal rights and, implicitly, aiming to determine what self-government meant, section 37 called for three constitutional conferences between Canada, the provinces, and Aboriginal peoples.[12] These televised meetings brought the self-government discussions into the homes of Canadians and introduced them to contemporary Indigenous leaders in conversation with members of the federal cabinet and the provincial premiers. The idea of self-government was hotly debated as many federal and provincial politicians questioned its legitimacy and foundations.

The Penner Report, 1983

As these discussions progressed, the House of Commons established a special committee chaired by Keith Penner to explore the issue of Indian self-government. The well-received Penner Report was released in 1983 and advanced a view of Indian government as enhanced municipal-style government within a federal legislative framework, though with three important differences: (1) Indian government should be a "distinct order" of government within Canada with a set of negotiated jurisdictions and fiscal arrangements; (2) the right of Indian self-government should be constitutionally entrenched with enabling legislation to recognize Indian governments; and (3) the areas of authority for Indian governments could be education, child welfare, health care, membership, social and cultural development, land and resource use, revenue-raising, economic and commercial development, justice and law enforcement, and intergovernmental relations (Penner 1983).

The Penner Report argued for a new relationship with Indigenous peoples based on Prime Minister Pierre Elliott Trudeau's comments at the First Ministers' Conference on Aboriginal Constitutional Matters, Ottawa, March 1983:

> Clearly, our aboriginal peoples each occupied a special place in history. To my way of thinking, this entitles them to special recognition in the Constitution and to their own place in Canadian society, distinct from each other and distinct from other groups who, together with them comprise the Canadian citizenry. (Penner 1983, 39)

The report recommended that "the federal government establish a new relationship with Indian First Nations and that an essential element of this relationship be recognition of Indian self-government" (Penner 1983, 114). It also recommended that:

> the right of Indian peoples to self-government be explicitly stated and entrenched in the Constitution of Canada. The surest way to achieve permanent and fundamental change in the relationship between Indian peoples and the federal government is by means of a constitutional amendment. Indian First Nations would form a distinct order of government in Canada, with their jurisdiction defined. (Belanger and Newhouse 2008, 11)

Finally, the report indicated that "virtually the entire range of law-making, policy, program delivery, law enforcement and adjudication powers would be available to an Indian First Nation government within its territory" (Penner 1983, 39–40).

The government of Canada accepted the Penner Report in March 1984: "The Committee's recommendations have a special importance because they were unanimously supported by Committee members of all Parties" (Belanger and Newhouse 2008, 11). In addition to identifying Indian communities as historically self-governing, the final report presented the need to establish a new relationship with Indian peoples: "The effect . . . is to call for the Government and Indian First Nations to enter into a new relationship. . . . Many of the details of the restructured relationship will have to be worked out after careful consideration and full consultation with Indian people" (Belanger and Newhouse 2008, 11). On the other hand, the government did not accept the idea of constitutional entrenchment, though a decade later it would read the Constitution in such a way as to include a right to self-government. This right, however, would still have to be negotiated within the confines of Canadian federalism. It is imperative to note here that the Indigenous belief in the historic nation-to-nation relationship was not considered the foundation of the emergent Indigenous–Canada relationship:

> The Government of Canada recognizes the inherent right of self-government as an existing Aboriginal right under section 35 of the Constitution Act, 1982. It recognizes, as well, that the inherent right may find expression in treaties, and in the context of the Crown's relationship with treaty First Nations. Recognition of the inherent right is based on the view that the Aboriginal peoples of Canada

have the right to govern themselves in relation to matters that are internal to their communities, integral to their unique cultures, identities, traditions, languages and institutions, and with respect to their special relationship to their land and their resources. (Canada 1995)

The Penner Report represents an important shift in that it was the first Canadian government report to present historical evidence reinforcing the FSI (and other Indigenous peoples') argument that Indian nations have always been self-governing. The report's acceptance by the House of Commons and the detailing of a plan for recognition of Indigenous self-government represent the end of a phase in the debate about Indigenous self-government. The first phase of the debate had asked whether Indigenous peoples have the right to govern themselves. The second phase began when the federal government responded in 1984 by answering yes, though within the Canadian federation (Belanger and Newhouse 2004).

Subsequent debates about Indigenous self-government during the Meech Lake and Charlottetown constitutional talks in the late 1980s and early 1990s were thus concerned with the details of Indigenous self-government rather than its validity. The Charlottetown Accord, in particular, proposed a distinct order of Aboriginal government, which foreshadowed the RCAP's recommendations. These discussions involved federal, provincial, and municipal governments. The role of provincial government representatives was crucial since it meant that the debates included not only questions surrounding government authority, jurisdiction, and funding in the areas of natural resources, social services, and education, but also issues of service delivery. Notably, Indigenous input in the Charlottetown Accord discussions represents the last substantive Indigenous participation in federal–provincial–territorial discussions, demonstrating how little space officials are willing to afford Aboriginal governments (Slowey 2007).

The Royal Commission on Aboriginal Peoples

What became evident was state representatives' reluctance to fully endorse Aboriginal self-government despite Canada accepting the Penner Report's recognition of the right to self-government. Aboriginal leaders, concerned about the weak nature of a right they believed could be taken away, demanded that self-government be recognized as inherent rather than granted. Discontent also resulted in a series of confrontations across the country. In response to a violent confrontation during the summer of 1990 between the Mohawk people of Kanesatake and the Canadian military over Aboriginal lands at Oka, Quebec, the Conservative government of Brian Mulroney established the RCAP in 1991 to investigate the evolving Canada–Indigenous political and social relationship. The 4,000-page, five-volume RCAP *Report* tabled in 1996 recommended restructuring these relationships while identifying the "third pillar," a political vision of Canada in which, as distinct political communities, Aboriginal nations would have a formal place within the country's governing structure. It proposed that each nation would have a defined jurisdiction and authority as well as a role in relation to Parliament through a First Peoples House and, similar to the *Wahbung* report, also called for a major effort to improve Aboriginal peoples' social and economic conditions. Canada had agreed just prior to the release of the RCAP *Report* to adopt Aboriginal people's view of self-government in the 1995 Inherent Right of Self-Government Policy, now known as the Inherent Rights Policy (IRP). Although there would continue to be much debate about the implications of the term "inherent," the state's acceptance of the Aboriginal view of self-government meant that a key element of the "Canada problem" had been addressed.

The RCAP *Report* presented three models of Aboriginal governments: (1) national governments, (2) Aboriginal public governments, and (3) community-of-interest governments, representing an expansive taxonomy that extended far beyond the limited municipal-style governments proposed by Hawthorn and endorsed by the Indian Chiefs of Alberta. The RCAP model envisioned Aboriginal governments being informed by a distinct Aboriginal political culture rooted in local governance traditions. It also imagined a continuing confederation of Canada with Aboriginal peoples occupying a distinct and constitutionally protected place within. The RCAP embraced the notion of complexity in its vision and rejected a one-size-fits-all view of Aboriginal governance while further calling for a new round of treaty-making to give shape, form, and substance to the development of relations between Canada and self-governing Aboriginal Nations.

As noted above, Indigenous peoples' ideas of self-government were not developed in some abstract political philosophical vacuum. The creation of the land claims process and various land settlements and agreements beginning in 1975 led to the negotiation resulting in self-government being devised and instituted in various regions. Post-RCAP agreements such as the Nisga'a Treaty (2000) and the Nunavik Inuit Land Claims Agreement (2005) lend further substance to the RCAP recommendations. Within the Indigenous community, critics argue that the land claims process was not conducted on a nation-to-nation basis. Non-Indigenous critics argued that these agreements were leading to race-based governments inconsistent with the principles of Canadian democracy.

What is apparent is that the nation-to-nation governance model advocated by most Indigenous leaders remains elusive due to Canada's refusal to formally acknowledge Indigenous peoples as operating legitimate alternative forms of government, thus privileging federal and provincial parliaments (Papillon 2009). This institutional inability to reconcile different governing traditions, which could result in a form of political interdependence evolving in Canada, has many Indigenous leaders identifying treaties as *the* fundamental building blocks of a nation-to-nation relationship. Judge David Arnott, the former Treaty Commissioner for Saskatchewan, stated:

> The treaties are an integral part of the fabric of our Constitution. They form the bedrock foundation of the relationship between the Treaty First Nations and the Government of Canada. It is from the treaties that all things must flow in the treaty relationship. They represent the common intersection both historically and politically between nations. They created a relationship, which is perpetual and unalterable in its foundation principles. The treaties are the basis for a continuous intergovernmental relationship. (Office of the Treaty Commission 2007, vii)

In summary, the idea of self-government as conceptualized by Canada has broadened considerably over the past three decades from: (1) an initial conception of local municipal-style government rooted in the Indian Act to (2) a constitutionally protected inherent right, with its most recent expression in the idea of "Aboriginal national government" as a third order of government within the Canadian federation, as envisioned by RCAP.

These conceptions are based on the premise that self-government is negotiated and thus remains subordinate to federal and provincial governments. In contrast, Indigenous leaders have advanced the idea of nation-to-nation relationships that envision a different starting point: a recognition of a unique political and constitutional relationship between Indigenous peoples and Canada that is grounded in and informed by the 1763 Royal Proclamation, the Treaty of Niagara of 1764, and the 2007 United Nations Declaration on the Rights of Indigenous Peoples (UNDRIP) (see Borrows 1997; Henderson 2008; Macklem 2001). Indigenous governments in this conception are *sui generis* (self-generating, or unique), with an exclusive but as yet to be negotiated relationship with Canada.

Into the Twenty-First Century

The last years of the twentieth century and the first two decades of the twenty-first century have seen Canada starting to come to terms with its colonial heritage. The Canadian government has begun to publicly acknowledge and atone for its past actions as well as promise that it will not engage in the same actions again. One of the earliest moments occurred in January 1998, when the Minister of Indian Affairs and Northern Development, Jane Stewart, read a statement of reconciliation before the House of Commons. Much debate has followed over whether it was an apology and what the words meant, whether or not she should have made the statement, whether it was sincere, whether it went far enough, and what its effect, if any, might have been. These are important discussions, but it is crucial to consider the statement in another light. It is the first formal statement by a national government of the Americas—e.g., the United States, Mexico, Brazil, Argentina, Peru—or any government that colonized the Americas—e.g., England, Spain, France, Portugal—to acknowledge wrongdoing regarding its treatment of the original people of the land on which it settled.

A profoundly different view of Indigenous peoples and Canadian history was also presented in that the statement explicitly identified thousands of years of Aboriginal occupancy and that, along with operating their own distinct government models and national cultures, the Indigenous peoples had contributed significantly to Canada's development. Deliberate and wrongful attempts both to suppress Aboriginal cultures and values and to dispossess Aboriginal peoples of their lands/territories based on attitudes of European racial and cultural superiority on the part of the Canadian government were noted. As well as vowing to change, the statement also painted a picture of Aboriginal peoples as having remarkable strength, resilience, and endurance. Stewart added:

> Reconciliation is an ongoing process. In renewing our partnership, we must ensure that the mistakes, which marked our past relationship, are not repeated. The Government of Canada recognizes that policies that sought to assimilate Aboriginal people, women and men, were not the way to build a strong country. We must instead continue to find ways in which Aboriginal people can participate fully in the economic, political, cultural and social life of Canada in a manner which preserves and enhances the collective identities of Aboriginal communities and allows them to evolve and flourish in the future. Working together to achieve our shared goals will benefit all Canadians, Aboriginal and non-Aboriginal alike. (Stewart 1998)

Even more remarkable was the statement of apology made a decade later by Prime Minister Stephen Harper. On 11 June 2008 the Prime Minister stood in the House of Commons to deliver a formal apology that stated in part:

> In the 1870s, the federal government, partly in order to meet its obligation to educate Indigenous children, began to play a role in the development and administration of these schools. Two primary objectives of the residential school system were to remove and isolate children from the influence of their homes, families, traditions and cultures, and to assimilate them into the dominant culture. These objectives were based on the assumption that Indigenous cultures and spiritual beliefs were inferior and unequal. Indeed, some sought, as it was infamously said, "to kill the Indian in the child."
>
> Today, we recognize that this policy of assimilation was wrong, has caused great harm, and has no place in our country. . . . The government now recognizes that the consequences of the Indian residential schools policy were profoundly negative and that this policy has had a lasting and damaging impact on Indigenous culture, heritage and language. . . . The legacy of Indian residential schools has contributed to social problems that continue to exist in many communities today. It has taken extraordinary courage for the thousands of survivors that have come forward to speak publicly about the abuse they suffered. . . .
>
> The government recognizes that the absence of an apology has been an impediment to healing and reconciliation.
>
> Therefore, on behalf of the government of Canada and all Canadians, I stand before you, in this chamber so central to our life as a country, to apologize to aboriginal peoples for Canada's role in the Indian residential schools system. . . . We now recognize that it was wrong to separate children from rich and vibrant cultures and traditions, that it created a void in many lives and communities, and we apologize for having done this. . . . The burden of this experience has been on your shoulders for far too long.
>
> The burden is properly ours as a government, and as a country. The Government of Canada sincerely apologizes and asks the forgiveness of the aboriginal peoples of this country for failing them so profoundly.
>
> We are sorry. (Canada 2008, 6849–57)

On the surface these are both extraordinary statements since they seem to acknowledge the colonial history of the country. Yet, less than a year later, in 2009, Prime Minister Stephen Harper stated at a meeting of the G20 that "Canada has no history of colonialism" (see Shrubb 2014). This statement represents the ongoing challenge in trying to address the Canada problem: the unwillingness of state representatives to acknowledge that colonialism lies at the heart of past and present relations between Canada and Indigenous peoples, even when presented with overwhelming evidence of it from Indigenous peoples—in scholarly writing, in public inquiries, and in legal cases in which judgements have consistently ruled against the government.

Despite Canada's refusal to acknowledge its colonial past and present, Indigenous political mobilization continues to ascend in a wide variety of political, cultural, economic, and educational contexts. John Ralston Saul argues in *The Comeback* (2014) that a new generation of Indigenous scholars, artists, politicians, and community leaders are drawing on Indigenous values, gaining power, and disrupting the conventional narrative in ways that are fundamentally altering our understanding of Canada's past, present, and future.

The generation that these and many other individuals represent will have experienced aspects of self-government in education, health care, economic development, social work, housing, cultural programs, and language training. Some of them will have grown up within the context of land claim agreements and new treaties. They have also done much to ensure that federal and provincial policy in particular becomes more consistent with Indigenous principles and visions. For example, in 2003, Indigenous political leaders, scholars, and community activists succeeded in forcing the federal government to retract the First Nations Governance Act (FNGA), which the government had developed to provide a legislative basis for Indian band councils. This new generation of Indigenous people, well versed in their own political history, has demonstrated their skill at crafting and putting forward a position that reflects their ideals. They recognized the FNGA as being incongruent with their principles and the foundations of Indigenous self-government.

The Idle No More movement is an excellent example of contemporary Indigenous activism (Coates 2015; Kino-nda-niimi Collective 2014). Initiated in 2012 in Saskatoon by four women, three of whom are Indigenous and one a settler, Idle No More based its position and actions in Indigenous conceptions of responsibility for water and the natural environment and adopted the Round Dance as its central act of resistance. They are imbued with a post-colonial consciousness: an awareness of the fact of colonization and its impacts; a determination to engage in acts of resistance and resurgence that build on the strengths and capacities of Indigenous individuals, communities, and Nations; a desire to assist in the recovery from this colonial legacy; and the development of knowledge and skills to undertake these tasks (McAdam 2015). Members of this emerging generation of leaders deliberately, consciously, and systematically endeavour to deal with the ongoing legacy and operation of colonization.

Although some analysts point to the positive rise in recent years of certain general economic indicators, there is widespread agreement that the many remarkable political, legal, and economic developments, as well as artistic and entrepreneurial achievements of the past 40 years, have not yet resulted in an overall improvement in the quality of life for Indigenous people in this country. While Canada is consistently ranked as one of the top five countries in the world in which to live, according to UNESCO measures of socio-economic development, First Nations are consistently ranked near the bottom of these same measures. In their efforts to solve the socio-economic consequences of the "Canada problem," Indigenous leaders, organizations, and academics, as well as community members and their supporters, have persisted in their efforts to advocate for additional resources to address the social and economic disparities experienced by Indigenous people (Graham, Dittburner, and Abele 1996a, 1996b). While there are diverse perspectives on how the socio-economic and other consequences of the "Canada problem" ought to be meaningfully addressed, many agree that *Time* magazine's description in 1997 of the Canadian lands claim process as "one of the boldest experiments in social justice in Canada's history" can be read in any number of (at best) cautiously optimistic ways.

The Truth and Reconciliation Commission

There is an emerging and compelling desire to put the events of the past behind us so that we can work towards a stronger and healthier future. The truth telling and reconciliation process as part of an overall holistic and comprehensive response to the Indian Residential School legacy is a sincere indication and acknowledgement of the injustices and harms experienced by Aboriginal people and the need for continued healing. This is a profound commitment to establishing new relationships embedded in mutual recognition and respect that will forge a brighter future. The truth of our common experiences will help set our spirits free and pave the way to reconciliation. (TRC 2015)

The Indian Residential Schools Settlement Agreement in 2008 resulted in the largest class action settlement in Canadian history. One of its components was the establishment of the Truth and Reconciliation Commission (TRC) to document the history, experiences, and impacts of Indian residential schools (Miller 2017). The TRC was expected to lay a foundation for a reconciled Canada after it conducted research and hearings over a period of six years; it submitted its final report in June 2015. The report documented in detail the history and experiences of Indigenous people in the schools as well as the continuing impact on survivors and Indigenous societies across Canada (Regan 2010). The Commission used the term "cultural genocide" to describe the purpose and intent of the Indian residential school period.

The TRC framed its 94 recommendations for wide-ranging reform in all sectors of Canadian society as "Calls to Action," and these have stimulated many sectors of Canadian society to take action. Many in the university sector have created Indigenization plans to help them respond to Indigenous needs; public schools at the primary and secondary levels have started reforming curricula; some corporations have developed their own Indigenization plans, including formal policy statements and renewed practices around community consultation and engagement. Indeed, some believe that the TRC has helped to usher in a new era with the potential to transform the Indigenous–Canada relationship. Prime Minister Justin Trudeau, speaking to a special assembly of First Nations chiefs on 8 December 2015, declared: "It is time for a renewed, nation-to-nation relationship with First Nations Peoples. One that understands that the constitutionally guaranteed rights of First Nations in Canada are not an inconvenience but rather a sacred obligation" (Trudeau 2015). In his speech he laid out five government priorities:

1. Launching a national public inquiry into missing and murdered Indigenous women.
2. Making significant investments in First Nations education.
3. Lifting the 2 per cent cap on funding for First Nations programs.
4. Implementing all 94 recommendations of the Truth and Reconciliation Commission.
5. Repealing all legislation unilaterally imposed on Indigenous peoples by the previous government.

Perry Bellegarde, National Chief of the Assembly of First Nations (AFN), responded to the first AFN visit of a sitting prime minister in a decade: "We are being heard, and I believe understood, like never before . . . and the new Government's plan is aligning with the AFN's vision" (Bellegarde 2015). The prime minister's priorities mark a change in tone and signal a willingness to restart the relationship in hopes of getting it right this time.

Many are hopeful that reconciliation as a Canadian political project that is moving from apologetic words to positive actions represents a different approach than past government attempts to address "the Indian problem." It took almost two decades—from the 1998 statement of reconciliation by Indian Affairs Minister Jane Stewart, to the 2008 statement of apology for Indian residential schools by Prime Minister Harper, to the December 2015 release of the report of the Truth and Reconciliation Commission—for reconciliation to become an important part of the Canadian public dialogue and public policy landscape. Of note, framing the recommendations of the TRC as "Calls to Action" was a brilliant move that created a policy frame to help guide the concrete efforts of Canadians, their governments, and their institutions towards reconciliation.

The TRC identified the United Nations Declaration on the Rights of Indigenous Peoples as an important catalyst for change since it recognizes the basic human rights of Indigenous peoples as well as rights to self-determination, land, language, education, culture, and equality with other citizens in nation-states. This document was endorsed by Canada in 2010 and fully supported without qualification in 2016, and Canada, through the Minister of Indigenous Affairs, committed the government to the use of the Declaration as a foundational document for reconciliation and rebuilding the relationship with Indigenous peoples.

It seems clear that the "Canada problem" in Indigenous politics is being addressed by Indigenous leaders with a long-term vision for their peoples and in their relations with Canada. They recognize that creating a Canada that respects the original peoples of this land requires fundamental reform of federal and provincial institutions in ways that honour Indigenous nations and governments and that include Indigenous peoples as real and significant political actors. They assert that reform must result in the development of a set of Indigenous institutions that are adequately resourced and directed by Indigenous people to serve their needs, the reimagining of non-Indigenous institutions to meet the needs of Indigenous people and deliver services in culturally appropriate ways, and the institution of laws to ensure that reforms do not disappear. Fundamental reform also requires that racism and discrimination be addressed through schools and other public education efforts. In addition, while there has been significant support for reconciliation-focused initiatives, much debate continues about what reconciliation means in the Canadian context and whether it is the best way for relations between Indigenous peoples and settler society to move forward.

Concluding Remarks on a Way Forward

Given the preceding discussion, what is a good way forward in relations between Indigenous peoples and the rest of Canada? Two fundamental aspects of the "Canada problem" obviously need to be addressed. The first is overcoming poverty and its effects, which envelop many rural and urban Indigenous communities and are rooted in often obscure and frequently outdated federal legislation and policies. Despite positive political developments, many Indigenous people still live in very difficult circumstances. That they continue to do so is the legacy of colonialism as identified by the 2014 *Report of the United Nations Special Rapporteur on the Rights of Indigenous Peoples . . . in Canada*, which noted "daunting challenges" ahead. Meeting these challenges will require Canada and the provinces to commit to change in many realms, including relinquishing their exhaustive claims to resources. The reawakening of the entrepreneurial spirit among many Indigenous people will remain important, but the Indigenous private sector alone cannot respond to this challenge. Continued development of an economic infrastructure that supports Indigenous–non-Indigenous business collaborations is needed to address this problem. It is also vital for other Canadians to recognize the need for reduced poverty, increased education levels, improved housing, and increased employment among Indigenous people as important imperatives, and not merely because these changes stand to benefit Canada but because they are fundamental issues of justice.

A second set of challenges involves finding ways to alter Canada's governing structures and institutions to better accommodate Indigenous self-governance—that is, to tackle the founding error in Confederation head-on. At first glance this would seem to be a difficult and perhaps almost insurmountable challenge. Precisely where do we start? First, all Canadians and their governments must recognize that Indigenous peoples have ideas about Canada, about how it ought to be governed, and about their place within the governance structure. Second, Canada must recognize that Indigenous people have ideas about their own governments—the principles and ideas that ought to inform them. In many cases these ideas are based in traditional political thought that was grounded in experience.

The Guswenteh, or two-row wampum, has been put forward as one of the ways we can do this. The Guswenteh symbolizes two nations, separate and distinct, engaged in a relationship of mutual friendship and non-interference. The wampum depicts two solid blue or purple parallel lines separated by a row of white space. Much public discourse on Indigenous self-government focuses on the ideas of separateness, distinctiveness, and non-interference, yet what has largely been missing from the discourse is the idea of dialogue and learning (Elliott 2018).[13] The spaces between the rows are not empty spaces. They are and can be places of conversation, dialogue, debate, discussion, and sharing. They are places where one can learn from the other. This is the place where diverse people can learn to use our "good minds." The dialogue in this space is not about cultural diversity, ethnocultural accommodation, or multiculturalism and how to support it. The dialogue is about how to recognize and develop nation-to-nation relationships between Canada and Indigenous peoples in a meaningful and significant way.

In 1983, the House of Commons Special Committee on Indian Self-Government (the Penner Committee) reported to the House that "contrary to the view held by non-Indians that political structures were unknown to Indian people prior to contact with Europeans, most First Nations have complex forms of government that go far back into history and have evolved over time." The Committee recommended "that the federal government establish a new relationship with Indian First Nations and that an essential element of this new relationship be recognition of Indian self-government." Notably, the Penner Report was accepted by the House in a rare all-party agreement.

This event represented, in our view, the end of the philosophical debate about whether Indigenous people had a right to govern themselves: individually and collectively, they had convinced Canadians and their government that they have this right. The first part of the debate lasted from 1867 until 1983: 116 years. The second part of the debate, post-1983, has expanded to include two broad themes: the overall jurisdictions, powers, and financing of nation-to-nation relationships and the details of day-to-day Indigenous governance. The debate about details has now been fully engaged and currently rages passionately within Indigenous communities, as well as between Indigenous peoples and the rest of Canada. Though the second part of the debate may be with us forever, we should not be afraid of it. After all, European societies have been debating similar issues for at least the last few hundred years. And so Indigenous people and the rest of Canada now join in a long tradition of debate about the origins, nature, structuring, uses, and limits of political authority.

It is also important that we turn our attention to examining the process of government development within Indigenous communities and bring to bear the accumulated wisdom and understanding of both our own traditions and those of others. Indigenous people bring their own political thought to the table and want to see it taken seriously by the governments of Canada. A major challenge is fostering the development of positive public attitudes towards Indigenous peoples and their governments. A major RCAP recommendation involved the establishment of a significant public education effort aimed at educating Canadian citizens about Indigenous aspirations, cultures, nations, and ways of living. An important part of this education will involve cultivating deeper awareness among Canadians of how the racism embedded in the colonial ways of the past is evident today. Fortunately, there is some indication of changing attitudes among Canadians: support for the honouring of treaties, for example, increased from 75 to 80 per cent between 2006 and 2008 (Belanger and Newhouse 2008). Regional work conducted in the Canadian prairies in 2016 demonstrates similar trends of acceptance (Berdahl et al. 2017). A 2016 report on *Canadian Public Opinion on Aboriginal Peoples* indicates a growing awareness of the challenges that Indigenous peoples face. This survey notes that the majority of Canadians believe it is important to find ways to address challenges (Environics 2016). Education and cultural initiatives are widely supported but support for increased control over lands and resources remains problematic.

Clearly, Indigenous peoples continue to face fundamental challenges in their efforts to address the "Canada problem," whether it is through the development of new treaties, the settlement of land claim agreements that include forms of self-government, or the continued seeking of a nation-to-nation relationship. Some argue that it is important, as a first priority, to focus on rebuilding Indigenous nations, cultures, languages, and territories; then, once all of this is accomplished, the focus can shift to the larger nation-to-nation relationship. In seeking to solve this problem, the actions of Indigenous leaders have been informed by Indigenous political philosophies based on collaboration and co-operation, accommodation and coexistence, and acceptance of diversity. These philosophies also inform contemporary expressions of reconciliation that were called for in the RCAP *Report*. For example, the purpose of the Truth and Reconciliation Commission was to "guide and inspire Aboriginal peoples and Canadians in a process of reconciliation and renewed relationships that are based on mutual understanding and respect." Similarly, the ongoing actions of the Idle No More movement are grounded in Indigenous ideas of nation-to-nation and respect for Indigenous sovereignty. Although there may appear to be signs that Canada is being transformed into a post-colonial state,[14] this transformation is proving to be problematic and challenging, and many still view settler colonialism in Canada as an "ongoing ideology and practice" (Battell-Lowman and Barker 2015, 35). Despite all the good policies and practices that focus on improving the quality of Indigenous people's lives, settler colonialism continues to attempt to absorb Indigenous lands, waters, and peoples into its system (Wolfe 2006).

Perhaps there is hope. The "Canada problem" in Indigenous politics has two parts: how to live as Indigenous peoples within this new entity called Canada and how to live in relation to this new entity called Canada. In *A Fair Country* (2008), John Ralston Saul argues that the political culture of Canada has been heavily influenced by Indigenous ideals of the well-being of all citizens, egalitarianism, a balance between the individual and the group, and preference for negotiation over violence as way of settling political disputes. By placing Indigenous ideals at the heart of Canada, he invites Indigenous peoples and the rest of Canada to cultivate a new vision for our country, based in Indigenous and European values that will enable its original inhabitants to live with dignity and respect as Indigenous peoples. However, as scholars such as Andersen (2011), Gaudry (2011), and others have noted, Saul's attempts to remythologize the Canadian identity ignore the second and more fundamental part of the "Canada problem," which is that Canada has consistently refused to acknowledge that colonialism lives within the heart of its relations with and treatment of Canada's Indigenous peoples. Moving to address this requires that Canada repudiate its repressive and assimilatory policies, past and present. This has started to happen through the various apologies for past state actions towards Indigenous peoples that have occurred since 1998. As the resolution to reject the 1969 White Paper approved by the Liberal Party of Canada at its 2014 biennial convention states: "Whereas Indigenous philosophies require the past be recognized and accounted for to foster better relationships and a path forward" (Policy Resolution 21, 2014). As other chapters in this collection discuss, Indigenous political activism and scholarship are increasingly focusing on the resurgence of traditional Indigenous political, economic, and cultural ideals, which in the political realm will hopefully translate into the development of fully "nation-to-nation" relations. Perhaps returning to Guswentah political philosophy can help Indigenous peoples and representatives of the Canadian state to navigate these challenging waters in a good and hopeful way. This will require a generation of leaders educated in Indigenous political philosophies as well as in the state's legal and political discourses, and they will need a keen willingness to engage in the difficult work of bringing Indigenous philosophies to the table.[15]

Discussion Questions

1. Has the "Canada problem" changed over time? If so, what important elements have changed, and what are its current elements?

2. What do you see as elements of the solution to the "Canada problem"?

3. If your perspective of the "Indian problem" has changed over time, in what ways has it changed and what contributed to the change?

4. From the perspective of Canada, what are the contemporary aspects of the "Indian problem"?

5. If you were the prime minister of Canada, how would you address the "Indian problem"?

6. If you were an Indigenous leader, how would you address the "Canada problem"? How might your response to this question differ if you were a First Nation, Métis, or Inuk leader?

Recommended Reading

Abley, Mark. 2013. *Conversations with a Dead Man: The Legacy of Duncan Campbell Scott*. Madeira Park, BC: Douglas & McIntyre.

Alcantara, Christopher, and Jen Nelles. 2016. *A Quiet Evolution: The Emergence of Indigenous–Local Intergovernmental Partnerships in Canada*. Toronto: University of Toronto Press.

Asch, Michael. 2014. *On Being Here to Stay: Treaties and Aboriginal Rights in Canada*. Toronto: University of Toronto Press.

——, John Borrows, and James Tully, eds. 2018. *Resurgence and Reconciliation: Indigenous–Settler Relations and Earth Teachings*. Toronto: University of Toronto Press.

Belanger, Yale D., ed. 2008. *Aboriginal Self-Government in Canada: Current Trends and Issues*, 3rd edn. Saskatoon: Purich.

—— and David Newhouse. 2004. "Emerging from the Shadows: The Pursuit of Self-Government to Promote Aboriginal Well-Being." *Canadian Journal of Native Studies* 24, no. 1 (2004): 129–222.

Borrows, John. 2010. *Canada's Indigenous Constitution*. Toronto: University of Toronto Press.

——. 2010. *Drawing Out Law: A Spirits Guide*. Toronto: University of Toronto Press.

Irlbacher-Fox, Stephanie. 2009. *Finding Dahshaa: Self-Government, Social Suffering, and Aboriginal Policy in Canada*. Vancouver: University of British Columbia Press.

Joseph, Bob. 2018. *21 Things You May Not Know about the Indian Act: Helping Canadians Make Reconciliation with Indigenous Peoples a Reality*. Vancouver: Indigenous Relations Press.

Kelm, Mary-Ellen, and Keith D. Smith. 2018. *Talking Back to the Indian Act: Critical Readings in Settler Colonial Histories*. Toronto: University of Toronto Press.

Ladner, Kiera. "Negotiated Inferiority: The Royal Commission on Aboriginal People's Vision of a Renewed Relationship." *American Review of Canadian Studies* (Spring/Summer 2001): 241–64.

Newhouse, David, Cora Voyageur, and Dan Beavon. 2007, 2010. *Hidden in Plain Sight: Aboriginal Contributions to Canada and Canadian Identity*, 2 vols. Toronto: University of Toronto Press.

Niezen, Ronald. 2017. *Truth and Indignation: Canada's Truth and Reconciliation Commission on Indian Residential Schools*, 3rd edn. Toronto: University of Toronto Press.

Saul, John Ralston. 2008. *A Fair Country: Telling Truths about Canada*. Toronto: Viking Canada.

——. 2014. *The Comeback: How Aboriginals Are Reclaiming Power and Influence*. Toronto: Viking Canada.

Simpson, Leanne Betasamosake. 2017. *As We Have Always Done: Indigenous Freedom through Radical Resistance*. Minneapolis: University of Minnesota Press.

Additional Resources

Royal Proclamation of 1763. 7 Oct. https://www.solon.org/Constitutions/Canada/English/PreConfederation/rp_1763.html.

We Can't Make the Same Mistake Twice. National Film Board, 2016. Dir. Alanis Obomsawin. https://www.nfb.ca/film/we_can_t_make_the_same_mistake_twice/.

Six Miles Deep. National Film Board, 2009. Dir. Sara Roque. https://www.nfb.ca/film/six_miles_deep/.

Inuuvunga—I Am Inuk, I Am Alive. National Film Board, 2004. https://www.nfb.ca/film/inuuvunga_i_am_inuk_i_am_alive/.

Two Worlds Colliding. National Film Board, 2004. Dir. Tasha Hubbard. https://www.nfb.ca/film/two_worlds_colliding/.

Is the Crown at War with Us? National Film Board, 2002. Dir. Alanis Obomsawin. https://www.nfb.ca/film/is_the_crown_at_war_with_us/.

Kanehsatake: 270 Years of Resistance. National Film Board, 1993. Dir. Alanis Obomsawin. https://www.nfb.ca/film/kanehsatake_270_years_of_resistance/.

Tisdale, Dawn. 2015. "The Impact of Residential Schools on Aboriginal Healthcare." TEDx Comox Valley. https://www.youtube.com/watch?v=kMvn_mSsykE&feature=share.

Harvest of Hope, Symposium on Reconciliation. 2013. https://www.youtube.com/watch?v=Jd6MQdBNfjU&list=PLS6nSmuURFJC8fMILcb0PZt-GBPyRk3dU.

Notes

1. This chapter uses the terms "Indian," "Aboriginal," and "Indigenous" as appropriate to the historical context. In 2016, the government of Canada moved to use "Indigenous peoples" to describe the original inhabitants of the continent, and this term is used throughout in speaking more generally of the constitutionally recognized Indians, Métis, and Inuit. The singular "Indigenous people" is used in reference to an agglomerate of people as individuals.

2. An extensive literature now documents racism towards Indigenous peoples and its impact in general and in specific sectors of Canada: Royal Commission on Donald Marshall Jr, *Prosecution* (Halifax: Queen's Printer, Dec. 1989); Public Inquiry into the Administration of Justice and Aboriginal People, *Report of the Aboriginal Justice Inquiry of Manitoba* (Winnipeg: Queen's Printer, 1991); *Report of the Task Force on the Criminal Justice System and Its Impact on the Indian and Metis People of Alberta* (Edmonton, 1991); Commission of Inquiry into Matters Relating to the Death of Neil Stonechild (Regina, Sask.: Queen's Printer, 24 Sept. 2004); Billie Allan and Janet Smylie, "First Peoples, Second Class Treatment: The Role of Racism in the Health and Well-Being of Indigenous Peoples in Canada" (Toronto: Wellesley Institute, 2015), document racism in the health-care system. The Urban Aboriginal People Studies of 2011 (https://uaps.ca) documents racism towards Indigenous people living in urban environments in Canada. Racism against Indigenous women is the subject of the National Inquiry into Missing and Murdered Indigenous Women and Girls (http://www.mmiwg-ffada.ca).

3. The Royal Proclamation states: "And whereas it is just and reasonable, and essential to our Interest, and the Security of our Colonies, that the several Nations or Tribes of Indians with whom We are connected, and who live under our Protection, should not be molested or disturbed in the Possession of such Parts of Our Dominions and Territories as, not having been ceded to or purchased by Us, are reserved to them, or any of them, as their Hunting Grounds." Borrows (1997) argues one must read the Proclamation alongside the 1764 Treaty of Niagara to see that the Crown acted on its belief that Indians of the day comprised nations.

4. The report does not discuss the existence of rights inherent to Indigenous nations, for this conception did not exist in Canadian political thought of the time. This is something that Indigenous leaders still struggle to have acknowledged.

5. See [2004] 3 S.C.R. 511 [*Haida Nation*] and [2004] 3 S.C.R. 550 [*Taku River*].

6. See *Tsleil-Waututh Nation v. Canada (Attorney General)*, 2018 FCA 153. https://decisions.fca-caf.gc.ca/fca-caf/decisions/en/item/343511/index.do#_Remedy.

7. A government white paper is a policy proposal released to invite comment and stimulate discussion. In this case, it did just that. In addition, the government proposal achieved lasting notoriety within Aboriginal communities by proposing that, for all intents and purposes, Indians become white.

8. See, for instance, the Supreme Court's determination that the treaties must be interpreted in a liberal way so as not to harm or denigrate the Aboriginal interpretation of events. *R. v. Sparrow* (1990), 1 S.C.R. 1075.

9. See *Calder v. Attorney General of British Columbia* (1973). For an excellent examination

of the importance of the *Calder* decision, see Foster (2008).

10. For a discussion on the concepts of universal versus differentiated citizenship, see Maaka and Fleras (2005).

11. The word "includes" led to much speculation by Aboriginal leaders that perhaps there were other, yet undiscovered Aboriginal peoples.

12. The provinces have an interest in the discussion as it involves land, natural resources, and possible amendments to the Constitution, all issues within their purview. Over the next two decades, provinces became increasingly involved in Aboriginal affairs, in many cases establishing ministries and departments to deal with Aboriginal peoples within their borders. Aboriginal leaders were initially reluctant to include provinces, since they saw their relationship as one with the Crown, refusing to accept the fanciful notion of the division of the Crown.

13. Elliott consolidates and elaborates on the ideas of Taiaiake Alfred, Glenn Coulthard, and Leanne Simpson, to name some of the more prominent theorists.

14. For further discussion surrounding the term "post-colonial," see, e.g., Alfred (2005); Borrows (2002); Kernerman (2005); Tully (1995); Turner (2006).

15. This call has also been advanced by Dale Turner (2006) as a need for "word warriors." With strong community connections and an education in European philosophy, "word warriors" can act as a bridge between Indigenous philosophers and dominant culture political philosophers, politicians, lawyers, and scholars.

3 Nishnaabeg Brilliance as Radical Resurgence Theory

Leanne Betasamosake Simpson

Gilbert drove the kids from the reserve into town for school every morning, and sometimes when we would come to visit, he would drive another lap around the reserve to pick up all the Elders in his yellow and black bus, driving us to the treatment centre or out to the community trapline on the edge of the reserve. I was in my mid-twenties. Young. I didn't yet know which things in life are rare and which things happen all the time if you remain open and happen to be in the right place at the right time. Over two years, spending time with a group of 25 Elders who had known each other and their land for their entire lives was an extremely rare situation. One that in the next 20 years of my life wouldn't be repeated with the same depth.

I've gone back to this experience over and over again in my head and in my writing because it changed the way I think in a fundamental way. It changed the way I am in the world. I want to reconsider it here because this experience is foundational to work on resurgence and to who I have become. I considered parts of this story in the short story "lost in the world where he was always the only one," published in *Islands of Decolonial Love,* although somewhat fictionalized, as a way of linking our current reality to the Nishnaabeg sacred story of a little boy who is taken to the skyworld to learn from seven Elders and then returned to the earth to share his new knowledge with the Nishnaabeg (L. Simpson 2013; Benton-Banai 1988, 61–8). Meaning, we all have to be, in some way, that little boy. Like that boy, those Elders that I learned from for two years actually gave me something that has propelled my writing and thinking ever since. It was the greatest gift.

I was working with Professor Paul Driben, an anthropologist from Lakehead University at the time. We had been hired by the Effects on Aboriginals from the Great Lakes Environment (EAGLE) project of the Assembly of First Nations (AFN) to work with the Anishinaabeg reserve community of Long Lake #58, located in the boreal forest of northern Ontario, about 300 kilometres northeast of Thunder Bay, to create a land-use atlas. The band council sent us to the Elders. This was not a unique project in the 1980s and 1990s. Traditional ecological knowledge was in its heyday in the eyes of white policy-makers, academics, and even Indigenous organizations. The idea was that if we documented on

This chapter is reprinted from, Leanne Betasamosake Simpson, *As We Have Always Done: Indigenous Freedom through Radical Resistance* (University of Minnesota Press, 2017).

lastdjedai/Shutterstock

Tee Harbor Beach at Sleeping Giant Provincial Park, about 300 km southwest of Long Lake #58, where the author was working for the Effects on Aboriginals from the Great Lakes Environment (EAGLE) project. EAGLE, which was started by the Assembly of First Nations in 1990, aimed to use the traditional knowledge of First Nations people from participating communities as well as mainstream scientific technologies to document the impact of environmental contamination in the Great Lakes Drainage Basin of central Ontario.

paper the ways that we use the land, policy-makers would then use the information to minimize the impacts of development on our lands and ways of life. The idea was that clearly documented land use would bring about less dispossession, as if dispossession occurs by accident or out of not knowing, rather than being the strategic structure it is. The project was to gather the individual cognitive, territorial maps Elders held in their heads into a collective, a visual remapping and translation of some aspects of Indigenous Knowledge into a form that would be recognized by industry and the state.

Of course, I don't think the Elders involved in these studies were naive. I think what I saw, and perhaps what they saw, was a process that could be used as a tool to generate cohesion, pride, and rebuilding within our own communities when our own people saw visually and so clearly what dispossession, displacement, encroachment, and industrial extractivism look like over our territories across time. Laid out in a visual way, the magnitude of the loss cannot be explained away, the strategic nature of colonialism cannot be ignored. The driving force of capitalism in our dispossession cannot be denied.

I was suspicious of Dr Driben in the beginning. He wasn't Native, he was an anthropologist of all things, but he had created these maps before with other Nishnaabeg communities. Sitting in his windowless cement office in the basement of a building at Lakehead University eating subs, I could tell by the details on the maps that Elders trusted him.

I could tell by the bunker-like nature of his office far removed from the upper echelons of the university that perhaps the university didn't. This boded well for our relationship.

Paul did something that has stayed with me and has always informed my approach to working with communities and to research. He was invited into the community to do a specific task, which in the end he delivered, but he actively and continually divested himself of the false power the academy bestowed upon him when he drove onto the reserve. He asked the Elders if they thought the project was a good idea. They said it was. He asked them how best to proceed. They told him. He asked them if they would be the decision-makers. They agreed, and then they were, and he got out of their way.

This was an overwhelmingly different way of conducting research than I had experienced in two biology degrees. At the time, I could only frame it within collaborative or participatory or community-based methodologies, but it was really none of those. Those kinds of methodologies to some degree privileged Western theories, epistemologies, or knowledge systems, and the process that emerged in this situation was Nishnaabeg to the core. These methodologies assume there is a role for the academic. Paul did not. He came into their circle on the terms of experts, the Nishnaabeg Elders, not the other way around.

Which enabled me to come into their circle, as a young Nishnaabeg person with very few useful skills to them other than youth. Western education does not produce in us the kinds of effects we like to think it does when we say things like *education is the new buffalo*. We learn how to type and how to write. We learn how to think within the confines of Western thought. We learn how to pass tests and get jobs within the city of capitalism. If we're lucky and we fall into the right programs, we might learn to think critically about colonialism. But post-secondary education provides few useful skill sets to those of us who want to fundamentally change the relationship between the Canadian state and Indigenous peoples, because that requires a sustained, collective, strategic long-term movement, a movement the Canadian state has a vested interest in preventing, destroying, and dividing. Post-secondary education provides very few skill sets to those who want to learn to think in the most complex ways possible within the networked system of Indigenous intelligence. In fact, I needed to leave all of that kind of education behind in order to come into this without hesitation and an open heart. The parts of me that I drew on in this circle of Elders were liabilities at university—gentleness, humility, carefulness, and the ability to proceed slowly.

During the next two years, the Elders, who in my memory are now eagles, took me under their wing. I wrote down on large topographical maps every place name for every beach, bay, peninsula, and island they could remember—hundreds and hundreds of names. We marked down all of their traplines, and the ones before that and the ones before that. We marked down hunting grounds and fishing sites, berry patches, ricing camps, and medicines spots. We marked down birthplaces and graves. We marked down places where stories happened. We marked down ceremonial sites, places where they lived, places where life happened. We also marked down the homes of their relatives—places where moose and bears lived, nesting spots and breeding grounds. We marked down travel routes, spring water spots, songs and prayers. Places where feet touched the earth for the first time. Places where promises were made. The place where they blocked the tracks during the summer of the so-called Oka Crisis.[1]

We also recorded pain. The prisoner-of-war camp, the internment camp and its school that some Nishnaabeg kids attended so they could continue to live with their families and not go to residential school. The 150 years of clear-cuts. The hydroelectric dams, the direction the lake was supposed to flow. The flood, the road, the railway tracks, the mines, the pipeline, the hydro lines. The chemical sprays, the white people parks and campgrounds. Deaths.

The overlays showed decade after decade of loss. They showed the why.

Standing at the foot of a map of loss is clarity.

Colonialism or settler colonialism or dispossession or displacement or capitalism didn't seem complicated any more. The mess I was wrapped in at birth didn't seem so inevitable. It seemed simple. Colonizers wanted the land. Everything else, whether it is legal or policy or economic or social, whether it was the Indian Act or residential schools or gender violence, was part of the machinery that was designed to create a perfect crime—a crime where the victims are unable to see or name the crime *as a crime*.[2]

But this isn't even the most important thing I learned from the Elders of Long Lake #58 in the middle of the 1990s. They gifted me with my first substantial experience with Nishnaabeg thought, theory, and methodology in a research context, and of Nishnaabeg intelligence in life context. Paul showed me the kind of researcher I thought I wanted to be, but in reality I wanted to be able to think like those Elders, not like him. By taking such a radically different approach to both community and research, Paul divested his power and authority as an academic that had been placed on him by the academy and then by an Indigenous organization, and placed that responsibility where it belonged: with the leaders and the intellectuals of the community. Paul was a holder of space. He created the space for Elders to not just say the prayer and smudge us off at the beginning of meeting but to be the meeting. He created the space to put intelligence at the centre and to use its energy to the project. Those Elders gave me my first glimpse of Nishnaabeg brilliance—theory, methodology, story, ethics, values all enmeshed in Nishnaabeg politics and encircled by the profound influence of the world. They pulled me into an alternative Nishnaabeg world existing alongside the colonial reality I knew so well. This has propelled my life.

This experience more than anything else opened my mind and heart to the brilliance and complexity of Nishnaabeg embodied thought. It resonated in a profound way in me and has driven two decades of living, making, writing, and research. Sometimes it is the only thing I am absolutely sure of, and more than that, I am absolutely sure that we as Nishnaabeg cannot survive as a people without creating generations of artists, thinkers, makers, and doers that live in Nishnaabeg worlds, that are in respectful relationship with each other, that create a movement that joins us to other Indigenous nations to protect the land and bodies. We need to live deliberately and with meaning.

I think about the maps those Elders carried in their bodies as two-dimensional representations of the networks they live and their parents and grandparents lived. I think about the maps my generation carries in our heads or maybe in our phones. I think about the networks the next generation will carry in their bodies. I think about how the networks we have in our heads today create the networks our children have in their heads as adults. It is this experience, more than any others, that has led me to centre Nishnaabeg intelligence in my life, in my work, and in my thinking about resurgence.

Years later, when I would begin thinking and writing about Indigenous resurgence as a set of practices through which the regeneration and re-establishment of Indigenous nations could be achieved, the seeds those Elders planted in me would start to grow, with a strong feeling, more than thinking, that the intellectual and theoretical home of resurgence had to come from within Indigenous thought systems, intelligence systems that are continually generated in relationship to place. I realized that the Elders of Long Lake #58 had pulled me into a Nishnaabeg world, and that this world was a very fertile place for dreaming, visioning, thinking, and remembering the affirmative Indigenous worlds that continue to exist right alongside the colonial worlds. I got a strong sense from them that our intellectual systems are our responsibilities, that they are an extension of our bodies and an expression of our freedom. There was no room in their Nishnaabeg world for the desire to be recognized and affirmed by the colonizer. There was no room in their Nishnaabeg world to accommodate or centre whiteness.

The Nishnaabeg brilliance those Elders pulled me into was profound. Their world—a cognitive, spiritual, emotional, land-based space—didn't recognize or endlessly accommodate whiteness, it didn't accept the inevitability of capitalism, and it was a disruption to the hierarchy of heteropatriarchy.[3] Thinking about it now, I see that it was my first flight path out of settler colonialism. In their very quiet, non-demonstrative, and profoundly gentle way, those Elders refused settler colonialism, driving along the Trans Canada in a children's school bus, laughing all the way to their trapline. They refused and generated something different. Every day. Just like their Ancestors and their Ancestor's Ancestors.

Biiskabiyang and Flight

Biiskabiyang—the process of returning to ourselves, a re-engagement with the things we have left behind, a re-emergence, an unfolding from the inside out—is an individual and collective process of decolonization and resurgence (L. Simpson 2011; Geniusz 2000, 9–10). To me, it is the embodied processes as freedom. It is a flight out of the structure of settler colonialism and into the processes and relationships of freedom and self-determination encoded and practised within Nishnaabewin or grounded normativity. In this way, it is a form of marronage.[4] Neil Roberts describes the concept of marronage (derived from Awawak and Tainos thought) in his book *Freedom as Marronage* "as a group of persons isolating themselves from a surrounding society in order to create a fully autonomous community" (Roberts 2015, 4–5), like the act of retreating to the bush or resurgence itself. Breaking from contemporary political theory's vocabulary to describe this flight, Roberts writes:

> marronage is a multidimensional, constant act of flight that involves what I ascertain to be four interrelated pillars: distance, movement, property, and purpose. Distance denotes a spatial quality separating an individual or individuals in a current location or condition from a future location or condition. Movement refers to the ability of agents to have control over motion and the intended directions of their actions. Flight, therefore, is directional movement in the domain of physical environment, embodied cognition, and/or the metaphysical. (Roberts 2015, 8–9)

It necessarily, then, must be rooted in the present. Black feminist theorist and poet Alexis Pauline Gumbs, in an interview about her book *Spill: Scenes of Black Feminist Fugitivity*, says, "I am interested in presence and the present tense. I think fugitivity requires being present and being with, which are both challenges" (Johnson 2016).

Those Elders of Long Lake #58 knew present and being with, they knew flight—distance, movement, land as relationship, purpose. They watched the freedom of eagles, our messengers, moving effortlessly between worlds as expert communicators. Through ceremony, they shifted through physical realities to heightened spiritual ones. They constructed the world according to the structures, the processes, and the relationships Nishnaabewin illuminates. To me, they were marronage. My flight to escape colonial reality was a flight into Nishnaabewin. It was a returning, in the present, to myself. It was an unfolding of a different present. It was freedom as a way of being as a constellation of relationship, freedom as world-making, freedom as a practice. It was biiskabiyang.

No matter what we were doing together, those Elders always carried their Ancestors with them. They were in constant communication with them as they went about their daily lives engaged in practices that continually communicated to the spiritual world that they were Nishnaabeg. I didn't understand this. I kept asking them about governance, and they would talk about trapping. I would ask them about treaties, and they would take me fishing. I'd ask them what we should do about the mess of colonialism, and they would tell me stories about how well they used to live on the land. I loved all of it, but I didn't think they were answering my questions. I could see only practice. I couldn't see their *theory* until decades later. I couldn't see intelligence until I learned *how* to see it by engaging in Nishnaabeg practices for the next two decades.

It would be 15 more years after my experiences at Long Lake #58 before I would sit down and begin to write what would become *Dancing on Our Turtle's Back*. I had completed a PhD at the University of Manitoba and was spending a good deal of time with Robin Greene-ba, a Treaty 3 Elder, and Elder Garry Raven-ba, and the community of Hollow Water First Nation on the east side of Lake Winnipeg. I had moved home to Michi Saagiig Nishnaabeg territory to learn from my own Elders and had connected with Curve Lake Elder Doug Williams, as well as Wikwemikong Elder Edna Manitowabi. They all confirmed my experiences in Long Lake #58: that centring ourselves in this Nishnaabeg process of living is both the instrument and the song.

I set out initially in *Dancing on Our Turtle's Back* to find Nishnaabeg knowledge of how to rebuild from within after devastation because I thought this knowledge would be instructive about how to continue to resist and resurge in the face of ongoing colonialism. I did this not so much through discussion, although there was discussion, but through deep engagement with the Nishnaabeg systems inherent in Nishnaabewin—all of the Nishnaabeg practices and ethical processes that make us Nishnaabeg—including story or theory, language learning, ceremony, hunting, fishing, ricing, sugar-making, medicine-making, politics, and governance. Through this engagement, a different understanding emerged. This is entirely consistent with Nishnaabeg thought, although I did not appreciate it at the time.[5] It became clear to me that *how* we live, *how* we organize, *how* we engage in the world—the process—not only frames the outcome, it is the transformation. *How* moulds and then gives birth to the present. The *how* changes us. *How* is the theoretical intervention. Engaging in deep and reciprocal Indigeneity is a transformative act because it fundamentally changes modes of production of our lives. It changes the relationships that house our bodies and our thinking. It changes how we conceptualize nationhood. Indigenous intelligence systems set up, maintain, and regenerate the neuropathways for Indigenous living both inside our bodies and within the web of connections that structure our nationhood outside our bodies.[6] Engagement changes us because it constructs a different world within which we live.

We live fused to land in a vital way. If we want to create a different future, we need to live a different present, so that present can fully marinate, influence, and create different futures. If we want to live in a different present, we have to centre Indigeneity and allow it to change us.[7]

I talk about this in *Dancing on Our Turtle's Back* as emergence, but emergence isn't quite the right concept because it isn't just a recognition of the complexity and multi-dimensionality that we might not fully understand at work. It is also a strategic, thoughtful process in the present as an agent of change—a *presencing of the present* that generates a particular kind of emergence that is resurgence. Kinetics, the act of doing, isn't just praxis; it also generates and animates theory within Indigenous contexts, and it is the crucial intellectual mode for generating knowledge. Theory and praxis, story and practice, are interdependent, co-generators of knowledge. Practices are politics. Processes are governance. Doing produces more knowledge. This idea is repeated over and over again in Nishnaabeg story and for me, ultimately, comes from the Seven Fires creation story as told to me by spiritual leader Edna Manitowabi and recorded in *Dancing on Our Turtle's Back* (L. Simpson 2011, 31–49). Through this story, she taught me that knowledge or existence itself is a function of intellectual thought, emotional knowledge, and kinetics or movement. Gzhwe Manidoo (The Creator, the one who loves us unconditionally) didn't research about creating the world or think about creating the world. Gzhwe Manidoo created the world by struggling, failing, and by trying again and again in some of our stories (L. Simpson 2011, 46).[8] Mistakes produce knowledge. Failure produces knowledge because engagement in the process changes the actors embedded in process and aligns bodies with the implicit order. The only thing that doesn't produce knowledge is thinking in and of itself, because it is data created in dislocation and isolation and without movement.

The Seven Fires creation story confirmed to me in an epic way that the original knowledge, coded and transmitted through complex networks, says that everything we need to know about everything in the world is contained within Indigenous bodies, and that these same Indigenous bodies exist as networked vessels, or constellations across time and space intimately connected to a universe of nations and beings. All of our origin stories do this, and, really, in the complex reality networked emergence generates, Nishnaabewin itself is a continual generation and iteration of these stories and principles.

The Seven Fires creation story sets the parameters for Nishnaabeg intelligence: the commingling of emotional and intellectual knowledge combined in motion or movement, and the making and remaking of the world in a generative fashion within Indigenous bodies that are engaged in accountable relationships with other beings. This is propelled by the diversity of Indigenous bodies of all ages, genders, races, and abilities in attached correlations with all aspects of creation. This is the exact opposite of the white supremacist, masculine, heteropatriarchal theory and research process in the academy, which I think likely nearly every Indigenous body that has walked into the academy in some way has felt. We need (to continue) to refuse that system or refuse to let our presence in that system change who we are as Indigenous peoples (A. Simpson 2014). We need to continue and expand rooting the practice of our lives in our homelands and within our intelligence systems in the ways that our diverse and unique Indigenous thought systems inspire us to do, as the mechanism for our decolonial present, as the primary political intervention of our times. This means struggle. Struggle because we are occupied, erased, displaced, and disconnected. Struggle because our bodies are still targets for settler-colonial violence. Struggle because this is the mechanism our Ancestors engaged in to continuously rebirth the world.

And our struggle is a beautiful, righteous struggle that is our collective gift to Indigenous worlds, because this way of living necessarily continually gives birth to ancient *Indigenous* futures in the present.

Nishnaabewin as Grounded Normativity

What I learned from *Dancing on Our Turtle's Back*, from the process that created it and through the process of engaging in conversations about it over the past five years, is that although I found lots of stories within Nishnaabeg thought about rebuilding, struggle, and self-determination, these were not all crisis-based narratives, and they certainly were not victim-based narratives, nor were they about mere survival. These stories relied upon a return to self-determination and change from within rather than recognition from the outside. They all pointed to invigorating a particular way of living. A way of living that was full of community. A way of living that was thoughtful and profoundly empathetic. A way of living that considered, in a deep profound way, relationality. When I look back at it now, my experience with the Elders of Long Lake #58 was my first substantive experience of Nishnaabewin, or what Dene political theorist Glen Coulthard, author of *Red Skin, White Masks: Rejecting the Colonial Politics of Recognition*, calls "grounded normativity," ethical frameworks generated by these place-based practices and associated knowledges (Coulthard 2014, 60). In academic circles, particularly theoretical ones, this is an important intervention because grounded normativity is the base of our political systems, economy, and nationhood, and it creates process-centred modes of living that generate profoundly different conceptualizations of nationhood and governmentality—ones that aren't based on enclosure, authoritarian power, and hierarchy. The term itself is far less important in Indigenous circles; we've always known our way of life comes from the place or land through the practice of our modes of intelligence. We know that place includes land and waters, plants and animals, and the spiritual world—a peopled cosmos of influencing powers. We know that our practices code and reveal knowledge, and our knowledge codes and reveals practices. We know the individual values we animate those lives in turn create intimate relationships with our family and all aspects of creation, which in turn create a fluid and collective ethical framework that we in turn practise. I think in the context of my own nation, the term "Nishnaabewin"—all of the associated practices, knowledge, and ethics that make us Nishnaabeg and construct the Nishnaabeg world—is the closest thing to Coulthard's "grounded normativity." I use the term interchangeably with Nishnaabeg intelligence, like Coulthard, as a strategic intervention into how the colonial world and the academy position, construct, contain, and shrink Indigenous knowledge systems.

In this sense, in the past, Nishnaabeg woke up each morning and built Nishnaabeg life every day, using our knowledge and practices because this is what we are encouraged to do in our creation stories; these are our original instructions. This *procedure* or practice of living, theory and praxis intertwined, is generated through relations with Michi Saagiig Nishnaabeg land, land that is constructed and defined by our intimate spiritual, emotional, and physical relationship with it. The procedure is our grounded normativity. Living is a creative act, with self-determined making or producing at its core. Colonized life is so intensely about consumption that the idea of making is reserved for artists at best and hobbies at worst. Making is not seen as the material basis for experiencing and influencing the world. Yet, Nishnaabeg life didn't rely on institutionality to hold the structure of life. We relied upon process that created networked relationship. Our intelligence system is a series of interconnected and overlapping algorithms—stories, ceremonies, and the land itself are procedures for solving the problems of life. Networked because the modes of communication and interaction between beings occur in complex nonlinear forms, across time and space. There is necessarily substantial overlap in networked responsibilities, such that the loss of a component of the network can self-correct and rebalance.

Governance was *made* every day. Leadership was embodied and acted out every day. Grounded normativity isn't a thing; it is generated structure born and maintained from deep engagement with Indigenous processes that are inherently physical, emotional, intellectual, and spiritual. Processes were created, practised. Daily life involved making politics, education, health care, food systems, and economy on micro- and macroscales. I didn't need to look for catastrophe or crisis-based stories to learn how to rebuild. The Nishnaabeg conceptualizations of life I found were cycles of creative energies, continual processes that bring forth more life and more creation and more thinking. These are the systems we need to recreate. The structural and material basis of Nishnaabeg life was and is process and relationship—again, resurgence is our original instruction.

What does Nishnaabeg grounded normativity look like? What is the ethical framework provided to me living my life on the north shore of Lake Ontario? What are these practices and associated forms of knowing? Nishnaabeg political systems begin in individuals and our relationships to the implicate order or the spiritual world. The ethics and values that individuals use to make decisions in their personal lives are the same ethics and values that families, communities, and nations use to make decisions about how to live collectively. Our ethical intelligence is ongoing; it is not a series of teachings or laws or protocols; it is a series of practices that are adaptable and to some degree fluid. I don't know it so much as an "ethical framework" but as a series of complex, interconnected cycling processes that make up a non-linear, overlapping, emergent, and responsive network of relationships of deep reciprocity, intimate and global interconnection and interdependence, that spirals across time and space. I know it as the algorithm of the Nishnaabeg world. I wrote about many of these in *Dancing on Our Turtle's Back*, the seven grandmother teachings, ethics of non-interference, and the practice of self-determination, the practice of consent, the art of honesty, empathy, caring, sharing, and self-sufficiency, for example. Our economy, fully integrated with spirituality and politics, was intensely local within a network of Indigenous internationalism that included plant and animal nations, the Great Lakes, the St Lawrence River, non-human beings, and other Indigenous nations. Its strength is measured by its ability to take care of the needs of the people, all the peoples that make up the Nishnaabeg cosmos. Colonialism has strangulated grounded normativity. It has attacked and tried to eliminate or confine the practice of grounded normativity to the realm of neo-liberalism so that it isn't so much a way of being in the world but a quaint cultural difference that makes one interesting. When colonialism could not eliminate grounded normativity, it tried to contain it so that it exists only to the degree that it does not impede land acquisition, settlement, and resource extraction. It is this situation—the dispossession of Indigenous peoples from our grounded normativities through the processes of colonialism and now settler colonialism—that has set up the circumstances that require a radical Indigenous resurgence as a mechanism for our continuance as Indigenous peoples.

I feel grateful, looking back, that I was able to interact with the Elders of Long Lake #58, these Nishnaabewin theorists, on their own terms, as opposed to as a graduate student.

Had I gone into their community as a student, I would have inevitably written about this project within the confines of the academic literature and thinking of the academy in the 1990s, and this perhaps would have become my record of these events. Instead, I didn't write about this experience until now, but I held it as a seed that in the right Nishnaabeg context grew and gives credence to the idea that the fuel for our radical resurgence must come from within our own nation-based grounded normativities because these are the intelligence systems that hold the potential, the theory as practice, for making ethical, sustainable Indigenous worlds.

I believe our responsibility as Indigenous peoples is to work with our Ancestors and those not yet born to continually give birth to an Indigenous present that generates Indigenous freedom, and this means creating generations that are in love with, attached to, and committed to their land. It also means that the intellectual and theoretical home for our nation-based resurgences must be within grounded normativity and, for me specifically, within Nishnaabewin, our lived expression of Nishnaabeg intelligence.

Discussion Questions

1. How does engagement with Nishnaabeg intelligence as radical resurgence theory differ from the ways in which Indigenous knowledge is typically regarded in mainstream institutions?

2. How might ideas of relationship, rights, and responsibility change when they are grounded in Indigenous place-based knowledges and ethical norms rather than generalist terms?

3. What are the challenges and transformative possibilities of thinking about governance beyond Western ideas and orientations?

4. What is the significance of focusing on the "everyday" politics inherent in individual actions and interactions?

5. What would personal self-determination look like for you? What systems/structures attempt to prefigure or contain this vision?

Recommended Reading

Belcourt, Billy-Ray. 2016. "A Poltergeist Manifesto." *Feral Feminisms*, 6: 22–32.

Coulthard, Glen. (2014). *Red Skin, White Masks: Rejecting the Politics of Colonial Recognition*. University of Minnesota Press.

Hunt, Sarah, and Cindy Holmes. 2015. "Everyday Decolonization: Living a Decolonizing Queer Politics." *Journal of Lesbian Studies* 19, no. 2: 154–72.

Simpson, Audra. 2014. *Mohawk Interruptus: Political Life across the Borders of Settler States*. Durham, NC: Duke University Press.

Simpson, Leanne. 2011. *Dancing on Our Turtle's Back: Stories of Nishnaabeg Re-creation, Resurgence and a New Emergence*. Winnipeg: ARP.

Additional Resources

Leanne Simpson's website. https://www.leannesimpson.ca
Alexis Pauline Gumbs' website. http://alexispauline.com
Dialogue between Leanne Simpson and Glen Coulthard on Dechinta Bush University, Indigenous land-based education, and embodied resurgence. https://decolonization.wordpress.com/2014/11/26/leanne-simpson-and-glen-coulthard-on-dechinta-bush-university-indigenous-land-based-education-and-embodied-resurgence/

Notes

1. The Oka Crisis occurred during the summer of 1990 as a response to the expansion of a nine-hole golf course into a sacred area of the Mohawk community of Kanesatake, west of Montreal, and involved a large-scale mobilization of land protectors with sites of physical resistance in Kanesatake and Kanawake and solidarity protests across Canada.

2. I heard Justice Murray Sinclair say this about residential schools at Queen's University on 27 May 2015 in his capacity as head of the Truth and Reconciliation Commission.

3. I use the term "heteropatriarchy" as an umbrella term to mean the intertwined systems of patriarchy and heterosexism, which include its manifestations as heteronormativity, transphobia, and cis-normativity.

4. Retreating to the bush was a common practice to escape the control of Indian agents, residential schools, coerced farming practices, encroachment, and many of the other impositions of settler colonial society.

5. As with *Dancing on Our Turtle's Back*, this is based on my own interpretation of Nishnaabeg thought. I do not speak for all Nishnaabeg people. I do not speak for anyone but myself. Like all nations and cultures, there are many ways of understanding our stories, histories, theories, and intellectual traditions within our collective system of ethics. There has always been and is lots of healthy and robust conversation about these interpretations.

6. Michael Yellowbird's "Decolonizing the Mind: Healing through Neurodecolonization and Mindfulness" is an excellent exploration of how ceremonial practices generate or regenerate neuropathways that provide the capacity to uphold Indigenous ethics and operationalize Indigenous political systems (Yellowbird 2015).

7. Some of our people are already doing this, and many of our people have always done this, in particular, language speakers, hunters, trappers, fishers, and medicine people.

8. I learned this from Doug Williams.

4 Colonialism, Gender Violence, and the Making of the Canadian State

Heidi Kiiwetinepinesiik Stark

The roots of sexual violence in Canada are as deep as colonialism itself.

—Sarah Hunt 2010

Colonialism cannot be fully understood or separated from the gender violence that animates it. Too often the gendered forms of discrimination experienced by Indigenous women, men, two-spirit people, and children are obscured by the processes of colonialism that code Indigenous bodies and lands into categories that naturalize[1] gender violence. This chapter explores the role and function of gender and Indigeneity relative to the structure of colonialism in Canada. In examining gendered constructions of Indigeneity, it contemplates the role of law, political legislation, and social and cultural representations. It engages these processes as integrated, co-constitutive, and collectively contributing to the particular forms of gendered violence faced by Indigenous people. Moreover, it engages these forms of violence not just as an effect of Canada's history of colonialism, but as actively functioning to produce colonialism in contemporary Canada. As Kwagiulth scholar Sarah Hunt observes, the categorization of Indigenous people and their lands functions as enabling categories for Canada by affirming the finality of settlement and the subjugation of Indigenous peoples as colonized subjects. She asserts that:

> categories of "Indians" (and the contemporary equivalent, Aboriginal) and "Indian space" have become naturalized in Canadian society and in much scholarship on Indigenous–government relations, and they continue to be enforced through a set of state-determined power relations, and histories of physical and epistemic violence. This system of categorization is foundationally gendered, as the rights and socio-legal standing of "Indians" have always been delineated along gender lines, resulting in distinct experiences of violence for "Indian" men, women and two-spirit people. (Hunt 2014, 58)

Through the codification of Indigenous peoples as subjects of Canada and the reduced lands as "reserves," Indigenous people are cast as subordinate minorities of the state, devoid of political authority and legal systems. Their lands become seen as merely small demarcated parcels where "Indians" are subject to live, naturalizing both the settlement of all other spaces as Canadian and Canadian political and legal domination over Indigenous peoples (Hunt 2014). This process is largely achieved by and compounded through the criminalization of Indigenous people whenever they seek to assert political authority over their lands and resist containment on their reserves. Indeed, the high rates of Indigenous incarceration and the ongoing tragedy of missing and murdered Indigenous women and girls can readily be traced to the core tenets of colonial expansion into North America. Jaskiran K. Dhillon, detailing the highly gendered and sexualized nature of colonial relationships, asserts that the state is actively engaged in ensuring that Indigenous girls and women continue to disappear and be murdered: "This is not an unexplainable phenomenon, it is not a mysterious 'crime problem.' It is a reworking of the gender violence that has been targeting Indigenous girls and women since the point of first contact, since before Canada became Canada" (Dhillon 2015). This violence was instrumental to the making of Canada. As Sherene Razack notes, the gender violence perpetuated against Indigenous women is a quite specific kind of violence, "a colonial violence that has not only enabled white settlers to secure the land *but to come to know themselves as entitled to it*" (Razack 2002, 129). While gender violence was essential to the colonial project of usurping Indigenous authority and lands, it has continued to condition Indigenous life as it is interwoven into law, policy, and social perceptions pertaining to Indigenous peoples.

Domesticity and the Construction of Indigenous Deviancy

It is important to understand how gender violence enabled historical processes of colonialism in order to see its continued legacy in Canada. The story of Canada is often told as one of settler–Indigenous partnership that is mutually beneficial and enabled the creation of Canada. In this narrative Indigenous women are often framed as contributing participants who consensually and voluntarily serve as cultural mediators and brokers. This narrative is seen, for example, in the American story of Pocahontas's life, which has been radically reconfigured again and again (including by Disney) to produce an account that renders European settlement of North America as both inevitable and desirable. In Canada, the eighteenth-century stories of Thanadelthur and Mikak, among others, exemplify the same motif of the helpful, enabling Indigenous woman, although neither of these women's stories reach into the popular culture and historical accounts have questioned the extent of their own personal agency (see, e.g., Houston 1989; Fay 2014). Resistance becomes framed as backward and misguided. This is also a narrative of white masculinity, proclaiming men must explore, conquer, and tame both Indigenous women and Indigenous lands and then ultimately settle and civilize/cultivate. As will be detailed later in this chapter, these kinds of depictions of both Indigenous women and white men persist today through cultural and social representations that serve to entitle white men and dehumanize Indigenous women, naturalizing violence against Indigenous women and girls as well as two-spirit people who are seen as disrupting these discrete categories.

This section details how Canada sought to avert attention from its own fabricated claims of sovereignty and illegal settlement of Indigenous lands by casting Indigenous people as a savage people in need of civilization. In the process, Canada constructed Indigenous lands as lawless spaces in need of colonial law. This colonial process was highly gendered. For example, Indigenous men's political authority had been recognized in the public sphere through the treaty-making process. Therefore, in order to invalidate their authority while ensuring that the treaties they "authorized," which were essential for Canada's "legitimacy" to land, remain intact required the depiction of Indigenous men as savage, lawless figures who were incapable of coping with modernity. For Indigenous women, whose political authority had already been dismissed and denied during the treaty process, further reduction of their social and political status was largely carried out in the private sphere through a demarcation of the proper attributes of domesticity (Stark 2016). Discourses focused on domesticity brought Indigenous women and other colonized peoples into relation with white men and were founded on a gender hierarchy that served to reify male supremacy. This gendered set of social relations was built into the mechanics of empire itself. Anne McClintock notes that "knowledge of the unknown world was mapped as a metaphysics of gender violence . . . and was validated by the new Enlightenment logic of private property and possessive individualism." In her analysis of the connections between gender violence and land acquisition, she asserts that "In these fantasies, the world is feminized and spatially spread for male exploration, then reassembled and deployed in the interests of massive imperial power" (McClintock 1995, 23). Cartographers laid out a "virgin territory" and filled blank seas with sirens and mermaids. Ships had female figures bound to their prows and were christened with women's names.

Imperial fantasies were the catalyst for the gender violence that animated colonialism. For example, manifest destiny was gendered spatially, with the private sphere of the home being a feminized safe haven constructed as a bounded and ordered interior space while the public sphere of males is a boundless, infinitely expanding frontier in want of territorial conquest. Amy Kaplan states:

> To understand this spatial and political interdependence of home and empire, it is necessary to consider rhetorically how the meaning of the domestic relies structurally on its intimate opposition to the notion of the foreign. *Domestic* has a double meaning that links the space of the familial household to that of the nation, by imagining both in opposition to everything outside the geographic and conceptual border of the home. (Kaplan 2002, 25)

While on the one hand drawing strict boundaries between the private and the public, domesticity, on the other hand, served as the engine of national expansion, reaching beyond its bounds to render the exterior as interior through the violent appropriation of Indigenous lands (Kaplan 2002, 29, 50; see also Piatote 2013).

The appropriation of Indigenous lands by the colonizers further required that Indigenous nations be defined as foreign entities whose sovereign political authority was requisite for treaty-making. As the colonial empire "settled" into power, Indigenous nations and their members were reconstituted as individual subjects of the colonial state. This made it easier for their political authority to be criminalized, thereby facilitating the imposition of settler law. Through the gendered expansion of its criminal jurisdiction, the settler state was able to bring Indigenous bodies, through colonial gendered norms, into the national polity, and in the process, domestic Indigenous nations and their lands.

Much like their male counterparts, Indigenous women found their mobility restricted and their activities constructed through the lens of criminality and savagery. While

Indigenous men's political authority was transformed within the public sphere, Indigenous women's authority was relegated to the private sphere and configured through the lens of domesticity. Domesticity became another mechanism to bring Indigenous women's bodies and Indigenous lands inside the state system by monitoring Indigenous women's behaviours and determining the boundaries between savage and civilized. Through Anglo-American conventions of modern domesticity, the colonial state sought to liberate Indigenous women from their "natural" yet "unreasonable" state of "savagery" (McClintock 1995, 35).

The discourse of domesticity sought to determine boundaries and delineate defined spaces. Imperialism had produced fear that the loss of boundaries would be catastrophic. This fear of boundary loss was generated by discourses centred on "an *excess* of boundary order coupled with fantasies of limitless power" (McClintock 1995, 26). McClintock (1995, 24) notes that "the feminizing of the land represents a ritualistic moment in imperial discourse as male intruders ward off fears of narcissistic disorder by reinscribing, as natural[,] an excess of gender hierarchy."[2] Further, Kaplan suggests that "Domesticity . . . refers not to a static condition, but to a process of domestication, which entails conquering and taming the wild, the natural, and the alien. 'Domestic' in this sense is related to the imperial project of civilizing, and the conditions of domesticity often become markers that distinguish civilization from savagery" (Kaplan 2002, 25).

In this domesticizing environment, Indigenous women's bodies, much like Indigenous lands, became marked as both criminal and lawless spaces solely because of their racialized gender and the accompanying Western constructions of Indigenous women's sexuality. As Gavigan (2012, 106) explains:

> One theme in the historical literature concerning Aboriginal women and Canadian law and society concerns the rapid and pervasive construction, by settlers, missionaries, and government officials alike, of Aboriginal women as a menace and as sexually promiscuous, such that any expression of sexual independence or agency was interpreted as illustrative of a "wildness" that had to be "tamed" while being simultaneously exploited by male newcomers.

As such, Indigenous women's bodies were constructed as inherently deceptive, cunning terrains, lawless frontiers, and virgin territory in need of conquest and civilization. Consequently, Indigenous women's bodies were to be strictly controlled through law because of the perilous threat they posed as lawless spaces.

Policies aimed at the assimilation of Indigenous nations also targeted many different aspects of Indigenous family life. Sex, marriage, and domesticity rapidly fell under colonial surveillance (Smith 2009), and progress towards civilization increasingly became measured by home life. Agents of the government and Christian denominations sought to impose virtues that were tethered to domesticity, such as modesty and cleanliness (Carter 1993, 18–19). As Adele Perry notes, "Christian missionaries of all denominational stripes were interested in Aboriginal women and, more particularly, in reforming their relationships to domesticity, to conjugality, and to work." She asserts:

> This triple program reflected missionaries' profound unease with the different ways that First Nations people experienced and understood manliness and womanliness. The collective, moveable, and matrilineal households; their plural, mixed-race, or

consensual relationships; and their physical labour or apparent lethargy all signaled a world of irreparable and dangerous difference. (Perry 2005, 125)

Government officials blamed Indigenous women's lack of domesticity for the "backward conditions" on many reserves. Carter (1993, 180) notes that "Indian women were often blamed for the squalid living conditions and poor health of reserve residents; their abilities as housewives and mothers were disparaged as were their moral standards." Indeed, the depiction of Indigenous women and their sexuality as "out of control" gradually became a popular way for state and religious leaders to deflect attention from failing government policies and unsuccessful missionary work (Barman 1997–8, 257). Furthermore, the sexualization of Indigenous women became a mechanism for colonial officials to justify the imposition of settler law and policy so they could reorder Indigenous life and subordinate Indigenous authority with impunity (Barman 1997–8, 257).

The application of the "deviant" label to Indigenous women coincided with the need to save not only these women but all Indigenous people from their demoralizing family structures. This gave rise to a number of restrictive policies that stripped Indigenous women of their political authority (Piatote 2013, 23). Under the Indian Act, the principal legislation through which Canada administers its paternalistic relationship with First Nations, widows could only inherit their husband's property if they could prove they were of a good, moral character (Carter 2005, 139). And, of course, Indian agents had the power and authority to decide what constituted a valid family unit in distributing treaty annuities. While Canada did not have the capacity to fully administer the marriage of Indigenous people, it had decided that Indigenous law would only be recognized if their marriages followed Euro-Canadian Christian norms. Furthermore, Canada sought to do away with polygamy by making it illegal, which then allowed for charging Indigenous men and women with a crime. Indigenous people were also accused of bigamy when they remarried, for the colonial state did not recognize Indigenous divorce law (Carter 2005; Harring 1994). And the ultimate domestication of Indigenous women's political authority occurred through the loss of their Indian political status under the Indian Act when they married a non-Indian (Palmater 2011).

Marking Indigenous Bodies for Death

Discourses of Indigenous deviancy and the simultaneous need to save Indigenous people persist to this day. Unlike in the past, however, law no longer has to be weaponized in order to impose colonial order over Indigenous lands and bodies. Rather, it "simply" renders the death of Indigenous people as inevitable and the usurpation of Indigenous lands as a consequence of colonial entitlement. For example, in her study of inquests and inquiries into Indigenous deaths in custody, Sherene Razack reminds us that "the failure [of state actors] to provide care, indeed to *care*, marks the body as a lower form of humanity, one that is already between life and death." Demonstrating how inquests and inquiries certify racial hierarchies as lawful and natural, she asserts: "Through the legal performance of Indigenous people as a dying race who are simply pathologically unable to cope with the demands of modern life, the settler subject is formed and his or her entitlement to the land secured" (Razack 2015, 6). For Razack, this process is necessary because Indigenous presence throws into question settler entitlement to and legitimacy over the land.

Young Inuit throat singers perform at a vigil for missing and murdered Indigenous women and girls at Parliament Hill.

Discourses of Indigenous deviancy and promiscuity also make gender violence permissible in the present. As Sarah Hunt notes, "stereotypes about the sexual availability and willingness of Aboriginal girls and women has resulted in generations of sexual violence and abuse continuing outside the law, as though it were not illegal to rape or batter an aboriginal woman" (Hunt 2010, 28). Indigenous women in Canada experience sexual assault at a rate 3.5 times higher than that for non-Indigenous women. This daunting statistic, coupled with the rising numbers of murdered and missing Indigenous women, has led many to designate violence against Indigenous women as an epidemic. Yet, Sarah Deer reminds us that the rape of Indigenous women has not been a short-term, isolated problem as the word *epidemic* may imply. Nor is it separate from the long-standing history of violence and oppression against Indigenous people. She argues against this framing, noting how it enables rape to be depoliticized by pointing out that "An epidemic is a contagious disease; rape is a crime against humanity" (Deer 2015, x).

Beyond the displacement and sometimes outright dismantling of the Indigenous legal and political institutions that are best positioned and best suited to respond to violence against Indigenous women, Canadian colonial culture and institutions have largely produced the environment that renders this violence both permissible and lawful. Colonization has always been characterized by the interrelationships between legal and sexual forms of violence. Amy Casselman (2016) notes that in the United States, "So important were both legal and sexual violence to the project of American colonization that they, in fact, became enmeshed. Throughout the history of Euro-American colonization, sexual violence became central to federal law and policy, while federal law and policy itself became structured by the logic of sexual violence." Such a conclusion fits the Canadian context as well, for as Casselman further asserts, all "modern jurisdictional conflicts in Indian country are not only *legacies* of colonialism but actively *maintain* and *inscribe* colonial violence on the bodies of Native women" (Casselman 2016, 8).

Casselman argues that under Euro-American colonization, Indigenous women were constructed as having a savage sexuality and were thus seen as inviting rape. She says: "As bodies were constructed as analogous to land that had yet to be dominated and was therefore for the taking, Native women were constructed as simply occupants of a body that was destined to be dominated by European power. Because Native sexuality, like Native land, was 'free' and 'unbridled,' it was not for Native women to control" (Casselman 2016, 71). Therefore, their sexuality was cast as something that had to be subdued by men. Like the land, control and ownership of Indigenous women's bodies could only rightfully come from colonial patriarchal domination and the violence that accompanied this form of conquest. These acts of violence, much like the constructions of Indigenous savagery in the nineteenth century, serve to justify the further regulation of Indigenous lands and bodies by colonial forces. As Dian Million notes, "Unspeakable acts of violence against Indigenous women effectively police them and their communities, but rarely the perpetrator" (Million 2013, 23). Such tendencies continue to be evident in the treatment of Indigenous women in the contemporary criminal justice system, such as in the trial of Bradley Barton, accused of the murder of Cindy Gladue. The initial trial in this case included more than 50 references to Ms Gladue as a "native," "a prostitute," and even "a specimen" as the court introduced her pelvic tissue into courtroom as evidence. The Alberta Court of Appeal has since set aside the acquittal and ordered a new trial, indicating that significant errors in the initial trial impacted the jury's ability to apply the law. Specifically, the Court of Appeal noted that "Despite our society's recognition of individual autonomy and equality, there still remains an undeniable need for judges to ensure that the criminal law is not tainted by pernicious and unfair assumptions, whether about women, Aboriginal people, or sex-trade workers" (Trimble 2018). This case and others like it speak to the ways in which discourses about Indigenous women continue to materialize within Canadian institutions to render violence against Indigenous women permissible or, at the very least, to situate Indigenous women as partially culpable in the high rates of violence that mark their lives.

Freezing Indigenous Identity in the Past

The legacy of colonialism in Canada continues to structure and animate gender violence today. By casting Indigenous bodies and lands as *wastelands* (Voyles 2015), vacating them of meaning, authority, and legitimacy, settlers are able to re-inscribe over and onto them. Indigenous women's roles, rather than representing legal political-economic or social authority, instead become caricatures, empty costumes that can be engineered and appropriated at will.

Indigenous people have long had to fight against stereotypes and dominant narratives that depict Indigenous suffering not as the result of destructive state policies but as the natural consequence of Indigenous poverty. Moreover, Indigenous legal and political traditions were not honoured as vibrant institutions but as relics of an ancient past that are incapable of meeting the challenges and aspirations of contemporary societies. Images that situate Indigenous people as a lawless people frozen in time have been relied on to strip Indigenous peoples of their rights. The widespread stereotypical view that Indigenous people are savage enabled Canada to reframe Indigenous assertions of sovereignty and political authority in the nineteenth century as criminal activities, which resulted in the execution of numerous Indigenous leaders (Stark 2016). Indeed, the largest mass executions in both the US and Canada resulted from the hyper-criminalization of Indigenous people. On 26 December 1862, 38 Dakota men were hanged before a crowd of some 4,000 spectators in Mankato, Minnesota (Berg et al. 1993; Chomsky 1990). Twenty-three years later at Battleford, Saskatchewan, six Cree and two Assiniboine leaders were hanged in front of hundreds of witnesses. Yet, these were neither isolated nor exceptional events. Numerous Modoc, Tlingit, and Nisqually leaders in the United States along with Tsilhqot'in, Ojibwe, and Métis leaders in Canada were executed under the pretense of criminality within colonial law (see Cothran 2014; Harring 1994, 1998; Blee 2014). Countless other Indigenous individuals have also been prosecuted and imprisoned for alleged criminal activities under the jurisdiction of these two colonizing states.

While the historical conceptions of Indigenous peoples as savage and criminal have thoroughly worked their way into the political and legal imagination of Canada, cultural appropriation now serves to perpetuate these stereotypical images. Cultural appropriation refers to a process wherein members of one cultural group use, "draw inspiration" from, commodify, or capitalize on the cultural expressions, labour, and resources of another group. Appropriation can take many forms; from the war chants heard at sporting events or remixed in songs like P. Diddy, Nelly, and Murphy Lee's "Shake Ya Tailfeather" to the recasting of historical actors such as Pocahontas into narratives of cross-cultural exchange that serve to legitimate English settlement and claims to possession of Indigenous lands, these seemingly harmless narratives both establish and reinforce cultural stereotypes and expectations.

Regardless of whether appropriation takes place in a piecemeal way or in the form of broader narratives, these forces combine to reinforce popular mythologies about Indigenous people that find their way into dominant social, legal, and political interactions. This can be seen in the *Delgamuukw* decision, for example, when one of the Elders testifying was asked whether they ate pizza, implying that their engagement with modernity diluted their Indigenous authenticity (Garoutte 2003). In the process, the settler state further entrenches its position as the arbiter of Indigenous identity and authenticity, originally asserted through the Indian Act but reinforced through multiple court decisions and pieces of legislation over the years. The point here is that the everyday representations and assumptions surrounding Indigenous peoples and the systemic forces and institutions that impact Indigenous peoples are deeply intertwined and often function to reinforce one another.

Returning to the everyday scale, there are seemingly endless examples of cultural appropriation in contemporary society and media. The appropriation of Indigenous headdresses and tribal elements has been a subject of critique in the fashion world for decades, as far back as the 1990s when then 15-year-old Kate Moss was photographed wearing a feathered headdress for *The Face*. Cultural elements such as headdresses and other "native-inspired attire" have been a continuous presence on fashion runways, including those of Chanel and Victoria's Secret, in stores such as Urban Outfitters, in the costumes of musicians such as Ke$ha (Keene 2010) and Pharrell (Celescoop 2014), and in the "everyday lives" of reality TV celebrities on shows such as *Dance Moms* and *Keeping Up with the Kardashians* (*Indian Country Today*, 3 Sept., 27 June 2014).

In 2011 Miss Universe Canada, Chelsae Durocher, wore a headdress and a "First Nations inspired" dress for the "National Dress" portion of the competition (Keene 2011a). When confronted with backlash for engaging in cultural appropriation, she said her dress paid homage to the Haida. She was not alone. Both the 2008 Miss Universe Canada and the 2015 Miss Universe Canada contestants wore culturally offensive costumes that appropriated Indigenous imagery and cultural items (*CBC News* 2015). Designers Dsquared also declared they were paying "homage to the beauty and strength of the indigenous peoples of Canada, who shaped our country's cultural identity," following criticism of their 2015 line called .dsquaw (*CBC News* 2016). Indeed, as two-spirit writer Gwen Benaway highlights in their analysis of Rihanna's "Savage X Fenty" lingerie line, the reclamation of derogatory terms associated with Indigenous peoples is not necessarily empowering or subversive for those whom these terms have historically been employed to dehumanize. Benaway notes that the implications of terms such as "savage" are not just located in the past, but they still signify "an entire set of racist beliefs that continue to endanger Indigenous peoples" (Benaway 2018).

It is important to also recognize that these aesthetics are not mere "fashion trends" but are representative of a broader impulse to derive amusement or, at the very least, some sort of social capital from the act of embodying stereotypical representations of Indigenous people. Thus, every year hordes of privileged individuals don clothing, accessories, headwear, and hairstyles "borrowed" from Indigenous cultures as they flock to music festivals such as Coachella and Burning Man, where they gather in "a field for a weekend, sleeping under canvas (and, in some cases, teepees), possibly on drugs, and some are bound to explore fantasies of escaping modern society and embracing their 'natural' selves via the otherness of older cultures" (Lynskey 2014). Here, Indigenous identity is appropriated as a temporary transgression or vacation from "normal life" through a foray into the Indigenous female identity, which is seen as a racy or provocative act precisely because of how representations of Indigenous women have historically been constructed and reproduced. As described earlier in this chapter, Indigenous women's bodies "were constructed as inherently deceptive, cunning terrains, lawless frontiers, and virgin territory" to be controlled and civilized through settler-colonial law and authority. While many now recognize these representations to be problematic, they nonetheless continue to be reproduced in the present day as they are insidiously embodied by the "nature-loving," "socially subversive," or "free-willed" hipster seeking to assert her or his own difference from mainstream society. In the process, festival attendees and others who engage in similar processes of cultural appropriation operationalize caricatures of Indigeneity for personal and social purposes with little or no engagement with the underlying cultural significance of the elements they are appropriating, and with even less regard for the implications of their collective actions. Cherokee scholar Adrienne Keene, speaking about cultural appropriation, states:

> for the communities that wear these headdresses, they represent respect, power and responsibility. The headdress has to be earned, gifted to a leader in whom the community has placed their trust. When it becomes a cheap commodity anyone can buy and wear to a party, that meaning is erased and disrespected, and native peoples are reminded that our cultures are still seen as something of the past, as unimportant in contemporary society, and unworthy of respect. (Quoted in Riley and Carpenter 2016)

While many forms of cultural appropriation continue to abound, Indigenous people have worked diligently to call attention to and prevent their growth. For instance, when a Toronto art gallery circulated promotional materials surrounding the upcoming exhibit of a non-Indigenous artist whose paintings were "inspired by" and clearly mirrored many elements of the works of Anishinaabe artist Norval Morrisseau, public outrage resulted in the cancellation of the exhibit (Nasser 2017). Indeed, the Indigenous art world has been a central site of resistance to cultural appropriation with anti-appropriative mobilization increasingly taking place online. Such efforts are evidenced in the works of Adrienne Keene (*Native Appropriations*), Jessica Metcalfe (*Beyond Buckskin*), and the collective efforts of northern Indigenous women (*ReMatriate*). These initiatives use social media to post real-time stories of cultural appropriation and to engage in discussions about the impacts these stereotypes have on Indigenous people and communities, not least of which include their highly gendered impacts.

At the same time, these and other online sites promote the works of individual Indigenous artists and art collectives, pointing to locations where individuals can find authentic works created by Indigenous people. They have also sought to nuance the conversations surrounding cultural appropriation and provide information into the measures that non-Indigenous people can take to address instances of appropriation and to pursue productive partnerships with Indigenous artists. For instance, when designer Paul Frank held an "Indian"-themed party for Fashion's Night Out in Hollywood in 2012, Metcalfe wrote an open letter to the company detailing why this event was harmful. In response, Paul Frank deleted all the images from Facebook and Twitter and issued an apology. The company then followed up with Metcalfe, took full responsibility for the event, and expressed a commitment to learning more. These dialogues resulted in Paul Frank pulling all Indigenous-inspired designs and, instead, partnering with Indigenous designers to release a new line that "fuses the iconic Paul Frank brand with four different artists' aesthetics, each rooted in their heritage" (Keene 2013).

Despite these and other positive examples, stereotypes that portray Indigenous women as hyper-sexualized and Indigenous men as hyper-savage continue to abound. Speaking to the impacts of racist Halloween costumes, Adrienne Keene (2011b) notes:

- The misogyny and stereotyping is so blatant, it almost reads like satire.
- But unfortunately these are real products, for sale on websites and in thousands of Spirit stores nationwide.
- Thousands of people are seeing, reading, and internalizing these messages.
- These costumes are hurtful and dangerous because they present a false and stereotyped image of Native people.
- The public sees these images, and it erases our current existence, so the larger, contemporary issues in Indian Country then cease to exist as well.
- When everyone only thinks Indians are fantasy characters put in the same category as pirates, princesses, and cartoon characters, it *erases our humanity*.

As Taté Walker (2015) notes in her blog on the hypersexualization of Indigenous women, "How our daughters see their cultures and themselves represented in the media, how products are marketed to them and how society built on colonial violence treats them in real life affect every aspect of their existence." These stereotypical representations normalize misogyny and sexualized behaviours, which puts Indigenous girls and women more at risk for violence. While the cultures of Indigenous peoples in general are fetishized, cultural symbols and messages related to Indigenous girls and women are sexualized. One of the most common of these is that Indigenous girls are seen to be in need of being rescued by the white, heterosexual cowboy hero. "The message is not only that a Native girl's value lies in her exotic, leather-clad (yet idyllically Western) body, but also that heteronormativity—a system of ideas that reinforce heterosexuality and rigid gender roles for men and women—is the foundation upon which relationships stand" (Walker 2015).

Margot Francis also examines this issue in her book-length study of whiteness, Indigeneity, and the Canadian national imaginary. Francis (2012, 95) asserts that "the simultaneous fetishization and erasure of Indigenous men in the new space of the wilderness (looking at Banff) has served to bolster Euro-Canadian masculinity and agency at the expense of those others, who, through the same process, were most often rendered primitive, static, and lacking." She argues that the "Indians," who are both acknowledged and refused in Canadian national symbols, do not mythologize a national character forged through violent struggles; instead, they re-inscribe Canada's peculiarly benign self-image. "They signify Canada's commitments to the values of justice and racial harmony, and consequently, they assist primarily white Canadians, as well as a wide range of others, to bask in the warm glow of being from a nice country that is innately given to tolerance and civility" (Francis 2012, 95). As Patrick Wolfe explains, settler-colonial logics often necessitate the appropriation of selective elements of Indigeneity to construct the national identity of settler-colonial states, allowing the state to subsume and use Indigenous difference to construct its own distinctiveness while also affirming its own authority over processes of identity construction such as those institutionalized through the Indian Act.

Yet, Indigenous scholars and activists have continually worked to assert our own agency and reclaim authority over questions of authenticity and identity. Indigenous people have found particular success harnessing social media to actively disrupt these trends and to problematize their implications. Indigenous youth have been especially successful in combatting negative images, stereotypes, and cultural appropriation with the #ImNotYourMascot and #mycultureisnotatrend hashtags; the Idle No More movement's poster campaigns such as "We're a Culture Not a Costume;" the National Congress of American Indians' "Proud to Be" advertisement against the Washington professional football team; the YouTube channel of sketch comedy group the 1491s; and blogs such as *Re-Matriate*, *Native Appropriations*, and *Beyond Buckskin*. Through these efforts, Indigenous people are effectively bringing the humanity back into representations of Indigenous people and instituting our own measures to mitigate new challenges that present themselves in contemporary contexts.

Conclusion

Whether through discourses of Indigenous deviancy and criminality, the construction of Indigenous bodies as inherently violable, or the dehumanizing caricatures of Indigenous people in the media, it is important that we be attentive to the gendered ways colonialism has shaped Canada and Canadians' perceptions of Indigenous peoples. The impacts of historical discourses of deviance and decency are perhaps more insidious today and require us to take special care to unpack the processes that enable the lives of so many Indigenous men, women, and children to be dismissed or even destroyed with impunity. We must ask why Indigenous life continues to be treated as disposable.

This chapter has outlined the many forms and scales of gendered norms and violence that implicate Indigenous peoples, past and present. Within this discussion, I have also sought to describe the myriad ways that Indigenous women are refusing these many forms of representation and repression. In blogs, scholarship, and activism and in the sheer refusal to disappear or perform gendered conventions of Indigeneity, Indigenous women continue to carve out spaces for their voices to be heard. Moving forward, it is important that we look out for and continue to critically examine the insidious ways that gender violence and colonialism persist in shaping Indigenous peoples' lives.

Discussion Questions

1. How have gendered norms helped produce and sustain structures of colonialism in Canada?
2. How do the historical aspects of colonialism continue to play out in contemporary contexts?
3. What gendered stereotypes have you heard about Indigenous peoples? Who benefits from these stereotypes? What is their social or political function?
4. What do the terms "cultural authenticity" and "co-optation" mean? Why are Indigenous people concerned about co-optation?
5. How are questions of gender and sexuality relevant to contemporary decolonization or reconciliation projects?

Recommended Reading

Dhillon, Jaskiran K. 2015. "Indigenous Girls and the Violence of Settler Colonial Policing." *Decolonization: Indigeneity, Education and Society* 4, no. 2: 1–31.

Doenmez, Caroline. 2016. "The Unmournable Body of Cindy Gladue." In *Forever Loved: Exposing the Hidden Crisis of Missing and Murdered Indigenous Women and Girls in Canada*, edited by Dawn Memee Lavell-Harvard and Jennifer Brant. Bradford, ON: Demeter Press.

Hunt, Sarah. 2014. "Law, Colonialism and Space." In "Witnessing the Colonialscape: Lighting the Intimate Fires of Indigenous Legal Pluralism," Chapter 3, pp. 58–80. PhD diss., Simon Fraser University.

Perry, Adele. 2005. "Metropolitcan Knowledge, Colonial Practice, and Indigenous Womanhood: Missions in Nineteenth-Century British Columbia." In *Contact Zones: Aboriginal and Settler Women in Canada's Colonial Past*, edited by Myra Rutherdale and Katie Pickles. Vancouver: Univesity of British Columbia Press.

Razack, Sherene. 2002. "Gendered Racial Violence and Spatialized Justice: The Murder of Pamela George." In *Race, Space and the Law: Unmapping a White Settler Society*, edited by Sherene Razack. Toronto: Between the Lines.

Additional Resources

Native Appropriations. http://nativeappropriations.com
#StandingRockSyllabus. https://nycstandswithstandingrock.wordpress.com/standingrocksyllabus
ReMatriate Collective. https://www.facebook.com/ReMatriate
Indian Country. https://newsmaven.io/indiancountrytoday

Notes

1. To naturalize in this context means to make seem natural, normal, and inevitable. Colonial processes that code Indigenous people as savage and Indigenous lands as lawless spaces produce narratives that imbue Indigeneity with this sense of naturalness and inevitability so that the average Canadian comes to see Indigenous people as backward savages who are incapable of coping with modernity. In the process, the high rates of Indigenous women's deaths are coded as inevitable and explained away by saying these women were engaged in a "risky" lifestyle. Indigenous poverty becomes seen as a "natural" outcome due to Indigenous peoples' inability or unwillingness to modernize and properly engage with a capitalist market. Addiction and health disparities become understood as the fallibility of Indigenous bodies, and the mass incarceration of Indigenous people is not understood through systemic racism and colonialism but instead determined as an inevitable outcome of Indigenous people's savage nature. In these ways, Indigenous people are always a threat. Indigenous men are coded as criminal and Indigenous women as lewd, sexual beings that either threaten civility or are ready for exploitation.

2. Gendering the land isn't in itself problematic. Indeed, many Indigenous nations understand creation in relational terms that are gendered, such as Mother Earth, Grandmother Moon, Father Sun, etc. However, Western conceptions of "Mother Nature" largely operate within a hierarchical system that serve to diminish the character and value of both creation and women by naturalizing their colonization and conquest. See Women's Earth Alliance and Native Youth Sexual Health Network, Violence on the Land, Violence on Our Bodies: Building an Indigenous Response to Environmental Violence. http://landbodydefense.org/uploads/files/VLVBReportToolkit2016.pdf.

5 Piecing Together Modern Treaty Politics in the Yukon

Lianne Marie Leda Charlie

> In honoring the disconnected, inexplicable, irresolute and relative, collage process
> engenders an inclusive reality where disintegration, disorder, and even destruction
> can be coincidental paths to meaningful renewal, and insists that restoration and
> insight are not easily rationalized and prescribed.

—Davis 2008, 250

Introduction

*Paper Politics. A committee of five community members has been appointed by the council,
the elected governing body of the First Nation, and tasked with determining the criteria
and process for citizenship in the Nation. They sit in a small conference room, inside an
office trailer. It is Monday night. Six o'clock. The summer sun is still high in the sky. Binders
overflowing with loose paper cover the table. A lawyer is present, paid upwards of $150 an
hour to help the committee navigate the legal transition from Indian band to self-governing
Nation. The committee spends the first hour clarifying terms—status Indian, non-status
Indian, beneficiary, band member, effective date, enrolment—and debating whether citizens' personal information should be stored in an online database or in hard-copy files. In
this moment, they're leaning towards hard-copy files. The majority of the Nation's members
descend from just over 40 original families. Everyone knows who is who. The conversation
about citizenship uses Canadian legal terms and draws upon the laws stipulated by the
Indian Act, the Umbrella Final Agreement, the Self-governing Agreement, and the Nation's
12-year-old constitution. Ancestral or cultural laws, values, or practices, if present, are sup-
plemental to Canadian terms and processes. Council has mandated that a citizenship act
be drafted as soon as possible. Decisions tonight will shape the foundation upon which the
Nation's citizenship is determined and legally enforced on their settlement lands. The doors
are closed. The rest of the self-government administration has long since gone home. Apart
from a few kids playing across the street in a gravel-covered field, the surrounding village
is quiet. One of the women gets up from the conference table and pours herself another cup
of coffee.*

Lianne Marie Leda Charlie

In this chapter, I use collage as a metaphor and an arts-based, Indigenous research methodology to understand modern treaty politics in the Yukon in northern Canada. A collage in its most basic and accessible form is the result of combining an assortment of images and texts that are cut from a magazine, for example, and reconfiguring the pieces into an entirely new and reimagined image. This chapter is organized as a collage that brings together a number of different pieces—images, stories, poetry, and analysis—in order to understand Indigenous politics in the Yukon differently.

Collage is a useful metaphor for understanding Indigenous politics because Indigenous peoples are having to navigate political worlds made up of many different, often incommensurable, pieces. For example, Indigenous and settler Canadian governance systems are fundamentally different because they are rooted in vastly different ways of understanding the world (ontologies or world views), yet we often consider them using similar terms and approaches. As Deborah McGregor explains in Chapter 11, Indigenous peoples and settler Canadians and their governments also have vastly different ways of relating to the land. Indigenous peoples have practices rooted in a deeply reciprocal relationship with the land; Indigenous peoples are essentially *of* the land. Canada sees the land as a commodity and extracts resources from it in pursuit of economic gain. This is further complicated by the fact that Indigenous peoples are dealing with a host of socio-economic pressures—lack of quality housing, underfunded education and health care, pervasive substance abuse, and poverty. Meanwhile, Canada insists on expanding natural resource extraction, forcing Indigenous communities to compromise and redefine their relationship with their land. The result is a very real tension between two divergent value systems: capitalism and the sacred.

Theories on how to navigate this political context are also divided: some scholars argue for more informed participation and Indigenous representation in Canada's settler state governance systems and capitalist pursuits, while others argue for disengagement and a de-prioritization of Indigenous participation and representation in favour of a turn inward towards more resurgent Indigenous-focused nation-(re)building (see Leanne Simpson, Chapter 3 of this volume).

These pieces that make up Indigenous political worlds are incommensurable, in that they reflect profoundly different ways of understanding and being in/with the world: e.g., capitalism and the sacred; land as relation and land as resource.

Collage, as a metaphor, helps us bring seemingly unrelated and diverse pieces together, not just Indigenous and settler governance but everything else that informs our political worlds—people, places, texts, images, contexts, experiences, practices, stories, histories, traditions, ontologies or world views. Chadwick Allen (2012) uses the phrase "purposeful and productive juxtaposition" to explain how this coming together of diverse pieces can be done intentionally and creatively so as to learn or reveal something new in their interconnections. This idea of productive juxtaposition within collage allows for multiple and sometimes irreconcilable elements to be deliberately placed within new proximities to one another. It is this purposeful and intentional act of creation that I think reveals new options for Indigenous peoples as we navigate our complex political lives.

I also use collage as an Indigenous research methodology. An Indigenous research methodology is a way of conducting research that flows from an Indigenous world view or way of knowing. Collage as methodology emerged out of my own art practice of creating digital photo collages and drawings, some of which can be seen throughout this chapter. When viewing these images, I invite you to explore how they bring divergent and sometimes incommensurable images and texts into new proximity to each other. When you look at these images, can you see how they are made up of divergent pieces that are then invited to be in relationship with each other differently within the collage? Collage allows them to be together physically on the page and metaphorically in ways that we may not have imagined, essentially allowing for new ways of understanding or seeing the world. It is this principle that I apply to modern treaty politics in the Yukon.

Modern Treaty Politics in the Yukon

The complexities of Indigenous politics are particularly evident in the Yukon, home to over 37,000 people, 23 per cent of whom identify as Indigenous. The Yukon is unique in contemporary Indigenous politics because the majority of the territory has been settled by comprehensive land claims (also known as final agreements or modern treaties).

In 1973, Chief Elijah Smith and a delegation of representatives from Yukon First Nations travelled to Ottawa to deliver to Prime Minister Pierre Elliott Trudeau a position paper called *Together Today for Our Children Tomorrow*, which called for a "fair and just" settlement with Canada and captured a desire, at the time, for redress: recognition of Indigenous rights and title to land in the form of a legal settlement (Council for Yukon Indians 1973, 17). This process was seen as a way of moving respectfully and responsibly towards a better future with Canada. The submission of *Together Today* and its

We still think of the Yukon as our Land.

acceptance by Trudeau initiated a land claims process in the Yukon.

Fifteen years of difficult negotiations later, the landmark Umbrella Final Agreement (UFA) was reached in 1988, and then finalized in 1990, between the Council of Yukon First Nations (at the time known as the Council for Yukon Indians), the Yukon territorial government, and the government of Canada. The UFA is a 309-page document made up of 28 chapters on a range of topics relevant to self-governing First Nations, including taxation, enrolment, water management, fish and wildlife, land-use planning, and implementation. The details of each chapter were meticulously negotiated by the three parties. Each chapter outlines the rights, powers, and jurisdiction of each party and how they are to relate to each other. The UFA is a framework that includes the general provisions for each individual First Nation's final agreement. An individual Yukon First Nation's final agreement will include all the provisions from the UFA plus individually negotiated special provisions.

Since 1990, 11 of 14 Yukon First Nations have signed comprehensive land claims and final agreements under the UFA and have been transitioning from "Indian bands," that is, governing bodies designed and administered under the Indian Act, to political entities that are, in theory, organized and managed by the First Nations themselves. The remaining three Yukon First Nations—White River First Nation, Ross River Dena Council, and Liard First Nation—continue to be administered as Indian bands under the Indian Act.

The UFA has ushered in a suite of political changes in the Yukon. The Indian Act ceases to apply to First Nations that have signed a self-government agreement, and each First Nation's specific treaty rights are now outlined in individual agreements. Self-governing Yukon First Nations have jurisdiction and law-making abilities on their settlement land. "Settlement land" is the term used in the UFA to describe land that is owned and managed by a First Nation (I explain more about the land categories under the UFA later in the chapter). A self-governing Yukon First Nation can determine its nation's citizenry and can design and implement its own justice, heritage, and social programming. It can also engage in economic development, as well as modify its governing structure to reflect more traditional governance practices.

The agreements signed under the UFA are celebrated as "modern treaties." A modern treaty is an example of a recent trend in Indigenous rights movements initiated by Canada that uses land claim settlements and self-government agreements to negotiate renewed legal and political relationships with First Nations in places where land rights have not previously been dealt with by, for example, historical treaties or other legal means. The government of Canada claims that this approach is based on mutual recognition and "true reconciliation" between Indigenous nations and Canada (Canada 2015). For Canada, processes like comprehensive land claims and final agreements are important for establishing "certainty"; in other words, the final agreements replace the ambiguity surrounding Indigenous rights and title to land with defined treaty rights and title in clearly defined areas. These agreements also extinguish or eliminate treaty rights and title in other areas. Thus, scholars such as James Tully (2000) and Taiaiake Alfred (2001) have argued that the term "modern treaty" is in fact a misrecognition of the nature of historic treaty relationships, described in greater detail by Gina Starblanket in Chapter 1 of this volume.

Today in the Yukon, 41,595 square kilometres of the territory (approximately 8.5 per cent) is settlement land, where Indigenous title for 11 Yukon First Nations remains. For these 11 First Nations, title to land has been extinguished on the remainder of their traditional territory. This is due to Canada incorporating a "cede, release, and surrender" clause into the final agreements. This clause states that First Nations that sign a final agreement are essentially agreeing to "cede, release, and surrender" to Canada all of their "claims, rights, titles, and interests" to their traditional territory (apart from the agreed-upon settlement land) and its land, water, and minerals. In exchange, a new set of negotiated rights can be expressed in designated areas, all of which is outlined in the final agreements (Government of Canada, Council for Yukon Indians, and Government of the Yukon 1993, 15).

Thinking about Collage

Now that you've read the above section on modern treaty politics in the Yukon, go back and look at the image "We still think of the Yukon as our Land" at the beginning of this section. The latter phrase is from *Together Today for Our Children Tomorrow*. The text in the bottom right corner of the image is the "cede, release, and surrender" clause from the Umbrella Final Agreement, the framework for Yukon's modern treaties. Read it out loud. I discuss this clause later in this chapter, but what stands out to you now about what it says? How does it relate, or not, to the statement at the top of the image: "We still think of the Yukon as our Land"? What about the woman in the image? Do you know what she is doing? She is wringing out a moosehide as part of the hide-tanning process. What do you notice about how the land is depicted in the image? Now look at the whole image. How would you describe the relationship between the text, the woman, and the land?

Critiques and Concerns

A text collage of words and phrases taken from *Together Today for Our Children Tomorrow* (1973):

*One hundred and thirty-two million five hundred and
twenty-eight thousand*

Lianne Marie Leda Charlie

*Six hundred and
forty acres*

We still think of the Yukon as OUR LAND

*What would be fair and just?
We used to be independent and free
Born and raised on land that we always thought of as our land*

*We will not accept promises
because we have very little faith anymore in Whiteman promises*

While the UFA extends certain, limited powers to Indigenous peoples via modern treaties, it also facilitates government-backed industry access to Indigenous lands and resources. Consider, for example, how the land under the UFA has been surveyed and categorized. The UFA settlement lands are divided into three categories: Category A settlement land, Category B settlement land, and fee simple settlement land. Under Category A, First Nations own both the surface and the subsurface, including oil, gas, and minerals. Where First Nations have subsurface rights, they can regulate mining activities as they wish, issue title to minerals, and collect royalties. Under Category B, First Nations own the surface only; the subsurface rights are under the administration of the Yukon government. Fee simple settlement land is settlement land where a Yukon First Nation has the same fee simple title as other land registered in the Land Titles Office, which means the First Nation is essentially a private landowner. In addition to these different categories of settlement land, there is also non-settlement land, which is basically all the land that's not settlement land and includes mines and minerals in Category B settlement land and fee simple land. Indigenous title no longer exists on non-settlement land; it was ceded to the government under the UFA. Non-settlement land is essentially Crown land that is administered and controlled by the Yukon government. Non-settlement land is now the majority of land in the Yukon.

It is important to look at the specifics of how land under the UFA has been categorized because it reveals how Indigenous rights and title to large swaths of land in the Yukon have been undermined. Consider, for example, that the Yukon has legislated a free-entry system, which means that any mining prospector (an individual or a multinational corporation) has the right to enter Crown lands to explore for minerals and acquire rights to those minerals. While the ratification of the UFA has put some restrictions on industry access to Category A settlement land, it has opened up large swaths of Indigenous traditional territory because of the "cede, release, and surrender clause." Only 8.5 per cent of the Yukon is settlement land, and part of that includes Category B and fee simple lands that are open to mineral staking. Despite the positioning of the modern treaty as a victory for Indigenous control of the land, industry and settler-state government bodies still have a significant say when it comes to resource extraction. As a result of modern treaties, industry can now operate with certainty in areas where Indigenous rights and title have been extinguished and where these lands are now largely controlled by the state.

The UFA has created a number of co-management and environmental assessment processes (for example, the Yukon Environmental and Socio-Economic Assessment Board [YESAB]) in order to protect lands and resources and to increase Yukon First Nations

Lianne Marie Leda Charlie

representation on bodies that oversee various resources. However, YESAB and other boards and committees can only put forward recommendations to the territorial government. Despite the intention to balance power and increase Indigenous decision-making power in the territory, the UFA allows the territorial government to have final say on what can and cannot happen on ceded land.

While the UFA has bolstered access to previously curtailed decision-making power and law-making abilities, the benefits of which should not be minimized, we still must ask: What kind of future might we create if we prioritize the implementation of the agreements we have with our ancestors and our lands, rather than those we have with the Canadian nation-state?

Conclusion

Resurgence. The forest floor is damp; the moss is thick and soft. My feet are wet and they're getting cold. I'm going to wear my insulated rubber boots next time, I think to myself. I see my cousin through the trees. She's gone back to the car to check on her baby, who is sleeping in the back seat. I scan the ground for bright clumps of blood-red cranberries. The ripe ones hang heavy on their little branches, drooping into the moss—they are hard to see. I learn quickly that the trick is to get low. At moss-level, the ground comes alive with bursts of red against a backdrop of green lichen. I haven't picked nihtl'ät before. I'm not sure of the technique I'm supposed to use to pull the berries off their branches. I opt for a gentle tug with my fingertips. The ripe ones practically fall off with the lightest touch. I crouch on the moss in a spot surrounded by berries. I pick all the ripe ones at an arm's distance and then stand up and take a couple steps, careful not to crush any berries underfoot. I crouch and pick all the ripe berries at arm's distance again, then stand up, scan the ground, spot red, step, crouch, pick. The berries make a light drumming sound as they land in my handle-less ice cream bucket: da-da-dum. I hear a twig crack in the distance and I look up to make sure it is not brother bear. It's not. It's just the forest making forest sounds.

I scan the ground, spot red, step, crouch, pick.

da-da-dum.

da-da-dum.

da-da-dum.

Land claims and self-government agreements are mechanisms of "the politics of recognition." Some liberal scholars, and certainly the Canadian state, consider recognition of Indigenous and treaty rights to be capable of righting the wrongs of historical and contemporary colonialism and state-initiated injustices. From this view, legal and political recognition can result in an affirmation of Indigenous inherent rights and legal security, state-backed protection from development and encroachment, cultural protection and renewal, and material redistribution and economic gain.

But as Joyce Green explains in Chapter 14 of this volume, some Indigenous scholars are drawing attention to how the state maintains control of Indigenous peoples and their land by using mechanisms of recognition, which are carefully constructed so as to restrict Indigenous peoples' ability to make autonomous decisions and ultimately to dispossess Indigenous peoples of large tracts of their traditional territories, as exemplified by what is happening in the Yukon. Yellowknives Dene scholar Glen Coulthard (2014) argues that the politics of recognition are state-serving at their core and merely extend the colonial project by repackaging land dispossession as self-determination.

This raises a number of questions and considerations for moving forward in the Yukon. How are Indigenous peoples to navigate a political landscape in which their rights and title have been legally extinguished in the majority of the territory? What does self-determination look like in a political landscape that pressures Indigenous peoples to create and uphold governance structures that mimic Canada's rather than those of their ancestors? How can Indigenous peoples express their ancestral values and enact their ancestral practices in their homelands where Indigenous jurisdiction is limited to a fraction of the territory?

Scholars of Indigenous resurgence, like Leanne Betasamosake Simpson (2011, 2016) and Glen Coulthard (2014), maintain that self-determination requires revitalizing Indigenous ancestral values and governance practices free of settler-state control and interference. For these scholars, Indigenous self-determination is grounded in the resurgence of our people, lands, languages, and laws. Self-determination is enacted intentionally in the everyday and steadily advances us towards a radically alternative future, perhaps one that our ancestors might recognize.

Collage as metaphor, arts-based practice, and theory can help us not only imagine but create a desired future. Collage offers a space for Indigenous historical realities, present political realities, and desired futures to intersect in innovative and unexpected ways. Collage is offered here as one way of augmenting our current view of our political context in a way that better reflects the realities of our communities, while also accounting for the distinct and diverse contexts we must navigate and the tools (i.e., theories and practices) we have to do so.

Chadwick Allen's (2012) use of purposeful and productive juxtaposition is important to restate here, as his language alludes to a place for agency and empowered, informed, and intentional decision-making as to how we can attend to power embedded within the political structures that Indigenous people are confronting. For example, collage-making as an art form requires manipulating images into any shape or size that is desired by the collagist, who chooses the pieces and how they interact with each other in the layout and the design. Choice is available at every stage of the collage-making process. While some pieces can be added, removed, reshaped, cropped, and expanded with the addition of new materials, others can be "refused" (Simpson 2014) or avoided by "turning away" (Alfred 2005; Coulthard 2014). A continuous, active engagement with the collage elements happens at both conscious and unconscious levels. From a theoretical standpoint, then, as described by Davis (2008, 247), "The artistic creation of collage may thus furnish a means to take back a measure of power over spectacular representations and renegotiate them versus everyday experience."

Beyond the physical form that collage can take, it can also represent an important theoretical and methodological practice. In theory, Indigenous collage can help us think

Lianne Marie Leda Charlie

in ways that circumvent and collapse the dichotomies listed at the outset of this chapter; it reveals new access points into seemingly incommensurable political divides. Outside of collage, there might be disorder, confusion, disempowerment, and exclusion as a result of continued colonialism. Within collage, however, there is room for purposeful engagement and empowered, creative productivity as these incommensurable pieces have a place to come into contact with one another. Just as collage as an art form requires a collagist, Indigenous collage theory requires an active and creative agent to engage in the process of identifying the pieces and their placement within the larger, theoretical collage. Indigenous collage as theory allows for an Indigenous individual, family, community, or nation to be the collagist, and not only invites but requires their creative and subjective input. Therein lies collage's potential to disrupt incommensurability and create a space for alternative realities to come into existence.

Indigenous collage, as theory, invites us to manoeuvre with(in) a political context that has, in some cases, been cast as fixed, rigid, and too massive to unsettle. In Indigenous collage theory, the "collage-makers" are outfitted with tools and optics that enable them to dismantle and reconfigure the pieces in ways that reflect their needs, desires, and responsibilities as Indigenous peoples. At the same time, collage acts as a metaphor for the emergence of alternative governance forms and a means to creatively extend our understanding of Indigenous contemporary politics and Indigenous research methodologies.

Continuance. There is little light coming in the window. It is too early. The smooth, cool logs of the cabin wall are pressed hard to my back. I'm facing the middle of the bed, where my cousin's seven-month-old baby is—or, rather, was—sleeping. He's awake now and wiggling around. His little hand touches my face. His tiny fingers go in my mouth. At home, in his crib, he'd have toys to occupy him, so his parents could get a few more minutes of sleep. Here at the cabin, the two people trying to sleep either side of him have become his toys. I try to sleep more, but it's impossible. His cooing sounds are too cute to ignore. I have to open my eyes and watch him. His mom is awake, too. The two of us lie there, smiling. His wide eyes stare back at us. In this moment, he is the centre of our world. Just outside the cabin door, Tagé Cho | Big River flows by, just as it did when our ancestors lay with their families in the early mornings, staring lovingly at their future.

Discussion Questions

1. How do metaphors and arts-based methodologies help you understand complex issues differently? Can you think of another metaphor that could help capture and explain some of the complexities in Indigenous politics?

2. Collage is used here to help illustrate some of the complexities in modern treaty politics in the Yukon, and it is offered as a tool for helping us create and imagine ways of navigating these complexities. Try making your own collage. How can the practice of making a collage and collage as theory help us think differently about Indigeneity or Indigenous identity, citizenship and belonging, cultural revitalization, trauma and healing, and decolonization?

3. The government of Canada is committed to using "comprehensive claims" (e.g., land claims and/or modern treaties) as the negotiating framework to "deal with the unfinished businessoftreaty-makinginCanada"(https://www.aadnc-aandc.gc.ca/eng/1100100030577/1100100030578). What cautions need to be taken when considering this route?

Recommended Reading

Coulthard, Glen Sean. 2014. *Red Skin, White Masks: Rejecting the Colonial Politics of Recognition*. Minneapolis: University of Minnesota Press.

Council for Yukon Indians. 1973. *Together Today for Our Children Tomorrow: A Statement of Grievances and an Approach to Settlement*. Whitehorse, YT: Council for Yukon Indians.

Nadasdy, Paul. 2005. *Hunters and Bureaucrats: Power, Knowledge, and Aboriginal–State Relations in the Southwest Yukon*, revised edn. Vancouver: University of British Columbia Press.

Simpson, Leanne. 2017. *As We Have Always Done: Indigenous Freedom through Radical Resistance*. Minneapolis: University of Minnesota Press.

Additional Resources

Yukon First Nation self-government agreements and implementation plans. https://cyfn.ca/agreements/

Indigenous collage artists.

   Lexx Valdez: https://lexxdigs.wordpress.com/

   Henry Payer: https://www.instagram.com/hochunkhenry/

   Lianne Marie Leda Charlie: https://www.instagram.com/littlesalmonwoman/

6 "The Place Where the Hearts Gather"

Against Damage-Centred Narratives of Urban Indigeneity

Dallas Hunt

> *To his right, a table away, sat a family of ruined Indians. They had all let themselves go.*
>
> —Richard Van Camp, "Sky Burial"

> *Nearly everyone had left that bar / in the middle of winter / except the hardcore. / It was the coldest night of the year, / every place shut down, but not us / . . . We were Indian ruins.*
>
> —Joy Harjo, "Deer Dancer"

Introduction

This chapter[1] begins with failure. I started conceptualizing the project that informs this chapter as one focused on urban Indigeneity in general, and I had intended to address this topic through the notion of "ruins" in particular. However, from my reading and the research process, I decided that a deficit-oriented/damage-centred reading of Indigenous communities and ruination was not how I wanted to proceed. Rather, I wanted to focus on something much more generative. The strongest impetus for change came from attending two Canadian literature conferences in Toronto in the summer of 2017—in a city that is arguably the pinnacle of what people think of as Canada, and during the year of Canada's 150th birthday. After presenting on a panel at a conference that overwhelmingly presented Indigenous people in city spaces as mired in damage or ruin, I did not want the research I was currently conducting to reproduce the same tropes or conceptions of urban Indigeneity. Ultimately, what I originally wanted to highlight, and caution against, is the tendency for damage-centred and depoliticized narratives about urban Indigenous people to predominate in these academic contexts, largely for the consumption of well-meaning white settlers (Tuck 2009). When I refer to well-meaning white settlers, I mean the so-called progressive white liberals who may have some basic critique of colonialism, yet seek to transcend their complicity in it without actually giving anything up (Jefferess 2012) or engaging with the challenges to their moral authority that are issued by Indigenous-led decolonization efforts. When such people consume and (re)produce damage-centred narratives, these narratives are read as the horizon of what urban Indigeneity can look like, which is precisely why these representations are so dangerous: they foreclose on more radical forms of Indigenous existence and modes of Indigenous political and social life.

While it is certainly the case that at times Indigenous people ourselves may produce these "damage-centred" or trauma-focused narratives, we also produce generative representations of Indigenous experience such as the ones offered by Leanne Simpson described later in this chapter. Furthermore, it is important to note that the limited set of imaginaries of Indigeneity that are palatable for settler consumption (such as "the tragic Indian") and supported by mainstream literary studies in Canada privilege particular kinds of Indigenous cultural production over others. Specifically, in their engagements with urban Indigeneity, predominantly non-Indigenous literary studies scholars receive and read Indigenous texts in narrow and damage-centred ways that foreclose on the texts' rich complexity and generative political potential. This is something I explore further in other work, but my primary concerns in this chapter are to problematize the engagement of Indigenous texts by non-Indigenous literary scholars, to broadly sketch how diverse and layered narratives and other forms of cultural production by Indigenous artists depict, respond to, or engage with the intimate, everyday acts of violence inflicted by settler colonialism in urban environments, and to highlight the number of profound effects that Indigenous cultural productions are having (or, more tentatively, "can have") on land-based practices, spatial relations, and kinship obligations.

I begin by briefly outlining the histories of urban Indigenous representation in literary texts, as well as these texts' reception, and then proceed to articulate Unangax scholar Eve Tuck's contrasting notions of "damage-centred" and "desire-based" research. I then gesture to alternative approaches to reading urban Indigenous texts, or Indigenous texts set in urban environments, by engaging in an analysis of Anishinaabe writer (and *Visions of the Heart* contributor) Leanne Simpson's short story, "Plight," from her book, *This Accident of Being Lost*.

Historical and Literary Contexts

This chapter addresses urban Indigeneity within Indigenous literary studies in a way that expands beyond common readings centred on questions of authenticity or identity.[2] In no way do I disparage those readings, but I find that "the urban" as a concept and as "a geography" is a generative site, a lens through which to look at everything from Indigenous community formations, land-based practices, and governance to gender issues and kinship, among many other things beyond notions of cultural alienation or individual belonging. Such a perspective speaks to the history of Indian policy in Canada and associated practices of colonial cultural production and analysis, both of which I review briefly in this section. Throughout Canada's history, colonial ideas, practices, and policies have perpetuated the idea that Indigenous peoples are incongruent with the city, even as they contribute to their migration to urban centres.

Although reserves were purportedly established as spaces in which Indigenous communities could prepare (and be prepared) to join Euro-Canadian society (regardless of whether or not this was what they desired), they effectively "reinforced First Nation people's economic and geographic marginalization" (Peters 1998, 670). As Evelyn Peters and Chris Andersen (2013, 22) note, "Most reserves were intentionally established away from urban areas, ostensibly to reduce contact between settlers and First Nations peoples but also to ensure that prime land was not under control of First Nations governments." However, the reduction of "reserve lands [over time] and the systematic underdevelopment of reserve economies" (Peters and Andersen 2013, 22), as well as the ongoing destruction of traditional Indigenous economies, have resulted in massive migrations to urban centres. Also contributing to Indigenous migration were the gendered effects of Indian Act policies. As a result, Indigenous women "have been overrepresented in urban areas since at least the 1960s" (Peters 1998, 674).[3] These gendered policies included provisions that stripped Indigenous women of their status if they married non-Indigenous or non-status Indigenous men, effectively barring them from treaty rights and the right to live on reserve, vote in band elections, and lay claim to inheritances (both monetary and land-based) (Lawrence 2004, 53).

These historical and political circumstances have led to the creation of a colonial imaginary that separates Indigenous peoples from city spaces—that is, circumstances and the settler state have cultivated the culturally accepted colonial myth that Indigenous peoples do and should only inhabit reserve or rural areas (with little regard to the possibility that reserves can exist in urban environments). Indeed, the dominant colonial view is that Indigenous communities are only compatible with "the savage space" of the wild, whereas urbanity remains a strictly European construct, a demarcated zone of white civility, despite the fact that, prior to European "discovery," thriving urban centres were not uncommon in agricultural and coastal areas of the Americas, including in what is currently called Canada. As Mandee McDonald explains in Chapter 13 of this volume, the exclusion of Indigenous peoples from urban spaces can also be perpetuated by Indigenous people through contemporary discourses that situate Indigenous belonging and futures in strictly land-based (rural/bush) contexts.

These portrayals work on a broader societal and cultural level to alienate Indigenous populations in urban settings and to naturalize a (white) Western view of urban Indigenous individuals as "inferiors" who engage solely in acts of "depravity" in urban settings. While there are rich, complex, and entangled histories of urban Indigeneity to unpack, what I am interested in is how the field of literary studies (specifically in relation to Canadian literature and American literature), which has undoubtedly been influenced by these historical and political processes, almost always approaches urban Indigeneity from the starting point of shortcoming or lack, with protagonists or speakers who are constantly obsessed with questions of individual identity or authenticity (even if it is only to invite/challenge readers to question these parameters of identity).

Craig Womack, in *Reasoning Together*, narrows concerns with authenticity down to the proliferation of "narratives of return," or the "'homecoming' impulse" (Womack, Justice, and Teuton 2008, 16), present in a multitude of influential Indigenous texts and examined in the field of literary criticism on Indigenous peoples, often at the expense of more complex historicized and political analyses. For Womack, the texts of the "Native American Literary Renaissance" can be read as homecoming impulse narratives, though he asserts that is not *all* that they are, even though they generally prompted criticism that engaged them in this way, specifically through the narrow lens of authenticity or identity.[4] A few examples of these influential texts include Leslie Silko's *Ceremony* (1977), M. Scott Momaday's *House Made of Dawn* (1968), and in the Canadian context, Richard Wagamese's *Keeper'n Me* (1994). Womack suggests that interpreting these novels primarily through this homecoming impulse results in readings that view them as stories of Indigenous people being "stuck between two worlds" (Womack 1999, 139), as they depict characters struggling to rectify living in "the Western world" and in "an Indigenous world." The readings of these texts within mainstream literary criticism (Kenneth Lincoln's *Native American Renaissance* [1985] and Andrew Wiget's *Native American Literature* [1985] being two salient and pervasive examples) are almost always preoccupied with notions of authenticity (among other issues), and usually cast the urban setting as a site or locus of disruption/incoherence in relation to "authentic Indigenous identity" in rural/reserve spaces. In commenting about the "stuck between two worlds" motif, Womack (1999, 140) notes that this type of thinking is "root[ed] in the tragic Indian notions of the early part of the [twentieth] century, the half-breed torn between cultures, and all of the either/or assumptions that go along with this type of thinking." Womack continues: "Someone even more cynical might try to point out that the bicultural arguments work out nicely for white critics who, by deconstructing insider/outsider status, can carve out a huge place for themselves in Native literary studies" (Womack 1999, 141). This problematizing of Indigenous people in urban contexts by white critics, I think, is a primary problem with literary studies' engagements with urban Indigeneity, since it recasts issues of authenticity as *the* issues within Indigenous literary studies, instead of reading an urban Indigenous community/nation/geography as "a real, viable, ongoing political entity," an entity that still participates in Indigenous ways of being in the world in urban environments (with land-based practices being just one example) (Womack 1999, 141).

The problem with whitestream literary studies' engagement with Indigenous studies is that many literary scholars appear not to read Indigenous critics or theorists in a substantive, contextualized way—which is to say, they do not engage with Indigenous thought(s), practices, and world views, including but not limited to the academic field of Indigenous studies.[5] Put simply, I am less interested in whether one *is* Indigenous or what it *means to be* Indigenous than I am in what one *does* as an Indigenous person who has obligations to communities in urban environments and beyond. While I know that literary and other scholars do read Indigenous texts, and increasingly so in the present era of reconciliation and in a moment during which the Canadian literature establishment has been very publicly called to account for its enduring whiteness, the questions they choose to engage in their reading of these texts in relation to urban Indigeneity almost always orbit around notions of authenticity or cultural authority, instead of engaging with the breadth and depth that these texts (may) have to offer.

Indigenous (Re)Framings of Urban Indigeneity

In this section, I reframe urban Indigeneity away from deficit-based or individual identity-focused engagements that dominate the Canadian literary studies landscape in order to emphasize the generative, resurgent practices and forms of Indigenous cultural production that occur in cities. Renya Ramirez refers to the diversity and complexity of urban Indigenous experience(s) as the manifestation of urban "native hubs." An urban native hub, to Ramirez (2007, 2), is a "a collecting center, a hub of Indian peoples' new ideas, information, culture, community, and imagination that when shared back 'home' on the reservation can impact thousands of Native Americans." Providing a description that has several resonances with "native hubs," Leanne Simpson explains that in

Anishinaabemowin, the word for "city" translates to "the place where the hearts gather." Elaborating further and supplying a Nishnaabeg-specific reading of the urban, Simpson writes: "I thought about how Odemin Giizis is June, or the moon when the heart berries (strawberries) are ready. I pictured those odeminanm, or heart berries, and their runners connecting the plants in a web of inter-relationships, much like cities" (Simpson 2011, 94). Urban native hubs, then, are acts of resurgence; they are tactics by Indigenous people in urban contexts that disrupt the colonial ordering and confinement of Indigenous bodies to particular spaces and challenge the predominant representations of where and how Indigenous peoples can live and thrive. Therefore, "[t]he beauty of culturally inherent resurgence," Simpson writes, "is that it challenges settler colonial dissections of our territories and our bodies into reserve/city or rural/urban dichotomies" (Simpson 2014, 23).

Indeed, the demarcation of different geographical areas as hospitable to Indigenous presence and habituation (or not) elides the fact that "[a]ll Canadian cities are on Indigenous lands," and, as such, are subject to the various ways in which Indigenous peoples decide to re-inscribe their active presence in these spaces (Simpson 2014, 23). As Matthew Snipp (2013, 174) notes, when "taking a long view of history, American Indians . . . have lived in urban areas since before the time of Columbus." What would it mean if the "return narratives" so prevalent in Indigenous texts were reversed? What if, contrary to the massive amounts of literature proclaiming them to be strangers, Indigenous people were exactly the opposite in urban spaces (Woodsworth 1909; Krotz 1980; Newhouse and Peters 2003)? As Jay T. Johnson (2013, 219) suggests, the "urbanization of First Nations people over the last several decades is, in some ways, merely a reclaiming of our rightful place within urban centres."

This reclaiming of our space within city environments, however, has been difficult, as centuries of colonial policy have regulated the movement and place-making of Indigenous communities. While Indigenous peoples have been relegated to reserve spaces and remote settlements (both in legislation and in the popular imaginary), they have simultaneously been removed from urban areas. As Jean Barman (2007, 5) has articulated, early Canadian settler urbanization "caused reserves in or near cities to be especially coveted." This resulted in Prime Minister Wilfrid Laurier dictating in a parliamentary session that "where a reserve is in the vicinity of a growing town, as is the case in several places, it becomes a source of nuisance and an impediment to progress" (quoted in Barman 2007, 5). Shortly thereafter, an amendment was made to the Indian Act whereby any Indigenous communities in close proximity to an urban (or urbanizing) environment could and would be relocated. Quoting from the Indian Act, Barman (2007, 5–6) explains, "the Indian Act was amended so that the residents of any 'Indian reserve which adjoins or is situated wholly or partly within an incorporated town or city having a population of not less than eight thousand' could be legally removed without their consent if it was in 'the interest of the public and of the Indians of the band for whose use the reserve is held.'"[6] Unsurprisingly, the interests of the Canadian public and "Indians" were regularly at odds, and ultimately this resulted in the removal of Indigenous people from urban environments in the interest of the Canadian "public good." These removals have bolstered the colonial myth that Indigenous peoples "naturally" belong solely to rural or reserve environments and that Indigenous people in urban settings are just as naturally "out of place" in the city. The removal of Indigenous people from city settings has therefore sedimented the notion that our ability to exist as political entities (albeit at times circumscribed) is only recognized in reserve geographies, that we can only govern on reserve, and that our laws and political orders cannot and must not exist outside of these bounds.

In part because of these complicated histories, my intervention, then, is to move beyond facile images of urban Indigenous people that are predominantly preoccupied with ideas of authenticity or cultural degradation or deficiency, and to provide a more nuanced view of Indigenous political and social life in urban environments. These more nuanced views not only exist in capital "L" Indigenous Literature, but they are also available in a variety of other forms of cultural expression that literary studies purportedly engages with (such as film, visual art, and other genres of Indigenous print culture), though it is my contention that it does not seem to read them in any critical or retentive way.

Ultimately, this chapter raises the following questions for further consideration and conversation rather than attempting to answer them all in any kind of satisfactory way: Why do literary engagements with Indigenous studies and Indigenous peoples continue to perpetuate the same tired tropes and questions about urban Indigenous people, primarily that the issues affecting Indigenous people are ones of cultural alienation or issues of authenticity? What other issues are elided or neglected when cultural alienation becomes a focal point or the point of emphasis? How can literary engagements with Indigenous studies and Indigenous peoples simultaneously attend to issues of cultural alienation and material issues facing Indigenous communities, such as land disputes and jurisdictional issues? Can settler scholars only conceive of Indigenous peoples within these very limited frames and only when they adhere to narrow scripts that allow for limited representations? Does the preoccupation with damage-centred research foreclose on the ability for literary scholars to read texts on urban Indigeneity in other, more generative ways? What might these more expansive readings of Indigenous literature offer to Indigenous communities? How can we support the production and circulation of diverse narratives and literary forms within Indigenous literatures, especially given the colonial political economy of literary production? How might it be possible to interrupt the settler desire for damage-centred literary narratives, and how can the labour of this interruption be distributed in a way that does not simply reproduce colonial relations?

Methodology

Eve Tuck, in her letter to communities entitled "Suspending Damage," cautions against "reinforc[ing] and reinscrib[ing] a one-dimensional notion of . . . [Indigenous] people as depleted, ruined, and hopeless" (Tuck 2009, 409). In a similar vein, queer Creek-Cherokee scholar Craig Womack warns against readings and critical responses that are "deficit-oriented," ones that foreground "some problem with [an Indigenous] nation's coherence" above all else. Indeed, Womack outlines how "deficit-oriented" engagements with Indigenous texts, especially literary engagements with these texts, prioritize and are mainly interested in "relatively conservative fiction that prioritizes issues of personal . . . recovery over political analysis" (Womack, Justice, and Teuton 2008, 80). Dian Million has outlined how readings of Indigenous peoples, in a Canadian context, are now overdetermined by trauma since the formation of the Truth and Reconciliation Commission; that is, Indigenous peoples are only legible through their private, personal, and individual traumatic experiences, and not through their "substantive Indigenous political empowerment" as political entities (Million 2013, 6). These predetermined narratives fail to account for what Tuck, following Avery Gordon, refers to as the "complex personhood" of Indigenous people and, indeed, the complexity of our communities. "Complex personhood," Tuck writes, "draws on Indigenous understandings of collectivity and the interdependence of the collective *and* the person rather than on the Western focus on the individual" (Tuck 2009, 420; emphasis mine). While I'm not interested in dismissing anyone's truth or personal history, I am curious about the way Indigenous narratives are received by the largely white audiences that attend the academic talks like the ones I mentioned in the introduction to this chapter. Rather than rehearse a litany of examples in which white literary critics receive/read Indigenous narratives in ways that pathologize them and in an effort to refuse what these damage-centred or deficit-oriented readings of Indigenous narratives reproduce, I prefer to focus on an alternative approach to reading urban Indigenous experiences. I hope to illustrate all that is lost in damage-centred readings by showing what other kinds of readings are possible and what they create. In doing so, I enact what Tuck describes as a "desire-based" reading of Indigenous literature.[7]

Although damage-centred research tends to index problems faced by Indigenous communities that are in fact the product of historical and ongoing contexts of colonization, "the significance of these contexts," to quote Tuck (2009, 414), "is regularly submerged." In other words, "[w]ithout [attending to] the context of racism and colonization, all we're left with is the damage, and this makes our stories vulnerable to pathologizing analyses" (Tuck 2009, 415). In response and counter to these modes of analysis, Tuck suggests a framework of desire-based research, one "concerned with understanding complexity, contradiction, and self-determination of lived lives." These alternative modes of analyzing are "intent on depathologizing the experiences of dispossessed and disenfranchised communities so that people are seen as more than broken and conquered," and even if "communities are broken and conquered, they are so much more than that—so much more that this incomplete story is an act of aggression." For Tuck, desire-based frameworks are "an antidote to damage-centered research," in that "[a]n antidote stops and counteracts the effects of a poison, and the poison [she is] referring to here is not the supposed damage of Native communities, . . . but the frameworks that position these communities as damaged" (Tuck 2009, 416). Desire-based reading practices, it should be noted, are not intended to be the mirror opposite of damage-centred frameworks—they do not uncritically celebrate our Indigenous communities. Neither do they suggest that there is harmony where there is conflict, that Indigenous people do not have contradictory desires, or that we do not in fact feel our wounds deeply. Rather, they account for all of these things, *and more*, in ways that generally cannot be accounted for within the narrow genres that Canadian literature reserves for us—that is, within the limited and conditional spaces we are granted and for which we are nonetheless expected to be grateful. Ultimately, desire-based frameworks "docu[ment] not only the painful elements of social realities but also the wisdom and hope" (Tuck 2009, 416).

Since Canadian literary scholars by and large have no problem envisioning Indigenous peoples as solely ruined, as culturally "broken," as permanently and terminably traumatized, as too angry to function in polite, political discourse, as well as a range of other positionalities framed by "deficiency," I look to narratives of urban Indigeneity that do not foreclose on active and vivacious Indigenous political and social lives. In particular, I look to resurgent, urban land-based practices as one means of countering damage-centred narratives. And while I also do not intend to reify or re-inscribe borders or distinctions between the urban and the rural, I am also not trying to easily cast aside these conceptual categories as though they do not exist and are not meaningful, something that happens just as frequently in Canadian literary preoccupations with troubling or deconstructing binaries. Rather, what I am interested in is how land-based practices, commonly thought of as happening *solely* in rural, reserve, or bush spaces, are conceived of in urban environments, and how might this reconfigure "conventional" notions of Indigenous engagements with the land more broadly. Now, I turn to one of these urban land-based texts to show not only how an urban Indigenous community navigates complicated and often difficult city environments, but also how such a community can demonstrate the hope, love, and *survivance* of collective urban Indigenous political and social life.

Resurgent Indians

For the remainder of this chapter, I provide a desire-based reading of Leanne Simpson's short story "Plight," and the resurgent potentials it offers. In "Plight," the speaker, along with other Anishnaabe women, form The Fourth World Problems Collective, a politically oriented group of women and two-spirit people engaged in land-based practices in an "urban" environment. Worth noting from the outset, however, is that although the territory in which they are enacting these practices may be considered an urban space— to be specific, the city of Mississauga, Ontario—this territory is actually the land of the Mississauga Nishnaabeg. As Simpson's speaker states plainly: "we are Mississaugas and . . . this is us acting on our land" (2017, 7). And yet, Simpson still refers to this land-based practice as the Collective's "urban sugar-making adventure," one that allows her speaker, Lucy, Kwe, and other characters from Nishnaabeg cosmologies to participate in resurgent processes (2017, 6).

Also worth emphasizing here is not only the collective nature of this urban Indigenous narrative, that is, it is neither depoliticized nor individualized, but also the way in which it resists being read as damage-centred. Indeed, Simpson is keenly aware of the predominant imaginaries that the white settlers of the neighbourhood hold of her and her compatriots. She flags this immediately in naming the short story "Plight," referencing the seemingly endless "plight" that Indigenous people presumably experience and that settler Canadians both bear witness to and for which they pity Indigenous communities. For Simpson, this group that pities Indigenous people consists predominantly of well-meaning white liberals who feel relief when they vote for progressive political parties, since this small act gestures to their innate "goodness" and simultaneously absolves them of having to engage in any wider political acts of restitution for Indigenous peoples, such as changing the structural arrangements that perpetuate the material conditions they face. Describing the members of this Mississauga neighbourhood, Simpson states they are people who "mostly vot[e] NDP or liberal in provincial and federal elections, and feel relief when they do," while simultaneously not "rent[ing] their extra floors to the lower class" (Simpson 2017, 5). Wryly recognizing the deficit-oriented imaginaries white settler communities have of her and other Indigenous people, urban or not, Simpson explains that the women "know how to do" these land-based practices "so [the white settlers] will be into it." She elaborates on this by outlining how they "Hand out the flyers first. Have a community meeting. Ask permission. Listen to their paternalistic bullshit and feedback. Let them have influence. Let them bask in the plight of Native people so they can feel self

Michael Thessel

A street art performance in Kahnawake.

righteous" (Simpson 2017, 5). Simpson is clearly aware of how frameworks of damage cast urban Indigenous people as historically and currently depleted/ruined, and how urban Indigenous lands "become spaces saturated in the fantasies of outsiders" (Tuck 2009, 412). She continues: "Make them [i.e., white liberals] feel better, and when reconciliation comes up at the next dinner party, they can hold us up as the solution and brag to their friends about our plight." Simpson (2017, 5) ends this passage with the sardonic line: "I proofread the flyers one more time because everyone knows white people hate typos." At work in Simpson's text is not only the recognition of the colonial conditions at play, and the way in which this collective of Indigenous people have to navigate the craving that this predominantly white neighbourhood has for damage-centred portrayals of Indigeneity, but also how the collective's shrewd and strategic deployment of these narratives allows them to create space for their earnest desires for resurgent practices, ones that occur on the land, in their home territory.

Beyond the recognition and refusal of the ways in which she and her kin are framed as depleted, Simpson provides a very practical guide to making syrup in a city space. Simpson's text is full of details on how to make sugar and engage in land-based practices in Mississauga. Their "urban sugar-making adventure" involves "mar[king] each [tree] with a spray-painted purple thunderbird so that when [the tree's] leaves [are] gone [they] would know which ones were the sugar maples the following spring." One character, Lucy, makes "a stencil so the thunderbird would look like a thunderbird and not the death mark the city puts on the trees when they are about to cut them down for safety reasons." Further, Simpson not only identifies the season in which the maple sugar-making should take place, but she also provides a list of equipment needed to engage in this activity: "Now it's March, and we have thirty tin buckets, thirty new spigots, tobacco, a drill with two charged batteries, a three-eighths-of-an-inch drill bit, and thirty flyers" (Simpson 2017, 5). In this single crucial sentence, Simpson outlines not only the season best-suited for maple syrup production, but also lists the equipment needed to engage in these resurgent practices. Once the equipment is secured and the timing is right, Simpson needs "[h]elp collecting the sap . . . and boiling it down for twelve hours in [her] backyard" (Simpson 2017, 7). This description takes place in the span of three pages, and when paired with her recreation of a sugar bush story in a chapter of *Dancing on Our Turtle's Back*, Simpson ultimately has provided a practical guide for Nishinaabeg and, by extension, other Indigenous communities for how to engage in land-based practices (specifically maple syrup-making) in urban spaces. This act is a resurgent one, one that escapes facile engagements that focus solely on identity and/or authenticity and details notions of protocol, land use, governance, and political orientations. These notions, combined with Simpson's descriptions in *This Accident of Being Lost* of Indigenous law, health, treaty, and various other facets of Indigenous life, counter the all-too-easy narratives of Indigenous ruin in city spaces, and potentially provide a path forward and beyond damage-centred readings.

Conclusion

While narratives of personal recovery and painful, individual, experiential knowledge of city spaces are important, it is equally if not more important to foreground how other readings of Indigenous engagements with urban environments are possible, because these engagements are occurring every day. What I have highlighted in this chapter is that it is not only possible, but it is also necessary to bypass the damage-centred, depoliticized, and at times highly individualistic narratives of urban Indigeneity that predominate in literary studies. This need also exists in Indigenous studies scholarship and in engagements with urban Indigeneity across disciplines, which often reproduce the same deficit-centred representations of "the urban Indigenous experience." Yet I also want to encourage people to engage in the necessary reflexive work of asking what exactly damage-centred approaches do for those who continue to (re)produce them—that is, what is it that leads so many people to read, write about, and generally conceptualize Indigenous peoples in this way? Though I have intentionally offered a reading that centres *Indigenous* desire, literary scholars must ask themselves: what are the settler desires that drive the reproduction of damage-centred interpretations of the lives of Indigenous people? Without isolating and interrupting these desires, the narratives might never cease. In the meantime, Indigenous authors like Simpson will continue to create works about urban Indigenous life that refuse to be contained by the narrative tropes that so many settlers desire.

These forms of refusal, present in Leanne Simpson's short story, carry great political significance. Indeed, writers like Simpson show the existence of vibrant and dynamic political formations that Indigenous peoples inhabit in a variety of geographies; that we are not exclusively focused on the losses of the past, but theorizing deeply about how we want to live our lives and what types of futures we want to create. While Indigenous people certainly experience violence, racism, and crises in urban and other contexts, stories about our experiences are largely read by whitestream literary critics in totalizing ways that diminish our experiences and dehumanize our lives. In contrast, Indigenous scholars, creative writers, and other artists engaged in creative expression are seeing and telling our stories in humanizing, vibrant, and hopeful ways. And importantly, we are generating new and healthy relations in many different spaces, including urban ones—Indigenous people are here, many of us are thriving, we are engaging in land-based practices in a range of contexts, adapting traditions, and creating them anew.

Discussion Questions

1. Why do literary (and other disciplinary) engagements with Indigenous studies and Indigenous peoples continue to perpetuate the same tired tropes and questions about urban Indigenous people, primarily that the issues affecting Indigenous people are almost solely ones of cultural alienation or issues of authenticity?

2. What other issues are elided or neglected when cultural alienation becomes a focal point or the point of emphasis?

3. Does the preoccupation with damage-centred research foreclose on the ability for literary and other scholars to read texts on urban Indigeneity in other, more generative ways?

4. What are some examples you can think of that depict urban Indigeneity in complex and nuanced ways?

Recommended Reading

Goeman, Mishuana. 2013. *Mark My Words: Native Women Mapping Our Nations*. Minneapolis: University of Minnesota Press.

Kino-nda-niimi Collective. 2014. *The Winter We Danced*. Winnipeg: ARP Books.

Peters, Evelyn, and Chris Andersen. 2013. *Indigenous in the City: Contemporary Identities and Cultural Innovation*. Vancouver: University of British Columbia Press.

Ramirez, Renya K. 2007. *Native Hubs: Culture, Community, and Belonging in Silicon Valley and Beyond*. Durham, NC: Duke University Press.

Simpson, Leanne Betasamosake. 2017. *As We Have Always Done: Indigenous Freedom through Radical Resistance. Minneapolis*: University of Minnesota Press.

Notes

1. The title for this chapter is drawn from Leanne Simpson (2011, 94), who explains that, in Anishinaabemowin, the word for "city" translates to "the place where the hearts gather."

2. "Authenticity" here refers to preoccupations over what being an Indigenous person means or entails. While I think these are potentially important questions (depending on who is asking them), the field of Canadian literary studies has been preoccupied with them for several decades, in a way that detracts or potentially distracts from questions of governance, land, jurisdiction, kinship relations, and the like that are just as important. Thomas King, addressing and participating in these same conversations, coined a well-worn phrase ("I'm not the Indian you had

in mind") in his 2003 Massey Lecture collection entitled *The Truth about Stories*. Much of settler Canadian literary engagements with Indigenous texts has not moved beyond this phrase or the debates and discursive terrains it is embedded and circulates within. In many cases, white settler literary preoccupations with Indigenous identity can appear to be a strategic way of "engaging" with Indigenous issues, without having to address the more complex and difficult topics of land, colonial violence, and everyday settler colonialism.

3.   Although Indigenous women's positions in their community differed from community to community, Bonita Lawrence (2004, 33) outlines how colonial interaction with women of eastern Indigenous nations (such as the Haudenosaunee), in which women had a direct role in land management, would later go on to influence the Canadian government's interactions with all nations and provide much of the reason for targeting women in particular in Indian Act policies.

4.   The Native American Renaissance refers to Indigenous literary texts from the late 1960s through 1980s, usually beginning with the publication of M. Scott Momaday's *House Made of Dawn* (1968). These publications coincide with the beginnings of the Red Power movement as well as the establishment of Native American or American Indian departments in the US universities (Womack, Justice, and Teuton 2008). What looked to be an explosion of Indigenous cultural production to outside observers (predominantly American studies and American literary studies scholars) was actually just the continuation of a rich history and long legacy of Indigenous cultural production, dating back to D'Arcy McNickle's *The Surrounded* (1936) and earlier texts. However, the supposedly "explosive" arrival of these texts was deemed as a "Renaissance," a term many Indigenous scholars repudiate and/or critique since it erases the centuries of literary and textual cultural production that was and has always been occurring in Indian Country, but has not yet received as much critical and mainstream attention (Brooks 2008; Warrior 1994; Womack 1999).

5.   According to Sandy Grande (2003, 330), "whitestream" refers to a discourse "principally structured on the basis of white middle-class experience; a discourse that serves [white people's] ethno-political interests and capital investments."

6.   Of course, these were not the only restrictions placed on Indigenous people and their mobility by the Canadian state. In 1885, in the immediate wake of the Northwest Rebellion, the Canadian government introduced the pass system, a policy limiting whether individuals were "allowed" to leave their home reserve, a decision usually at the discretion of the local Indian agent (and these agents were government bureaucrats who often harboured racist ideas of what spaces Indigenous people belonged to or were allowed to exist in). According to James Daschuk, the pass system "was implemented to limit the mobility of treaty Indians, keeping them on their reserves and away from European communities." Further, the imposition of the pass system "undermined access to game and crippled the economic prospects of reserve communities" (Daschuk 2013, 161), as well as "curtail[ed] broad participation in Indigenous religious ceremonies" (171). In addition, the policy effectively made any pan-Indigenous political or military organizing impossible.

7.   Tuck (2009, 420) uses the term "desire-based" "because it is an assemblage of experiences, ideas, and ideologies, both subversive and dominant, [and] necessarily complicates our understanding of human agency, complicity, and resistance." However, a desire-based framework, Tuck clarifies, is not intended to be the complete opposite of a damage-centred focus; in other words, it is not a kind of rose-coloured analysis that ignores or elides complicated issues or negative affects and makes little room for disagreement or strife. Rather, a desire-based research orientation is "an argument for desire as an epistemological shift" (Tuck 2009, 419), as a mode of engagement that accounts for the complexities and nuances flattened out by simple binaries, such as between repression and resistance.

7 Why Calgary Isn't Métis Territory

Jigging towards an Ethic of Reciprocal Visiting

Daniel Voth and Jessie Loyer

On old-time jigging: You gotta know your fiddlers and you really have to listen. Listening is your key to dancing. You really have to listen, as soon as there is a change, you got to change and if he's playing fast, you got to give 'er, you know? If he's playing slow, you can take it easy. But there's always that little rivalry between fiddlers and jiggers, because with dancers they like to tease some fiddlers and say, "you know, I'll keep going man, I am going to play you out" and they are always challenging each other and that's the way it used to be.

—Brent Potskin, Batoche

Introduction

Territorial acknowledgements have steadily grown in popularity and frequency over the last 10 years. Before the era of widespread acknowledgements, they were done by Indigenous academics, activists, and their allies to unsettle preconceived notions of what a settler relationship to land means, and to point out what most people give no thought to: the land under their feet is the territory of Indigenous people. The power of the statements emanated from their rarity (see Vowel 2016); these acknowledgements use words to give thought and form to Indigenous territoriality, something settler-colonial states like Canada have been trying to erase for centuries.[1] Growing in popularity in recent years, there is now a territorial acknowledgement at the beginning of many different events, including hockey games, university and other public meetings, school days, major TV broadcasts, and concerts as well as festivals. While more research is needed on the power dynamics wrapped up in this now pervasive form of acknowledgement, this chapter explores the unsettling questions of whose territory is being acknowledged and what it means to acknowledge the wrong people. More specifically, the Métis Nation is acknowledged in Calgary, an action that seems misplaced.

Both of the authors have a very personal stake in this investigation. Jessie Loyer is Cree on her mother's side from Michel First Nation, and her father is Métis; she grew up in Calahoo, Alberta. Daniel Voth is a member of the Métis Nation and grew up in Manitoba's Interlake region as well as the inner city of Winnipeg, the heartland of the Métis people. We both work in what is now called the city of Calgary at major universities in the territory of Treaty 7 peoples. Both universities have developed land acknowledgements that appear in their respective Indigenous strategic plans. Mount Royal University (MRU), which employs Loyer, acknowledges the territory it is on in the following way:

> Mount Royal University is situated in an ancient and storied place within the hereditary lands of the Niitsitapi (Blackfoot), Iyarhe Nakoda, Tsuut'ina and Métis Nations. It is a land steeped in ceremony and history that, until recently, was used and occupied exclusively by peoples indigenous to this place. (Mount Royal University 2016)

The University of Calgary, which employs Voth, offers its formal territory acknowledgement in its "Indigenous Strategy":

> The University of Calgary, located in the heart of Southern Alberta, both acknowledges and pays tribute to the traditional territories of the peoples of Treaty 7, which include the Blackfoot Confederacy (comprised of the Siksika, the Piikani, and the Kainai First Nations) as well as the Tsuut'ina First Nation, and the Stoney Nakoda (including Chiniki, Bearspaw, and Wesley First Nations). The University of Calgary is situated on land adjacent to where the Bow River meets the Elbow River, and notes that the traditional Blackfoot name of this place is "Moh'kins'tsis", which we now call the City of Calgary. The university recognizes that the City of Calgary is also home to Region III of the Métis Nation of Alberta. By virtue of the signing of Treaty 7 in 1877, the university recognizes that we are all treaty people. . . . (University of Calgary 2017)

You'll note that both universities explicitly acknowledge the city of Calgary as part of the territory of the Métis Nation.

Both of us are from peoples who are not signatories to Treaty 7, and, as will be pointed out below, both of us are from peoples who were party to an inter-Indigenous alliance that actively and militarily challenged Blackfoot territoriality and power in the region around Calgary.[2] So should Calgary be acknowledged as Métis territory? What does it mean to be Métis in Treaty 7 territory? Our core argument is that Calgary is not Métis territory and that, therefore, Métis people need to have an ethic of reciprocal visiting in these spaces. This argument is animated by inter-Indigenous relationships rooted in tradition, respect, and openness.

This chapter begins by first defining who the Métis are within a complex, multinational Indigenous milieu. This is followed by a historical and political argument for delineating Blackfoot space from Métis space, and will include an examination of the Blackfoot and Métis perspectives on territoriality. We then present a theoretical approach rooted in Métis kinship practices that can inform what we are calling an ethic of reciprocal visiting for Métis people. By "ethic," we mean a set of culturally informed principles designed to inform how individuals move through complex worlds in a good way. In the final section of the chapter we discuss the demands of our ethic in inter-Indigenous politics and inquire into what ways this ethic can inform how we act in other Indigenous peoples' territory. The chapter concludes by asking you, the reader, how you can live well in other peoples' territory.

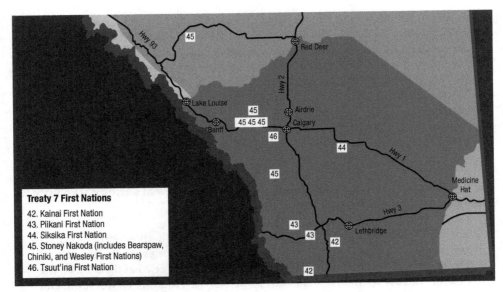

Figure 7.1 Treaty 7 Territory and First Nations
Source: Indigenous and Northern Affairs Canada.

Who Are the Métis?

Métis identity has emerged as one of the most controversial questions in Indigenous politics and Indigenous studies. Métis people, plagued by centuries of racialized impositions on our peoplehood and personal identities, have been writing back against the focus on race and racialization in recent years (Andersen 2014; Gaudry 2013; Vowel 2016). If you were to peruse most high school Canadian history textbooks or Wikipedia pages you would find that the Métis people are described as a mixed or mixed-race people that emerged from unions between European men and Indigenous women. Much of this stems from a literal translation of the French word "métis," which means "mixed" in English. But this translation has also come to mean that being mixed means something for the Métis as a people (Andersen 2010).

Yet, racial mixing alone does not create a people.[3] All peoples of the world are mixed. The notion of a racially pure people is a fallacy. As Chris Andersen (2014, 207–8) has pointed out:

> we can think about and analyze the Métis as an instance of a "post-contact" Indigenous people, one of many instances of Indigenous ethnogenesis that sprung up in the wake of global imperial intrusions into Indigenous territories. While historians and ethnohistorians have been happy—eager, even—to note the ethnogenesis of Métis self-consciousness, virtually none of this analysis has extended to a comparative discussion of other post-contact Indigenous peoples such as Comanche, Lumbee, Oji-Cree, and Seminole.

What Andersen is pointing out is that a number of Indigenous peoples emerged after fur traders and other non-Indigenous people showed up in Indigenous peoples' territories. So, this means that there are more important factors than mixed ancestry in the making of the identity of the Métis people.

The Métis people have a very particular language, history, set of economic engagements, relationships with other Indigenous peoples, culture, and most importantly, a collective sense of being politically self-aware. This has been outlined well by Adam Gaudry and Darryl Leroux (2017). These scholars point out that Métis identity has nothing to do with finding a Mi'kmaq ancestor in the 1600s, or taking a DNA test, or finding a long-dead Algonquin, Haida, or Cree woman in your ancestral tree. These things do not make a Métis person. Rather, being Métis is about belonging to a sociological, political people. From this perspective, the Métis are a people primarily from the Northwest Plains. Gaudry and Leroux (2017, 117, 127–30) point out that Indigenous–European intermarriages in Quebec and Acadia were part of a program of Indigenous assimilation, not the awakening of a post-contact Indigenous people. Further, the Indigenous history in those places does not include the rise of a politically distinct, collectively aware "Métis" people like it did on the Northwest Plains. In contrast, we Métis of the Northwest Plains are a people that waged military and political conflicts alongside and against other Indigenous peoples. We are a people that are parties to peace treaties made with our allies and adversaries. We are a people that have our own governments, run our educational institutions, disagree with each other, take part in collective and individual economic activities, speak our own language, and sing our own songs. All of this we have done, and continue to do, in our own name, not because we are mixed, but because we were, are, and will continue to be *a people*. Generally, the Métis are one of the Indigenous peoples of the Northwest Plains.

Defining Métis territory (and, subsequently, Métis territorial acknowledgements) is complicated. The tools of colonization that defined First Nations territories created visible reserve boundaries and numbered treaties that are associated with particular swaths of land. Métis are mappable in a different way. Métis lawyer Jean Teillet highlights this when she argues that: "contemporary Canadian maps do not show the outlines of the Northwest Métis territory, indicate important Métis sites, travel routes or show kinship connections. . . . On these maps the Métis simply do not exist" (Teillet 2008, 36). Instead, Métis kinship connections exist within a Métis territory that Michel Hogue (2015, 5) calls a "complex and shifting set of Indigenous homelands." These prairie homelands make up Métis territory. While Hogue is concerned with how the border between Canada and the United States affects the treatment and recognition (or lack thereof) of the Métis in the US, his assertion that Indigenous borders prior to the medicine line[4] were "shaped by local interactions—of commerce, family, and politics—within Plains borderland communities" (Hogue 2015, 8) helps us to understand that while Indigenous borders shift, they are certainly not arbitrary. Therefore, territory cannot be arbitrarily claimed: Indigenous peoples have long-standing histories of existing in relation to territories that are not their own. We now take up this question of non-arbitrary territory in understanding Blackfoot and Métis engagements with each other and with each other's homelands.

Being in a Place Does Not Make It Yours

Can just being somewhere make a territory yours? You may have heard of "squatter's rights," or of the tradition in international law that if you can't defend your territory from outsiders and incursions then you may not be able to continue to claim it as your own (see Cassese 2005, 81–4). These theories of territory tend to be incredibly self-serving since they are written by powerful people or nation-states with a vested interest in justifying their takeover of other people's territory. What if we instead focused on Indigenous peoples' understandings of their space and their own appreciations of where they are from and where they are not from? Doing so helps to weave a richly contextualized tapestry of territories and borders between Indigenous peoples. Much of this tapestry's context is informed by Indigenous orientations towards and relationships with outsiders. By understanding how Indigenous peoples view their and others' territoriality, one can better get a sense that, in the area that is now Calgary and central-southern Alberta, there seems to be a clear consensus of where Métis are from, and where they are not. Let's start with Blackfoot expressions of their territory.

The Blackfoot Confederacy includes four peoples: the Siksika, which means Blackfoot; the Kainai, or the Blood Tribe; the Piikani; and the Amskapi Piikani. This confederal political arrangement became one of the key nodes of Indigenous political, military, and economic power in what is currently western Canada and the United States. Historian Hugh Dempsey argues that prior to the formation and installation of the North West Mounted Police (NWMP) in and near Blackfoot territory, the Blackfoot were still largely able to chase out those who entered their territory to engage in unwelcome behaviour. For example, in the 1870s, during the height of the trade in alcohol and spirits in Blackfoot territory, Dempsey (1995, 100) argues that the Blackfoot were able to chase out whisky traders. Whisky traders are noted by many Elders of the Blackfoot Confederacy to have had a terrible impact on the health and well-being of the nation's people (Hildebrandt, First Rider, and Carter 1996). From an inter-Indigenous perspective, the Confederacy also did a lot of "chasing out" of members of a rival political and military alliance that was referred to as the Nehiyaw Pwat, or in English, the Iron Alliance. The Nehiyaw Pwat included Métis and Cree people along with the Assiniboine and Saulteaux. Dempsey finds that "[e]ven during the whiskey days, the Blackfoot tribes had been able to keep most of the unwelcome strangers out of their land. Cree and half-breed hunting parties [the Nehiyaw Pwat] ventured in at their own risk" (Dempsey 1995, 100).

In the fall of 1875, the encroachment on Blackfoot territory by non-Indigenous settlers as well as Cree and Métis peoples was a major concern for all nations within the Confederacy. The Métis, in particular, were reported to be a concern to the Blood Tribe since they had established permanent Métis settlements at Fort Macleod, Fort Calgary, and Fort Walsh (Dempsey 1995, 100). To confront this, "[a]s was the custom when a problem arose that needed to be considered by the three tribes, a general council was called. Held in the autumn of 1875," and attended by a large cross-section of the Confederacy's leadership, the council produced a petition stating:

> That the Half-breeds and Cree Indians in large camps are hunting buffalo, both summer and Winter, in the very centre of our lands.
> That the land is pretty well taken up by white men now and no Indian Commissioner has visited us.
> That we pray for an Indian Commissioner to visit us at the Hand Hills, Red Deer River, this year and let us know the time that he will visit us, so that we could hold a Council with him, for putting a stop to the invasion of our Country, till our Treaty be made with the Government.

That we are perfectly willing the Mounted Police and the Missionarys [*sic*] should remain in the country, for we are much indebted to them for important services. (HBC Archives, Alexander Morris Fonds, P5284.8; see also Dempsey 1995, 100–1)

Importantly, there are several drafts of this petition between the Blackfoot and the Crown, with one version noting that this poor hunting behaviour on the part of the Cree and Métis had been happening for four years.

The petition is a Blackfoot expression of their territory that emerged from a political gathering of the Confederacy and was given weight by the governing body under the authority of the people of that place. It is a statement of collective will to deal with problematic and troublesome outsiders. The petition also indicates that only some outsiders, such as the NWMP, are allowed access to the territory since they serve the Confederacy's interests. Stated differently, it is the Blackfoot's pleasure that these outsiders remain in Blackfoot territory. This helps illuminate a simple but often overlooked point in inter-Indigenous politics: one need not make generous invitations into one's territory to everyone. Some will be welcome for a period of time or for a particular purpose, while others will not be welcome at all. A permanent Métis presence in Blackfoot territory does not make a Métis claim to the territory they inhabit legitimate simply because of the permanence of their presence. The Blackfoot are asking the Métis to conform themselves to the political authority of the Blackfoot Confederacy.

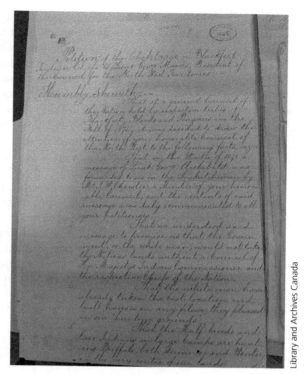

Petition from Blackfeet

Library and Archives Canada

Dempsey also records a protest among the Bloods and the other members of the Confederacy about the hunting behaviour of Métis buffalo-hunting brigades in Blackfoot territory. The Métis were accused of killing buffalo and only harvesting the hides for robes while leaving the carcasses to rot. This infuriated the Blackfoot, and Dempsey quotes a member of the Fort Macleod community to have said "[t]he Indians look with no favorable eye on these Red River half-breeds . . . . They say that their medicine is bad for the buffalo, and I think they are pretty nearly right" (Dempsey 1995, 102). In this moment, the Blackfoot resentment is not only colouring the way settlers in Fort Macleod view the Métis, but in the process, the exact part of the Métis Nation that is accused of the transgression is named. In addition, disrespecting the herds is not just an affront to the people in and near the Bloods at Fort Macleod; it is really a crime against all peoples, inside and outside the Confederacy, who rely on the herds for their livelihood. If true, this disrespectful hunting behaviour helps explain why the Métis were not welcome inside the territory of the Blackfoot Confederacy.

In addition to Blackfoot perspectives on others in their territory, the Blackfoot also negotiated the borders of their territories through diplomacy. The act of peacemaking also establishes the distinctions between where people are from and where they are not. For example, there were a series of treaties and treaty breaches between the Cree and the Blackfoot Confederacy in 1827–8. The Confederacy had made peace with the Cree, only to see it fall apart months later, which then required that a new peace be negotiated to take its place. The renegotiated peace in 1828 is reported to have lasted for five years, during which "enemy tribes deliberately [chose] not to hunt in areas occupied by their foes" (Dempsey 2015, 21–2). From an Indigenous political perspective, this peace was an agreement of respect for other Indigenous peoples' territories for the life of the treaty, meaning that the Blackfoot would not venture out to hunt in Cree territory and the Cree would not hunt in Blackfoot territory. These peace treaties therefore give us a glimpse into what was and what was not delineated as Blackfoot space. Indeed, the treaty suggests that there was a level of agreement about the boundaries of these spaces.

The expressions of tension between the Blackfoot and the Nehiyaw Pwat were part of a broader public discourse that took place before the large-scale settling of the West. During the 1885 Northwest Resistance, in which the Métis and Cree launched a military campaign against Canada, much ink was spilled over whether or not the Blackfoot would

Library and Archives Canada

Calgary from the Bow River (1880–1900). There has been a Métis presence in Calgary for many years, but Métis are guests in Blackfoot territory.

join the Métis and Cree cause.[5] The *Fort Macleod Gazette* published an opinion piece in 1885 calling for Canada to enlist the Confederacy in its fight against the Métis and Cree in the north, because "[The Blackfoot Confederacy] are the natural and bitter enemies of the Crees, and would hail with enthusiastic joy the prospect of marching against their old enemies" (Dempsey 1995, 178). The *Calgary Herald* published a response challenging this call on the grounds that to do so would be as immoral and un-Christian as pushing whisky as a solution to troubles with Indigenous peoples. This newspaper also covered tensions between the two nations on several other occasions, reporting that Blackfoot Chief Crowfoot had offered the Crown support in the conflict if needed (*Calgary Herald*, 16 Apr. 1885, 2; see also 30 Apr. 1885, 1).[6]

Interestingly, much of what was opined by the *Fort Macleod Gazette* was not wild speculation. While the Métis and Cree attempted several times to forge an alliance with the Confederacy during the conflict, all the attempts were unsuccessful. Crowfoot would not act without the other nations in the Confederacy and was pushed into the Crown's camp by the Crees, who promised to wipe out Crowfoot and his people if he didn't back the resistance. Red Crow, chief of the Bloods, commented that he was more interested in joining the conflict on the side of the Crown, and if the NWMP "would give the word they would be ready at any time to fight the Crees" (Dempsey 1995, 177). Bull Shield informed the government to "[g]ive us the ammunition and grub and we'll show you how soon we can set the Crees afoot and lick them" (Dempsey 1995, 178).

While all of these interactions paint a picture of Blackfoot expressions of their territory and relationships with outsiders, you should also begin to see that a counter political entity to Blackfoot military, economic, and political power was starting to emerge from this rich contextual inter-Indigenous tapestry. In the nineteenth century, the Confederacy took part in making war, peace, and treaties of trade and safe passage with other peoples on the Plains. Much of that activity was with, or oriented to, the Nehiyaw Pwat. Robert Innes (2013) describes the Nehiyaw Pwat as a political, social, military, and economic alliance among different Indigenous peoples that was woven together by kinship ties. The Plains Cree, Métis, Assiniboine, and Saulteaux peoples that made up the Iron Alliance all had kinship links that pulled them together and forged responsibilities of mutual support. These nations came together for shared self-defence and to advance the goals of the alliance. As we can see, these goals frequently brought them into conflict with the Blackfoot Confederacy.[7]

Robert Innes has studied the kinship ties that stretched across overlapping territory and gave rise to this alliance. Indeed, Innes points out that the alliance provided key strategic benefits in a region with adversaries like the Confederacy and the Sioux. He argues:

> By the early 1800s, Plains Cree and Assiniboine bands, augmented by a few Saulteaux and Métis bands, had formed a formidable military alliance. Stonechild, McLeod, and Nestor have called this the Iron Alliance. Their main enemies, according to Milloy, were the Gros Ventre, Blackfoot, Sioux, and Mandan/Hidasta. (Innes 2014, 60)

Covering some of the key conflicts between the two spheres of political and military power, Innes explains that "[b]etween 1810 and 1870, hostilities between the Cree/Assiniboine/Saulteaux/Métis and the Blackfoot confederacy increased until the defeat of the Iron Alliance [by the Blackfoot] in 1870" (Innes 2013, 61). This was by no means the end of military hostilities, as we can see from the number of fights and petitions after 1870.

In this light, the hesitancy to rush into supporting the 1885 Resistance in the north and the eventual promise to oppose it makes sense. The willingness of the Métis and the Cree to come together to fight Canada in the north was likely helped by their long-standing kinship alliances in the Nehiyaw Pwat. For the Blackfoot, these were the same political and military adversaries they had been engaging for a long time in order to keep them from imposing themselves on Blackfoot territory.

Another way we can understand territoriality is to look at how the Métis talk about the boundaries of their own spaces. For example, in a letter that appeared in the *Nor'Wester* newspaper, a prominent paper published in Red River, a well-respected member of the Métis community by the name of George Flett discussed the potential of Red River people getting into the gold-mining business in the Rocky Mountains. In describing the best way for folks in Red River to get to the mountains, he said:

> The most direct route would be through the Blackfeet country. Mr. James Sinclair crossed the Mountains twice by this route, and from parties who accompanied him, I learn that the road is a good one. But the thought will suggest itself,—How could we get through the Blackfeet? They are hostile and dangerous. My answer is,—If we do not trouble the Indians, they will not trouble us. Our object should be to find the Indian camps on our route, and once there we would be safe as within the walls of Fort Garry. (*Nor'Wester*, 22 Jan. 1862, 1, col. 2)

There are several points we can pull out of this passage. By way of context, this was published in a paper whose readership was mostly Métis people, and it was a type of advertisement that called people to take up this mining endeavour. In this light, Flett was aware that any Métis people reading his letter would have the same question he was asking about getting to the Rocky Mountains: what about the Blackfeet? Notice he doesn't ask "what about the Assiniboine, or what about the Crees?" He only addresses one other nation directly and sets out to assuage his readers' fears. What does he mean by saying first that the expedition should not trouble the Indians, and then that Indian camps should be found, and once there he and others who accompany him will be "as safe as within the walls of Fort Garry"? While it's not totally clear, there are at least three possible ways to understand Flett's comments. First, he is not referring in the second half of that sentence exclusively to Blackfoot camps. Earlier in the letter Flett says "[t]hat we have every faculty for enabling us to make such a trip to advantage, is easily proved. We are, many of us, well acquainted with the country—we can converse with the inhabitants the Red Men, in their native tongue—we are familiar with Indian habits and traditions,—and we would not, under the circumstances, be scared by even the dreaded Blackfeet. We can live comfortably on such a journey where strangers would almost infallibly starve" (*Nor'Wester*, 22 Jan. 1862, 1, col. 1). Flett was confident that they could spend time in camps with other members of the Nehiyaw Pwat, where they would find friends, kin, and safe haven. Second, the tenor of Flett's words may indicate that if the Métis were clear that they would be moving through with no intention to stay or hunt in Blackfoot territory, then they would be welcome to camp alongside Confederacy parties. Lastly, Flett was clearly communicating a sense of being from somewhere else. He, along with all the Métis people reading his letter, was aware that *they were not from Blackfoot territory*. They were from Red River and other parts of the Northwest, and since Blackfoot places are not Métis places Flett knew that he and his Métis readers needed to govern themselves differently when moving through those spaces.

This is not to say there is no history of Métis people in Blackfoot territory. All one need do is think of all the conflicts and fights noted above and it becomes clear that there is a long history of Métis people being in Blackfoot territory. However, some historians have sought to tell a different story of Métis presence in central and southern Alberta. Heather Devine has argued that there are Métis families in Blackfoot territory and that "[t]he earliest Métis trading families in central Alberta were descended from Northwest Company and Hudson's Bay Company *engagés* who married into Blackfoot communities and established the family ties necessary to conduct business unmolested. Four families that fit this profile include the Birds, the Munros, the Salois, and the Dumonts" (Devine 2010, 29). For Devine, these four mixed European and Blackfoot (or other Indigenous heritage families) show a Métis presence in Blackfoot territory.

She notes that James Bird was the son of an HBC chief factor and a Cree woman (who Divine does not name). Bird lived his life in Blackfoot territory, "marrying a Peigan woman, Sarah, in 1825." Hugh Munro lived his life on the Plains and Devine reports that he died on the Blackfeet Reservation in Montana. Joseph Salois married a mixed-blood woman, Angelique Lucier. The mother of famed buffalo hunter and 1885 Resistance military leader Gabriel Dumont was Josette Sarsi, or Sarcisse, from Tsuut'ina Nation (Devine 2010, 29–30).

Devine's work outlines some important points about both the definition and contours of the Métis Nation, and the way that definition gets taken up in questions of territoriality. Devine uses these examples of racial mixing to assert:

> From this nucleus of individuals, all of whom had established an early presence in Central Alberta by the 1820s, grew a loosely knit community comprised of a minimum of fifty Métis families living in the general vicinity of Central Alberta by the 1870s. As an old man, Jimmy Jock Bird used to boast of being the first resident of Calgary, having occupied Old Bow Fort in the 1830s. (Devine 2010, 30)

However, this is an assertion that relies on uncompelling views of Métis politics and identity. Devine's four families appear to be more individual instances of mixed bloods spending their lives in Blackfoot territory than of families that are part of the politically self-aware Métis Nation *in* Blackfoot territory. More to the point, it isn't clear whether or not these families would have been viewed by themselves and others as Blackfoot or Tsuut'ina.[8] For example, what happens to the Dumonts if we note that Gabriel Dumont was born in the Red River Settlement, the heart of the Métis Nation, rather than in a Blackfoot or Tsuut'ina community? What happens if we shift our gaze away from the mixed-race heritage of these families and think about how they moved in, between, and through the political collectivities that make up the Indigenous world on the Northwest Plains? Indigenous people from the nineteenth century until today have varied kinship ties to other nations, including European nations. By focusing exclusively on mixed heritage in her analysis, Devine paints a picture of mixed-race people being everywhere. And she would be right about that. Anyone could look anywhere and find mixed-race people.

But did she find Métis political collectivities? Her analysis cannot be used to make conclusions on this. A "loosely knit community" might be a start, but it is not a place to
finish. While there is no shortage of Métis presence in Alberta, the question remains as
to whether Blackfoot territory is *also* Métis territory? We would argue that it is not and
should not be conceived of in that fashion.

Other historians have also examined the development of permanent Métis spaces
in Blackfoot territory. As mentioned above, Dempsey points out that after the arrival of
the NWMP in Blackfoot territory "the Crees, Half-breeds, and white men were streaming into the country unchecked. Some of the half-breeds . . . even established permanent
settlements at Fort Macleod and at the newly-built posts at Fort Calgary and Fort Walsh"
(Dempsey 1995, 100). While Jimmy Jock Bird may have boasted about being the first resi-
dent of Calgary, *settlers* also boast about those things all the time. Such boasting exposes
an uncomfortable fact for the Métis: their hunting activities and permanent settlements
in southern Alberta had long been safeguarded by the NWMP, the same coercive arm of
the settler state that protected early settlers. The benefit that the Métis gleaned from their
relationship with the NWMP was best captured in communication between the Blackfoot
Confederacy and Colonel Macleod of the NWMP. Dempsey writes:

> Angry at the repeated invasions by their enemies [Crees and Métis] and the mas-
> sive buffalo slaughter, a delegation of Blood and Blackfoot chiefs went to see Col-
> onel Macleod, who had been appointed the new commissioner of the police. They
> told him that if his men were not in the country, the Blackfoot would destroy the
> half-breed hunters. (Dempsey 1995, 102)

Macleod recorded in a letter that Red Crow of the Bloods along with other Blackfoot
leaders recognized that "now that we [the NWMP] have come into his country he finds that
from all sides his old enemies, who he dare not attack, *are under our protection* pressing
upon him" (Dempsey 1995, 103; emphasis added). Indeed, the nations of the Blackfoot
Confederacy were well aware that in the late 1870s they had Cree and Métis hunting brigades in their territory from the Belly River all the way to the Bow River, or roughly between Lethbridge and Calgary, and could not remove them as they once would have done.

A Métis presence can be found in Calgary without Jimmy Jock Bird or his boasting.
But the reason that the Métis are still there and were not chased out by the Confederacy
is because an armed force of settler police protected the intruders, and all involved parties knew it. The Métis knew that without using settler police as a shield they could not
establish themselves in space that was not theirs. Proximity to settler power was used
to advance Métis goals that could not otherwise have been advanced. The proximity
took several forms, the first being geographical proximity to settler military power and
the second being a conceptual one linked to a proximity to whiteness. It is important
to remember that some contemporary Métis people have benefited from the ability to
keep outward manifestations of their Indigeneity secret. Certain proximities to whiteness (not racially, but socially) mean that, for some, the ability to disappear due to shame
was possible.[9] This, too, is a privilege. However, instead of exercising that privilege as a
weapon for one's personal gain, we wonder if it is possible to use it to advocate for shared
Indigenous concerns. The next section will develop a framework that will help engage
this question.

The Northwest Plains was not a place with border checkpoints staffed by Indigenous border guards checking people's passports. Rather, borderlands were fluid, overlapping territories. Still, there was a clear sense of where a people were from as well as where they were not from. There was a sense of what was needed when travelling away from one's territory into the territory of another or other Indigenous nations. Some people in the Métis Nation had, and continue to have, kinship ties both through marriage and other forms with people in the Blackfoot Confederacy. But those kinship ties do not allow Métis people to claim Blackfoot space as Métis space any more than Blackfoot people with Métis kinship ties can claim Red River as Blackfoot space. What we need in all of this is a thoughtful way of engaging other peoples when we are away from our home territories.

How to Jig in Treaty 7 Territory While Being a Good Guest

Both authors have been dancers, growing up at Métis dances or being performance jiggers. Jigging is a dance done in many different Métis communities, and one can often tell where someone is from by the way they jig. But getting together to dance is not exclusively about the dance: jigging is wrapped up in and animated by a number of social activities that give form to spaces that are Métis, and spaces that are not. So how might we jig in Treaty 7 territory? In the previous section we examined the delineation of different Indigenous spaces by looking at the politics and battles between the Nehiyaw Pwat and Blackfoot Confederacy. This section takes a different approach and engages cultural and gendered forms of understanding space. As such, it lays out the beginnings of a theory of living well in places that one is not from and is informed by the growing scholarship concerned with wahkotowin. Kinship shapes Métis political and social life, though kinship is much more than ancestral blood ties. The very specific ways that Métis social relationships are created, defined, and maintained inform the structures of relationality for Métis movement and territory. These relationships are complex, strict, and defined, which, as Anderson and Ball explain in Chapter 9, make kinship not so much an anthropological or genealogical list of cousins, but part of the body of the law and practice of wahkotowin. This law provides Métis people with guidelines of how to behave when in relationship with family, extended family, and non-family, including how to be a good guest.

Brenda Macdougall's definition of wahkotowin[10] notes the wide swath of relationships that the law relates to:

> As much as it is a worldview based on familial—especially inter-familial—connectedness, wahkootowin also conveys an idea about the virtues that an individual should personify as a family member. The values critical to family relationships—such as reciprocity, mutual support, decency, and order—in turn influenced the behaviours, actions, and decision-making processes that shaped all a community's economic and political interactions. Wahkootowin contextualizes how relationships were intended to work within Métis society by defining and classifying relationships, prescribing patterns of behaviour between relatives and non-relatives, and linking people and communities in a large, complex web of relationships. Just as wahkootowin mediated interactions between people, it

also extended to the natural and spiritual worlds, regulating relationships between humans and non-humans, the living and the dead, and humans and the
natural environment. (Macdougall 2010, 8)

One of the benefits of Macdougall's discussion of wahkotowin is that it helps us understand the Nehiyaw Pwat as a political framework. In this light, the aggressive relationship between the Nehiyaw Pwat and the Blackfoot Confederacy stemmed from a shared
understanding of Blackfoot as *non-relatives* to Métis people. Indeed, in the Cree language,
spoken by many Métis, the Blackfoot are referred to as ayahcininiw, which in English
means "strangers." Blackfoot territory is more aggressively defined as ayahciyinînâhk,
which means enemy territory. In Macdougall's definition of wahkotowin, this complex
web of relationships also governs the patterns of behaviour we have with non-relatives
(Macdougall 2010, 8). Wahkotowin does not position relationality as universal and equal,
which means that it does not propose that *we are related to everyone*. For those who are not
related to the Métis, there are expected behaviours through wahkohtowin, as any kinship
system has limits. Because the Blackfoot are strangers from enemy territory, the Nehiyaw
Pwat has no territory in the land of the Blackfoot Confederacy.

As part of the Nehiyaw Pwat, the Métis had clear expectations of how to be in relationship with others, but particularly, how to be a good guest. Macdougall (2010, 44–5)
captures this well when she argues "[t]he Métis, like their Indian and fur trader relations,
lived in a social world based on reciprocal sharing, respectful behaviour between family
members, and an understanding of the differences between themselves and outsiders. The
Métis were part of the economic structure of the fur trade, facilitating its success by embodying the principles of family loyalty, accountability, and responsibility." Reciprocity,
mutual support, decency, and order, or what Macdougall calls "values critical to family
relationships," influenced "the behaviours, actions, and decision-making processes that
shaped all a community's economic and political interactions" (Macdougall 2010, 8). In
negotiating space, Métis people are guided by boundaries based on this reciprocal sharing
and understanding of outsiders.

The long-term presence of Métis in southern Alberta means that Métis people who
have lived here have had generations to become responsible guests. How do Métis people
live as good guests in the territory of our non-relatives? Though we may not be relatives
to the Blackfoot, we do have a relationship to them as our hosts and to this land where we
live. Remember, we noted above that the Blackfoot were calling on Cree and Métis people
to affirm Blackfoot authority in this land. Because that call has not changed with the passage of time, how do we as Métis people now act in good relationship with the Blackfoot?

Wahkotowin can inform an ethic of visiting on the land; being in relationship with
the land also guides other behaviours. As Jean Teillet argues, "constant visiting on the
land continually renews the relationship between the people and the land. It is a large
vision and mobility is the Métis way of renewing the relationship to their friends, family
and land. In this way, there is little distinction between terms such as residence, home
and community; terms that are heavy with meaning for outsiders" (Teillet 2008, 39). This
is a holistic and balanced sensibility within wahkotowin. Maria Campbell takes this idea
further and highlights various reciprocal relationships within wahkotowin: "Human to
human, human to plants, human to animals, to the water and especially to the earth. And
in turn all of creation had responsibilities and reciprocal obligations to us" (Campbell

2007, 5). There is a distinct reciprocity in the way Métis culture emerges directly from the land, as the land is changed by Métis emergence:

> Métis society emerged and gained strength because of its connection to indigenous worldviews that were predicated on the children's ancestral connection to the lands of their female relations. Over time, the region itself was transformed into a Métis homeland not only by virtue of the children's occupation of the territory, but also through the relationships with the Cree and Dene women and fur trader men from whom they were descended. (Macdougall 2010, 44)

Wahkotowin structures the very creation of the Métis nation: it is kinship with other Indigenous nations, their non-human relatives, and the land that forms the foundation of Métis culture.

Because reciprocal responsibilities to the land are the foundation of wahkotowin, Métis political and economic decisions about the land, about hunting rights and pipelines, must also contend with how we recognize and engage the territory of other Indigenous peoples, even in the areas where we are guests. As history shows, the Métis have not always lived up to their obligations as good guests in this respect—recall the buffalo hunting brigades and their wastefulness that disgusted the Blackfoot. How then do we do better? Christie Belcourt's work sees people needing the earth and the earth as needing people, and gives us a framework of care to help us understand how we can be a good guest on the land (Hogue 2017): a recent art piece by her is titled *The earth is my government* (Belcourt 2018). We are directed by wahkotowin to maintain an active relationship with the land, not in terms of stewardship but as an enriching reciprocity.

The concept of enriching reciprocity is well articulated in the work and teachings of Métis and other Indigenous women. This chapter opened with an examination of the Blackfoot perspective on territoriality, though a number of writers have rightly criticized this perspective as hyper-masculinist. Jennifer Brown resists the "patrifocal" reading of Métis texts by looking at the way mothers pull their children to them and view the familial tie as a core component of their lives. In this way, Métis women transmit Métis culture. Brown notes that it is largely female-headed family units that begin to contribute to an emerging Métis sensibility as Indigenous people (Brown 2007 [1980], 42). Once we shake Métis history from its masculinist moorings, we can more clearly see how kinship, as rooted in wahkotowin, guides Métis ideas about reciprocity. By focusing on women's orientations and teachings on wahkotowin, rather than on its connection to the great battles of the past, it becomes clear that the protocols for visiting are a cornerstone of Métis culture and contribute to a more robust and hopeful set of guidelines for being a good guest.

The centrality of maternal Métis culture sits firmly with elderly Métis women. It is important that old women tell and retell stories, for doing so serves as a mechanism of sharing information from one generation to the next as well as a means of explaining what behaviour is and is not acceptable. For example, one story was told to remind everyone about the law against incest and its consequences:

> The old ladies used to tell those stories. They would be telling the kids the stories, but everybody was sitting around because you are all in the same room. My dad

would be working at snowshoes with my uncles, too, if they were there. They were hearing it over and over; by repetition, it was really engrained in everybody's head. It reminded us that those things were wrong. And everybody was getting different things from different places. Like the story tells you what a mother is supposed to do if this happens. She didn't do anything when she suspected him for the first time. She could have prevented it. So the story tells you all of this, and when you hear it over and over again you start to think about it. (Anderson 2011, 142–3)

Thus, Métis women are instructors, carrying cultural values and educating others about Métis values, telling and retelling stories beyond leisure and into instruction. As well, the stories told by elderly Métis women have a function of outreach besides cultural transmission and affirmation. Stories that educate about wahkotowin are told to children as the primary audience and to the secondary audience of adults in the community who overhear these stories throughout their lives. And importantly for our purposes in this chapter, stories are also intended for an audience of *non-relatives*, those outsiders and visitors to the community: "If you were a strange man coming to visit for the first time, the message was, 'Watch it, young man. This old lady has been around the block and knows what the laws are'" (Anderson 2011, 143). The telling of these stories ensures that the boundaries of domestic life are strict and that listeners also understand the basis of laws for political identity.

In addition to stories, reciprocity also extended to spaces *within* Métis communities. For example, we see a gendered split in physical spaces that can inform our understanding of respecting different realms: "women and men held different spaces. These environments were respected to the extent that it was considered inappropriate to go into another group's territory because it could interfere with the authorities and powers within that group" (Anderson 2011, 102). Held within this notion is not simply the way that spaces are gendered, but also how it is a political act to maintain the borders within different realms. What seems to be happening here is a commitment to *non-interference* in gendered boundaries, and this non-interference can be extrapolated into a need to uphold political boundaries with other Indigenous groups, extending from the way that balance and well-being are "contingent on respecting boundaries" (Anderson 2011, 103).

To recap, reciprocity with the land and the people living on it and a commitment to non-interference outside our spaces form essential components of building a reciprocally grounded ethic of being a guest with the land and on the land of others. Being a good guest means not claiming the spaces of others as one's own, respecting the traditions and authority of those peoples in whose territory you are in, and working to not undermine or attack the authority of other peoples. It is important to note that these ethics require practice and negotiation. Guidelines around gender are not oppressive binary gender roles, but instead create balance.[11] Maria Campbell states that it was "inappropriate to go into another group's territory because it could interfere with the authorities and powers within that group" (Anderson 2011, 102), with the phrase "another group" here meaning men and women; there are echoes in the way that the Nehiyaw Pwat and the Blackfoot Confederacy negotiated boundaries in southern Alberta by considering each other's power and authorities as animated by their territories.

Boundaries are both affirmed and negotiated when visiting happens, with men, women, and Elders physically occupying different parts of the home. Kim Anderson shared the memories of one Elder who remembered how different groups of people, guided by clear kinship protocols, would use space in the home in different ways while visiting: how the use of outdoor space expanded into a communal arbour for shared meals and socializing, Elders in a tent, women near the kitchen, men in her father's log cabin in the bush. Men, in particular, respected these protocols and did not come around the house. "As Maria remembered, 'Those rules were really strict. We never went in that shack of my dad's. That was a men's house. And the men never came into the house for meal time if it was summer. If they were around the house, they were on the side where the arbour was'" (Anderson 2011, 102). Note that these gendered spaces have strict (though flexible if necessary) rules, but that visiting happens in a negotiated communal space like the arbour. In places that are not our own territories, communal spaces like the arbour exist as places of negotiation and visiting, and other spaces are more like the houses or tents, with specific groups of people animating the spaces.

But what happens if these rules and boundaries are transgressed? It is important that an ethic of reciprocal visiting also include an appreciation for the space and time needed for negotiation, and the opportunity for correction. People make mistakes. Intentional or unintentional, malicious or benign, political interactions across spaces are messy and full of conflict and disagreement. An ethic of reciprocal visiting doesn't mean we always get it right. Instead, it commits us as a people from somewhere else to receive correction thoughtfully and to recommit ourselves to living well in places we are not from.

This becomes clearer if we think about what it is to be a child in the Métis nation. In these gendered spaces, "children would move back and forth between the women and elders, with the youngest typically staying close to the elders" (Anderson 2011, 102). Métis children are parented by their community, and visiting was and remains integral to instilling an ethic of reciprocal visiting: "Growing up in a small community where children were welcomed into every home, we learned how to relate to one another. When invited to visit 'for tea,' if we made a mistake, adults gently corrected our behaviour" (Anderson 2011, 113). This illustrates a number of things: first, that visiting culture helps do the work of maintaining the relationships that guide Métis culture; second, that boundaries of home are fluid for children; and third, that *correction* is a feature of visiting. Being a good guest is often about learning from the experience inherent in making mistakes, or getting it wrong, and demands we be humble when receiving correction. For all of us who live outside our home territories, this is an important reminder to listen and receive correction from our hosts. But the notion of an ethic of reciprocal visiting need not be a solemn, burdensome act.

Visiting in Métis tradition is also an act of joy. Métis visiting has always been tied to parties, balls, and an all-around good time. For a long time these principles were interpreted in racist ways by settlers as laziness. One MLA in Saskatchewan complained that the Métis were always having picnics: "They do little but spend their time having picnics and galloping their horses around" (Anderson 2011, 114). This outsider's perception of visiting as laziness rather than as a kin-focused ethic ignores the way that being together on the land is a subtly political act, affirming kinship relationships while sharing the workload needed for life on the Plains. In the nineteenth century, Bishop Taché commented that "the most striking fault of the Half-breeds appears to me to be the ease with which they resign themselves to the allurements of pleasure. Of lively disposition, ardent and playful, gratification is a necessity to them, and if a source of pleasure presents itself they sacrifice everything for its enjoyment" (quoted in Ens 1996, 46). Perhaps most compellingly, Métis visiting culture provides a model for playfulness and rowdiness as a basis for negotiating, transgressing, and maintaining boundaries. A culture of visiting doesn't just revolve around shared work, but also games, gambling, dances, and parties. Métis dances have always been a feature of Métis culture, with hosts sometimes not realizing they were hosting until guests showed up at their door after "pass[ing] from house to house, certain of an invitation to come in" (Ens 1996, 46). What others incorrectly perceived variously as the behaviour of common peasants or quaint lazy barbarians was in fact an important activity of building, of renewing relationships of space and bonds with kin, non-kin, and the land.

If we return to jigging as a Métis methodology, we might start to see how this ethic comes together. Jigging requires your steps to be co-ordinated with the music played by the fiddler. The idea that a good jigger stays in time with the fiddle player helps us to consider that even this dance, one that is flashy with fancy steps, is governed by negotiation and co-ordination between the jigger and the fiddler: "A good dancer is always 'in time' and 'in sync' with the melody of the fiddler's rendition of the 'Red River Jig'; that is, when the fiddler begins the second part of the tune, the dancer begins his or her varying steps. Ideally, the dancer is no sooner or later than the exact moment that the fiddler begins the lower notes within this section" (Quick 2017, 49). For dancers who might encounter fiddlers with a different way of playing this tune, the co-ordination must be assessed quickly. If we think about jigging in Blackfoot territory, those Métis people moving through it must tune our ears to the twang of a different fiddle. We are required to adjust *how* we jig, and the *way* we jig to these new tunes that are not from our home territories. To not do so would be deeply insulting to our host fiddlers, and as all jiggers know, fiddlers are boss. Jigging is a social dance but it's more than that: it can inform Métis people about how to listen. Champion jigger Brent Potskin (2005) says, "Listening is your key to dancing. You really have to listen, as soon as there is a change, you got to change."

Jigging shows us that correction does not simply refer to scolding children, but that in this ethic of reciprocal visiting adults may also have missteps and need to find their footing. The point of thinking about jigging in Blackfoot territory is that it encourages Métis people to engage in ethics of relationality that are both informed by their own philosophical foundations and by the traditions of the territory they are visiting.

Towards an Ethic of Reciprocal Visiting, or How Not to Be an Asshole Outside Your Territory

As Leanne Simpson argues in Chapter 3 of this volume, Indigenous people have a body of theory, traditions, and laws that are more than simply cultural practices. An ethic of reciprocal visiting, seen through jigging or gendered spaces, is a theory of being in the world in relation to others. This theory informs our behaviour when we are in the territory of other Indigenous peoples. Métis traditions of visiting our kin and those who are not our kin can shape how we move respectfully through territories of other peoples.

Being Métis in Calgary gives us lessons that may be helpful for other Indigenous peoples navigating complex spaces: to be an Indigenous guest outside of your territory requires a navigation of space and a commitment to understanding your own protocols of visiting as well as the protocols of your host nations. Reciprocity undergirds it all. What are we doing to enable Indigenous resurgence where we live? For Indigenous folks living outside of our territories, we need to educate ourselves and listen closely to the music around us. What agreements existed to enable our presence in these spaces? We move through the territories of our non-relatives and need to be reciprocal. What can we do to be better guests? What is being asked of us?

As Indigenous people living outside of our territories, we have a responsibility to be gracious guests and to affirm the needs of Indigenous peoples in the territories where we live. In their investigations of Métis misrecognition in spaces where there is no Métis terri-tory, Gaudry and Leroux (2017) and Thistle (2016) note the way Métis claims to non-Métis territory are actively harmful to the other Indigenous peoples fighting for their authority to be respected. For Thistle, Métis territorial acknowledgements in Toronto harm Anishi-naabe, Haudenosaunee, and Wendat territory claims in that area. And for Gaudry and Leroux, the demands of fake Métis organizations in the East[12] have undermined Mi'kmaq treaty rights in the Maritimes. This lateral violence can occur when Métis guesting isn't gracious and instead takes up space, visibly.

But doesn't visiting also imply that you go home at some point? Much of the frustration that the Blackfoot Confederacy had with the Nehiyaw Pwat was that they set up a perma-nent presence in Blackfoot territory and, as noted above, used the NWMP, the coercive arm of the settler state, to do so. If this ethic of reciprocal visiting is to be respectful and attuned to the Blackfoot and the land, it requires the establishment of a new political relationship.

Relationships between the Blackfoot Confederacy and the Nehiyaw Pwat were fraught with tension and filled with acrimony. But that doesn't mean that needs to continue. What if we opened up new dialogues as Métis people with the Blackfoot and other signatories to Treaty 7, and asked to build a new set of revisable treaties that would allow us to continue to visit in their territory? Doing so would come with risks, because the Blackfoot and other Treaty 7 peoples may say no. We would then have to confront that, and if we are living an ethic of reciprocal visiting, we would need to leave or at least accept that we are bad visitors and unwanted guests. But engaging these acts of respecting territory and authority allows for moments of correction that should have happened a long time ago. When the Métis were forcibly moving into Blackfoot territory, that was a moment for correction, humility, and more thoughtfulness. The Blackfoot asked us to respect their authority, and in response we were bad guests for undermining Blackfoot authority as we poorly negotiated those bound-aries and demarcated spaces. A new political relationship informed by an ethic of reciprocal visiting can change those relationships and ultimately build an inter-Indigenous politic that is rooted in support for your hosts and the sounds of your host's fiddle.

Conclusion

We have argued that a good way forward in inter-Indigenous relationships would be to root them in a commitment to reciprocity with the land and the people living with it, respectful non-interference in spaces one is not from, and a commitment to listen to the tune of your host fiddler. But that's not where it ends. As we pointed out above, Indigenous people may be tempted to use a settler logic that emphasizes long-standing presence in a place supported by settler military power to help absolve them of the need to act ethically in other people's territories. This needs to be resisted, and at the same time those primarily settler logics also need to be confronted by settlers. Settlers must confront their own daily practices that strip away Blackfoot authority and the authority of the land in Treaty 7. The Métis ethic of reciprocal visiting and all the complexities it entails might be a good starting point for both other Indigenous people as well as non-Indigenous people to think about how they live in the territories of Indigenous peoples. It is an ethic rooted in theory and legal protocols and presents us with a call to action.

In our introduction, we noted how territorial acknowledgements often misrepresent Métis presence in Calgary; the complex diplomacies between Indigenous nations are silenced by formulaic and inaccurate acknowledgements, which undermine the resurgence of Indigenous protocols around visiting. We now return to the question: should Calgary be considered Métis territory? Based on Métis relationships to the land, the answer is no. So how then do we be Métis in Calgary? By renewing cultural protocols and living an ethic of reciprocal visiting and listening to our hosts. This may mean becoming absent from territorial acknowledgements in Calgary in order to make space for our host nations. It may also involve actions that are not prescribed, but learned through careful reflection: what are your obligations to your hosts, and what practical steps can you take to uphold Indigenous resurgence in the spaces where you live and work?

Discussion Questions

1. Can an ethic of reciprocal visiting reshape inter-Indigenous relations in your context? Why or why not?

2. Though the chapter has focused on what it means to be Indigenous in other Indigenous peoples' territory, these spaces are also shared with many non-Indigenous people. What is required of non-Indigenous people to live well in Indigenous peoples' territories? What are some of your daily practices that strip away the authority of the Indigenous peoples in the territory you live in?

3. Maybe you think the authors are wrong about Métis territory in Calgary. Keeping in mind the structure of analysis in this chapter, what evidence would you need to see to believe that Calgary *is* Métis territory?

4. Métis kinship protocols can include and exclude. Develop a list of the ways that kinship is including and also excluding people. Are there ways this is happening that the authors missed or under-appreciated? Where else do you see kinship being enacted?

5. The chapter began with a discussion of misplaced territorial acknowledgements. What happens when we get these territorial acknowledgements wrong? What harm can this cause?

6. As Métis people, we don't speak for Blackfoot in this chapter. Yet turning to our hosts for their perspectives is necessary. How can Blackfoot ideas about visiting and hosting teach us about being better guests?

Recommended Reading

Gaudry, A. 2017. "Métis Are a People, Not a Historical Process." https://www.thecanadianencyclopedia
.ca/en/article/metis-are-a-people-not-a-historical-process/.

Drops of Brandy, and Other Traditional Metis Tunes. 2002. Saskatoon: Gabriel Dumont Institute.
(Four CDs, with sheet music, fiddler biographies, and cultural discussion.)

Native Youth Sexual Health Network (NYSHN). n.d. "What We Believe In." http://www
.nativeyouthsexualhealth.com/whatwebelievein.html.

Notes

1. For a deeper discussion on the relationship between settler colonialism and Indigenous relationships to the land, see Wolfe (2006); Goeman (2015).

2. In this chapter, "inter-Indigenous" refers to the political relationships and interactions that take place between different Indigenous peoples. See Voth (2018).

3. For the most theoretically robust enunciation of this idea, see Andersen (2014); see also Vowel (2016).

4. Indigenous peoples have talked about the border between Canada and the United States in a variety of ways. One of those ways is by referring to its imposition on Indigenous peoples, and the bifurcation of a number of contiguous nations, as the "medicine line."

5. A great many historical studies have been written about the Resistance, with some historians calling it a Rebellion. See Stanley (1960); Friesen (1987); Reid (2008).

6. Dempsey also finds that while the Cree messengers seeking the support of Crowfoot were welcomed into the camp, Crowfoot would not act without knowing the minds of the other nations in the Confederacy. Dempsey argues that Crowfoot was tempted to join the resistance, but several factors militated against a Blackfoot alliance. The other members of the Confederacy were mostly opposed, and Crowfoot was deeply insulted when the Cree suggested that if Crowfoot did not join them, after the war was won by the Métis and Cree, the victors would march on Blackfoot territory and wipe out Crowfoot and his people. Shortly after this, Crowfoot announced in public that he would not join the fight and would support the Crown militarily if necessary (Dempsey 1972, 171–89).

7. The Great Sioux Nation was another node in the fabric of Northwest Indigenous political life, but discussion of it is beyond the scope of this chapter.

8. Devine's own language here is interesting. Note that she describes these families as marrying *into* Blackfoot communities. They are not marrying into *Métis* communities because the Métis are not from Blackfoot territory.

9. For an interesting examination on this topic as it pertains to Métis people, see Adams (1975) or Lutz (1991).

10. Wahkotowin can be spelled in a variety of ways. We have chosen a standardized spelling here, unless a source has indicated otherwise.

11. Though this particular story may seem to reify cishet categories despite a discussion of balance, queer Cree thinkers who consider kinship clearly outline this concept of care beyond these normative categories. See, for example, Nixon (2017); Wilson (2015).

12. Gaudry and Leroux (2017) discuss the way some settler organizations make claims of being Métis through genealogical revisionism: believing a distant ancestor to be Indigenous. This then gives rise to fake Métis organizations, with no connection to living or contemporary Indigenous peoples or communities.

8 Transforming Toxic Indigenous Masculinity

A Critical Indigenous Masculinities and Indigenous Film Studies Approach to *Drunktown's Finest*

Renae Watchman and Robert Alexander Innes

Sick Boy: *You wanna hear su'um funny? When I was growing up, I used to think that being a drunk was just a part of life everyone went through.*
Felixia: *What do you mean?*
Sick Boy: *I mean, first you were a kid, and then you hit puberty, then you became a drunk. And if you made it, you became an adult. So here's to becoming adults and shit and getting the fuck out of here! (shot glasses clink).*

—*Drunktown's Finest* [2014]

Introduction

The transformation from childhood to adulthood is marked in Diné (Navajo) culture for both girls and boys by Kinaaldá. The word "Kinaaldá" refers to the person who achieves puberty.[1] The Kinaaldá is also a four-day ceremony that was originally practised by Asdzą́ą́ Nádleehé, Changing Woman, upon her first menses. She is "one of our most benevolent and compassionate of the Holy Deities. She is the Mother of the Diné peoples" (Denetdale 2014, 78). As such, healthy Diné strive to mimic Asdzą́ą́ Nádleehé. At the end of a Kinaaldá ceremony, not only does the person become an adult, they become Kinaaldá. The opening quote, from the 2014 feature film *Drunktown's Finest*, written and directed by Diné filmmaker Sydney Freeland and executively produced by Robert Redford, illustrates the cultural disconnect between Diné epistemologies and how young people understand transformation when surrounded by alcoholism, dysfunction, toxic masculinities, and other realities brought upon by colonialism and internalized from the time they are very young.

Within the context of settler colonialism, Indigenous people have undergone an intense process of cultural genocide through federal and provincial governments' formal assimilation policies and through everyday informal interactions with white people. The assimilation process used, and continues to use, white supremacist heteronormative patriarchy as a means of colonizing Indigenous people's bodies, minds, and lands, leaving a lasting and negative impact on Indigenous communities.[2]

For Indigenous men specifically, the assimilation process meant, among other things, that Indigenous social and political relations had to be reconfigured to conform to a masculinity that upheld white supremacist heteronormative patriarchy.[3] As a result of assimilation efforts, many Indigenous men, to varying degrees, have internalized white supremacist heteronormative masculine ideals. In many cases, as Maori scholar Brendan Hokowhitu writes, this internalization is then represented as the Indigenous masculine ideal: "Productive heterosexual patriarchy became the model, the norm—the post-contact tradition, reflecting invader culture, yet also reproducing the focus of Indigenous cultures on genealogical lineage" (Hokowhitu 2015, 89). Indigenous communities are suffering long-term negative impacts from the imposition of the hegemonic masculinity that has usurped the various traditional Indigenous forms of masculinities.[4] The process of colonization attempted to erase, disregard, and deem reprehensible the various forms of Indigenous masculinities and replace them with a simplified and singular form of masculinity that celebrates men who exhibit the traits that uphold the white supremacist heteronormative patriarchy.

For most Indigenous people, the specificities of cultures, people, and historic experiences conveyed in Indigenous films transcend nation-state borders. Though there are different historic contexts, Indigenous people, especially in former British colonies, share a similar relationship with settler colonialism. *Drunktown's Finest* takes place in New Mexico on the Navajo Nation. The relationship Navajo, and indeed Native Americans in general, have with the US federal government is different from the relationship Indigenous people in Canada have with the Canadian federal government. However, Indigenous people on both sides of the border share a similar kind of relationship with the nation-states through treaty-making and the racist laws and policies enacted against them. Both share experiences of their federal government's assimilation processes, which included removing children from homes and sending them to residential schools (though in the US they are typically referred to as boarding schools, which is not surprising as the Canadian government's residential school system was based on the US boarding schools). They also share many cultural activities. For example, the largest and best-known powwow in North America, known as the Gathering of Nations, is held in Albuquerque, New Mexico, and attracts thousands of Indigenous people from Canada. In addition, Indigenous people in the US and Canada share the same anti-Indigenous racism directed towards them from white people. They also share in the same repercussions of colonization, like the internalization of white supremacist heteronormative patriarchy, apparent in *Drunktown's Finest*.

Analyzing Indigenous films provides an accessible way to explore these and other complex issues facing Indigenous people.[5] In this chapter, we will focus on how Sydney Freeland depicts issues of Indigenous masculinities in *Drunktown's Finest*. The film centres on the lives of three young Diné people, framed by the motif of changing and transformation through Diné teachings. Their stories are rich and complicated, and we unpack and focus on two of the three protagonists and the ways the film raises questions about what it means to be a man for the character of Sick Boy. Sick Boy is Luther Maryboy's nickname, and this nickname is tied to the hip hop or youth vernacular and an accurate appellation that suits his current state. The chapter also tackles the topic of homophobia and transphobia through the character of Felixia. Both of these topics are often difficult to talk about in many contemporary Indigenous homes, but through visual media we can explore these difficult experiences from the perspectives offered by the scholarship on critical Indigenous masculinities and Indigenous film studies.

Critical Indigenous Masculinities

Critical Indigenous masculinities is a nascent field of study within Indigenous studies. The emergent nature of the field is evidenced by the panels, articles, and books explicitly focused on masculinities.[6] Brendan Hokowhitu and Ty P. Káwika Tengan are the leading scholars in the area, publishing many articles on Maori and Kanaka Moali masculinities. Tengan (2008) and Diné scholar Lloyd Lee (2013) have published the only two monographs to date on the topic. In 2014, Sam McKegeny published *Masculindians: Conversations about Indigenous Manhood*, the first book to gather scholars and artists to talk about issues facing Indigenous men and the idea of masculinity. In 2015, Kim Anderson and Robert Alexander Innes edited the first anthology on Indigenous masculinities.[7]

Critical Indigenous masculinities studies, as Anderson and Innes (2015, 4) envision it, "seeks to deepen our understanding of the ways in which Indigenous men, and those who assert Indigenous masculine identities, perform their identities, why and how they perform them and the consequences to them and others because of their attachment to those identities." The critical study of Indigenous masculinities builds on theories and praxis of Indigenous feminist and queer scholars to question the hegemonic nature of the "masculine" in attempts to examine negative Indigenous male behaviour (see, e.g., Green 2007; Suzack, Hundorf, Perrault, and Barman 2010; Driskill, Finley, Gilley, and Morgensen 2011; Arvin, Tuck, and Morrill 2013; Flowers 2015; Tatonetti 2015; Anderson 2016; Kermoal and Altamirano-Jiménez 2016; Simpson 2016). The term "Indigenous masculinities" acknowledges the existence, significance, and legitimacy of the multiple, overlapping, and sometimes contradictory gender identities of Indigenous people and explicitly counters the notion of a singular masculinity.

Some scholars examine how the process of colonization has been imposed on Indigenous men and has led to the internalization of the ideal masculine traits and characteristics based on the white supremacist heteronormative patriarchy. This internalization acts to simplify and make uniform the ways a masculine identity can be exercised. Indigenous masculinities theorists ask how, and to what degree, Indigenous men have adopted and adapted the Western heteronormative notions of maleness that serve to subjugate and erase Indigenous women and queer people in violent and non-violent ways, and while these notions lead many to inflict violence on each other, others become trapped in the cycle of institutional incarceration. The results act to reinforce stereotypes of Indigenous men while contributing to the maintenance and strengthening of colonial structures that oppress all Indigenous people (Hokowhitu 2007; McKegney 2012). Indigenous men who exhibit these behaviours thus continue to personify and reproduce many colonial dynamics, even when their aims are represented as decolonial.

At the same time, other scholars examine how Indigenous men are trying to overcome the negative and toxic masculinities that have engulfed them. Indigenous men lead in various categories indicative of the social conditions they have to overcome. As some Indigenous men become aware of the forms of violence and hierarchy they are reproducing, they strive for change by creating pathways for themselves and others to address their issues so they can turn their lives around and become positive, contributing members of their families and communities. Some communities and organizations have started to institute programs designed specifically for Indigenous men, typically in relation to men's roles in reducing incidents of violence against women. The growing number of initiatives by Indigenous individuals and communities that are committed to creating healthy men coincides with an increased number of researchers focused on detailing and assessing these initiatives to determine their effectiveness in counteracting toxic masculine behaviours and creating spaces for the expression of multiple masculinities (Tengan 2014; Anderson et al. 2015). The act of transforming the lives and behaviours of Indigenous men is an act of decolonization.

Indigenous men's lives are complicated by multiple and varied factors, and Indigenous masculinities studies scholars, like Indigenous studies scholars in general, aim to understand and clearly articulate the intricacies that inform Indigenous people's lives so that we can start to better understand how to regenerate our families and communities in positive ways. As Heidi Stark notes in Chapter 4 and as Kim Anderson and Jessica Ball explain in Chapter 9, representations of Indigenous identity and experience, such as the archetypal Indigenous man/woman, exist in a broad range of cultural and political forms that merit critical engagement. Thus, another important way to explore these intricacies is through the study of film that engages the intersection of issues in Indigenous lives in a tangible and accessible medium.

Indigenous Film Studies

Film scholarship about the representations of Indigenous peoples in visual media has abounded since the 1980s (e.g., Bataille and Silet 1980, 1986; Kilpatrick 1999; Aleiss 1991, 1995, 2005; Pavlik, Marubbio, and Holm 2017; Bird 1996; Buscombe 2006; Casebier 1991; Diamond 2010; Hilger 1995; Howe and Markowitz 2013; Marubbio 2006; Rollins 1998). Scholarship about the self-representation (Bataille and Silet 1980, 1986; Kilpatrick 1999; Aleiss 1991, 1995, 2005; Pavlik et al. 2017; Bird 1996; Buscombe 2006; Casebier 1991; Diamond 2010; Hilger 1995; Howe and Markowitz 2013; Marubbio 2006; Rollins 1998) of Indigenous peoples in Indigenous-directed films is also rich and comprehensive.[8] Seneca scholar Michelle Raheja's *Reservation Reelism: Redfacing, Visual Sovereignty, and Representations of Native Americans in Film* offers distinct theoretical avenues that include redfacing, the virtual reservation, and visual sovereignty. Redfacing is the act of performing Indigeneity by all actors whether or not they are Indigenous, though this is not synonymous with self-representation. Redfacing was an important development because it "allowed Native directors and performers to exercise agency in participating in image production at the same time it revealed the powerful hegemonic forces Hollywood exerted in controlling those images" (Raheja 2010, 22).

The virtual reservation is an epistemological site in and through which Indigenous knowledges are privileged over tired stereotypes and, more importantly perhaps, where "Indigenous people recuperate, regenerate, and begin to heal. . . . It is a decolonizing space" (Raheja 2010, 149). The decolonizing space that is the virtual reservation is an Indigenous aesthetic that Freeland deploys in *Drunktown's Finest*. As a Diné filmmaker, Freeland's gaze is the epitome of visual or cinematic sovereignty, concepts that film scholars continually refine.

Joanna Hearne (2012, 15) connects Raheja's theoretical tenant of visual sovereignty with others that have come before and offers a definition of visual sovereignty or cinematic sovereignty as "an expansive framework that creates a critical space to privilege a range of Indigenous aesthetic strategies and access to traditionality in a political world."[9] The characters Sick Boy and Felixia are at once protagonists and allegories for Diné cultural and political identities, and their transformation to embody Indigenous epistemologies, or traditionalities, are recognized through k'e (kinship), Nádleehí (third gender), and Kinaaldá. These epistemologies are necessary to Raheja's notion of visual sovereignty, and when employed in film they effectively correct misrepresentations found in many other films and media. She says visual sovereignty is "a practice that takes a holistic approach to the process of creating moving images that locates Indigenous Cinema in a particular historical and social context while privileging tribal specificity" (Raheja 2010, 194). We embrace Raheja's challenge to approach film "through the lens of a particular Indigenous epistemic knowledge . . . on the virtual reservation" (Raheja 2010, 148). Although she demonstrates the prophetic as epistemic knowledge in her analysis,[10] we anchor our work through the lenses of critical Indigenous masculinities scholarship and the Diné epistemology of becoming Kinaaldá.

In addition to Raheja's and Hearne's work, film criticism has considered the growing body of nation-specific cinema (e.g., Peterson 2011). Specifically, Randolph Lewis's "New Navajo Cinema" identifies common tropes among the work of three Diné filmmakers: Larry Blackhorse Lowe, Nanobah Becker, and Bennie Klain. Lewis asserts that "the preservation or restoration of familial ties, cultural continuity, Native language, individual wellness, and tribal land" are crucial. He further notes that these filmmakers' work reveals their deep connection to a "politics of geography" of "their ancestral landscape" (Lewis 2010, 57), which is not necessarily the case for two of the principal characters in *Drunktown's Finest*. Sick Boy and Felixia do not see the value in their land and home and seek ways to leave, but ultimately the end of the movie suggests they both come full circle and stay. Like others, Lewis also recognizes the "cinema of sovereignty" to suggest that Indigenous films are "the embodiment of an insider's perspective, one that is attuned to cultural subtleties in the process of image making as well as in the final image itself" (Schweninger 2013, 180). *Drunktown's Finest* exemplifies verisimilitude by offering not just a Diné-centric film, but one that also centres a trans woman. Writer and director Sydney Freeland has been very open in online venues where she discusses her process of making this Diné-centric film and its subtleties:

> The grandma and grandpa characters represent the more traditional aspects of Navajo culture. And one of those aspects includes the concept of 3rd and 4th genders.[11] The mindset on the reservation tends to be more conservative, but because this is part of the culture, it made perfect sense that they would be accepting of Felixia. . . . Now here is the ironic part—I grew up on the reservation but had no idea about this aspect of Navajo culture. The first time I really heard about it was when I moved to San Francisco. I met a trans woman who, when learning that I was Navajo, was like "Wow, the reservation must be so loving and accepting of the trans people!" I didn't know what she was talking about at the time, but I was able to research and learn more about this. It ended up that I had to move to San Francisco to learn about my own culture. . . . I am a member of both the Native community and the LGBT community. (Wissot 2014)

Freeland's own self-discovery has manifested into an accessible film that youth and adults alike can learn and grow from. Freeland aims to promote the survival of Diné epistemologies, because her personal story of finding out about Nádleehí, albeit in San Francisco, highlights issues around the ongoing Diné diaspora, which is a direct result of fleeing what is akin to a Diné dystopia on the rez. At stake for Freeland is confronting through fiction the aggressive, conservative Christian heteronormative ideologies that colonization perpetuates by showing acceptance of Nádleehí identities, and complicating what it is to be a man or male in the context of Indigenous identities. The trajectory and transformation of Freeland's life inform the storylines in *Drunktown's Finest*, and while this chapter does not explicitly engage in debates about who is Indigenous and what constitutes Indigenous film, we do acknowledge the work of Marubbio and Buffalohead, who write: "As is evident, naming Indigenous film necessarily embeds the politics of Indigeneity . . . and what it means to call oneself, or be called, Indigenous or Native or First Nations" (Marubbio and Buffalohead 2012, 15).

Drunktown's Finest

Freeland's hometown, a border town of the Navajo Nation called Gallup, New Mexico, is the inspiration and setting for *Drunktown's Finest*. Gallup was called "Drunk Town, USA" in a 1980s feature of ABC's *20/20* that focused on the town's alcohol problem. In *Drunktown's Finest*, Dry Lake, New Mexico, is the fictional name of the border town. In the movie, Freeland captures the lives of three individuals, Nizhoni Smiles (played by MorningStar Angeline), Luther "Sick Boy" Maryboy (Jeremiah Bitsui), and Felixia John (Carmen Moore) over four days. They exemplify three archetypes specific to the Navajo Nation: the Christianized, urban-educated "Bible Lady" who wants to be a missionary, the reckless macho thug who wants to be a warrior, and a transgender woman whose dream is to be an international model. Their contemporary stories mirror the monstrous violence that pervades the Diné nation: domestic and gang-related violence, homophobia and transphobia, internalized racism, jealousy and hostility perpetuated by substance abuses, and sexual and gambling addictions.

Jeremiah Bitsui and Carmen Moore as Sick Boy and Felixia in *Drunktown's Finest*.

The film opens at dawn, with the voice-over narration of Nizhoni Smiles. The establishing shot is of the town of Dry Lake, captured atop a hill in fast-motion from the darkness of early morning to just past sunrise. Nizhoni laments why people choose to stay in Dry Lake. Dry Lake is a place name that conceptualizes two disparate realities: although the reservations are legislated as being "dry" the people are drowning in alcoholic behaviour, which Freeland highlights in the opening montage of *Drunktown's Finest*. While Nizhoni's voice sets the tone of the film, the stories of Sick Boy and Felixia are brought into focus to answer her query of why people stay in Dry Lake.

In *Drunktown's Finest,* Sick Boy and Felixia's connection to traditional teachings, to Diné creation stories, is fleeting. The teachings of clan relations (k'éí) and kinship relations (k'é), what it is to be a warrior, the role of Nádleehí, and the implementing of the Kinaaldá are told and taught by Harmon John (Richard Ray Whitman), who symbolizes the characteristics of what Lloyd Lee says epitomizes Diné masculinities. In Diné Bizaad (the Navajo language), the word "Hastiin" means man, husband, wise, and Elder. Harmon is all of these, as well as a grandfather and a medicine man (Hataałii). Harmon could be the shortened form of the word "harmony," which is one facet of understanding the Diné philosophical foundation of hózhǫ́:

> the essence of the meaning of hózhǫ́ could be interpreted as a fixed or constant idea to imply a state of peace and harmony, it can also be interpreted and understood as an ever-changing, evolving, and transformative idea, especially in how an individual applies and interprets its meaning to his or her life. (Werito 2014, 27–9)

Harmon lives by hózhǫ́, and as a Hastiin and Hataałii he embodies Diné masculinities.

Diné masculinities, according to Lee's study, were aimed to ensure "Diné continuance." Lee examined Diné identity and perspectives through interviews with 30 Diné men "whose experiences reflect a combination of Diné thought and an American education" and whose stories inform what it means to be a Hastiin (Lee 2013, 1, 3). He asked them questions of what it means to become a Hastiin in terms of: (1) male development, (2) male performance, and (3) the impact of colonization that aligns with critical Indigenous masculinities frameworks from a Diné perspective. What it means to be a man, in English, does not convey the same message as what it means to be a Hastiin. There are stages in Diné lives, where one is guided by healthy individuals and Diné epistemologies, marked by stories and ceremonies. To transform from childhood to adulthood requires more than reaching an eighteenth birthday. The four-day Kinaaldá begins when girls menstruate for the first time and when a boy's voice changes. Felixia (nor Felix) did not become Kinaaldá through ceremony. Similarly, Sick Boy also did not go through the male Kinaaldá, as is evidenced by his behaviour from the outset of the movie.

In *Drunktown's Finest*, the critical role of K'e, or kinship, is nearly invisible. In fact, the role of kinship, of clans and family, is fragile, and only Felixia depicts this insider knowledge when she is asked, in Diné Bizaad, what her clans are. The Diné clan system establishes relationships and if one identifies as Diné, one should—at the very least—know two of their four clans, per clan protocol. The primary two clans to know begin with one's maternal clan, as Diné are matrilineal and matrifocal, followed by the person's paternal mother's clan whom one is "born for." Where possible, the continuation of the clan introduction continues with the maternal father's clan and concludes with the paternal father's clan, for a total of four clans.

Clan introductions are usually spoken in Diné Bizaad publicly, are often place-based, and serve to establish relations among strangers, which at once secures relatives and fends off forbidden sexual partnerships. Lee (2013, 47) writes: "K'é and K'éí represent the relationship and clanship systems for the people to know and understand their relations. . . . In Diné thought, K'é teaches the people that all creations in the world are intertwined with one another, and no one is alone." Felixia demonstrates her knowledge and understanding of K'éí, which earns her a spot for the Women of the Navajo Calendar (WON is a real-life enterprise; Cooms 2006) swimsuit edition (not part of the actual WON calendar)[12] after two other Navajo women are disqualified for not understanding the basic question posed to them: "Há'áát'íishadóone'é?" [sic][13] (What are your clans?) When Felixia is asked, she does not hesitate to respond—in Diné Bizaad:

> "Shíéí Felixia John yinishyé." (My name is Felixia John.)
> *Her first clan is inaudible.*
> "Tsi'naajinii báshíshchíín." (I'm born for the "Black Streaked Wood
>   People" Clan.)
> "Ma'ii Deeshgiizhnii da shicheii." (My maternal grandfather is from
>   the "Jemez Clan"; some also translate this as "Coyote Pass People" Clan.)
> "Hónágháahnii da shinálí." (My paternal grandfather is from the "One
>   Who Walks Around" Clan.)

Felixia impresses the judges and acknowledges that her "pretty traditional" grandparents raised her. Her grandfather is the Elder named above, Hastiin Harmon, who later tells Felixia the story of the Nádleehí, as she decides whether or not to leave Dry Lake for New York City, ostensibly to pursue her dreams of becoming an international model, financed by a client who found her on Facebook. Nádleehí means "one who is constantly changing" or simply "changing," as in Asdzáá Nádleehé, the female deity Changing Woman of the Diné Creation stories[14] (introduced at the beginning of this chapter). Though Felixia knows her four clans, this scene is indicative of the loss of cultural knowledge by young Navajos who have embraced Western constructs of beauty, including Felixia. Felixia's hair is dyed strawberry blonde and the judges ask her if she'd change her hair back to its original colour if chosen for the WON calendar. Still not recognizing her own complicity in embracing the erasure of Diné notions of hózhǫ (beauty/balance/harmony), she eagerly agrees to do so because she'll do anything to become a model. Though reviewed relatively favourably, some viewers do not catch the Diné cultural nuances in *Drunktown's Finest* (see Denetdale 2015; Sujsik 2015; Edwards 2014; Gatewood 2014; Graver 2015; McDavid 2014; Solis 2015) that are rooted in the Diné language.

Sick Boy has custody over his younger sister, Max, whom we meet sitting on the steps to his apartment, practising her Diné vocabulary. Sick Boy is just now coming home, after a night spent in jail, and helps her with the flash cards and gives her a mnemonic device on how to maintain certain words, which reveals his own command of Diné Bizaad. This loving scene with his sister is in stark contrast to many others in the film, where his toxic, hegemonic masculinity prevails. Further to this, the film never discloses Sick Boy's knowledge of k'é or k'éí, hinting at the rupture of Diné epistemologies through his own self-inflicted sicknesses (hence his name). When Sick Boy leaves Max on the porch and joins his wife, Angela, he asks why Max is wearing Navajo jewellery and Angela relates that Max has begun her transition from childhood to womanhood through beginning her menses on this very day. Sick Boy reveals his ignorance of the Kinaaldá by wanting to delay the ceremony for a few months. Angela, angry and frustrated with him, tells him that they have to begin and complete the Kinaaldá in the first four days of Max's first period. Sick Boy grimaces and exclaims: "woah, way too much information!" As Max's closest male relative, he has responsibilities to uphold for her Kinaaldá, but his own state of sickness and his lack of cultural knowledge prevent this. His response shows his internalization of the patriarchal view of a woman's period as disgusting and dirty, which is in contrast to hózhǫ́.

Today in Navajo land, the female Kinaaldá is practised regularly, but few know that there are puberty ceremonies for boys that Diné practice. They are also dictated by the stories from the Diné Creation narratives. Asdzą́ą́ Nádleehé's twin sons, Naayéé' Neezghání (Monster Slayer) and Tó Bájísh Chíní (Child Born for Water), are said to be the first two to partake in the male Kinaaldá. Through the Kinaaldá, the one who is changing faces challenges that are to prepare them for life (Toledo-Benalli 2003). Whether male or female, the person must rise before the sun and run towards the east, further each time to learn stamina and endurance and to build strength; the young man or young woman must also learn cultural and life teachings throughout the four-day ceremony. Furthermore, girls must grind corn and keep busy all day long; boys, on the other hand, must endure a purification táchéii/sweat and consume a cleansing herbal tea. Lee (2013, 53) says the main teaching for males, through a two-part ceremony, is to "acquire the necessary skills to live in this world and ensure the community's well-being." Lee's study reveals that not many Diné men undergo their own Kinaaldá, and the majority of young men are not learning the life skills needed through ceremony. This poses the question: then how and what are they learning?

In the film, Luther's mother is not depicted as a matriarch, but rather as a woman struggling with her own addictions while in an abusive relationship, exemplifying Luther's comment quoted at the outset of this chapter. She doesn't pass on teachings of becoming Kinaaldá; rather she models what it is to become a drunk, stuck in Dry Lake. There is no mention of his father, or of other healthy adult relatives to guide him towards adulthood. He, like many Indigenous male youths, is forced to learn about what it means to be an Indigenous man from friends, many of whom have learned their understanding of maleness from their dysfunctional and/or absentee male and female relatives who are suffering from intergenerational colonial trauma. Indigenous masculinities are simplified to conform to a singular type of masculinity that adheres to the white supremacist model of heteronormative patriarchy, and this model is reinforced through institutions (such as education, social agencies, media, jail, and the army) and by face-to-face interactions with white people (Innes 2015, 53). The challenges that the film's protagonists undergo are not induced by relatives through the Kinaaldá for didactic purposes, but rather they result from the ongoing colonialism and systemic violence brought on by heteropatriarchal ideologies that have been internalized.

Sick Boy is depicted as careless and abusive of alcohol. He is also a womanizing, violently aggressive deadbeat dad-to-be. He is depicted as a party animal, and is friends with the local drug dealers. For these reasons, Sick Boy is actually hoping to enlist in the army, so that he can become what he sees as a warrior, in order to clean up his act, provide for his growing family, and leave the rez behind, as if the rez is the source of his oppression rather than settler colonialism. His toxic behaviour typifies the internalization of the white supremacist heteronormative patriarchy by Indigenous males.

When Sick Boy meets Hastiin Harmon for the first time, he introduces himself as Luther Maryboy, which was the name given to him at birth. His reverence for the Hataałii (a medicine man, cultural practitioner) is noted and reciprocated in teachings about being a warrior. Harmon John is not only conducting the Kinaaldá ceremony for Max and her family, he is also the sole person preparing for the ceremony by chopping the wood (which male relatives of the family should be doing) when they meet. While Harmon takes a break from chopping wood, Luther "Sick Boy" tells him he is joining the army. Harmon asks Sick Boy:

"So, you wanna learn what it is to be a warrior?"

Sick Boy responds: "I never thought of it like that, but I guess . . . yeah."

Hastiin Harmon responds that there are two things that make one a "true warrior": knowing how to fight for and protect those who cannot defend themselves, and "the mark of a true warrior is one who knows when to retreat." Sick Boy is taken aback and mocks this teaching: "Retreat, man, how's that a good thing? It's like losing!" Losing and self-invoked defeat are not in line with Sick Boy's understanding of warriorism, for retreating is viewed as backing down or chickening out and is something that "real" Indigenous men/warriors don't do. Unfortunately, this strategy for living has resulted in many Indigenous men becoming caught in the recidivist cycle inherent to the corrections system.

It remains unclear in the film exactly what Sick Boy believes constitutes a warrior, but he ultimately listens to Hastiin Harmon and retreats instead of joining Julius (Kiowa Gordan) and Ruckus (Naát'áanii Nez Means) in an armed robbery. Julius and Ruckus would have considered Sick Boy's retreat as chickening out because he is scared. However, instead of robbing a store, Sick Boy chooses to run at dawn with his sister Max on the last day of the Kinaaldá, towards the east, making the transformation to adulthood with her. He demonstrates that he, too, is becoming Kinaaldá and transforming from Sick Boy to Luther, which is on the pathway towards hózhǫ́ and not to jail, as his friends, Julius and Ruckus are, as they do get caught and arrested at the very same time the family is running eastward in ceremony.

Felixia is a transgender woman (as is the actress, Carmen Moore, who plays the part), and she seeks love, respect, and recognition amid the capitalist, patriarchal, heteronormative ideologies that pervade the Navajo Nation. She accepts cash from Navajo men for sexual services, and we first meet her in the front seat of a family van, getting a blow job from a john (jáahn). Later in the film, this same man is too ashamed to be seen with Felixia in public. In another instance, Felixia calls Julius in response to his eager anonymous Facebook message and they spend the night together. By morning, Julius does not want to have anything to do with Felixia and has to be reminded to pay for her services. He takes out a roll of money, flips her cash, and tells her to be gone by the time he gets out of the shower. These two instances epitomize the ostensibly straight men's covert desire and their overt disdain for Felixia.

In his analysis of colonial masculinity, Scott Morgensen recognizes that these normalized ideologies "enforce colonial masculinity and whiteness" and put transgender individuals in further danger and "exposure to colonial, racist, gendered, and sexual violence." He continues:

> With respect to Indigenous peoples, just as heterosexuality helped white settlers enforce colonial masculinity and whiteness, its adoption by Indigenous communities served as a further tool of colonization by turning them into policing agents for a patriarchal and now *heteronormative* settler society. Modern notions of sexuality, and of heterosexuality in particular, appear to be crucial aids to European colonization. (Morgensen 2015, 53)

The internalization of Western views of sexuality forces Indigenous transgender, queer, and gender non-conforming people to the margins, susceptible to violence and shaming from community members.[15] Felixia has late-night sexual rendezvous with "straight" Diné men who later ignore her in public. They do not want to be seen or associated with her as they believe it will damage the heteronormative masculinized images they have constructed and performed as husbands, fathers, or gang members. The Diné men who are sexually attracted to Felixia must disassociate themselves from her to protect themselves for fear of being accused of losing their manhood, which encompasses asserting a heteronormative persona.

Felixia's experience is similar to those described in a focus group interview with two-spirit men in Winnipeg for the Bidwewidam Indigenous Masculinities project. Participants spoke about secret sexual rendezvous they had with "straight-acting" Indigenous men on their reserves in Manitoba. One participant explained that he had many rendezvous with one particular young man who was considered the reserve's star hockey player. Their last rendezvous was discovered. The participant, who identified as a male in the interview but acknowledged that he presents as female, explained that community members were angry at him because they believed that he seduced the naive hockey player. The result was that he had to leave the reserve to get away from the hostility directed at him. The hockey player was excused for his indiscretion as it was "not really his fault." The fallout not only justified the need for secret rendezvous but reinforced what the penalty is for not conforming to heteronormative behaviours, and it demonstrates one way in which patriarchy deems masculine traits in males as superior to feminine traits. Similarly, in *Drunktown's Finest* the fear of repercussions for being caught having sexual encounters with Felixia guides how men from her community treat her in public and highlights the ways in which the lives of gender non-conforming individuals are affected by those fears.

While modernity and colonization have taught hate and intolerance, teachings from the Diné Creation oeuvre provide a counter-narrative and offer different attitudes towards transgender individuals (Silversmith 2013). On the third day of the Kinaaldá, Grandpa Harmon learns of Felixia's imminent departure when he finds her e-ticket to New York in the printer. This prompts him to share a version of the separation of the sexes and the role of Nádleehí from the Navajo Creation emergence stories:

> Long time ago, all Navajo lived alongside the great river: The men, the women, and the Nádleehí. One day they began to argue over who was more important than the other. The men said they were, because they hunted. And the women

said they were, because they tended the crops. On and on they argued until finally, they decided maybe they were better off without each other. The men rafted across the great river and they took the Nádleehí with them. And for a while everything was fine; then the men begin to miss their wives and children, but they were too proud to go back. So, they sent the Nádleehí back to check on things. And the Nádleehí returned with the message: that things weren't so well with the women and that they missed the men and that they had no one to hunt for them. It became apparent both sides needed each other; the men needed the women and women, in turn, needed the men. And they both needed the Nádleehí. To this day we carry this lesson. This balance. And I know you, you struggling with acceptance and this world can be cold and hard on our people. But, you must always remember: wherever you go, whatever you choose to do, you always have home here. This place, for you.

Felixia becomes aware that she personifies and embodies the balance that is needed in this world. She has a place as Nádleehí. As Jennifer Nez Denetdale notes: "'There is an indication that there have always been multiple genders in societies including the Navajo society.'" Denetdale explains that "What's important about the current issues facing Navajo LGBTQ is the significance of the creation stories, in which they draw upon the story of Nadleeh [sic] to validate their places in society" (Silversmith 2013). Grandpa Harmon asks if Felixia will be part of the final night of the Kinaaldá, which commences with the pre-dawn run, washing, and moulding of the young girl and symbolizes her transformation from girl to woman. Felixia initially says she will be on her way to New York, but at the end of *Drunktown's Finest*, Felixia has dyed her hair back to natural black and chooses to help her grandma in the kitchen with making fry bread for the final feast. Her physical transformation and self-acceptance as a Diné woman is indicative of becoming Kinaaldá.

Diné historian Jennifer Denetdale's critique of the film takes aim at the loftiness of art and at refocusing our gaze on the hopelessness that pervades contemporary border towns like Gallup (Dry Lake):

> In hopes of redeeming her hometown, Freeland ends her film with the trope of finding healing and redemption in tradition and culture. When Native peoples are traumatized, they need only channel tradition and healing will begin. . . . Sometimes art is about making us feel good so we don't have to do anything about a problem that seems insurmountable. (Denetdale 2015)

Of course, Indigenous people address their trauma and begin the difficult process of healing in many ways. The concerted effort to impose hegemonic masculinity was meant to erase the multitude of masculinities that were expressed in Indigenous cultures. However, there are still people within Indigenous communities who have retained the cultural knowledge that can assist in healing, as exemplified by Hastiin Harmon. As a result of over 40 years of cultural revitalization, a significant number of Indigenous people are looking to traditional ways to recover from their trauma.

Indigenous knowledge has traditionally been transmitted through ceremony and storytelling. Visual media are another way to tell such stories. *Drunktown's Finest* universalizes problems faced by everyday people who can turn to collective memory, or ancestral memory as previous scholars[16] have grappled with, to relearn, reclaim, and reframe what it means to be Indigenous. Denetdale puts it this way, "In this way, our ancestors' memories become our memories, and we become part of the vehicle of oral history. . . . Native American perspectives on the past focus on the creation as a time of perfection, and the narratives become instructional tools about how to return to those philosophies and values" (Denetdale 2014, 74).

The film does not reflect the ongoing work that citizens and community members of the real community of Gallup are doing to restore their defamed image, from grassroots efforts to sustain the local treatment centre to the tourist industry installing new running pathways and marketing Gallup as a recreation hotspot (Colorado School of Public Health 2017). Not surprisingly then, there are also a plethora of programs throughout Canada that employ traditional philosophies in dealing with Indigenous male dysfunctions, dealing with victims of violence or perpetrators of violence, such as the Native Youth Sexual Health Network, kizhaayanishinaabeniin: I'm a Kind Man, Warriors Against Violence, the Moose Hide Campaign, and the Dudes Club.[17] The healing process is long and difficult since much of it involves countering the internalization of the white supremacist heteronormative patriarchy. Commencing the healing process is not the end of the story but the beginning. For Indigenous men, they must face their fears of living up to an imposed foreign notion of masculinity and their shame of what has been done to them and what they have done to others. For Felixia and Sick Boy, like many who have been damaged by Western ideals of masculinity, the end of the movie is actually the beginning of their long journey to recovery.

The *mise-en-scène* at the end of *Drunktown's Finest* is a shot that focuses on an eagle circling overhead. Hataałii Harmon fixes his eyes upon it and tells Luther, Nizhoni, and Felixia that brother eagle's visit means that "it's a sign of good things to happen." The scene cuts to Max's emergence from the hogan for her final run of the ceremonial Kinaaldá; Max is followed by her family of supporters, which includes Luther. Shortly after he emerges from the hogan, he stops and turns to share a loving glance with Angela Maryboy, who is carrying their unborn child, that speaks volumes as her smile conveys the hope of good things to come. Behind her, framed by the doorway, which is draped with a Diné woven rug, is Grandma Ruth.[18] They approvingly watch Luther and the family run east, towards rebirth and renewal. The Kinaaldá ceremony frames this film and it symbolically transforms one from childhood to adulthood, while conveying positive teachings through hard work, enabling them to become Kinaaldá.

Drunktown's Finest highlights the transformational possibilities that visual sovereignty affords to characters whose lives have been profoundly affected by internalized colonialism. Through their stories, they challenge mainstream notions of heteronormative masculinity by performing active Indigenous presence that subverts stereotypes and strives for inclusivity, love, and acceptance, and for good things to come for Indigenous people and communities. Approaching *Drunktown's Finest* using critical Indigenous masculinities and Indigenous film studies allows us to see how internalized toxic Indigenous masculinity, as shown through Freeland's characters, Sick Boy and Felixia, can be transformed and expressed in a multiplicity of ways.

Discussion Questions

1. What is visual or cinematic sovereignty, and how exactly does it correct misrepresentations in *Drunktown's Finest*?

2. The Kinaaldá is both ceremony and metaphor in this chapter. How do you understand positive transformative changes?

3. The recognition and acceptance of Nádleehí is particular to the Diné. Identify some mainstream practices of adopting similar ideologies for positive, inclusive change.

4. What are the two areas critical Indigenous masculinities scholars explore?

5. How are those areas applied in the analysis of *Drunktown's Finest*?

Recommended Reading

Driskill, Qwo-Li, Chris Finley, Brian Joseph Gilley, and Scott Lauria Morgensen, eds. 2011. *Queer Indigenous Studies: Critical Interventions in Theory, Politics and Literature.* Tucson: University of Arizona Press.

Innes, Robert Alexander, and Kim Anderson, eds. 2015. *Indigenous Men and Masculinities: Legacies, Identities, Regeneration.* Winnipeg: University of Manitoba Press.

Lee, Lloyd, ed. 2014. *Diné Perspectives: Revitalizing and Reclaiming Navajo Thought.* Tucson: University of Arizona Press.

Nibley, Lydia, dir. and prod. 2010. *Two Spirits* (65 minutes). Riding the Tiger Productions.

Raheja, Michelle. 2010. *Reservation Reelism: Redfacing, Visual Sovereignty, and Representations of Native Americans in Film.* Lincoln: University of Nebraska Press.

Notes

1. Non-Navajo anthropologist Charlotte Johnson Frisbie cites Father Berard Haile's translation of the word "kinaaldá" (Frisbie 1967, 8). He divides the terms of "kin" (house) and "naaldá" (to sit), which Casey Watchman (2018), a certified Navajo interpreter who works for the Diné Nation in the judicial system, says is not accurate. Watchman cautions from breaking the word up into components: "Kinaaldá is the person who becomes Kinaaldá after achieving puberty. Kinaaldá is also the ceremony itself." To claim that this is an isolated time (when the girl sits alone in a house/hogan)—"house sits"—is a grave misunderstanding of the communal involvement of Kinaaldá, which depends on all members of one's family, male and female alike.

2. The term "white supremacy" has been taken to apply to extremist groups such as the Ku Klux Klan and neo-Nazis who explicitly espouse white racial purity. Andrea Smith puts forward a model that positions white supremacy in a much larger context. Smith (2006, 1) proposes "the 'Three Pillars of White Supremacy.' This framework does not assume that racism and white supremacy is enacted in a singular fashion; rather, white supremacy is constituted by separate and distinct, but still interrelated, logics. Envision three pillars, one labeled Slavery/Capitalism, another labeled Genocide/Colonialism, and the last one labeled Orientalism/War, as well as arrows connecting each of the pillars together."

3. Of a similar phrase—"white supremacist capitalist patriarchy"— bell hooks states: "I started to use White supremacist capitalist patriarchy because I wanted to have some language that will actually remind us continually of the interlocking systems of domination that define our reality. . . . All of these things [gender, race, etc.] are acting simultaneously at all times in our lives. . . . I won't be able to understand it if only looking through the lens of race, won't be able to understand it

if only looking through the lens of gender, won't be able to understand it if only looking at how white people see me. For me, an important breakthrough was the call to use the term 'White supremacy' over 'racism' because 'racism' in and of itself did not really allow for a discourse of colonization and decolonization; the recognition of internalized racism within people of colour." See YouTube interview, "bell hooks Pt 2 cultural criticism and transformation," at https://www.youtube.com/watch?v=OQ-XVTzBMvQ.

4. Connell and Messerschmidt (2005, 832) outline how hegemonic masculinity has been understood: "Hegemonic masculinity was distinguished from other masculinities, especially subordinated masculinities. Hegemonic masculinity was not assumed to be normal in the statistical sense; only a minority of men might enact it. But it was certainly normative. It embodied the currently most honored way of being a man, it required all other men to position themselves in relation to it, and it ideologically legitimated the global subordination of women to men."

5. To date the intersections between critical Indigenous masculinities and film studies are scant. Relevant to our study include the following: Bayers (2016); Dowell (2006); hooks (1996); Marsh (2011); Wright (2016).

6. In 2007, a Native American and Indigenous Studies conference at the University of Oklahoma saw the first panel on Indigenous masculinities, comprised of Vicente Diaz, Lloyd Lee, Ty Tengan, and Brendan Hokowhitu. It is not a coincidence that the panel, "Native Men on Native Masculinities," had three Pacific scholars as this region has been a leader on research on Indigenous masculinities. For example, in 2008, *Contemporary Pacific* published a special issue titled "Re-membering Oceanic Masculinities" highlighting how much further ahead the Oceanic region was compared to Canada and the US in exploring Indigenous masculinities studies (see Jolly 2008).

7. This book emerged out of three panels organized for the 2012 NAISA conference. The panels included one on "Identities" and another on "Queer Indigenous masculinities," as well as a roundtable for dialogue and networking. The participants were from Australia, Canada, New Zealand, and the United States.

8. While outside the scope of this chapter, the debate about defining Indigenous film is also ripe. Schweninger (2013, 5) defines Indigenous film according to auteur theory: "Auteur theory of course places huge emphasis on a single person, usually the director, as the one who creates and controls the film and would clearly argue that for a film to qualify as Indigenous, the director must be Indigenous."

9. Marubbio and Buffalohead (2012, 10) write: "Both cinema of sovereignty and visual sovereignty are aspects of media sovereignty: the act of controlling the camera and refocusing the lens to promote Indigenous agency in the media process and in their own image construction."

10. Raheja suggests approaching film "through the lens of a particular Indigenous epistemic knowledge—prophecy—on the virtual reservation" (Raheja 2010, 148). Her suggestion comes because she analyzes two films, *Imprint* (2007) by Chris Eyre and *It Starts with a Whisper* (1993) by Shelley Niro. Raheja writes: "Native American ghostly images remind the nation of its brutal past, but ironically also give lie to the concerted national effort to render Native American communities extinct. Speaking against these silences instituted by historical uses of the ghostly effect, Native American writers and filmmakers often employ the figure of the ghost as a means to draw attention to the embodied present and future" (146).

11. In Lydia Nibley's 2009 documentary, *Two Spirits*, Wesley Thomas, Professor of Diné Cultural Studies, explicates four traditionally acknowledged genders: (1) Asdzàà, the feminine woman; (2) Hastiin, the masculine man; (3) the Nádleehí, or male-bodied person with a feminine essence; and (4) the Dilbaa', or female-bodied person with a masculine essence.

12. Owner Larry Thompson says the goal of the Women of the Navajo calendar is to promote culture and the Navajo concept of modest beauty. Email correspondence, 26 Sept. 2015.

13. Preferred: "Há'áát'ííshadóone'énílí?"

14. In addition to the oral stories shared among family, written accounts include Denetdale (2007); Zolbrod (1987).

15. The documentary *Two Spirits* (2009) by Lydia Nibley highlights the story of Diné transgender teen Fred Martinez. He was bludgeoned to death by a transphobic racist, a non-Indigenous man and not a community member. Fred's murder happened in Cortez, Colorado, a border town of the Diné Nation.

16. An in-depth, critical integration of "memory in the blood" or "blood memory" is beyond the

scope of this chapter, but see Allen (1999, 2002); Mithlo (2011); Momaday (1968, 1976).

17. See http://www.nativeyouthsexualhealth.com/; http://www.iamakindman.ca/; http://wav-bc.com/home.html; https://moosehidecampaign.ca/; http://www.dudesclub.ca/

18. This is not a critique of the usage of Diné tapestry as a prop (see Soliz 2008, on the exaggerated use of Navajo rugs as film props), but rather a reflection of the reality that many Indigenous households show their Native pride (and presence) through such decorative choices.

9 Foundations

First Nation and Métis Families

Kim Anderson and Jessica Ball

There is nothing more important and precious than family. As Native people, we believe that family is where we start.

—Albert Pooley, National Collaborating Centre for Aboriginal Health, Family Is the Focus National Gathering, 2014

Introduction

Thinking about family as a place "where we start," this chapter will address how family has always been an anchoring place for Indigenous peoples, a foundation for social relations but also for the economic, spiritual, and political systems that sustain them. With a primary focus on Canada, we will examine how the attack on Indigenous[1] children and families has been a key strategy of colonization; dismantling Indigenous families has been the way to grant access to lands and resources for the settler population. We provide a profile of Indigenous families today, demonstrating the legacy of this attack, and discuss how Indigenous family theory and praxis have continued to sustain Indigenous peoples over time in spite of it. As family is foundational for rebuilding and sustaining Indigenous peoples and nations, we conclude by sharing some contemporary practices related to strengthening Indigenous families.

Our understanding of family is grounded in the Cree term "wahkootowin," which can be simply translated as "relationship" or "relation" but holds much deeper meaning. In her book *One of the Family: Metis Culture in Northwestern Saskatchewan* (2010), Brenda Macdougall demonstrates how family, land, and identity are interconnected for Indigenous people. Wahkootowin describes how we are responsible to the web of "all our relations," human, non-human, ancestral. Macdougall (2010, 56) writes:

> In the context of wahkootowin, individuals were taught that who they were could only be understood in relation to others in their family and community, as well as in relation to the environment, the sacred world and outsiders. . . . Importantly, wahkootowin socialized an individual to the proper way of behaving toward all people (oneself included), the land itself, and all realms of existence.

According to the theory embedded in the word "wahkootowin," family involves how well we carry out responsibilities towards all other life forms, and this will determine the course of how life itself is sustained, now and into the future. Family is therefore critically important, as Albert Poole states in the epigraph above.

While drawing on a Cree word for the chapter's foundation, we acknowledge the challenge of writing broadly about "Indigenous families," since First Nations, Métis, and Inuit are extremely diverse, both between and within these populations. For example, First Nation coastal cultures are often matriarchal and have very different spiritual beliefs, languages, and social structures from Plains cultures. Métis people who come from different geographic and socio-historical locations differ greatly from one another and from other Indigenous groups. The various Inuit cultures in the Canadian North are all unique. However, certain common values, practices, and histories can be evoked to construct a cohesive portrayal of the past, present, and anticipated future of Indigenous families in Canada, and much of this is captured by the concept of wahkootowin. We begin by examining the family's historical function, with a focus on First Nation and Métis cultures.[2]

Foundations: Kinship and Historical Indigenous Societies

Historical traditions, values, and approaches are still practised in the everyday lives of Indigenous peoples, but prior to the second half of the twentieth century Indigenous families in land-based communities were strongly kinship-based. Generally speaking, people lived in extended family groupings that allowed them to harvest and share resources through hunting, trapping, fishing, gathering, and agriculture. These groups often changed in size depending on the season and the resources available, as conveyed in this description of the Anishinaabek (Ojibway) prior to confinement on reserves:

> Ojibwa familial units would have looked rather different to an observer at different times of the year. In early autumn, in shallow water areas where wild rice grew, extended-family groups gathered canoes full of grain and processed it for winter use. After the rice harvest, Ojibwa groups both shrank in size and multiplied in number as people scattered to hunting and trapping areas inland from main bodies of water. The more northerly the environment, the smaller the winter camps tended to be, but no group could easily survive without at least two male hunters and two or more women to care for children, process food and furs, make clothing and moccasins, and net snowshoes, among other things. (Peers and Brown 2000, 532)

Peers and Brown point out that the family was "the primary unit of economic production within Ojibwa culture," as it was in other traditional Indigenous societies (Volo and Volo 2007). Because so much of the economy depended on family well-being, marriages were decided based on how the extended family might ensure survival and well-being through resource procurement. Historians of the fur trade have demonstrated that the intermarriage of Indigenous women with traders was considered beneficial to Indigenous communities as well as to traders, since these unions consolidated alliances that served the trade (Brown 1980; Van Kirk 1980). Business was family business, and survival was a matter in which everyone in the family played a part.

Governance has always been managed through families and family alliances in Indigenous communities—this is true even to some extent today. But the Indian Act significantly disrupted systems of governance based on family. In hunting societies such as many Plains communities, extended families were typically led by elder men, and often there were different types of "chiefs"—for hunting, warfare, and so on (Peers and Brown 2000). Métis communities had chiefs and captains of the buffalo hunt, which were organized along family lines. In many west coast societies, hereditary chieftainships were passed to men or women. As leaders of the "house," Indigenous women also held political authority as clan mothers, through women's councils, or as leaders of extended families (Anderson 2016). First Nation and Métis Elders talk about "head women" in their families, women who governed large extended families through the authority they had earned during their lifetime. This authority came from recognition that the elderly women made decisions based on the best interest of the family and future generations, a principle that is evident in a number of Indigenous societies (Anderson 2016). Although elderly women maintained some of this governing role in First Nation and Métis communities well into the twentieth century, as Stark explains in Chapter 4, their authority was greatly eroded by the introduction of patriarchal Western governing systems. Remarking on how women lost the "public function" of organizing the community that existed when his people were more migratory, Saulteaux Elder Danny Musqua has stated, "This damn Indian Act and the control they [government] put upon us, they destroyed the women's place among us!" (Anderson 2011, 101).

First Nations peoples still organize to some extent according to clans, which represent broader kinship ties, both among humans and with the natural world (i.e., bear clan, eagle clan), but these systems have also been disrupted. Historically, clans were led by "head men" and "head women" who ensured adherence to community laws. One law was that people could not marry within their clan, which prevented marriage between "relatives." Indigenous societies often also organized community and stewardship/environmental responsibilities according to clan—one clan might be responsible for overseeing health, others for negotiating with outsiders, and so on. The family and clan one was born into thus prescribed one's greater role in society and the way in which one built family and community into the future (Dickason with McNab 2009).

In Indigenous societies, child-rearing was typically shared in family groups; traditional Indigenous communities were the prototypical model of "it takes a village to raise a child." Children were raised by aunts and uncles, grandparents and great-grandparents, great-aunts and great-uncles. In spite of Canadian state attempts to break these systems down, extended family models also continued to some extent into the twentieth century, as oral historians have noted (Anderson 2011) and as evident in the statistical information we present later in this chapter. Up until recently, although children knew their biological siblings, parents, and grandparents, other members of the extended family could be equally considered a parent, grandparent, or sibling. The names people used to refer to one another are telling in this regard: a child might refer to any elderly person in his or her community simply as "grandmother," Kohkom, or "grandfather," Mosom (to use Cree as an example). Likewise, elders would refer to young people in the community as "grandchild," *Nosim*, and treat them accordingly. In Algonquian and Haudenosaunee societies, similar words could be used to address one's mother and her sisters (nikowi, "mother," and nikowis, "little mother" or "aunt" in Cree), and the offspring of one's mother's sister or father's brother would be considered a sibling. Thus, a child could have many mothers and fathers, grandparents, and sisters and brothers who played intimate roles in their upbringing. Roles relating to discipline, teaching, and play were divided up in a systematic way among kin so that children received comprehensive and balanced guidance as they moved towards adulthood.

Through ceremonies, children were both challenged and recognized as they moved through different life-stage milestones, and these events were grounded in community support. Babies were held and passed around at naming ceremonies, children were collectively celebrated at walking-out ceremonies (first steps), and youth were taught by various community members in puberty fasts and seclusions (Anderson 2011).[3] These practices contributed to children's sense of belonging and responsibility, and are now being revived in many Indigenous communities.

It was considered vital to educate children about their roles and responsibilities in relationships because community survival depended on how well the family worked together and how well they managed their relationships with the animals and the land. Métis Elder Maria Campbell has explained the significance of interconnecting roles within family and community by calling on a diagram shared by her teacher, Peter O'Chiese (see Figure 9.1). Within this system, as Campbell explains, children were at the heart of the community. Everyone worked together for the children's well-being because children represented the future and the survival of the people. Elders sat next to the children because they were their teachers and typically their caregivers. It was understood that elders and children had a special bond, since they were closest to the spirit world on either side. In Campbell's description, women looked after the circle of home and community. It is important to note that women were not merely caregivers or servants within the family. Rather, it was among women's responsibilities to manage the home and community in ways that, as Voth and Loyer observe in Chapter 7, gave rise to important governance principles with applications beyond the domestic realm. Campbell also describes the roles of Indigenous men as protecting and providing for the community; they travelled outside the communities and brought in resources that women distributed and managed. In this system, everyone was thus involved in ensuring the health and well-being of present and future generations. Responsibilities were organized according to gender and age so that everyone cared for all their relations and was also cared for. Certainly, the division of labour and responsibilities described by Campbell was not universal; it varied from community to community or nation to nation. Yet a common thread was that gender and age generally did not carry the same hierarchies as in Western society, and gender was more fluid prior to colonial interference. Reciprocity in relationships was considered important in these systems, and could be seen, for example, in the relationships between elders and children: elders were teachers to children, who were expected in turn to help their elders through taking on physical or other types of work that required their youthful energies and capacities. These interconnecting responsibilities created an elaborate relationship web, and children were raised to know their responsibilities to this web (Anderson 2011).

As noted by Macdougall (2010) in her description of wahkootowin, and as echoed by McGregor in Chapter 11, Indigenous kinship practices and responsibilities extend to all life forms. Referring to Anishinaabe peoples, Amadahy and Lawrence (2009, 116) explain:

> All My Relations is used to honour a concept of family that does not stop with living blood relatives but includes ancestors, the generations to come and a whole host of "spirit beings" that inhabit another realm; all of whom play various essential roles not only in sustaining life on Mother Earth but in facilitating our spiritual development—collective and individual. It also includes, in a non-hierarchical way, the animal and plant life that are a necessary part of Indigenous survival.

This understanding of responsibilities to "all our relations" is elucidated in contemporary research about Indigenous families. In her study of caregiving on the part of Indigenous women in the Northwest Territory, Rebecca Hall (2016, 221) has documented "the expansion of the 'family' beyond the nuclear and through community and kin networks; and the expansion of relations of care to include the land." Her findings demonstrate that "The intimate relationship between land and people, and care and subsistence in northern Indigenous communities is a thread that tightly winds between different time and places" (Hall 2016, 234). The concept of "all my relations," sometimes heard at the end of prayer or giving thanks, thus captures an ethic of responsibility to all life and spirit. This is wah-kootowin in practice. The following section will discuss how such relationships, and thus life itself, have been and continue to be violated for Indigenous peoples through settler colonialism.

Dismantling the Foundation

From the earliest encounters, Indigenous peoples were coerced and threatened by European newcomers to change the way they managed their families. This was not simply because the newcomers didn't like the way Indigenous peoples raised their children. Indigenous family systems came under attack because they stood in the way of settler access to lands and resources.

In seventeenth-century New France, the Jesuits complained that Indigenous children enjoyed the liberty of "wild ass colts" and noted an "excessive love of their offspring" among the peoples they encountered (Miller 1996, 46, 55). This was problematic to the Jesuits because the autonomy and respect afforded to children in Indigenous societies made it difficult for them to "train" and assimilate children through the schools they were trying to establish. These early missionaries had ascertained that working with children held the most potential for converting populations to Christianity, but they were thwarted by the strength of these Indigenous families. Parents were reluctant to give up their children, and women were hostile to patriarchal family structures that would rob them of their power (Anderson 1991; Miller 1996).

Pressures to change Indigenous family systems intensified towards the end of the nineteenth century as Canada became a nation and (European) settlers were encouraged to move west. Rose Stremlau connects the dismantling of kinship to removal from the land in the United States. She describes how reformers during the late nineteenth century campaigned for allotment, the subdivision of tribal lands into individual homesteads, as

a way to dismantle "the kind of societies created by different systems of property ownership" (Stremlau 2005, 276). Kinship systems supported Indigenous relationships with the
land and vice versa, and all of these relationships would need to be dismantled to get rid of
"the Indian problem." Stremlau writes:

> Reformers concluded that kinship systems, especially as they manifested in
> gender roles, prevented acculturation by undermining individualism and social
> order, and they turned to federal Indian policy to fracture these extended Indigen-
> ous families into male-dominant, nuclear families, modelled after middle-class
> Anglo-American households. (2005, 265)

During this period, "field matrons" were sent out by the Office of Indian Affairs in the
US to train Native American women in the ways of Victorian womanhood (Emmerich
1991). Similarly, female missionaries in Canada took on a primary role in trying to convert
Indigenous women to Euro-Canadian standards of conjugality and domesticity (Perry
2005; Rutherdale 2002), and in the early twentieth century, matrons in the United States
used Indigenous women as domestic labour as part of their campaign to "civilize" (Jacobs
2007). Indigenous mothers were infantilized through global colonial narratives and practices that positioned white women as superior in their mothering and thus in a position
to oversee Indigenous women and their children (Jacobs 2011). Indigenous motherhood,
once widely understood as the foundation for governance and authority in Indigenous
communities (Anderson 2007), generally came under attack through the discourses of
domesticity and criminality described by Stark in Chapter 4, which depicted Indigenous
mothers and Indigenous women as dirty, lax in discipline, and in need of training (Carter
1997). Ongoing twentieth-century attacks on Indigenous mothering included subjection
to eugenics and involuntary sterilization, which has been documented as a widespread
policy across Canada and the United States (Ralstin-Lewis 2005; Stote 2015; Torpy 2000),
and which continues to this day as a recent class action lawsuit in Saskatchewan demonstrates (Longman 2018).

With these tools and pretexts, the heteropatriarchal nuclear family was forced
upon Indigenous peoples across North America, as it was in other colonies—a project
that caused disruption and damage to Indigenous men, women, children, and families
(Innes and Anderson 2015). Scholars have linked the imposition of a heteropatriarchal
order to violence on and within Indigenous communities (Driskill et al. 2011). Sarah Deer
writes that rape and sexual violence "are deeply embedded in the colonial mindset. Rape
is more than a metaphor for colonization—it is part and parcel of colonization" (2009,
15). Sandrina de Finney (2015) describes how Indigenous girls and women have been targeted for centuries by colonial institutions, stripped of their tribal rights and leadership
roles, in part because they are essential to the intergenerational transmission of culture
and thus to First Peoples' sovereignty and continuity. Today, Indigenous communities
suffer disproportionate levels of violence (RCMP 2014), which has been linked to the dismantling of families and the violence of colonialism (Bourgeois 2018). The United Nations
alerted the world that Canada is facing an "epidemic" of gender-based violence against
Indigenous girls and women (Anaya 2013). Thousands have had their rights violated, been
exploited, stolen, and murdered (TRC 2015). This violence is connected to violent and ex-
ploitative practices towards the land and runs counter to the principles of responsibility,

accountability, and respect for "all our relations" or wakhootowin (Anderson, Campbell, and Belcourt 2018).

All of these atrocities have been damaging to Indigenous families, with two twentieth-century strategies having particularly devastating and enduring impacts within communities: residential schools and the child welfare system. The attack on children was an emerging settler-state answer to intensified demands for lands and resources as part of nation-building. As McKenzie et al. write, "Although colonial disruption of Indigenous families predated the late nineteenth and early twentieth century, this was a critical time in the formation of Canadian state sovereignty and identity—what would later become the Canadian body politic." They add, "the project to eliminate Indigenous people served and continues to serve those who benefit from the appropriation of Indigenous lands" (McKenzie et al. 2016, 2). It is thus clear that twentieth-century colonialism can be characterized as a prominent and ongoing attack on Indigenous children.

Following long-standing efforts of churches to school and assimilate Indigenous children, the newly established Canadian state formed partnerships with various Christian churches to operate residential schools, beginning in 1879 and operating until the final one closed in 1996 (TRC 2015). Although they resisted, many communities lost whole generations of children; by 1930, almost 75 per cent of First Nation school-aged children were in residential schools (Fournier and Crey 1997, 61). Many of these children were abused physically, sexually, emotionally, and spiritually. Some took their own lives. Many never returned to their communities. Those who did usually found themselves alienated from their families, lands, and cultures. When residential school survivors became parents, many struggled because they had lost their traditional family structures but also had not experienced positive parental role modelling in the abusive institutions (TRC 2015). Residential schools thus disrupted wahkootowin in a way that no earlier policy or practice had done. In the wake of this devastation, child welfare authorities removed the next generation of Indigenous children from their homes in record numbers in what has come to be known as the "Sixties Scoop" (Miller 1996). By the early 1980s, Indigenous children represented less than 4 per cent of the population but made up 50, 60, and 70 per cent of the child welfare caseloads in Alberta, Manitoba, and Saskatchewan, respectively (Bennett and Blackstock 1992).

O'Chiese and Campbell would link colonization, residential schools, and child welfare interference by referring to the aforementioned diagram of social relations (Figure 9.1). In this narrative, men were the frontline of resistance to colonization through warfare and negotiations, and when these lines broke down, women protected the culture and family by resisting change. In spite of these colonial inroads, strong kinship systems and relationships with the land persisted. State authorities thus came to the same conclusion the Jesuits had centuries earlier: the fastest way to overtake Indigenous communities, deal with "the Indian problem," and gain access to land was to assume the education and rearing of Indigenous children. Anishinaabe educator Sally Gaikezheyongai explains that the mass removal of children from Indigenous communities was akin to ripping the heart and centre out of Indigenous worlds (Wemigwans 2002). Once the heart was taken, everything else began to fall away: Elders lost the children they had been responsible to teach, women lost the children they had cared for, and men lost the children they had protected and provided for. This created the conditions for an unravelling of family relations that communities struggle with to this day (see Figure 9.1).

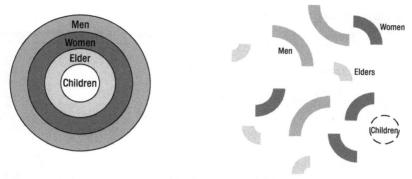

Figure 9.1 Attack on Family and Community Relations

The ongoing repercussions of these colonial interventions as well as the resilience of wahkootowin are evident in our discussion of the Indigenous family characteristics provided in the next section.

First Nation and Métis Families Today

We begin this section with some basic demographic and socio-economic information about contemporary First Nation and Métis families, followed by a discussion of the current quality of life and emerging trends among Indigenous families. While drawing from statistical data we are mindful that, as Tam et al. point out, "What is considered a 'typical family' may differ between people and between cultures" (2017, 243). They ask the question "How relevant is it to define Indigenous families using non-Indigenous family concepts and terms?" and point to the prevalence of complex household memberships, multiple caregivers, different kinship systems, and mobility among Indigenous families (Tam et al. 2017, 244, 246). Taken out of context, data about Indigenous families might easily be interpreted from a purely deficit perspective, while from an Indigenous perspective the data could be read as evidence of the resilience of wahkootowin. Thus, while providing data on challenging trends such as "lone-parent households," "churn/mobility," and "young parenting," we ask the reader to consider the strengths that these practices simultaneously represent and the histories that they come from. It is also important to remember that Indigenous families are diverse and thus not all are represented by the profiles we present here.

Some Demographic Characteristics of Indigenous Families in Canada[4]

Between 2006 and 2016, the total Indigenous population in Canada grew by 42.5 per cent, nearly four times faster than the 10.9 per cent increase of the non-Indigenous population over the decade (Statistics Canada 2016).

The most remarkable trend can be found in the increase in numbers of Indigenous children and families. In 2016, the average age for the Indigenous population was 32.1 years, which is nine years younger than the average of 40.9 years for the non-Indigenous

Table 9.1 Indigenous Populations in Canada, 2016[6]

	Number	% Indigenous Population	% Canadian Population
First Nations	977,235	58.4	2.8
Métis	587,545	35.1	1.7
Inuit	65,025	3.9	0.2

Source: Statistics Canada (2016).

population. The average age of Inuit was 28, First Nations was 30.6, and Métis was 34.7 years old. Indigenous children aged 14 and under make up 27.7 per cent of the Indigenous population and 7.7 per cent of all children in Canada. Indigenous youth aged 15 to 24 represent 16.9 per cent of the Indigenous population and 6.7 per cent of all youth in Canada.

The population of First Nations people living in land-based communities (designated by the government as Indian reserves or settlements) is also rapidly growing: of the 744,855 First Nations people who reported being registered Indians, nearly half (44.2 per cent) live on a reserve or settlement. Statistics Canada indicates that of the total population of 977,235 First Nations people, 334,385 currently live on reserve. (Table 9.1 shows the populations of the three constitutionally recognized Indigenous groups living in Canada.) However, First Nations and Métis people are also highly mobile, frequently moving in and out of land-based communities. As well, the last four censuses have shown a steady migration of Indigenous people to urban centres (mainly Winnipeg, Edmonton, Vancouver, Toronto).[5]

The average household income of Indigenous families in Canada in 2011 (the most recent available information) was little more than one-third of that of non-Indigenous families. First Nations children living in land-based communities are particularly affected by extreme poverty: approximately 43 per cent of First Nations children live in a household with an annual household income of less than $20,000 (Statistics Canada 2011). The 2011 census estimated that 41 to 52.1 per cent of Indigenous children live below the poverty line, depending on criteria for defining poverty and whether estimates are for Indigenous identity (a more exclusive criterion) or ancestry (a more inclusive criterion). A Canadian Press review of 2016 census figures for Indigenous communities found that about 81 per cent of Indigenous families on reserves had incomes below the low-income measure (defined by Statistics Canada as $22,133 for one person). One in four First Nations children in land-based communities lives in poverty, compared to one in six children in Canada as a whole. As a group, half—50 per cent—of status First Nations children live below the poverty line. This number grows to 62 per cent in Manitoba and 64 per cent in Saskatchewan.

Quality of Family Life

While some First Nation and Métis families are thriving, poverty and other socio-economic indicators show that many Indigenous families are struggling. In their literature review and analysis of First Nations child poverty, Brittain and Blackstock (2015, 12) found "the majority of literature links the overwhelming rates of First Nations child poverty to Canada's history of colonial laws that led, and continue to lead, to loss of land, and thus to [a loss of] economic self-sufficiency, loss of language and culture, break up of family and community and a plethora of other negative and enduring effects." Contrary to popular notions, assimilation into the mainstream is not, nor has it ever been, the answer to Indigenous well-being (Palmater 2018). Brittain and Blackstock (2015) call for attention to the structural determinants of poverty, and for self-determined, adequate services that are holistic, multi-faceted, and built out of respectful partnerships, arguing that action in these areas would significantly impact First Nations child poverty.

Drawing from decades of research as well as testimony, the Truth and Reconciliation Commission of Canada (2015) has connected struggles in Indigenous communities with the intergenerational repercussions of residential schooling.[7] Child welfare involvement, which increased as residential schools began to wind down in the 1960s, exacerbated the disruption of Indigenous families that began with the residential school debacle. Indigenous children have suffered a crippling loss of identity and sense of belonging when displaced from their homes, communities, lands, and cultures through these systems (Newhouse and Peters 2003). For Indigenous communities, where "nothing is more important" than children and family, this sustained practice of child removal by agents of the Canadian state has been devastating.

Beginning in the 1990s, scholars began to formulate historical trauma theory, writing about how the trauma of colonization is transferred intergenerationally (Duran 1990; Brave Heart 1998). While this theorizing has been important in advancing social justice, it is important to acknowledge the risks of associating trauma as an affliction of individuals passed down through families. Critics of the discourse on healing and historic trauma note that such a view can pathologize Indigenous people by seeking solutions in individual "healing" while ignoring the ongoing systemic injustices (Maxwell 2014, 2017; McKenzie et al. 2016; Million 2013). A more critical approach takes into account that many Indigenous families continue to suffer from the ongoing and pervasive influences of government policies and inequities in access to supports and services and that Indigenous family life is a function, in large part, of the quality of the contemporary environments in which they are embedded, including economic, political, physical, and social conditions. Risks and difficulties facing Indigenous parents and their children are compounded by ongoing racism, political oppression, environmental dispossession and degradation, and lack of community-based education, health, and family support programs that incorporate Indigenous knowledge or that are relevant to local circumstances (Salee 2006). These conditions produce a very different quality of life for most Indigenous families compared to non-Indigenous families in Canada (Macdonald and Wilson 2013).

Household Memberships

Today, half of all Indigenous children aged 14 and under (49.6 per cent) are living in families with both their parents, either biological or adoptive, compared to three-quarters (76 per cent) of non-Indigenous children living with both parents. Approximately one-third of Indigenous children (34.4 per cent) live in a lone-parent family, mostly with the mother (128,595 with female lone parent; 28,580 with male lone parent) compared with 17.4 per cent of non-Indigenous children who live with a lone parents (Statistics Canada 2016). Lone-parenting is associated with a greater probability of living in poverty (Weitzman 2003). This situation is more likely for adolescent mothers, and among First Nations the percentage of adolescent mothers is seven times higher than it is among mainstream Canadian adolescent females (Guimond and Robitaille 2008).

It is possible, however, that national survey data over-represent the numbers of children living in lone-parent households so care must be taken when interpreting such data. Legal marriage is not an Indigenous tradition, and many Indigenous partners may not be married; many may be re-partnered with a co-resident adult who functions as a father or mother figure for a child; and some adults may report being a lone parent for financial reasons. Evidence also suggests that many families still have extended and fluid family structures consistent with wahkootowin in traditional Indigenous cultures. The 2016 census found that more Indigenous (2.7 per cent) than non-Indigenous children (0.4 per cent) live in "skip-generation families"—that is, with one or both grandparents where no parents are present. In addition, 9.1 per cent of Indigenous children lived in multi-generational families with at least one of their parents and at least one of their grandparents, compared with 3.9 per cent of non-Indigenous children. A further 1.2 per cent of Indigenous children, compared to 0.2 per cent of non-Indigenous children, lived with other relatives in arrangements that did not include at least one parent or grandparent. Relatives included extended family, such as aunts, uncles, or cousins (Statistics Canada 2013). The benefits of these systems are evident, for example, in what Quinless (2013) describes as "networks of care": extended family systems that support young First Nations mothers.

Census and other survey findings as well as anecdotal reports from First Nation and Métis communities and family-serving agencies indicate that many First Nation and Métis fathers are elusive when it comes to family life. This information must be contextualized with statistical data that show that, compared to non-Indigenous men in Canada, First Nation and Métis men experience higher levels of poverty, homelessness, and unemployment (Akee and Feir 2018; Statistics Canada 2016). They also have higher rates of suicide, mental and physical health problems, and injuries requiring hospitalization (Health Canada 2003), and are more likely to be incarcerated. In 2015–16, Indigenous adults were greatly over-represented in admissions to provincial and territorial correctional institutions, accounting for 26 per cent of admissions while representing about 3 per cent of the Canadian adult population (Statistics Canada 2017a). Combined with negative social stigma, media stories, and expectations for their roles as fathers, First Nation and Métis men face formidable obstacles to developing positive and involved relations with their children.

In an inaugural study involving interviews with 80 First Nation and Métis fathers of young children (Ball 2010), the vast majority interviewed reported that three or more of the aforementioned problems create difficulties for connecting with their children, playing a positive role in family life, or sustaining connections with their children as their relationships with their children's mother or others change. Virtually all of the 80 men described past or current challenges with mental health or addictions, and most were struggling to generate a living wage and to secure adequate housing. These challenges, related to the legacy of colonialism, can hinder a significant factor in family life: father involvement. Research about non-Indigenous fathers shows significant correlations between father involvement and developmental outcomes for children, mothers, and fathers (Cabrera 2016; Palkovitz 2002). Father absence is associated with more negative developmental and health outcomes for children and fathers (Ball and Moselle 2007). Grand Chief Edward John of the BC First Nations Summit contends that "Indigenous fathers may well be the greatest untapped resource in the lives of Indigenous children and youth" (John 2003).

As Claes and Clifton (1998) and Mussell (2005) point out, the frequent lack of involvement of First Nation and Métis fathers in their children's lives can be misread as reflective of their indifferent attitudes. There is little acknowledgement in family support programs of the unique challenges faced by these men, many of whom have no memories of positive experiences with a father or father figure in their own lives as children and youth. While there is a trend towards increasing numbers of lone-father-headed households among First Nation and Métis men, few programs are specifically designed to help them learn how to effectively support their children's health and development.

Ongoing Child Removal and the Child Welfare System

One of the dire consequences of the residential school experience and ongoing structural inequities confronting Indigenous peoples is the persistent over-representation of Indigenous children in government care. Exact numbers are difficult to ascertain because each province and territory collects its own data and there is no national database. In some provinces, Indigenous children in care outnumber non-Indigenous children in care by a ratio of 8 to 1, and removals of Indigenous children from home into child welfare custody appear to be increasing. In 2016, an estimated 8,483 First Nations children were in government care. According to the 2016 Census of Population, although Indigenous children represent only 7.7 per cent of the total population aged 0 to 14 in Canada, they account for over half (52.2 per cent) of children in foster care. The majority of Indigenous children in foster care are registered Indians (69.1 per cent).[8] Further, according to Sinclair (2016), "three-quarters (76%) of Aboriginal foster children lived in the four Western provinces.... In Manitoba and Saskatchewan, 85% or more of foster children were Aboriginal children."

The largest study of child welfare investigations involving First Nations children, conducted in 2008 and released in 2011, is the First Nations component of the Canadian Incidence Study of Reported Child Abuse and Neglect (Sinha et al. 2011). The study examined data from 89 provincial and territorial agencies and 22 First Nations and urban Indigenous agencies. The rate of child maltreatment investigations involving First Nations children was 4.2 times the rate of investigations involving non-Indigenous children: for every 1,000 First Nations children living in the geographic areas served by sampled agencies, there were 140.6 maltreatment-related investigations in 2008, whereas for every 1,000 non-Indigenous children living in the geographic areas served by sampled agencies, there were 33.5 investigations in 2008. Indeed, First Nations incidence rates for investigations are significantly higher than non-Indigenous incidence rates in virtually every subcategory of investigation examined in the FNCIS study (Sinha et al. 2011). The study also identified caregiver and household risk factors that contribute to First Nations over-representation, including wellness challenges, overcrowded housing, and poverty. These factors make it difficult for some families to provide adequately for their children's wellness. Child maltreatment has not been found to be a leading precipitant of Indigenous child welfare investigations (Blackstock, Bruyere, and Moreau 2005; Trocme et al. 2005).

In 2007, the Assembly of First Nations (AFN) and the First Nations Child and Family Caring Society (FNCFCS) filed a human rights complaint, arguing that the federal government was discriminating against First Nations children by failing to provide equitable and culturally based services on reserve. A landmark ruling by the Canadian Human Rights Tribunal in January 2016 found Canada to be racially discriminating against 165,000 First Nations children (Blackstock 2016). In its decision, the Tribunal admonished the government of Canada for its continued reliance on an incremental approach to equality that fosters the discrimination and instigated the initial complaint. In February 2018, the Tribunal issued a fifth legal order (2018 CHRT, 4) against the federal government in an ongoing case for equity for First Nations children and families.[9]

The federal Ministry of Indigenous Services has acknowledged serious shortfalls in funding for prevention and early intervention services within child welfare services and across all types of services. The federal government has agreed to a six-point plan, which includes the following commitments: reforming child and family services; exploring the co-development of federal child welfare legislation; giving more focus to early intervention and prevention; supporting communities to draw down jurisdiction; accelerating the work of trilateral and technical tables across the country; supporting Inuit and Métis Nation leadership to advance culturally appropriate reform; working with provinces, territories, and Indigenous partners to develop a data and reporting strategy. As Cindy Blackstock argues, while the reforms would provide some fertile ground for reconciliation to grow, "ultimately the children's best hopes lie with the Canadian public knowing about the federal government's discriminatory conduct and standing up against such discrimination. . . . The best friends of systemic discrimination are public silence and inaction" (Blackstock 2016, 328, 326).

Health Consequences of Poverty and the Attack on Wahkootowin

On nearly every health indicator, Indigenous people experience poorer health than any other population group. In a review of research, Richmond and Cook (2016) found overwhelming evidence of disproportionately high rates of accidental deaths, youth suicides, problematic substance use, and mental illness among Indigenous adults and children. First Nations and Métis children are more likely to be born prematurely, to be diagnosed with fetal alcohol spectrum disorder, to have a physical disability, and to suffer accidental injury. They are 1.5 times more likely to die before their first birthday, and have a higher rate of hospitalization for acute lung infections. Acute-care hospitalization rates among Indigenous children and youth consistently surpass those of their non-Indigenous counterparts. Among children aged 0 to 9 years, the overall hospitalization rate was highest for First Nations children living on reserve (839 per 100,000), which is 1.8 times the rate for non-Indigenous children (478 per 100,000) (Statistics Canada 2016).

Between 2007 and 2010, First Nations adults living in urban areas and Métis adults reported poor overall health and higher rates of chronic conditions compared with non-Indigenous people (Gionet and Roshanafashar 2013). Household food insecurity is much more prevalent in Métis (15 per cent) and First Nations (22 per cent) households compared to non-Indigenous households (7 per cent) (Gionet and Roshanafashar 2013). Related in part to low availability of fresh and more nutritious foods, obesity is rapidly becoming the primary health concern among First Nations people living in urban areas (26.1 per cent) and in Indigenous settlements and on reserves (36 per cent), as well as among Métis (26.4 per cent) (Public Health Agency of Canada 2011). Mortality rates remain higher (and corresponding life expectancy remains lower) than they are among non-Indigenous people (Tjepkama and Wilkins 2011).

Frequent and often serious health problems experienced in Indigenous families cause a chronic sense of living with stress, in crisis, and with grief (Loppie and Wien 2009). Family life is often destabilized by long absences of family members needing health care provided in cities far from home, frequent disruption of family routines in order to travel to health services, and accommodations within the home environment and household routines to meet the needs of a family member with a physical disability, psychiatric disorder, or chronic disease (Ball 2008). Chronic disease, severe and pervasive learning disabilities, frequent illness, and overall poor health of children place enormous burdens on their caregivers in terms of finances, time, effort, competing parenting, grandparenting, and elder care demands in large families, parents' sense of adequacy in being able to meet their child's needs, and parents' overall experience of stress. These challenges are coupled with a widely recognized lack of access to needed screening, diagnostic assessment, early intervention programs, treatment, and occupational therapy programs, particularly on reserves and in rural communities.

Families in Motion

A distinctive feature of life in First Nation and Métis families is their high mobility. First Nations living off-reserve and Métis families move nearly twice as often as non-Indigenous families (Statistics Canada 2006). In addition to the general trend towards moving to cities, First Nation and Métis parents may relocate as a strategy for gaining access to needed resources, including professional services and specialized programs for children with disabilities or health conditions, or education or employment for an adult family member (Ball 2006). Norris and Clatworthy (2006) refer to this high mobility as "churn," noting the difficulties it can present and the effects it has on the delivery of programs, services, and education.

Mark Spowart/Alamy stock photo

Idle No More flash mob protest in London, Ontario, 10 January 2013.

While researchers have called attention to the disruptive effects of family mobility (National Council of Welfare 2007), Indigenous family mobility has also been more positively characterized as "non-random radical mobility" in which Indigenous children "move frequently between the residences of their relatives" (Morphy 2007; Tam et al. 2017). This can be seen as evidence of strength-based family fluidity, broader networks of care, and wahkootowin. Fluidity is evident in considering that First Nation and Métis family units tend to be permeable and family members often are in transition from one home or town to another, one set of relationships to another, or they divide their time among more than one place they call home. Sometimes an adult family member may leave the family unit temporarily or permanently because of difficulties in the primary-couple relationship. The remaining parent may welcome a new partner and one or more of his or her children or other relatives. Families may informally adopt a niece or nephew or even a neighbour. Families in urban centres may expand to include more distant relatives from rural or remote communities who come to the city for school, work, or special programs. The "open doors" found in many First Nation and Métis families, it would appear, are an extension of the traditional extended family structures that were commonplace before colonization.

Putting the Pieces Back Together

As noted previously, many First Nation and Métis families suffer the consequences of the attack on wahkootowin in their everyday lives. Rebuilding wahkootowin involves reinvigorating Indigenous relationships to territory while addressing poverty and structural injustices, all of which involves larger questions of decolonization. At the same time, needs exist for culture-based healing programs related to the residential school experience, education and support for mothers and fathers during the transition to parenthood, infant development programs, quality child care, family-strengthening initiatives, family literacy, community development, employment, and social justice. In this final section, we will identify some Indigenous family programming needs and profile some of the exemplary work undertaken by Indigenous peoples towards strengthening Indigenous families.

Preparation and the Arrival of Family

In terms of overall healing and support for adults who care for children, Anishinaabe investigator Chantelle Richmond and her colleagues (2008) found that First Nations and Métis adults report relatively high levels of social support from within their communities. This is a strength that could be enhanced through funding for initiatives regarding community-led outreach and accompaniment for vulnerable families, children transitioning out of care, partners becoming parents, and adults returning to community following institutionalization.

Relationship violence and peer pressure to engage in health-damaging behaviours are widely understood by Indigenous scholars and others as legacies of colonial disruptions of Indigenous family and community systems (Richmond 2009). Indigenous peoples and organizations such as the Congress of Aboriginal Peoples (2015) have taken up responsibilities for developing culturally appropriate curriculum and programming to address family violence in their communities. The Ontario Federation of Indigenous Friendship Centres has developed the Kahanawayhitowin (Taking Care of Each Other's Spirit) program to address abuse against Indigenous women in Ontario (http://www.kanawayhitowin.ca), as well as the Kizhaay Anishinaabe Niin (I am a Kind Man) program in which Indigenous men learn how to engage in ending all types of violence against women, with one goal being "to re-establish traditional responsibilities by acknowledging that our teachings have never tolerated violence and abuse towards women" (www.iamakindman.ca).

On a broader societal level, Indigenous women have long advocated for attention to the historical and sociological context of missing and murdered Indigenous women in Canada (Bourgeois 2018). Their efforts have resulted in many grassroots, community-led initiatives as well as a national inquiry into the high number of deaths and disappearances of Indigenous women, girls, and two-spirit people (http://www.mmiwg-ffada.ca). A number of initiatives also are geared towards Indigenous men, such as the Moose Hide Campaign, which encourages allies to wear a small square of moose hide as a symbol of support to end violence against women. This idea came to Paul Lacerte, an Indigenous father, while watching his daughter skin a moose along the Highway of Tears in British Columbia (a 720-km stretch of Highway 16 between Prince George and Prince Rupert where many Indigenous women and girls have gone missing). It is but one example of how Indigenous families draw on culture-based practices of engaging "all our relations"—in this case, relations between daughter, father, animals, the land—to create and rebuild safe and healthy communities (Innes and Anderson 2018).

Another critical means of preparing healthy families involves the growing practice of Indigenous midwifery. Birth can be a traumatic event for Indigenous mothers who have to leave home communities to give birth or who give birth in environments that are culturally unsafe (Tait Neufeld and Cidro 2017). The last few decades have seen a revitalization of Indigenous midwifery practices to address these and other challenges. With their determination that birth had to be returned to community, the people of Six Nations of the Grand River opened the first Indigenous birthing centre in their territory in 1996, and the National Aboriginal Council of Midwives now profiles 12 Indigenous birthing centres/midwifery practices on its website (https://aboriginalmidwives.ca). In addition to providing clinical care for women and babies throughout the life cycle, Indigenous midwives are also "keepers of ceremony like puberty rites," and "draw from a rich tradition of language, Indigenous knowledge, and cultural practice as they work with women to restore health to Aboriginal families and communities" (https://.aboriginalmidwives.ca). Some Indigenous midwives are also working to ensure that newborns are not removed by the child welfare system. One such incident occurred in British Columbia, where a group of women stepped into the hospital to form a protective circle around a new mother and baby at risk of being apprehended, enacting, instead, a community model of care and support (Hunter 2018). Indigenous midwifery thus encompasses not just clinical care, but acts of sovereignty connected to bringing forth new life. In this description of Indigenous birth during the pipeline resistance at Standing Rock in North Dakota, Tait Neufeld and Cidro (2017, 9) demonstrate the connections between land, responsibility, and the reclaiming of family practices:

> Midwives and families demonstrated the ultimate in Indigenous self-determination through the birthing of an Indigenous child at Standing Rock reservation during the resistance to the Dakota Access Pipeline. We saw midwives and birth workers supporting women who wanted to birth in a place of tradition

and ceremony, which reinforced a deep connection to land and water. Despite years of policies and practices, which have negated Indigenous maternal practices and birthing knowledge, a reclamation of the value of place and ceremony has been ignited within Indigenous women across the world, as they repossess their rights to protect water, starting with the water inside them.

Early Childhood as a Strong Foundation for Family Strengthening

National organizations representing First Nation and Métis peoples have identified early childhood care and development training and services as priorities within a holistic vision of social development, population health, and economic advancement (see Canada Council on Learning 2007). In its seminal report, *The Circle of Care*, the Native Council of Canada (1990) conceptualized a direct link between culturally relevant child-care services controlled by First Nations and the preservation of First Nations cultures. Cree scholar Margo Greenwood (2006, 20) underscored this link:

> Indigenous early childhood development programming and policy must be anchored in Indigenous ways of knowing and being. In order to close the circle around Indigenous children's care and development in Canada, all levels of government must in good faith begin to act on the recommendations which Indigenous peoples have been articulating for early childhood for over 40 years.

Unlike many high-income countries, Canada lacks a national child-care strategy to ensure access to quality early childhood programs. The current patchwork of child-care and preschool programs includes private, not-for-profit, and government services that come and go, and that tend not to integrate Indigenous culture or pedagogy. With poverty limiting the ability of many Indigenous families to pay for early learning programs, lack of access is more prevalent among Indigenous children: only about 20 per cent are enrolled in any type of program—often Aboriginal Head Start—with lower rates of enrolment in rural and remote communities (Ball 2014). Lack of access has been recognized by the current federal government, which is exploring the feasibility of a national child-care program. However, the federal government has also created a separate silo for Indigenous early learning programs (mainly in the form of Aboriginal Head Start) and it is unknown whether a national child-care program will include First Nation children on reserves.

Many community-based programs reach out especially to families seen as needing extra support to provide adequate supervision, nutrition, and nurturance for their children to stop the cycle of recurrent removal of children by welfare agencies. Some programs reach out to children with health or developmental challenges. Some communities have initiated home visiting programs, parent support, infant care, preschool, afterschool care, and youth programs that include culturally grounded elements and approaches (e.g., Ball 2012). These programs aim to reinforce the positive cultural identity of Indigenous youngsters and their families by using culturally based pedagogy and service models (Preston 2014). For example, program activities and materials often draw on traditional motifs in arts and crafts, drama, dance, and stories and provide opportunities to engage with positive Indigenous role models in caregiving, teaching, and mentoring roles. Many communities integrate or co-locate resources and services that respond to particular local needs, such as parent education, counselling, speech and language services, dental care, and referrals (Ball 2009).

A significant contribution to family strengthening has come in the form of the federally funded Aboriginal Head Start (AHS) preschool programs, although only about 11 per cent of Indigenous young children have access to these programs. AHS programs deliver culturally based, community-specific programs embodying six components: (1) parent/family involvement; (2) education and school readiness; (3) health promotion; (4) nutrition; (5) social support; and (6) culture and language. AHS programs have the flexibility to develop in ways that are family-centred, family-preserving, and delivered within a community development framework. The programs are informed by the communities' internally identified needs and vision for improving the quality of life of young children and their families (Mashford-Pringle 2012). Findings of a study by the Public Health Agency of Canada (Statistics Canada 2017b) built on previous evidence that Aboriginal Head Start in Urban and Northern Communities is successful in producing positive short-term school outcomes over the course of one year of programming (Public Health Agency of Canada 2012), and suggests additional positive impacts on health and education outcomes in elementary and intermediate/high school years.

AHS programs help to fill gaps in services to support families during the early stages of family formation, when parents—many of them very young and with few resources—need social support and practical assistance. Some AHS programs have the potential to reduce the high rates of removal of children from their families and communities. Anecdotal reports in the non-formal literature and at gatherings often describe how the programs help the families of participating children to gain access to food, warm clothing, income assistance, and physical health, mental health, and social services. This is an important aspect of AHS because many Indigenous children do not make it as far as the entry point in mainstream service delivery systems that seem designed to meet the needs of children in middle-class families in urban centres (e.g., families with ready access to transportation, knowledge of how service systems work, enough cultural safety to advocate for their child's service needs, etc.). The potential for early childhood programs to become an entry point for young children and their caregivers, gradually introducing families to a range of other services and opportunities, has been documented in First Nations early childhood programs in BC (Ball 2005).

Nurturing Children and Youth

For older children and youth, long-standing examples of support programs include the Akwe'go and Wasinabin programs operated by the Ontario Federation of Indigenous Friendship Centres (OFIFC). These programs for children 7–12 years old and 13–18 years old, respectively, use land-based activities, participation in cultural events, kinship models, and culturally grounded mentoring and leadership to promote young people's cultural identity, resilience, sense of belonging, and healthy choices (OFIFC 2014). A longitudinal study by the OFIFC demonstrates the increasing value these "at-risk" children and youth place on learning and practising their cultures as they progress through the programs. The children also demonstrate an understanding and practice of wahkootowin by stating that they highly value taking up responsibilities for their communities. Another example of rebuilding wahkootowin is the Gathering at Blackfoot Crossing organized by the Siksika Nation in Alberta. This event is held at a site where Indigenous people have been meeting for thousands of years and where Treaty 7 was signed. It is one of several activities sponsored by the Circle on Philanthropy and Aboriginal Peoples in Canada, which supports activities that connect people with the land and with their ancestors. In events such as these, supporting youth, mentoring, and nurturing and honouring their gifts, talents, and growth are seen as intrinsic to the survival of the community now and in the future.

Bringing Children Home and Recreating Family

Approximately one-quarter of children waiting for adoption in Canada are First Nation and Métis children (Adoption Council of Canada 2009). It is beyond the scope of this chapter to discuss how Indigenous child welfare organizations are developing to serve children and families, but it is important to note that the range of programs and the scope of delegated authority for child welfare vary from cultural consultation to mainstream agencies to a full range of family support, prevention, and early intervention services, as well as foster and adoption placement (Bala et al. 2004; National Collaborating Centre for Aboriginal Health 2017), and efforts are being made by Indigenous communities and agencies to reconnect children with their families of origin and/or with their cultural communities. In British Columbia, for example, the Métis Community Services Society operates a "Roots" program to ensure that each Métis child and youth in government care has a plan that respects and preserves his or her Indigenous identity and ties to the individual's community and heritage. Another Métis program in BC is called "The Circle of Life: Honouring the Spirit of the Family." This family preservation program works closely with families to provide education and support for Métis culture-based parenting, teachings from the medicine wheel, loss and grief counselling, family violence prevention, conflict resolution, life skills, and healing and spiritual growth. A third example is a program called *Nong Sila*, a Lekwungen term meaning "many grandparents, many grandchildren." This program arose in response to the fact that most First Nation and Métis children are placed with non-Indigenous parents and these adoptees risk losing their cultural roots in their communities. The goal of *Nong Sila* is to promote adoption strategies grounded in the needs and cultural traditions of urban Indigenous peoples.

Child welfare policy reforms and expanded funding are needed to create effective systems of in-community placements for Indigenous children needing temporary out-of-home care (e.g., kinship guardians and Indigenous foster care) so that Indigenous children and youth can maintain their identities and not be bereft of family, community, and the life that family and community provide. The practice of "customary care," in which children are placed with relatives, continues to be promoted by Indigenous child welfare agencies as an effective practice (di Tomasso, de Finney, and Grzybowski 2015).

Indigenous people have also used their adaptive capacity to create close social ties in the absence of blood ties. For example, Marlene Brant Castellano (2002, 1) notes that the traditional roles of extended families are sometimes assumed by Indigenous agencies that adapt mainstream practice models to reflect the cultures and needs of the Indigenous people they serve. She describes how some Indigenous adults, working on recovery, are finding their way "home," not by returning to their original families but by knitting together connections in an urban environment with Indigenous people who come from diverse nations, creating "families of the heart." This kinship model is also evident in a story shared by Métis writer Joanne Arnott, who participated in a "traditional parenting skills" program in Vancouver facilitated by "Grandmother Harris," a woman who took on the role of grandmother for younger women and parents in the urban context. Arnott's experience was one of "home making" in which she was able to benefit from kinship support through the program's "family of the heart" (2006).

Conclusion

In spite of the tremendous devastation caused by ongoing colonial attacks on the family, many Indigenous children continue to experience a rich and culturally distinct family life that can provide a strong foundation for development and for life. "All my relations," or wahkootowin, is used to honour a concept of family that does not stop with living blood relatives but includes ancestors, the generations to come, and a host of "spirit beings" that inhabit another realm; all of these relations play various essential roles not only in sustaining life on Mother Earth but in facilitating our collective and individual spiritual development. It also includes, in a non-hierarchical way, the animal and plant life that are a necessary part of Indigenous survival (Amadahy and Lawrence 2009, 116). Between extended families and "families of the heart," Indigenous peoples have worked to meet the needs of children in their communities, and they call upon the genius of their cultures to do so. Growing numbers of Indigenous families are sustaining or reclaiming practices to strengthen individuals and to rebuild families and communities. Naming ceremonies, walking-out ceremonies, puberty seclusions, fasts, and traditional infant care practices (e.g., using a cradle board) reinforce these vital relationships. Indigenous families continue to struggle against systemic poverty, dispossession from lands, practices of child removal, and inequitable service provision, but the resilience of Indigenous family systems and practices is ongoing.

In closing, we share a story told by Lakota scholar John Red Horse:

> The Anishinaabe family drove its station wagon into a tight parking space at the Regional Native American Center in Minneapolis. Everyone in the family above the age of toddler joined in unloading suitcases, folding chairs and bustles. A celebratory dance was being held tonight—the Wild Rice Festival—and the family was there to dance, sing, and visit kin as well as old friends. Once in the building, those family members who would dance this evening went to the dressing area and changed from street clothes to regalia. One daughter carried her 3-year-old son back to the dance area; he was dressed in the regalia of a grass dancer. They got to their chairs, and the mother laid out a star quilt. She put her son on the quilt, and this was the first glimpse that any stranger had of the boy outside his mother's arms. These strangers looked at him with a sympathetic expression. The boy was disabled from the waist down.
>
> As the evening wore on, the strangers were taken aback with the circle of care and concern organized around the boy by family and friends. He was the centre of attention. Elders, including grandparents and older aunts; older brothers, sisters, and cousins; and a host of teenage and adult friends joined together to meet the boy's needs: holding him when he became restive, carrying him around to retail stands, entertaining him with play, and supervising him when his mother was dancing. The strangers beamed with pride because the boy danced in his own way—from the waist up, with head and shoulders keeping time to the beat of the drums. He participated in every inter-tribal dance and entered the dance contest for little boys. (Red Horse 1997, 243)

Like all Indigenous stories, this one has many lessons and levels. The first observation might be that, in many cases, extended family and community still work together, with children at the heart and centre. The significant presence of children in community gatherings comes across here; anyone who has spent time in an Indigenous community will know that children are always around, even in business venues that might be considered off-limits in a mainstream setting. As with stories of fetal alcohol spectrum disorder gathered by the Ontario Federation of Indigenous Friendship Centres, Red Horse's story demonstrates that Indigenous communities often recognize and honour children with different abilities and that cultural activities can be a way of providing them with a place and a way to participate. Red Horse's story, then, is the story of Indigenous families, now and into the future—one of strengths and challenges; of time-honoured systems and cultures; of modern settings, emergent tools, and techniques; of children at the heart and a resolute wahkootowin falling into place.

Acknowledgements

For their helpful comments during the writing of this chapter, we are grateful to Sharla Peltier, Cathy Richardson, John Red Horse, and David Long. We thank Maria Campbell for permission to share her metaphor about the shattering of Indigenous families and communities and John Red Horse for permission to share his story.

Discussion Questions

1. Why do you think family was identified as the most fundamental area of concern and the starting point for healing and hope in both the Royal Commission on Aboriginal Peoples report and the Truth and Reconciliation "Calls to Action"?

2. Who took care of you as you grew up, and how did your early experiences of caregiving contribute to how you view family now? In what ways was your experience similar to or different from the ways that Indigenous peoples may have raised their children in the past?

3. What are Indigenous and non-Indigenous child and family social service agencies in your region doing to contribute to supporting and strengthening First Nation and Métis families?

4. What challenges and opportunities do you see in your community or area of work that may affect opportunities for First Nation and Métis families to a secure quality of life and social inclusion?

5. How might the concept of "families of the heart," described by Marlene Brant Castellano, inspire new kinds of "kinship" networks and communities, especially for people living in urban areas?

Recommended Reading

Ball, J. 2009. "Centring Community Services around Early Childhood Care and Development: Promising Practices in Indigenous Communities in Canada." *Child Health and Education* 1, no. 4: 183–206. http://web.uvic.ca/fnpp/documents/Ball_CenteringCommunity.pdf.

Lavell-Harvard, M., and K. Anderson, eds. 2014. *Mothers of the Nations: Indigenous Mothering as Global Resistance, Reclaiming and Recovery.* Toronto: Demeter Press.

National Collaborating Centre for Aboriginal Health. 2016. *Family is the Focus: Proceedings Summary.* Prince George. https://www.ccnsa-nccah.ca/495/Family_is_the_Focus_-_Proceedings_summary.nccah?id=155. There are also a summary report and DVD of this gathering and others about parenting, fatherhood, and child-rearing.

Rising Baldy, Cutcha. 2018. *We Are Dancing for You: Native Feminisms and the Revitalization of Women's Coming of Age Ceremonies.* Tucson: University of Arizona Press.

Siem'Smuneem Indigenous Child Well-being Research Network. 2011. *Honouring Our Caretaking Traditions: A Forum on Custom Indigenous Adoptions. Proceedings and Stories.* 18–19 Nov., University of Victoria. http://icwrn.uvic.ca/wp-content/uploads/2014/01/Honouring-Our-Caretaking-Traditions.pdf.

Additional Resources

CBC Radio. "163,000 reasons Why Cindy Blackstock Keeps Fighting for Kids." 4 Mar. http://www.cbc.ca/radio/unreserved/unreserved-honours-the-strength-of-indigenous-women-1.3472826/163-000-reasons-why-cindy-blackstock-keeps-fighting-for-kids-1.3476574.

We Can't Make the Same Mistake Twice. National Film Board, 2016. Dir. Alanis Obomsawin. https://www.nfb.ca/film/we_can_t_make_the_same_mistake_twice/.

Redvers, Tunchai. 2017. "Creating Environments for Indigenous Youth to Live and Succeed." TEDx KitchenerEd. https://www.youtube.com/watch?v=zwLR23fHBQU.

National Collaborating Centre for Indigenous Health. https://www.nccih.ca/en/

First Nations Child and Family Caring Society. https://fncaringsociety.com/

The Healing Journey: Family Violence Prevention in Aboriginal Communities. http://www.thehealing journey.ca/main.asp

Indigenous Early Learning and Child Care Framework. https://www.canada.ca/en/employment-social-development/programs/indigenous-early-learning/2018-framework.html

Early Childhood Development Intercultural Partnerships. www.ecdip.org

Aboriginal Head Start in Urban and Northern Communities. https://www.canada.ca/en/public-health/services/health-promotion/childhood-adolescence/programs-initiatives/aboriginal-head-start-urban-northern-communities-ahsunc.html

Aboriginal Head Start on Reserve. https://www.canada.ca/en/indigenous-services-canada/services/first-nations-inuit-health/family-health/healthy-child-dvelopment/aboriginal-head-start-reserve-first-nations-inuit-health-canada.html

Notes

1. In this chapter, we are generally using "Indigenous" to refer to First Peoples in Canada, which include First Nations, Inuit, and Métis, as recognized in section 35 of the Constitution Act, 1982.

2. Our chapter focuses on First Nations and Métis examples. We have not described Inuit families because we are not personally familiar with their distinct family practices and systems. Some of

our Inuit colleagues have explained to us that Inuit people do not relate to people of the "south" but live in a circumpolar world and have more in common with northern cultural groups living in various countries surrounding the North Pole.

3. These examples refer to Algonquian peoples.

4. Each source of data about Indigenous peoples in Canada offers an incomplete set of information because of widely differing sampling opportunities and methods and different ways of asking questions, analyzing data, and reporting findings across data collecting agencies (e.g., Statistics Canada, Indigenous and Northern Affairs Canada, Health Canada, National Indigenous Health Organization). Thus, constructing a picture of First Nation and Métis families' quality of life and their health and development requires a synthetic process relying largely on proxies and anecdotal and non-formal reports, along with a handful of program evaluations that are far from conclusive.

5. In 2016, 867,415 Indigenous people lived in metropolitan areas of at least 30,000 people, accounting for over half (51.8 per cent) of the total Indigenous population. From 2006 to 2016, there was a 59.7 per cent increase in the number of Indigenous people living in a metropolitan area over at least 30,000 people.

6. The number of residents in Canada who report Indigenous identity is considerably smaller than the number who report Indigenous ancestry. Sources of population-level data about Indigenous peoples are often conflicting and contested, and all are incomplete in terms of which populations of Indigenous children have been surveyed. Estimates of Indigenous people, their characteristics, and their life conditions are more affected than most by incomplete enumeration of certain Indian reserves and Indian settlements in the 2016 Census of Population. For more information on Indigenous variables, including information on their classifications, the questions from which they are derived, data quality, and their comparability with other sources of data, refer to the Aboriginal Peoples Reference Guide, Census of Population, 2016, and the Aboriginal Peoples Technical Report, Census of Population, 2016.

7. To find bibliographies and literature on the impact of residential schools, visit the Truth and Reconciliation website: www.trc.ca.

8. See the First Nations Child and Family Services Government of Canada website: http://www.aadnc-aandc.gc.ca/eng/1100100035204/1100100035205.

9. See the First Nations Child & Family Caring Society of Canada's report, "Canada Fails to Grasp the 'Emergency' in First Nations Child Welfare: Canadian Human Rights Tribunal Finds Federal Government Non-Compliant with Relief Orders," at: https://fncaringsociety.com/sites/default/files/Caring%20Society%20Press%20Release%202018%20CHRT%204_0.pdf.

10 Terminating Canada's Failed System of Injustice

Unmasking Colonialism, Redefining Relationships, and Re-establishing Balance

Lisa Monchalin and Olga Marques

> *When Christopher Columbus landed in North America in 1492 there was not one Aboriginal person in prison because there were no prisons. There were no prison guards, no police, and no lawyers and no judges. We simply did not need them because we had a vastly better way. The laws of the people were written in the hearts and minds and souls of the people. And justice was tempered with mercy.*
>
> —Solomon 1994, 80

Introduction: The Continued Failure of the Canadian Criminal Justice System

In his opening remarks to delegates at the 1975 National Conference and Federal–Provincial Conference on Native Peoples and the Criminal Justice System, the Solicitor General of Canada, Warren Allmand, stated:

> We said that we came here to solve some serious problems and I hope that we can move that along today. Some of these problems have been with us for a long time and have been ignored for a long time and we are trying to do something about them. . . . I hope we can set up continuing mechanisms to make sure that what we start here will be carried forward. (Solicitor General Canada 1975, 35)

Attended by governmental officials at both the provincial and federal levels, as well as representatives from various Indigenous groups, the Conference focused on the scope and nature of Indigenous peoples' involvement with the criminal justice system—namely, their over-representation within the system and under-representation as officials and employees. The Solicitor General noted in his final report of the Conference that: "concern over the jailing of a disproportionate number of Canada's native people promoted calling a national conference to consider issues of prime importance not only to native peoples but also to the governments under which they live" (Solicitor General Canada

1975, 3). Echoing countless previous governmental reports, surveys, and inquiries, the Conference produced several proposals for action, or what Jaskiran Dhillon (2017) has described as "neoliberal calls for participation" within mainstream Canadian institutions. These included: increased sensitivity towards the needs of Indigenous peoples; alternative judicial measures for Indigenous peoples who are in trouble with the law; implementation of Indigenous-centric penal programming; and a call for Indigenous persons to be more involved in the planning, policing, and delivery of criminal justice in their own communities.

In 2012, Canada's Correctional Investigator, Howard Sapers, observed that very little had changed since 1975, and that four decades of inquiries into the state of criminal justice in Canada had repeatedly identified the over-representation of Indigenous people in prisons (Office of the Correctional Investigator 2012). Major reports examining the many injustices Indigenous people have experienced at the hands of the Canadian criminal justice system include the 1983 report by the Ontario Native Council on Justice entitled *Warehousing Indians*, as well as the 1988 report of the Canadian Bar Association, *Locking up Natives in Canada*. Serious injustice was also clearly identified by a 1989 Royal Commission examining the wrongful conviction of Donald Marshall Jr, a Mi'kmaw man who spent 11 years in prison for a murder he never committed. The Commission's final report asserted that Canada's criminal justice system had not only "failed Donald Marshall, Jr. at virtually every turn from his arrest and wrongful conviction for murder . . . to . . . his eventual acquittal by the Court of Appeal," but that he had been treated this way because he was Indigenous (Hickman, Poitras, and Evans 1989, 1). The "utter failure" of the Canadian criminal justice system was also noted in the 1991 Law Reform Commission of Canada report. Indigenous participants in that study indicated that "virtually all of the primary actors in the process (police, lawyers, judges, correctional personnel) patronize them and consistently fail to explain adequately what the process requires of them or what is going to happen to them" (Law Reform Commission of Canada 1991, 5). Similar comments by Indigenous people can be found throughout the interim report from the Royal Commission on Aboriginal Peoples (RCAP), *Bridging the Cultural Divide: A Report on Aboriginal People and Criminal Justice in Canada* (RCAP 1995). Four years later, the opening statements in the Aboriginal Justice Implementation Commission's *Report of the Aboriginal Justice Inquiry of Manitoba* (1999) asserted that: "The justice system has failed Manitoba's Aboriginal people on a massive scale. It has been insensitive and inaccessible, and has arrested and imprisoned Aboriginal people in grossly disproportionate numbers."

All of this is to say that over 50 years of commissions, reports, studies, and inquiries have consistently found that the criminal justice system does not provide justice for Indigenous peoples in Canada. Despite government and justice representatives having been very aware of the over-representation of Indigenous people in the criminal justice system during this time, the continued increase in incarceration rates indicates that the situation has been getting worse. This fact led the Truth and Reconciliation Commission to call (yet again) for "federal, provincial, and territorial governments to commit to eliminating the overrepresentation of Aboriginal people in custody over the next decade" (TRC 2015, 3). If the past "commitments" of Canadian governments and justice officials to address this issue are any indication of things to come, there appears to be little hope for Indigenous people in Canada that anything will change for the better in such a short time frame. While it is common to hear critics speak of the need for governments to have the "political will" to effect meaningful change in the justice system, it is clear that the problem with Canada's criminal justice system is much deeper than Canadian politicians having to take more seriously their responsibility to ensure that justice is done in Canada.

In this chapter, we therefore argue that the contemporary crises related to law and justice must be understood as an extension or continuation of colonialism. Rather than locating colonialism as a historic moment, we recognize that all Canadian institutions, including criminal justice, continue to perpetuate the colonial project. Thus, we begin this chapter by providing an overview of the mass incarceration and disproportionate victimization of Indigenous people in Canada—in order to relay the extent of the crisis. We then critically examine the response of the criminal justice system, showing how the over-representation of Indigenous people in the criminal justice system and their disproportionately high rates of victimization are inherently problems of colonialism. This is followed by a brief outline of Indigenous justice strategies, at which point we conclude with a vision for moving forward towards reciprocal and equitable relations between Indigenous peoples and Canada.

The Mass Incarceration and Disproportionate Victimization of Indigenous Peoples

Despite many decades of commissions, reports, and inquiries on the Canadian criminal justice system by both federal and provincial governments, the mass incarceration and disproportionate victimization of Indigenous peoples in Canada has continually increased (Monture 2011). For instance, from 2007 to 2016 the population of Indigenous prisoners in Canada rose by a staggering 30 per cent while the population of Caucasian prisoners decreased by 14.7 per cent; during the same period the overall federal prison population increased less than 5 per cent. In 2017, Indigenous peoples represented 26.4 per cent of the total federal incarcerated population despite comprising only about 5 per cent of Canada's total population. Moreover, for over a decade now the proportional representation of Indigenous women has been the fastest-growing segment of the prison population, so that in 2017 Indigenous women accounted for 37.6 per cent of all imprisoned women in federal institutions in Canada (Office of the Correctional Investigator 2017).

Disparities in over-representation are even higher in Canada's prairie region, a geographical area marked by high concentrations of Indigenous people as well as the greatest relative disparity in wealth between First Nations and the settler population (Dhillon 2017, 11). In 2016, 47 per cent of inmates in the Prairie provinces were Indigenous. The institutions with some of the highest incarceration rates of Indigenous people are currently the Saskatchewan Penitentiary (59 per cent), the Stony Mountain Institution in Manitoba (58 per cent), and the Regional Psychiatric Centre in Saskatoon (61 per cent). Given such drastic over-representation, the Office of the Correctional Investigator (2016, 44) recently referred to some prisons on the prairies as essentially "Indigenous prisons."

Indigenous people in Canada are also disproportionately victims of crime. In 2014, Indigenous people experienced violent victimization at a rate more than double that of non-Indigenous people. Across most categories of violent crime, rates of victimization are higher for Indigenous people compared to non-Indigenous people. For example, rates of physical assault are almost double and rates of sexual assault are almost triple those of non-Indigenous people. There is also a discernible gendered dimension to victimization, as the rate of violent victimization experienced by Indigenous women is almost triple that for non-Indigenous women (Boyce 2016). In 2015, the homicide rate for Indigenous women was six times greater than that for non-Indigenous women (Mulligan, Axford, and Solecki 2016). Indigenous women and girls have experienced generations of physical, verbal, and sexual violence, and such violence has been fuelled by racializing colonial attitudes (Dhillon 2017). As noted by Heidi Stark in Chapter 4, such violence is often rationalized and even mythologized by mainstream culture as a matter of racial or cultural differences, which situates violence against Indigenous women as "natural" and thus a normative part of life in Canadian society.

The extensive number of unresolved cases of missing and murdered Indigenous women and girls clearly indicates that the police and the criminal justice system in Canada have not taken this matter seriously (Hunt 2015). As noted previously, politicians and other justice representatives have been aware of the steadily increasing levels of incarceration and victimization for decades, and yet their responses have remained largely reactionary and individualistic in scope. The Canadian criminal justice system has primarily sought to address all matters of "Indigenous justice" through three institutional arenas: police, the courts, and corrections. This is what we turn to next in our discussion.

The Colonizing Approach to Justice: Police, Courts, and Corrections

Anthropologist Rémi Savard (2003) contends that the Canadian criminal justice system lacks credibility in the eyes of many Indigenous people largely because of the way it has contributed to the systematic dismantling of Indigenous systems of justice. Interviews with 2,614[1] Indigenous people in 11 Canadian cities[2] during 2009 showed that over half (55 per cent) of the respondents reported little or no confidence in the Canadian criminal justice system (Environics Institute 2010). That Indigenous persons who took the survey were more than twice as likely as the general population to have low confidence in the Canadian criminal justice system is hardly surprising given their experience with it. This section explores the roots of this troubling relationship, traces its trajectory over time, and reviews ongoing issues in contemporary approaches to the administration of justice in Canada.

In his introduction to the final report of the RCAP in 1996, Dene leader and RCAP co-chair Georges Erasmus stated that "the roots of injustice lie in history." Mohawk scholar Patricia Monture (2007, 207) elaborated on this idea when she noted that "the past impacts on the present, and today's place of Aboriginal peoples in Canadian society cannot be understood without a well-developed historical understanding of colonialism and the present-day trajectories of those old relationships." Cree scholar Jeffrey Paul Ansloos notes the many ways that Indigenous peoples have been subjected to violence by Canadian society for generations, including treaty violations, racist legislation, abusive policies and practices, and more. He asserts that examining the way violence has impacted Indigenous people's lives both historically and today is, therefore, "essential to any discussion of the factors that lead to their involvement in crime" (Ansloos 2017, 22–3). In other words, any discussion of the highly disproportionate incarceration or victimization rates of Indigenous people must be placed within the context of colonialism.

Since the beginnings of policing in Canada, the state's crime prevention strategy has remained essentially the same—that is, to react punitively to whatever the police and the courts, with some legislative direction, deemed to be criminal. One of the primary reasons the North West Mounted Police (NWMP, which become the Royal Canadian Mounted Police or RCMP in 1920) was formed in 1873 was to address, in criminal justice terms, the "problem" of Indigenous resistance to settler colonization (Fleming et al. 2008, 99). According to Nettelbeck and Smandych (2010, 357), the government established the NWMP to deal with the so-called "obstacle" of Indigenous presence, and its officers were "actively required to ensure the submission of Indigenous peoples to colonial rule." If Indigenous people resisted the imposition of colonial rule they were often arrested, and in some cases charged with "treason." One of the most obvious examples of the criminalization of Indigenous attempts to resist colonization was when parents who refused to send their children to residential schools—and who hid their children so that they would not be detected by clerics and police who roamed First Nations communities looking for children—were imprisoned (TRC 2015).

Given Euro-Canadian support for Victorian ideals of racial superiority, racist attitudes and practices inevitably became embedded within the culture of the NWMP from very early on (Hildebrandt 2008; Comack 2012b). These racist ideals thoroughly informed the policies of the NWMP as well as the practices of its officers, who by viewing Indigenous people as inferior were able to legitimize their prejudiced and discriminatory treatment of them. As Campbell, Cater, and Pollard (2017, 272) note, Indigenous peoples in Canada were "over-policed first by the North-West Mounted Police and then its successor, the RCMP," by racially driven measures that affected all aspects of their operation.

From its origins, the Canadian criminal justice system has been used to assert Canada's jurisdiction over Indigenous peoples as non-violent, lawful processes. At the same time, it has used these same discourses to depict Indigenous assertions of rights and responsibilities to their ancestral lands as precisely the opposite, that is, as criminal acts or domestic threats against national security. Canadian national identity centres much around the imagery of vast unpopulated lands, as well as the "peaceful" ways in which lands were/are acquired and used.[3] However, as Lawrence (2002, 23–4) articulates:

> Canadian national identity is deeply rooted in the notion of Canada as a vast northern wilderness, the possession of which makes Canadians unique and "pure" of character. Because of this, and in order for Canada to have a viable national identity, the histories of Indigenous nations, in all their diversity and longevity, must be erased. Furthermore, in order to maintain Canadians' self-image as a fundamentally "decent" people innocent of any wrongdoing, the historical record of how the land was acquired—the forcible and relentless dispossession of Indigenous peoples, the theft of their territories, and the implementation of legislation and policies designed to effect their total disappearance as peoples—must also be erased.

Other chapters in this collection, including those by Starblanket (Chapter 1), Simpson (Chapter 3), Watchmen and Innes (Chapter 8), Stark (Chapter 4), and Hunt (Chapter 6), highlight that Canada's commitment to repressing and removing Indigenous peoples in order to clear the lands for settlement is absent from colonial depictions of this country's national identity. These authors also note that the promotion of a "purified" version of Canada's national identity narrative has made it much easier for state representatives in all institutional areas, including the criminal justice system, to pursue the colonial goal of eradicating Indigenous peoples in this country with impunity. Furthermore, Stark notes that discourses of criminality functioned to justify the extension of colonial law and authority over every aspect of Indigenous people's lives from the beginning of the colonial project, which legitimized settler-colonial assertions of jurisdiction over Indigenous bodies and lands. These discourses constructed Indigenous women as hyper-sexualized, deviant, and in need of domestication, while also depicting Indigenous men as savage, lawless, and uncivilized. Such representations have been continually (re)produced over time in response to shifting socio-economic contexts, which in the contemporary climate has often resulted in Indigenous people being characterized as homegrown terrorists (Monchalin and Marques 2014). This, in turn, has supported the ongoing colonial imperative of building an expanded carceral network to punish and even eliminate those who are committed to fighting for Indigenous sovereignty or personal agency.

A clear example of the criminalizing of Indigenous people for asserting their sovereignty and protecting their inherent rights and lands is evident in the responses by Canadian government, justice, and policing representatives to Indigenous people publicly challenging the interests of the state and private industry. Relatively recent instances of this happening include (to name a select few): the armed conflict in the summer of 1990 involving Quebec provincial police, the Canadian military, and the Mohawk people of Kanehsatà:ke when the Mohawk sought to defend their sacred burial grounds and pine trees from being taken over for an extension of a nine-hole golf course, during which a provincial police officer was killed; the 1995 occupation of an armed forces base due to a land dispute near Sarnia, Ontario, by members of the Stony and Kettle Point First Nation that resulted in the shooting death of one of the members of the First Nation; the armed standoff with the Canadian military near Caledonia, Ontario, in 2006 when members of the Haudenosaunee Confederacy resisted the development of properties on their lands; the conflicts with the RCMP and Canadian military forces between 2012 and 2014 over attempts by First Nations people and their supporters to protect lands on the unceded territories of the Elsipogtog First Nation in New Brunswick against industrial shale gas exploration. The framing of Indigenous peoples' assertion of their rights as a "threat" to the Canadian nation-state is also evident in government surveillance of those involved in Idle No More activities (Ling 2013) and even in the life of Gitxsan researcher and educator Dr Cindy Blackstock, whose work involves defending the rights for First Nations children in the child welfare system by demanding that the government treat them the same way it treats non-Indigenous children (Amnesty International 2013).

The current crisis of missing and murdered Indigenous girls and women can also be traced back to the deliberate attempts by patriarchal colonizers to destroy the lives of Indigenous women by dismantling their roles within their communities and normalizing the violence against them. As then prime minister Stephen Harper insisted in 2014, these many incidents were not "a sociological phenomenon" but individual crimes—no different from those involving non-Indigenous victims—to be pursued by the criminal justice system on a case-by-case basis (Kennedy 2014). Although the forms of political organization and governance varied greatly between Indigenous nations throughout Turtle Island prior to European contact, many Indigenous communities "generally secured the status of Native women" (Anderson 2016, 33). As Ball and Anderson explain in Chapter 9 of this volume, this often meant that women held higher degrees of decision-making authority and political power within their communities (Anderson 2016). In viewing Indigenous women as a threat to the patriarchal vision they had for their colonial empire, colonizers sought to strip them of their power and remove them from positions of authority in their communities through many different means (Riel-Johns 2016; Gunn Allen 1992). These included implementing the residential school system, child welfare apprehensions, and forced sterilization of Indigenous girls and women (Lavell-Harvard and Brant 2016). Add to these the significant number of unresolved cases of missing and murdered Indigenous women and girls in Canada, and it is difficult to deny that the criminal justice system in this country continues to be a central means for realizing the Canadian colonial project.

Colonial Continuity and Participatory Criminal Justice Programming

Unfortunately, the criminal justice system is operating in the same way in the lives of Indigenous youth in Canada. In her critical analysis of Indigenous–state relations in the city of Saskatoon, Jaskiran Dhillon (2017) argues that the multi-faceted and intergenerational impacts of the colonial project remain very much alive. Such effects are social, material, political, and discursive, and continue to negatively affect the lives of Indigenous youth despite the claims of state agents and community organizations that the purpose of intervening in the lives of Indigenous youth is to liberate them from dangerous circumstances. Institutional arenas involving criminal justice, education, and the child welfare system continue to cycle young people in and out of families and various areas of "institutional care," all the while sustaining systems of settler governance and legitimizing the same colonial relations of domination and colonial violence (Dhillon 2017).

According to Reiman and Leighton (2017), the government is more than capable of developing policies that will help reduce crime. However, Canadian governments at all levels have supported conservative, "get tough on crime" agendas that include hiring more police, tinkering with the colonial court system, and "enhancing" prison systems. Governments have continued to support this agenda in the face of significant empirical evidence that such an approach will do nothing to reduce the levels of crime (Waller 2008, 2014). Sociologist David Garland argues that crime control strategies are not implemented by governments because they view them as insightful and possibly effective. Rather, he asserts that governments tend to adopt strategies because they support certain ways of addressing crime-related issues that "fit with the dominant culture and the power structure upon which it rests" (Garland 2001, 26).

Crime prevention experts have known for decades that simply increasing the number of police officers to engage in the standard practice of "reactive policing" does nothing to reduce levels of crime. This understanding goes back at least four decades, when Kelling et al. (1974) ran a field experiment to gauge the effects of increasing the number of police officers conducting routine patrols in marked cars. In this case, the researchers concluded that increasing the number of police officers on the streets produced no discernible reduction in crime. Despite such data, Waller (2014, 36) notes that "a larger and larger portion of police budgets goes for more and more cars to respond to calls for service, thereby reinforcing isolated, reactive policing." In the absence of supporting data, the allocation of resources towards increased police presence in public spaces can be interpreted as a response to calls for more police and harsher sentences from the dominant majority—that is, from those whose bodies, identities, and spaces are not already subject to heightened degrees of surveillance, scrutiny, and policing. In the face of such policies, which are incorrectly touted as improving (read: rendering more punitive and deterrent) the carceral state as well as increasing social safety, we need to reflect critically on these purported paradigms of "improvement" and ask: Who does this improvement serve? Whose conceptions of safety is it designed to address? Who benefits from these changes, and at whose expense? And indeed, to what extent do these types of changes generate improvement in the lives of those who are most directly implicated by the systems themselves?

Beyond finding themselves policed primarily by non-Indigenous people, Indigenous people have to contend with a criminal justice system and body of laws grounded on Western understandings of land, property, relationships, hierarchy, and punishment. That there are currently some Indigenous police officers in Canada, as well as Indigenous people employed in various police service roles, does not negate the inherently colonial nature of policing or of the laws that are being enforced. In recent decades, the number and variety of strategies aimed at hiring Indigenous people into policing roles have increased. One of the initial efforts to do so was the Band Constable Program in 1969, which allowed band councils to hire band members to administer bylaws in their First Nation communities, and this program was expanded in 1971 to hire "special constables" to supplement senior police forces at the local level (Cummins and Steckley 2003). However, special constables held significantly less status and authority than regular police officers; they were not permitted to carry firearms, received a minimal salary, were expected to use their own cars, and in some cases did not even receive uniforms (Cummins and Steckley 2003, 20–1). The Special Constable Program was soon expanded to the federal police service, which resulted in a slight increase in the authority given to Indigenous police officers. Similar to the Special Constable Program that operated in Indigenous communities, the federal program had a number of problems. In addition to receiving lower salaries, Indigenous special constables received less training than their non-Indigenous counterparts. Special constables also reported being treated with hostility by community members and in general experienced feelings of social isolation. The Special Constable Program was replaced in 1990 with the Aboriginal Constable Development Program. Instead of creating "special" adjunct officers, this program sought to increase the number of Indigenous people who were qualified to become regular RCMP members. This outreach has remained largely intact to the present day: police agencies across Canada continue to actively recruit Indigenous people through impressive marketing campaigns deployed in a range of contexts.

While Canadian government representatives have presented the active recruitment of Indigenous people by policing agencies as a positive development in Canadian criminal justice, some view it as a means by which Indigenous people have become active participants in their own criminalization and dispossession. After all, such participation situates Indigenous people as agents of the colonial state who are responsible for enforcing laws that, in many contexts, are geared towards protecting the structure of settler colonialism. Rather than drawing on Indigenous laws or understandings of justice to change mainstream systems, Indigenous policing initiatives represent an attempt to "Indigenize" or "Indianize" the mainstream system by slotting Indigenous people into various roles within the justice system. Doing so gives the appearance that the system is fundamentally "good" and that it is only necessary to make minor changes for the system to be "good" for all people in Canada (Dickson-Gilmore and La Prairie 2005, 68). In the process, Indigeneity is co-opted by the state and used as evidence of inclusion and improvement, yet the underlying institutional structure remains unchanged. Thus, the vestiges of colonial rhetoric surrounding the surveillance, apprehension, and containment of the Indigenous "threat" remain at the core of policing. Rather than dismantling the colonial structure of the policing system, Indigenous people are called to "participate" in their own repression and incarceration. The success of this participation, however, has not been evidenced by a reduction in the number of Indigenous people who find themselves in conflict with the law, a dilemma we turn to in the following section.

Indigenous Peoples and Sentencing Initiatives

Over the years, government and the courts have sought to make several changes and amendments to existing laws with the aim of reducing the incarceration rates of Indigenous people. They have also at times supported the diversion of Indigenous people who have been convicted of a crime away from prisons and towards alternative programs. For instance, Parliament amended the Criminal Code in 1996 to include section 718.2(e), which made specific reference to Indigenous people in its wording:

> All available sanctions other than imprisonment that are reasonable in the circumstances should be considered for all offenders, with particular attention to the circumstances of Aboriginal Offenders.

Much like hiring special constables, these sentencing initiatives represent another attempt to Indigenize or Indianize the mainstream justice system by offering culturally appropriate measures for Indigenous people. In the case of *R. v. Gladue* (1999), the Supreme Court interpreted section 718.2(e) to mean that "the jail term for an Aboriginal offender may in some circumstances be less than the term imposed on a non-Aboriginal offender for the same offence" (*R. v. Gladue* 1999). The Court further ruled that "Aboriginal offenders must always be sentenced in a manner which gives greatest weight to the principles of restorative justice, and less weight to goals such as deterrence, denunciation and separation." In 2012, the importance of the *Gladue* ruling was reaffirmed in *R v. Ipeelee*. The Supreme Court stated in this case that judges must apply *Gladue* and consider broad and systemic background factors impacting Indigenous people's circumstances at sentencing.

Since the inclusion of section 718.2(e) and the *Gladue* decision, the over-representation of Indigenous people has not declined. In her examination of whether 718.2(e) had been successful in reducing the incarceration of Indigenous persons, Fennig (2002, iii) found that "Aboriginal over-incarceration levels had actually *increased*" since the introduction of section 718.2(e). According to Fennig, law reform alone clearly does not address the root cause of Indigenous over-incarceration, and disproportional incarceration rates are a symptom of a much larger issue related to political, social, and economic disadvantage as well as historic and intergenerational trauma.

In some cases, alternative sentencing can also pose particular challenges for Indigenous women and children. Métis scholar Emma LaRocque (2002) notes that attempts to incorporate Indigenous traditional forms of justice can result in certain contexts in the privileging of the offender's rights or the broader community interest over the individual rights of the victim. Moreover, she questions to what degree "alternative" sentencing programs are actually representative of Indigenous traditions, arguing that in some cases they may be reinvented or incorrectly interpreted Indigenous traditions. For example, LaRocque interrogates the merits of justice programs that attempt to put offenders of sexual violence together with their victims for mediation. She argues that such approaches may have drastic negative effects on the victim and community. As she states, "it has simply not been established that forcing mediation on victims is either helpful to the victim or 'rehabilitating' for the attacker" (LaRocque 2002, 81).

Beyond the courts, Canada's corrections system also has attempted to integrate measures tailored towards Indigenous people. For example, Correctional Services Canada (CSC) established a national healing program for incarcerated Indigenous people in all federal prisons and facilities after an extensive review of the system in 2009. It also introduced Indigenous-specific provisions into the Corrections and Conditional Release Act, including sections 81 and 84. Section 81 provides CSC the ability to "enter into an agreement with an Aboriginal community for the provision of correctional services to Aboriginal offenders," while section 84 allows Indigenous people in the system to be "released into an Aboriginal community" if the community and the person being released express an interest in this happening. Such changes have led scholars such as Martel, Brassard, and Jaccoud (2011, 237) to argue that "Canada is a forerunner in the Indigenization of its correctional apparatus."

Under section 81, two types of healing lodges have been established: CSC-operated lodges, and lodges run in agreement with CSC but operated by Indigenous communities. Currently, there are five healing lodges operated by communities and four CSC-run lodges. CSC (2016) outlines the purpose of its healing lodges as places "where we use Aboriginal values, traditions and beliefs to design services and programs for offenders. We include Aboriginal concepts of justice and reconciliation. The approach to corrections is holistic and spiritual. Programs include guidance and support from Elders and Aboriginal communities."

According to the Office of the Correctional Investigator, several problems with the implementation of sections 81 and 84 of the Corrections and Conditional Release Act include major discrepancies between funding support for healing lodges operated by Indigenous communities and those operated by CSC. In 2009–10, the yearly allocation per incarcerated individual at CSC-run healing lodges was $113,450, whereas community-operated lodges received only $70,845 per incarcerated individual. Moreover, employee salaries at community-run healing lodges were 50 per cent lower than those of employees who were doing similar work at CSC-run lodges (Office of the Correctional Investigator 2012).

Corrections Canada officials have stated that section 84 was intended to facilitate a process for Indigenous communities to set conditions for those who wanted to be released back to their home communities. In practice, however, the Office of the Correctional Investigator admitted that the process had become "cumbersome, time-consuming and misunderstood." The deeper problem, according to Martel et al. (2011), is that although numerous attempts have been made over the past two decades to adapt the carceral structure of prisons to better fit Indigenous persons and values, the structures and processes of Canada's entire corrections system continue to be informed by deeply entrenched colonial attitudes.

Healing lodges are meant to be places that incorporate Indigenous values, traditions, and beliefs. They are informed by Indigenous concepts of justice and reconciliation, and reflect a holistic and spiritual approach to well-being. In an analysis of initiatives intended to support Indigenous people, however, the Office of the Correctional Investigator (2012) found only limited understanding and awareness among CSC staff of Indigenous peoples, cultures, spirituality, and approaches to healing. Problems of underfunding also limited the number of Elders available to provide support, guidance, and ceremonies to incarcerated Indigenous people. The Correctional Investigator also found little understanding among CSC staff about the release plans and needs of urban Indigenous people, for while corrections employees typically assumed that Indigenous prisoners would be returning to a First Nation communities after release, many in fact had no plans to do so.

Although the Office of the Correctional Investigator revealed serious problems within Canada's corrections system, it is important to acknowledge that the integration of Indigenous cultures and perspectives into prison-based healing initiatives has benefited many Indigenous people who have been pulled into the system of incarceration. For example, in interviews with 68 previously incarcerated Indigenous persons, Heckbert and Turkington (2001) found that Indigenous cultures and spirituality within institutions, including ceremonies and Elders, greatly helped people turn their lives around and start them on a healing journey. As one participant in their study explained: "I used to go to sweats once a week when I was in Drumheller. It started my healing . . . give me time to think about, reflect back on what . . . happened in the end. And, to pray for those people who done what they done to me. For . . . forgiveness for them. And . . . that made me madder and made myself feel real good about myself and be at peace with myself and those people" (Heckbert and Turkington 2001, 37).

In many respects, the success of programs and supports for incarcerated people based on Indigenous traditions shows how impactful and effective Indigenous cultures can be, even within the confines of colonial structures. Indigenous cultures and traditions helped Indigenous peoples thrive for thousands of years, and since the arrival of Europeans in the Americas they have been the key to survival in the face of European attempts at physical as well as cultural genocide.

Despite the seemingly good intentions of some CSC officials, the incorporation of Indigenous traditions or cultures into the operation of CSC represents yet another attempt to "fit" or integrate elements of Indigeneity into a fundamentally colonial system. Even Canada's Correctional Investigator (2012, 12) noted that "the findings from various task forces and commissions all point to the *failure to adapt* correctional systems to meet the needs of the growing Aboriginal offender population" (emphasis added). The language of "adapt" here is central, as while it is framed as both a pressing imperative and potentially progressive development, the Correctional Investigator nonetheless continued to follow the well-worn colonial path in proposing that certain adjustments, modifications, and adaptations needed to be made *within* the current systems and structures, as opposed to overhauling the carceral structure by redesigning it from an Indigenous frame. In the process of making these adaptations, authorities have drawn on selective, idealized, and often essentialized visions of Indigeneity. A select number of these "adaptive" recommendations over the past several years have included: more funding for healing lodges and beds, including closing the funding discrepancies between CSC-run and Indigenous-run healing lodges; expanding section 81 capacity, such as an increase in healing lodge bed capacity for Indigenous women; more Indigenous awareness training for CSC staff; the development of new culturally appropriate assessment tools for Indigenous men and women; addressing funding shortages as well as service issues affecting the number and role of Elders working within prisons; and the appointment of a Deputy Commissioner for Indigenous Corrections (Office of the Correctional Investigator 2012, 2016, 2017). Clearly, these and many other recommendations propose to adjust the colonial system rather than seek to effect forms of change that lie outside the boundaries of the systems and structures of CSC. Despite the Canadian government's apparently strategic, political commitment to continue its colonial approach to justice, there has not yet been any empirical evidence to suggest that increasing the number of police, adjusting colonial laws, incarcerating greater numbers of Indigenous people, or offering alternate sentencing options will reduce the numbers of Indigenous people interacting with the criminal justice system as prisoners or victims. Rather, meaningful changes must begin by addressing the colonial foundations and structures of these systems, and by asking how and in what ways they might be dismantled. As long as the colonizing roots and branches of the Canadian justice system are not identified and called into question, official inquiries and reports will continue to identify ways that Canada's justice system is "failing" Indigenous people, and calls will continue for better policing practices, more alternative court procedures, and more culturally sensitive programs within CSC.

The Canadian criminal justice system has not provided justice for Indigenous people in this country, and increased spending on programs and initiatives such as those listed above have done nothing to reduce crime affecting Indigenous people. According to Story and Yalkin (2013), federal and provincial government departments spent $20.3 billion on the criminal justice system in Canada in 2011–12 to support the police, the courts (youth justice, legal aid, prosecutors, and judges), and corrections (including parole). They also note that national criminal justice expenditures steadily increased from 2002 to 2013. The problem, as Garland (2001, 65) notes, is that it is "notoriously difficult to overcome the inertia of an institutional system once it has become established." Such institutional inertia is particularly hard to overcome when those in positions of power cloud the general public's awareness of failures within the system through the rhetoric of benevolence (Cohen 1985, 20).

That the general public evinces a lack of concern for the treatment of those accused and imprisoned has been noted in the literature (Wozniak 2014), and is evident through a cursory scan of reader comments on online news items related to prisoner rights. This lack of concern is magnified when applied to Indigenous persons, particularly when assessed in light of rising incarceration rates and recent media attention of the killings of Indigenous men and women by non-Indigenous persons in Canada. And, as Razack (2015) highlights, even gestures of "benevolent concern" have a tendency to obfuscate the systemic racism and colonial violence perpetrated on Indigenous bodies, identities, and spaces.

Rather than continuing to ask what should be done about Indigenous over-representation in the *Canadian* criminal justice system, it is time for governments and policy-makers to contemplate the systemic harm and violence committed by the Canadian criminal justice system itself. Rather than framing the current situation in terms of the "problem" of over-representation of Indigenous people—which places responsibility on Indigenous people for not conforming to a foreign system—over-representation should be framed as the intended function of a colonial system that continuously creates and recreates the conditions whereby Indigenous people are rendered vulnerable, criminal, or both, and that contributes to their ongoing marginalization, precarity, and erasure. The system continues to impose foreign structures, institutions, discourses, laws, and cultures in the territories of Indigenous peoples, intentionally requiring the complicit assimilation of Indigenous peoples. As Wilson and Yellow Bird (2012, 4) have pointed out, "our un-critical participation in this colonial system undoubtedly increases the rate at which we are failing and failing."

Structurally Racist Criminal Justice System

Anyone in the justice system knows that lady justice is not blind in the case of Aboriginal people. She has one eye open. She has one eye open for us and dispenses justice unevenly and often very harshly. Her garment is rent. She does not give us equality. She gives us subjugation. She makes us second-class citizens in our own land.

—Chief Allan Ross, Norway House Cree Nation, quoted in
Aboriginal Justice Implementation Commission 1999

There is much more to explaining the over-representation of Indigenous people in Canadian prisons than simply saying they commit more crimes than non-Indigenous people. Rather, the highly disproportionate incarceration rates of Indigenous people are a consequence of ongoing legacies of colonialism, racism, and sexism in Canada. Racist and gendered attitudes and practices against Indigenous people are built into the policies and practices of the institutional structure of Canadian society, including the criminal justice system. While official sources such as Correctional Services Canada provide data emphasizing the over-representation of Indigenous "offenders" (Public Safety Canada 2017), readers should be mindful that these sources are part of a larger colonial discourse designed to tell a distorted story of Indigenous criminality to serve colonial interests.

Although it appears that there have been some improvements in police attitudes and practices, it is nonetheless clear that many of the racist beliefs, attitudes, and goals still pervade the criminal justice system in Canada. For instance, frequent and explicit cases of police abuse, such as those now referred to as "starlight tours," have continued to be documented in Canada (Comack 2012a). The term "starlight tour" has colloquially been used to describe instances when police have arrested Indigenous people on the streets and left them on the outskirts of town late at night or in early mornings in freezing temperatures. Such practices have resulted in several deaths and led to a commission of inquiry into the freezing death of Cree teen Neil Stonechild in 1990 (see Green 2006). As Joyce Green has observed, such incidents highlight deeply embedded systemic and institutional racism in Canada's political culture. She argues that "processes of colonialism are the impulse for the racist ideology that is now encoded in social, political, economic, academic and cultural institutions and practices, and which functions to maintain the status quo of white dominance" (Green 2006, 509). Several people have survived "starlight tours" and have come forward with their stories to describe the accompanying violence and racism they endured at the hands of police forces. For instance, Ken Thomas survived after being driven out of town by two police officers on a cold Saskatoon night in April 2018. The officers left him for dead in freezing temperatures and laughed at him as they drove away. Being a triathlon athlete and marathon runner, Ken was able to run back to town and stay warm (Irinici 2018). He filed a complaint with the Saskatchewan Public Complaints Commission and they are still investigating the complaint, including reviewing the GPS logs and in-car cameras from police cars.

In a separate but related context, a 1999 study examining First Nations people's experience with the police in Metro Toronto showed that Indigenous people are often subject to very harsh treatment by the police, including being persistently treated with disrespect. They are often mocked by the police in belligerent, hostile, and even cruel ways (Neugebauer 1999). Similarly, the Aboriginal Justice Implementation Commission (1999) noted that in Manitoba the police are often abusive and insensitive to Indigenous people. As sociologist Elizabeth Comack (2012b) explains, "racism pervades the practice of policing in Canada." She found that Indigenous men are subject to regular stops by the police, often under suspicion of their being gang-involved. One 20-year-old Indigenous man she interviewed in Winnipeg explained that he is stopped by the police "once a week, guaranteed. I can't even count the number of times where I've been stopped just for walking down the street wearing, like, all black or something" (Comack 2012b).

Much evidence also indicates that racism and injustice against Indigenous people continue to permeate Canada's court system. Consider the recent trials of Gerald Stanley, a non-Indigenous man accused of murdering 22-year-old Colten Boushie from the Red Pheasant First Nation, and Raymond Cormier, a non-Indigenous man accused of murdering 15-year-old Tina Fontaine from Sagkeeng First Nation. Just a few weeks apart, each

Canadian Press/Chris Donovan

Protesters gather in Toronto to protest the verdict of Gerald Stanley after an all-white jury acquitted him of second degree murder in the killing of Colten Boushie.

of these men were found not guilty by predominantly non-Indigenous juries, and both cases were followed by public outcry and demonstrations across the country surrounding the failures of the policing and court systems (Poisson 2018). While Tina's death was cited as a key factor in convincing Prime Minister Justin Trudeau to set up a National Inquiry into Missing and Murdered Indigenous Women and Girls (Poisson 2018), the acquittal signalled to the Indigenous community a failure not just of the police and of the court system but also of the other institutional systems that Tina was involved in during her life, including children's services. As Kim Anderson and Jessica Ball explain in Chapter 9, Indigenous children's and family services continue to receive significantly less funding and resources than that provided for similar non-Indigenous services in Canada, evidencing yet another form of systemic discrimination that intersects with the criminal justice system. Despite governmental avowals of advocacy and concern surrounding the plight of Indigenous persons in Canada, this facade of benevolence does not materialize into actual physical and structural changes.

The Way Forward: Re-establishing Peace, Friendship, and Indigenous Systems of Justice

Many early relations between Indigenous peoples and Europeans were based on peace and friendship. As the Two-Row Wampum suggests, Indigenous peoples and settlers were to travel down the river of life side by side in our own respective boats, remaining independent and not trying to steer the other's vessel (Morito 1999; Williams 1986). That the basis of our current relations has significantly diverged from these principles is evident across nearly every realm of Indigenous life, including the mass incarceration of Indigenous people within Canadian prisons.

The vision of non-Indigenous people walking beside rather than in front and going down the river of life in tandem with Indigenous peoples based on peace, friendship, and respect is a good way forward. Similar visions were expressed when the British and Great Lakes Covenant Chain Confederacy Wampum Belt was presented in 1764 by the superintendent of Indian Affairs to members of over 24 nations and approximately 2,000 chiefs. This wampum agreement reiterated that our relationships often tarnish—like silver—over time, so they also at times require polishing and repolishing (Borrows 2002; Gehl 2011).

Repolishing our relationships depends in part on every person in Canada acknowledging that Indigenous nations in Canada were thriving before the arrival of Europeans. Nations across Turtle Island have their own languages, customs, governance structures, and laws, including various methods of solving conflicts or harms that have maintained communities since time immemorial. Although approaches to justice differ from nation to nation, Indigenous laws and resources for conflict resolution and justice have much to teach us about maintaining harmony without the archaic use of prison bars, guns, segregation cells, and other instruments of fear that are so strongly relied upon by the Canadian state. As outlined elsewhere, "Indigenous people's ways of addressing victimization and offending tend to be rooted in their own respective world views, and these typically emphasize concepts such as respect, harmony, and the maintenance of balance" (Monchalin 2016, 53). Consequently, violations of Indigenous laws were quite rare prior to contact. If a violation of an Indigenous law did occur, communities had strategies in place to effectively deal with it. For example, Leanne Simpson (2011) notes that Nishnaabeg legal systems have always focused on restoration and the rebalancing of relationships. Similarly, Opaskwayak Cree Nation scholar John Hansen explains that traditional justice processes in Cree communities involve the full restoration of all community members. The Cree system of justice involves accountability whereby offenders acknowledge their wrongdoing and must learn about the consequences of the pain they have caused (Hansen 2012). According to Mi'kmaw Elder Daniel Paul, achieving justice in traditional Mi'kmaw societies involved bringing together disputing parties "for mediation and reconciliation" until everyone reached an agreement "based on justice and fairness." Any final agreement had to address all the main "concerns of the individuals, groups or governments involved" (Paul 2006, 9). Despite the diversity of world views and systems of justice, many Indigenous peoples, past and present, have continued to share a commitment to the principles of respect and maintaining balance within their communities. Accordingly, justice is much more than something to be achieved within the narrow confines of the *Canadian* criminal justice system; it is a way of relating with all others that is based on a commitment to peace and to treating all our relations with respect. It is time for Indigenous legal principles to play a major role in reconciliation. As Alfred (1992) explains, focus must be given to thinking beyond current Western political, social, and environmental conceptions, and instead look at Indigenous notions of justice. Indigenous approaches to justice are reflective of each nation's world views, which are best understood through each nation's own language, stories, and philosophies. An important way forward for justice in Canada, then, requires the reinvigoration of Indigenous languages, legal systems, and governance structures that rightly focus not only on reducing harm but also on cultivating peaceful relations between all peoples. As Hansen (2012, 15) notes:

> Indigenous justice systems have been dismissed or marginalized while our overrepresentation in the prisons increases. An Omushkegowuk response to wrongdoing encourages accountability, repairs harm, restores relationships, forgives wrongdoers and advocates peace. This is what our ancestors did, and this is what we should continue to do. The struggle for restoring justice and accountability should expand and develop in all policies concerning Indigenous justice.

Substantive change requires the revitalization and implementation of Indigenous systems of justice that the colonial project sought to destroy. For Indigenous peoples, this means drawing on the strengths, cultures, traditions, and ceremonies that reinforce our identities and enrich our well-being, while applying them to new and contemporary contexts. As Cree Elder Vernon Harper noted, "The Indian people have survived because we've been flexible, we adapt, we know how to keep the values of our ancestors and take things from other cultures and make use of them" (Johnson and Budnik 1994, 133). Rebuilding our communities will also include being supported by our non-Indigenous sisters and brothers, as all people must play a role in continuing to resist colonialism and dispelling the myths it propagates. Working together to challenge and change colonial structures so our relations move forward in a good way thus requires that everyone living in Canada be made aware of the truths of Canada's origins as well as the ongoing injustices that continue to occur in this country.

Discussion Questions

1. In what ways has Canada's criminal justice system been set up to "fail" Indigenous people in this country?

2. Why are Indigenous people over-represented within the criminal justice system as both victims and as those incarcerated?

3. What has your experience been with the Canadian criminal justice system, and in what ways does your experience support the view that the system works to support the interests and positions of colonialism?

4. How might harm and victimization affecting Indigenous people in Canada be reduced?

5. What does it mean to "Indigenize" or "Indianize" the Canadian criminal justice system, and why would this not provide a long-term solution to reducing harm and victimization affecting Indigenous people?

6. What role can all people in Canada play in achieving a good way forward towards justice?

Recommended Reading

Dhillon, Jaskiran. 2015. "Indigenous Girls and the Violence of Settler Colonial Policing." *Decolonization: Indigeneity, Education & Society* 4, no. 2: 1–31.

Green, Joyce. 2006. "From Stonechild to Social Cohesion: Anti-Racist Challenges for Saskatchewan." *Canadian Journal of Political Science* 39, no. 3: 507–27.

Hunt, Sarah. 2013. "Witnessing the Colonialscape: Lighting the Intimate Fires of Indigenous Legal Pluralism." PhD Dissertation, Simon Fraser University.

Monchalin, Lisa. 2016. *The Colonial Problem: An Indigenous Perspective on Crime and Injustice in Canada.* Toronto: University of Toronto Press.

Nichols, Robert. 2014. "The Colonialism of Incarceration." *Radical Philosophy Review* 17, no. 2: 435–55.

Stark, Heidi Kiiwetinepinesiik. 2016. "Criminal Empire: The Making of the Savage in a Lawless Land." *Theory & Event* 19, 4.

Additional Resources

Crozier, Cullen. 2017. "APTN Investigates: Indigenous People in Canada behind Bars." *Aboriginal Peoples Television Network*, 3 Nov. http://aptnnews.ca/2017/11/03/aptn-investigates-indigenous-people-in-canada-behind-bars/.

Correctional Service Canada. 2017. "Bringing the Grandchildren Home: Elders in Federal Correctional Facilities." http://www.csc-scc.gc.ca/media-room/009-1009-eng.shtml.

CBC. n.d. "Live Q&A: Indigenous Incarceration Rates." https://facebook.com/CBC.caIndigenous/videos/2141835185843896/.

Notes

1. The interviews took place between March and October 2009 (Environics Institute 2010, 7).

2. The cities were Vancouver, Edmonton, Calgary, Regina, Saskatoon, Winnipeg, Thunder Bay, Montreal, Toronto, Halifax, and Ottawa (Environics Institute 2010, 7).

3. Research on Canadian cinema speaks much to how these sorts of representations are central to Canada's visual national identity, as well as to how they are signified on screen through film as well as television (Melnyk 2007/2008).

11 All Our Relations

Indigenous Perspectives on Environmental Issues in Canada

Deborah McGregor

The environment is fundamentally important to First Nation Peoples. It is the breadth of our spirituality, knowledge, languages and culture. It is not a commodity to be bartered with to maximize profit, nor should it be damaged by scientific experimentation.

 The environment speaks of our history, our language, and our relationship to her. It provides us with nourishment, medicine and comfort. Our relationship and interaction was and is the basis and source of independence. We do not dominate her. We harmonize with her.

—AFN 1993, 39

Métis people have a holistic view of the world that is based on the concept of integration with the natural environment. Métis people have a very close connection to the landscape and its ecosystems; the land and water are relied upon by the Métis for food, medicine, and spiritual fulfillment and livelihood. The interconnected, interdependent nature of ecosystems, of which the Métis people are a part, means that all aspects of the environment are connected in some way.

—MNO 2012, 3

We, native people, have lived in our land since time immemorial. We know our lands, are experts in our environment. We do not study it for just a few years. It is a lifetime study. It is knowledge from the beginning passed on to us by our Ancestors. We have knowledge, true knowledge because it's our way of life.

—Titi Kadluck in McDonald, Arragutainaq, and Novalinga 1997, 1

Introduction

In Canada, it is commonly recognized that Indigenous peoples (First Nations, Métis, and Inuit) hold close and intimate ties to the lands and environments they inhabit (RCAP 1996). As the above quotations indicate, the health and well-being of Indigenous people stem directly from these unique relationships.

To fully appreciate the relationships between Indigenous peoples and the environment, it is important to understand Indigenous world views, ontologies, and epistemologies. While the diverse languages, governance systems, laws, and practices of Indigenous peoples shape their unique relationships with the environment, common environmental philosophies and shared values among the different nations are evident in their interactions with the natural world. This is also true internationally, where many diverse nations from around the world have expressed common principles that reflect their values and experiences (Clarkson, Morrrissette, and Regallet 1992).

While Indigenous peoples experience and express many of the same concerns relating to environmental challenges as other people in this country, the unique history, identity, culture, and constitutional status of Indigenous peoples mean that they experience such challenges in profoundly different ways. The land has represented the heart of our knowledge, language, culture, laws, and livelihood since time immemorial; since contact with European settlers, it has also been the source of our disempowerment and oppression. In Canada, Aboriginal and treaty rights are front and centre in every discussion of the environmental challenges faced by Indigenous peoples in this country (AFN 1993; MNO 2012).

This chapter will provide an overview of key Indigenous environmental perspectives and experiences and how these play out in the contemporary environmental governance landscape in Canada. Discussion will centre on the idea that *environment* is more than just the natural landscape, a home surrounding us. It includes aspects of Creation that are tangible and intangible, physical and spiritual. Environment is not just the observed landscape; it is the relationship itself that Indigenous peoples have with the world around them.

Three main strands form the basis of exploring Indigenous environmental perspectives in this chapter:

1. For thousands of years, Indigenous peoples flourished on their territories by using their own knowledge and legal systems to develop and maintain sustainable relationships. In this strand, Indigenous traditional environmental perspectives will be explored with a focus on Creation stories.
2. Indigenous peoples' relationships to their environment/lands/territories have been severely disrupted through the colonial practices of Europeans. Understanding this history is essential to understanding the current situation Indigenous peoples face in relation to environmental governance in Canada and the reasons behind their efforts to re-establish relationships with their territories.
3. After centuries of displacement and dispossession from their territories, Indigenous peoples have increasingly sought to reconnect with their lands through various processes, including comprehensive land claims, self-government agreements, and other collaborative environmental initiatives. This strand explores the mechanisms in place

that have the potential to lead to respectful coexistence between Indigenous peoples and Canadian society.

Indigenous Concepts of Environment: All of Creation

There are many different conceptions of the "environment." The *Oxford English Dictionary* defines "environment" as a noun:

1. The surroundings or conditions in which a person, animal, or plant lives or operates.
2. The natural world, as a whole or in a particular geographical area, especially as affected by human activity.

Similarly, the Canadian Environmental Protection Act (1999) states that:

"environment" means the components of the Earth and includes
(*a*)   air, land and water;
(*b*)   all layers of the atmosphere;
(*c*)   all organic and inorganic matter and living organisms; and
(*d*)   interacting natural systems that include components referred to in paragraphs (*a*) to (*c*).

In these commonly applied definitions, the environment is seen as separate from people, despite the fact that we are deeply interconnected in ways that require the environment for our very existence. The separation of humans from the rest of the environment is a key feature of the Western world view. Not everyone shares this view or sees it as constructive in the move towards greater sustainability.

The perspectives that Indigenous peoples have of the environment are significantly different from the views expressed above. Throughout this chapter I use the terms "environment," "the natural world," or "all of Creation" interchangeably since both tangible (material) and intangible features of the world, such as spiritual aspects, ancestors, and spiritual teachers, are equally important to Indigenous peoples. The following section explores Indigenous conceptions of "environment" through the lens of Creation or origin stories.

Starting at the Beginning: Creation and Origin Stories

Origin stories say a great deal about how people understand their place in the universe and their relationship to other living things. Creation stories are the means by which cultural communities ground their identity in particular narratives and particular landscapes.

—Johnston 2005, 1

Anishinaabe Creation stories inform us of our beginnings and provide the conceptual frameworks for an Indigenous understanding of our relationship to Creation and its many beings. Anishinaabe storytellers Basil Johnston (*Ojibway Heritage*, 1976) and Edward

Benton-Banai (*The Mishomis Book*, 1988) both begin their books with Creation. Below is part of the story as told by Johnston (1976, 12):

> Kitche Manitou (The Great Spirit) beheld a vision. In this vision he saw a vast sky filled with stars, sun, moon, and earth. He saw an earth made of mountains and valleys, islands and lakes, plains and forests. He saw trees and flowers, grasses and vegetables. He saw walking, flying, swimming, and crawling beings. He witnessed the birth, growth and the end of things. At the same time, he saw other things live on. Amidst change there was constancy. Kitche Manitou heard songs, wailings and stories. He touched wind and rain. He felt love and hate, fear and courage, joy, sadness. Kitche Manitou meditated to understand his vision. In his vision, Kitche Manitou understood that his vision had to be fulfilled. Kitche Manitou was to bring into being and existence what he had seen, heard and felt.

In Anishinaabe world view, Creation comes originally from *vision* and people come originally from the spirit world. In addition to generating living beings, the Creation process begins to lay out the key ideas and principles that comprise the foundation for Indigenous laws and codes of conduct: how every being will relate to the Creator and all other beings in Creation. These laws do not just apply to people, but to all of Creation (sun, moon, stars, animals, etc.).[1] Jim Dumont, Anishinaabe scholar and Elder, adds, "The very first concept at the centre of everything is the spirit. If we can understand the place of Spirit in the Indigenous world view, that will define for us the starting place, the centre of our understanding" (Dumont 2006, 4). This understanding, in turn, informs the rights and responsibilities that humans hold towards the living earth.

Richard Atleo, in his book *Tsawalk: A Nuu-chah-nulth Worldview*, observes that many questions about life are answered in the origin stories since they reflect the interrelationship between the physical and spiritual realms, and that it has always been well understood "that all things come from the spiritual realm" (Atleo 2004, 17). The origin stories, Atleo states, "consequently provide an orientation to the life and reality that, prior to colonialism, allowed the Nuu-chah-nulth to manage their lives and communities for millennia" (Atleo 2004, 5).

Origin or Creation stories inform us of our relationships with the natural world and guide our conduct within it. They outline our duties as humans to ensure Creation continues. They lay out principles (often implicitly) for how humans are to coexist with non-human relatives and beings. The Haudenosaunee Creation story "tells us of the great relationships within this world and our relationships, as human beings, with the rest of Creation" (Williams in HETF 1999, 2).

In their own ways, many other Indigenous Creation or origin stories also illustrate how humans were fully integrated into the rest of Creation. John Petagumskum (in McDonald et al. 1997, 5) provides the following example:

> Everything created on this earth was put in its natural place. The Creator decided where everything, including all plant life, should be. . . . People have their place in the environment along with the animals. In the time when only Cree and Inuit were out on the land there was nothing to disturb the animals and plants. At that time, everything in the natural world spoke for itself. People were so connected with

nature that they knew and read its signs. . . . The Elders watched and kept track of everything around them. They closely observed the animals in order to predict the weather.

People, then, were part of complex networks of interdependence with all of Creation. The interactions between humans and other beings (animals) were guided by natural and spiritual processes that were understood and respected by humans and all other beings to ensure harmony. Indigenous origin stories point to the centrality of spirituality in how one conducts himself/herself appropriately and respectfully in relation to the natural world. The teachings and lessons embedded in Indigenous peoples' stories that have provided them with guidance and key principles for living can thus be thought of as environmental principles.

Environmental Principles

Identifying basic Indigenous environmental principles embedded in the stories and the lived experiences of Indigenous peoples can help all peoples better understand Indigenous environmental world view and epistemology. It is important to keep in mind that each Indigenous nation and culture developed its own conceptual frameworks (stories) for understanding relationships with the natural world/environment based on where its people travelled and lived. Principles and practices derived from such frameworks have persisted and continue to be applied despite historical attempts to eradicate them (HETF 1999). Although Indigenous peoples who point to the ongoing relevance of Indigenous environmental principles are often criticized for wanting to "return to the past," such criticism indicates a narrowness of understanding and vision on the part of the critics. Such principles maintain relevance today; in fact, they are essential to achieving what is now commonly referred to as "environmental sustainability."

The purpose of developing a number of basic principles and practices associated with environmental thought, perspectives, and values has been to ensure that all members of each community would understand their role and conduct themselves in a sustainable, ethical, and respectful way in relation to the environment. It was believed by many that ethical behaviour would follow if people understood their responsibilities to "all their relations."

Such an approach has been beautifully expressed in *Words That Come Before All Else: Environmental Philosophies of the Haudenosaunee* (HETF 1999), one of the key resources provided by Indigenous peoples that explicitly speaks to Indigenous environmental philosophies and values. In Haudenosaunee tradition, the Thanksgiving Address, or *Ohen:ton Karihwetehkwen*, is given before any gathering begins. It is aimed in part at building consensus and acknowledging "the power and duties of every part of the world, and joining our minds and determinations together to fulfill the obligations of humans beings in the web of life" (HETF 1999, 1).

The principles and samples outlined in the following table are shown in artificially discrete categories and in no particular order since in reality the principles and practices overlap. These principles and their application have always operated in an open, flexible way to allow for adaptation to changing circumstances. This will be evident in our examination of some of the similar and different ways that Indigenous peoples have sought to gain control over environmental governance through self-government and comprehensive land claim processes.

Table 11.1   Key Indigenous Environmental Principles

Earth Is Alive	The notion of the Earth as a life-giving entity is closely linked to the view that the Earth is alive and filled with spirit (Dumont 2006). This principle emphasizes the animate nature and creative capacity of the Earth, as shared by humans and other living beings. If our identity as people is inseparable from the Earth itself, we are likely to treat the Earth the way we treat our relatives.
All Living Things Are Equal	From an Indigenous perspective, people should not view themselves as somehow above or separate from the other beings of the Earth, otherwise misfortune will occur (Clarkson et al. 1992). Instead, all living things are believed to be equal. Some beings may have greater power or more responsibilities than others, but all life is believed to be essential to the continuing work of Creation.
The Seventh Generation	Closely related to the environmental principle of equality is that of the seventh generation. Indigenous peoples have long believed that they must consider how their actions will affect all currently living things as well as those beings who will live in the future. Decisions are made to ensure that generations to come will have the opportunity to "live well." According to Lyons (1980), the abuses that Indigenous peoples and Mother Earth face today are due to decision-making that has failed to consider the seventh generation and the welfare of all living things.
All Things Are Related: Inter-connectedness and Interdependence	Integral to Indigenous sacred traditions is the idea that all things depend on one another. Humanity holds a special place within nature, though it is fully interdependent upon and interconnected with every other aspect of nature (Dumont 2006). The concept of interconnectedness is recognized and acknowledged in everyday activities (song, prayer) and in communal activities such as ceremonies, feasts, and other celebrations. The constant recognition that all things are related enables Indigenous peoples to be acutely aware of how their actions will affect all other beings.
Responsibility	Although most of the discourse regarding Indigenous peoples and the environment currently centres on Aboriginal and treaty rights, all people have a responsibility to care for the Earth (Walken 2007). According to traditional teachings, every child is raised to assume some part, however small, in this life-giving endeavour. In turn, some people have more responsibility than others, such as those with specialized knowledge, including healers or ceremonial leaders. In some traditional teachings women have a special relationship with water as a life-giving force (Mandamin 2003).
Reciprocal Relations: Achieving Balance and Harmony	Indigenous peoples have always had a close and intimate relationship with the Earth based on reciprocity rather than exploitation. One way that all relations within Creation are acknowledged is to ensure that when something is taken, something is given in return. For example, if one takes an animal's life, then that person is responsible to return something back to the animal or give something in exchange for that life. One must never take something and give nothing in return or imbalance will result (LaDuke 1994). Indigenous societies and their governments were structured around trying to ensure and maintain such balance.
Cyclical Thinking	Thousands of years of observation and intimate interaction with the Earth have enabled Indigenous peoples to develop an understanding of the world that envisions all parts of Creation as flowing in a cycle (Dumont 2006; LaDuke 1994). Instead of trying to make the world fit into linear or hierarchical patterns, Indigenous people learned long ago to follow what came naturally; following cyclical and seasonal teachings enabled them to act in minimally disruptive ways in relation to the environment and adapt to environmental changes when required.

Summary: All My Relations

The principles and practices outlined above are not exhaustive, though they do constitute the foundation for an Indigenous environmental ethics, again keeping in mind, every Nation has taken great care to develop their own principles and practices. It is important, as well, to remember that all of these principles are interconnected and that it is therefore not possible to fully adhere to one principle without simultaneously following the others. Without practising respect, for example, it is difficult to act responsibly. Also, without a basic understanding of the reciprocal relationship between all beings in Creation it is difficult, if not impossible, to achieve and maintain harmony and balance.

The common strand that ties together various expressions of Indigenous environmental principles is Indigenous people's holistic understanding of their spiritual and personal relationships with the environment (LaDuke 1999). These values and principles have been articulated by Indigenous peoples from around the world and expressed in various environmental declarations such as the declaration formulated at the International Indigenous Peoples Summit on Sustainable Development that was held in Khoi-San-San territory, Kimberly, South Africa, in 2002. The Indigenous participants at the summit prepared the Kimberly Declaration, which affirmed previous Indigenous environmental declarations and clearly articulated the relationships between the right to self-determination and sustainability:

> As peoples, we reaffirm our rights to self-determination and to own, control and manage our ancestral lands and territories, waters and other resources. Our lands and territories are at the core of our existence—*we are the land and the land is us*; we have distinct spiritual and material relationship with our lands and territories and they are inextricably linked to our survival as to the preservation and further development of our knowledge systems and cultures, conservation and sustainable use of biodiversity and ecosystem management.

On Earth Day in 2010 at the World People's Conference on Climate Change and the Rights of Mother Earth in Cochabamba, Bolivia, participants collaborated in developing the *Universal Declaration on the Rights of Mother Earth*. The Preamble to the Mother Earth Declaration states:

> We, the peoples and nations of Earth:
>   considering that we are all part of Mother Earth, an indivisible, living community of interrelated and interdependent beings with a common destiny;
>   gratefully acknowledg[e] that Mother Earth is the source of life, nourishment and learning and provides everything we need to live well . . . .

Article 1 describes Mother Earth in the following way:

> (1) Mother Earth is a living being.
> (2) Mother Earth is a unique, indivisible, self-regulating community of interrelated beings that sustains, contains and reproduces all beings.
> (3) Each being is defined by its relationships as an integral part of Mother Earth.
> (4) The inherent rights of Mother Earth are inalienable in that they arise from the same source as existence.

(5)   Mother Earth and all beings are entitled to all the inherent rights recognized in this Declaration without distinction of any kind, such as may be made between organic and inorganic beings, species, origin, use to human beings, or any other status.

(6)   Just as human beings have human rights, all other beings also have rights which are specific to their species or kind and appropriate for their role and function within the communities within which they exist.

(7)   The rights of each being are limited by the rights of other beings and any conflict between their rights must be resolved in a way that maintains the integrity, balance and health of Mother Earth.

Indigenous peoples' voices are gaining recognition and contributing to a distinct narrative of how humanity should be relating to Mother Earth through the expression of legal rights and responsibilities. Similar to the international narrative, Indigenous peoples in Canada have conveyed ideals based on their own world view and ontologies through the revitalization of Indigenous legal orders/systems.

Indigenous Legal Traditions and Environmental Responsibilities

Western and colonial laws continue to fail Indigenous peoples, as evidenced by the continuing economic, health, educational, and other disparities that to this day characterize the lived experience of Indigenous peoples (Anaya 2014; Borrows 2016). Indigenous peoples have called for recognition on their own terms not only of Indigenous rights, but also of Indigenous governance, legal orders, and intellectual traditions to support their own goals, aspirations, and well-being. As such, Indigenous peoples have expressed a concept of natural law distinct from that of Western legal jurisprudence. The natural law that many Indigenous peoples speak of is quite simple, although it is expressed in a variety of ways. Natural law is the requirement that we accept the way things are in nature, whether we fully understand them or not, and that we relate to all things in a respectful manner. Failure to adhere to this law could cause life as we know it to perish (Clarkson et al. 1992). There is nothing romantic about this view of our relationship to the Earth: it is based quite simply on the will to support all life. Anishinaabe/Métis legal scholar Aimee Craft (2014) identifies responsibilities at the heart of Anishinaabe legal structure, and that law is about *living* according to, and *sharing* the burden of, those responsibilities. John Borrows (2010, 59) adds that "[d]uties and obligations are central to relationships under Anishinabek law." He also states that natural law is one source of Indigenous legal orders and that natural law flows directly from:

- experiences in living and observing the natural world/Creation;
- understanding how the Earth maintains its functions;
- lessons on how to read laws from the land/water/nature.

Elder and educator Cecile King describes these laws as a:

code of conduct, a set of lessons, derived from the Law of the Orders. . . . They spoke of what was appropriate behaviour, what was forbidden, and the responsibility ensuing from each. These laws pertained to the relationships among human beings as well as the awesome responsibilities of co-existence with members of the other orders. (King 2013, 5)

Indigenous laws are meant to allow for good relations and ultimately for each living being to live well (Craft 2014). People do not make up natural laws; rather, they flow from Creation, the cycles of nature and knowledge contained herein. Understanding the natural law embodies the principles outlined in Table 11.1; for example, they require us to consider the seven generations principle (Lyons 1980). Indigenous conceptions of law are based on relationships and responsibilities to "all our relations" (McDermott and Wilson 2010). Such laws, treaties, and agreements also helped guide human conduct to ensure sustainable relationships with all of Creation. Indigenous laws convey particular types of relationships with and responsibilities to each other as peoples, the natural world or environment, the ancestors, the spirit world, and future generations (Borrows 2010; Johnston 2006). The revitalization and application of Indigenous legal traditions continues to gain momentum as Indigenous nations continue to seek self-determination on their own terms.

The assault on Indigenous peoples and lands continues and colonial laws and governments continue to undermine Indigenous sovereignty at every level and in every facet of life. As outlined in the preceding pages, Indigenous peoples acknowledge that they have obligations, duties, and responsibilities to care for the Earth. Their world view shapes how they experience and understand environmental challenges and speaks to why they remain concerned about the impact of environmental degradation on people, as well as on all other beings (relatives) and on Mother Earth herself. Concerns about environmental degradation are not merely about "natural resources" and who benefits from them. Rather, they reflect Indigenous peoples' concern for life itself in every form. It is in this light that Indigenous peoples in Canada understand why ongoing displacement and dispossession from their traditional territories have had, and continue to have, devastating impacts on their lives.

Historical Context: Dispossession of Lands and the Environmental Crisis

Various forms of environmental crisis have been a fact of life for Indigenous peoples for centuries. Anthropogenic environmental change has been imposed on Indigenous peoples by historical and ongoing colonialism, for example, the loss of land through resource extractive industries (Richmond 2015, Whyte 2017). Richmond argues that environmental dispossession brought on by colonialism is a "root" cause of many health challenges Indigenous peoples face (Richmond 2015). Loss of land and/or access to their traditional lands since the arrival of Europeans in the Americas almost immediately resulted in life-threatening situations. As discussed in the following section, current global environmental crises are intricately tied to the ongoing dispossession, colonialism, and exploitation of Indigenous peoples and their territories in Canada and many other parts of the world.

Dispossession of Lands and Resources

One of the most significant challenges that Indigenous peoples in Canada have faced since the arrival of European colonizers is the systematic loss of their lands to make way for European settlement and resource development (RCAP 1996).[2] As Starblanket explains in Chapter 1 and Charlie observes in Chapter 5, being dispossessed from their land has prevented Indigenous peoples from exercising their duties and responsibilities to "all their relations," and so it is hardly surprising that this issue continues to be a primary source of conflict between Indigenous peoples and the rest of Canada (Linden 2007).

Indigenous legal scholar John Borrows describes the connection between the dispossession of land and the impact of this dispossession on Indigenous peoples:

> Aboriginal peoples have a pre-occupation. It is *of* land. They occupied land in North America prior to others' arrival on its shores. Over the past two-hundred and fifty years Aboriginal peoples have been largely dispossessed of their lands and resources in Canada. This dispossession has led to another Aboriginal pre-occupation. It is *with* land. It is crucial to their survival as peoples. Its loss haunts their dreams. Its continuing occupation and/or reoccupation inspires their visions.
>
> Indigenous peoples want to continue living on territories that have sustained them for thousands of years. Yet the Crown now claims occupation of traditional Indigenous lands. (Borrows 2005, 3)

One key aspect of dispossession is exclusion from environmental decision-making, for Indigenous sovereignty, jurisdiction, and authority over decision-making have decreased as others have gained control over the lands through violent historical and ongoing colonial processes. Traditional Indigenous governance structures and regimes were systematically undermined through various colonial interventions, including the ongoing imposition of the Indian Act (RCAP 1996).

These facets—dispossession from their territories and exclusion from decision-making—together have contributed to virtually every environmental challenge facing Indigenous peoples today. In response, Indigenous peoples have been seeking to reclaim their rightful place in environmental governance through a variety of means. Many communities continue in their attempts to establish new forms of government and engage in land claims processes, though the experience of being excluded from decision-making or simply being ignored by environmental decision-makers has also resulted in leaders and/or other community members engaging in other kinds of action, including setting up blockades, various expressions of civil disobedience, and litigation (Borrows 2005).

Aboriginal and Treaty Rights

One often misunderstood aspect of contemporary environmental discourse is the role of Aboriginal and treaty rights. Even policy-makers and environmental practitioners frequently lack appreciation of the importance of this issue. In Canada, Aboriginal and treaty rights are protected under section 35 of the Constitution Act, 1982 (Doyle-Bedwell and Cohen 2001).

According to Linden (2007), the lack of recognition and respect for Aboriginal and treaty rights has been the main reason that Indigenous peoples in Canada continue to be dispossessed from their lands. Such a separation has had profoundly negative social, cultural, spiritual, and emotional impacts on people that have resulted in the deplorable living conditions now present in many Indigenous communities throughout Canada.

Environmental Injustice

Indigenous peoples struggle every day against resource development initiatives that negatively impact their lands and communities (LaDuke 1999). Many of the issues surrounding such development can be characterized as environmental injustice issues. Indigenous peoples throughout the world do not have access to the kinds of resources and environmental protection supports necessary to address the environmental injustice issues that affect them (Edgar and Graham 2008; O'Connor 2002). This includes Indigenous peoples in Canada, who also continue to be denied opportunities to participate in the development of laws, policies, and processes that impact their environment and lands, often with devastating results (Dhillon and Young 2010; RCAP 1996).

Throughout Canada, as a consequence of pollution and other forms of environmental degradation, Indigenous peoples face social, cultural, economic, and spiritual challenges in their communities and environments that are generally not experienced by people in other communities (Agyeman et al. 2009, 27–41).

The concept of environmental racism helps focus our analysis of why Indigenous peoples in Canada are over-represented in incidences of environmental injustice (Jacobs 2010). Dhillon and Young (2010, 26) define environmental racism as "the deliberate or intentional siting of hazardous waste sites, landfills, incinerators, and polluting industries in communities inhabited by minorities and/or the poor." Peoples and communities subject to this type of racism are often impoverished, marginalized, and excluded from dominant society in various ways. The ongoing drinking water crisis in First Nation communities in Canada is an example of an environmental injustice issue that continues to plague many communities (Collins et al. 2017).

In relation to climate justice, Kyle Whyte critiques the current environmental and climate justice frameworks for failing to acknowledge historical and ongoing colonialism. He calls for the decolonization of such ideas by calling for the recognition and renewal of Indigenous knowledge and the experiences of Indigenous peoples, including renewing relationships among humans and non-humans, a process he terms "renewing relatives" (Whyte 2017a, 158). Whyte draws our attention to the fact that Indigenous peoples experience environmental racism and climate injustice through the intensification of environmental change imposed on them by colonialism. To move towards a self-determined future thus requires reckoning with the continued disruptions of "colonialism, capitalism and industrialization" (Whyte 2017a, 154). From this standpoint again, Indigenous peoples cannot rely solely on Western colonial frameworks of justice to address their concerns adequately (Victor 2007). Many contemporary examples, including the Unist'ot'en camp formed by members of the Wet'suwet'en Nation to protect their lives, livelihood, and future generations, illustrate how Indigenous communities must and do act in opposition to state and corporate intervention.

In British Columbia, members of the Wet'suwet'en Nation continue to struggle against LNG Canada's efforts to construct a new liquid natural gas pipeline across their territory, with further arrests being made recently (Bellrichard and Ghoussoub 2019). Although both sides proclaim their commitment to a peaceful solution, it is clear that, with a $40 billion investment already being sunk into a new plant on the BC coast to receive the gas the pipeline will carry, both LNG Canada and the Canadian governments involved have no intention of accepting any resolution that doesn't involve completion of the pipeline. The BC government has stated that it *hopes* "all parties find a safe and mutually respectful resolution," yet the power imbalance and the resulting injustice remain: when the

"Force is not consent" reads a sign at a checkpoint leading to the Unist'ot'en camp near Houston, BC. The camp protects Wet'suwet'en land from an oil and gas company's planned expansion of a pipeline, which would have progressed without the consent of five Wet'suwet'en hereditary clan chiefs.

Thousands of people rally with Coast Salish leaders against the Kinder Morgan pipeline in Burnaby, BC, on 10 March 2018.

project proponents are finished consulting with Indigenous communities, the government is going to authorize the RCMP to ensure that the project goes ahead regardless. In an unfolding and tragic story that has played out countless times across North America over the last century, colonial environmental injustice remains (Bellrichard and Ghoussoub 2019).

Exclusion from Environmental Governance

Indigenous peoples have been excluded from participation in decisions that impact their lives and lands throughout Canadian history (AFN 1993; RCAP 1996). In many cases where the interests of Indigenous peoples have actually been considered, their input has been ignored or simply subsumed under that of other stakeholders. In other words, they have not been seen as a unique stakeholder with especially valuable input, but merely as one of several or many who hold an interest in land and its development or exploitation.

Due to historical exclusions, much of the legislation and regulations for environmental protection and conservation do not reflect the unique concerns or perspectives of Indigenous peoples. Current laws are therefore inadequate for protecting Indigenous peoples' traditional territories and rights since the knowledge that informs policies, laws, regulations, and programs for environmental and resource management is almost all based on a Western scientific world view and on knowledge derived from that paradigm (Berneshawi 1997). Despite the countless barriers and setbacks they have faced in having their voices heard, Indigenous peoples in Canada continue to have a keen desire to be involved in environmental governance at various levels. Recent court decisions involving the Haida (2004), the Taku (2004), the Mikisew Cree (2005), and the Tsilhqot'in (2014) indicate that some progress has been made in gaining legal support for Indigenous interests, although it has largely been achieved through lengthy, financially draining, and exhaustive legal processes. Various levels of government in Canada have responded by developing Indigenous consultation protocols to meet their legal obligations to consult and accommodate. For example, the Canadian government released *Updated Guidelines for Federal Officials to Fulfill the Duty to Consult* in March 2011 to provide direction on the government-wide responsibility of departments and agencies to fulfill the duty to consult with and to accommodate Indigenous interests.

Despite such gains, the constraints of relying on recognition of rights in a colonial governance and legal system have been evident as conflict and tensions over resource development continue unabated.

Environmental Degradation and Quality of Life

Indigenous peoples are increasingly asserting that their cultural identity, their very survival as peoples, is threatened when the environment is degraded (Richmond 2015). The impact of environmental degradation on Indigenous peoples can range from a change in diet (from country foods to highly processed foods) to a decrease in drinking water quality, an increase in exposure to toxic chemicals from fish and game, and a decreased ability to exercise rights or practise ceremonies, to name just a few core effects (AFN 1993; CIER 2005). Efforts to restore environmental health therefore represent far more than a "cause" for Indigenous peoples; it is a responsibility upon which the survival of their nations depends (CIER 2005).

Lack of Recognition of Indigenous Knowledge

Dispossession of land results not only in a people being unable to practise their cultural traditions, but also in the subsequent loss of knowledge about that land (CIER 2005). While much of Indigenous peoples' traditional knowledge (TK) has been disrupted, TK remains critically important and should be at the forefront of environmental governance. Canadian governments and non-profit organizations and institutions, including environmental non-governmental organizations (ENGOs), other NGOs, and academic institutions have also gradually acknowledged the legitimacy of Indigenous world views, cultures, values, and traditional knowledge in environmental governance. For example, the Great Lakes Water Quality Agreement (2012) explicitly recognizes TK along with Western science, as does the Great Lakes Protection Act (2015). Nonetheless, in many instances Indigenous peoples in Canada are still prevented from having regular and meaningful involvement in environmental decision-making (Bowie 2013).

Increasing Indigenous Control in Environmental Governance

Over thousands of years, Indigenous peoples developed intellectual traditions and knowledge systems that enabled sustainable relationships with all of Creation. These knowledge systems are rooted in our ancestral relationships, but also transform with time, incorporating new knowledge and insights to ensure that knowledge about how to relate properly with the natural world is maintained.

First Nations, Métis, and Inuit have distinct conceptions of TK, although there is some commonality in their perspectives. Following are examples of how each group conceives of TK:

> Inuit Qaujimajatuqangit is a body of knowledge and unique cultural insights of Inuit into the workings of nature, humans and animals. Inuit Qaujimajatuqangit has both practical and epistemological aspects that branch out from the fundamental principle that human beings are learning, rational beings with an infinite potential for problem-solving within the dictates of nature and technology. (Qikiqtani Inuit Association 2007, para. 3)

> Métis traditional environmental knowledge is built from community practices which form the foundation for understanding the natural world, building skills and behaviour adaptable and applicable to other facets of Métis life, maximizing use and benefit of natural resources within community accepted ethical boundaries, and contributing to personal and community spiritual, physical, intellectual and emotional health and development. While the phrase "traditional environmental knowledge" does not mention contemporary life, the purpose of understanding Métis traditional environmental knowledge is for adaptation and use in everyday life. Ancestral knowledge is an integral part of traditional environmental knowledge as it influences subsequent generations in understanding and interacting with the natural world. (MNC 2011, 1)

> The term Aboriginal Knowledge is understood to describe knowledge informed by aboriginal paradigms as applied to skills, understandings, expertise, facts, familiarities, beliefs, revelations and observations. Furthermore, AK is understood to include the customary ways in which aboriginal peoples have done or continue to do certain things, as well as the new ideas or ways of doing things that have been developed by Aboriginal peoples and which respect their traditions, cultures and practices. Many of these customary ways have been passed on from generation to generation and must be considered as sacred. (AFN 2010, 4)

There has been a worldwide surge of interest in TK in recent decades, in terms of understanding what it is as well as in recognizing its value in helping people move towards the establishment of more sustainable societies. This growing interest has resulted in opportunities for Indigenous peoples to become increasingly involved in resource management and other environmental governance initiatives in Canada. Increased interest in TK also has its risks for exploitation and inappropriate use (Barrister and Hardison 2006). In response, Indigenous nations are developing protocols to protect their knowledge (McGregor 2013).

The degree to which Indigenous people are able to exert influence and control over environmental and resource management in Canada nonetheless remains varied (Bowie 2013). In the North, where a number of comprehensive land claims have been settled and self-government agreements negotiated, new institutions of governance have been established that specifically provide for Indigenous involvement and the inclusion of TK (Natcher and Davis 2007; Spak 2005). In some parts of Canada, institution-building for the purposes of Indigenous environmental and resource management has been more difficult to establish and is practically non-existent. For example, the Indigenous environmental and resource management context in Ontario differs significantly from those areas in Canada where modern comprehensive land claims or modern-day treaties and other agreements have been established with the Crown. Nineteenth-century and early twentieth-century treaties dispossessed First Nations in that province of most of their traditional land base and set the "rules" for future relations with government to their disadvantage. Even where treaties do exist, it is clear that the Crown's view is that traditional Indigenous rights to lands and resources have historically been extinguished and that "the Crown now claims occupation of traditional Aboriginal lands" (Borrows 2005, 3). Indigenous nations dispute the Crown's view and continue to assert their jurisdiction and authority. Métis scholar and activist Jean Teillet has observed that the Crown's view has resulted in environmental conservation and protection processes in Ontario being used to deny Indigenous authority and jurisdiction over their traditional territories. The natural resource regulatory regime in Ontario has historically sought to dispossess Indigenous people of their lands, and "the dispossession is not finished" (Telliet 2005, 4). Consequently, in Ontario and elsewhere in Canada, Indigenous peoples often find themselves in the difficult position of striving to maintain ties to their territories through participation in Crown-led environmental and resource management regimes. And again, Indigenous people find themselves relegated to a place among various stakeholders at the table.

For Indigenous knowledges and practices to flourish, Indigenous peoples must be *part of the governance system*—they must, in fact, be decision-makers. Currently, the level of control of state-managed systems:

> continues to limit the extent to which First Nations are empowered to propose and implement change. . . . the pervasiveness of state management has in effect

perpetuated historical conditions where First Nations governments have gained little autonomy in the management of lands and resources. (Natcher and Davis 2007, 277)

Despite such challenges, Indigenous peoples continue to assert their own laws, values, knowledge, and traditions in environmental and resource management (Borrows 2010). Hundreds of recommendations put forward over the past two decades, including over 400 in the 1996 *Report of the Royal Commission on Aboriginal Peoples* (RCAP), reflect Indigenous peoples' desire for justice, and for creating the levels of change that are necessary to carry out their responsibilities to the living earth in a meaningful way. However, struggles are ongoing as Indigenous peoples and the Canadian state continue to vie for control of lands and resources. James Anaya, the United Nations Special Rapporteur on the Rights of Indigenous Peoples, made the following observations in May 2014:

One of the most dramatic contradictions indigenous peoples in Canada face is that so many live in abysmal conditions on traditional territories that are full of valuable and plentiful natural resources. These resources are in many cases targeted for extraction and development by non-indigenous interests. While indigenous peoples potentially have much to gain from resource development within their territories, they also face the highest risks to their health, economy, and cultural identity from any associated environmental degradation. Perhaps more importantly, indigenous nations' efforts to protect their long-term interests in lands and resources often fit uneasily into the efforts by private non-indigenous companies, with the backing of the federal and provincial governments, to move forward with resource projects. (Anaya 2014, 19)

Regardless of the numerous challenges posed by historical and ongoing colonization, many changes provide reason for optimism. For example, international agreements and conventions have influenced the recognition of TK in environmental resource management in Canada (Butler 2006; Higgins 1998; Settee 2000), and there is now reference to TK (or TEK, traditional ecological knowledge) in some federal and provincial environmental legislation. Moreover, modern-day treaty-making has entrenched TK as an integral part of many co-management regimes in northern Canada (Bocking 2005; Spak 2005; White 2006).

This trend towards increasing Indigenous control represents a considerable opportunity for TK to play a vital role in environmental and resource management, since Indigenous and non-Indigenous resource managers recognize a pressing need to incorporate TK as current Western scientific systems continue to fail (Houde 2007; Menzies 2006; Sable et al. 2006).

Indigenous peoples in Canada have also sought to develop strategies for decolonizing institutional frameworks that promote TK and Western science as equally valid ways of knowing. A recent example is *We Rise Together: Achieving Pathway to Canada Target 1 through the Creation of Indigenous Protected and Conserved Areas in the Spirit and Practice of Reconciliation*, a report focused on international and national biodiversity goals. The approach was developed by an Indigenous Circle of Experts (ICE) from across the country, and calls for the establishment of Indigenous protected and conserved areas based on Indigenous knowledge systems, legal traditions, and customary cultural practices (ICE 2018, iii). However, most current institutions and programs are based on a Western framework, and so merely inserting components of Indigenous knowledge at various convenient points will only serve to fragment TK and distort, and possibly destroy, its meaning (Stevenson 2006).

The dominance of Western-style environmental resource management regimes presents a significant challenge even to accommodating TK, let alone putting it on an equal footing with Western knowledge. It therefore seems that entirely new institutions and/or ways of envisioning new programs will have to be developed to meet this challenge in a way that supports Indigenous goals for self-determination. On Canada's east coast, the Unamak'ki Institute of Natural Resources (UINR) provides an excellent example of how Indigenous nations are incorporating TK into environmental and resource management work. UINR was established in 1999 to address the environmental concerns of the Mi'kmaq on Cape Breton Island, Nova Scotia. The goals of UINR include working co-operatively and collaboratively with others and ensuring Mi'kmaq traditions are maintained. The UINR incorporates the concept of Netukulimk, based on Mi'kmaq world view and environmental philosophy:

> Netukulimk is the use of the natural bounty provided by the Creator for the self-support and well-being of the individual and the community. Netukulimk is achieving adequate standards of community nutrition and economic well-being without jeopardizing the integrity, diversity, or productivity of our environment.
>
> As Mi'kmaq we have an inherent right to access and use our resources and we have a responsibility to use those resources in a sustainable way. The Mi'kmaq way of resource management includes a spiritual element that ties together people, plants, animals, and the environment. UINR's strength is in our ability to integrate scientific research with Mi'kmaq knowledge acquisition, utilization, and storage. (UINR 2011)

The approach taken by UINR does not exclude the use of Western science or its tools. Instead, ensuring respect for Netukulimk is based on what the Mi'kmaq refer to as the "two-eyed seeing concept" or "Etuaptmumk." "Two-eyed seeing" is offered as a guiding principle from which two knowledge systems can be respected and used to address environmental concerns. In Canada, as Indigenous peoples regain authority and jurisdiction over lands and resources, innovative collaborations based on Indigenous environmental philosophies can flourish, as UINR has shown.

Reconciliation with the Natural World

Established in 2008, the Truth and Reconciliation Commission (TRC) heard from over 7,000 residential school survivors willing to share their experiences. The final report, released in 2015, found that the residential school system was implemented within the context of other coherent "Aboriginal policies" of the colonial and later Canadian governments, whose clear intent was the *cultural genocide* of Indigenous peoples in Canada (TRC 2015, 5). The Commission defines "reconciliation" as "an ongoing process of establishing and maintaining respectful relationships. . . . Establishing respectful relationships also requires the revitalization of Indigenous law and legal traditions" (TRC 2015, 121). However, as John Borrows recently declared: "Colonialism is not only a historic practice, it continues to be acted upon and reinvented in old and new forms to the detriment of Indigenous Peoples" (Borrows 2016, 142). Indeed, all the contributors to this volume echo Borrows's statement. Within this context, it is reasonable to assume that continuing to rely on state-conceived and state-sponsored conceptions of reconciliation may not serve Indigenous peoples in the manner necessary and may in fact be to our detriment. After all, what can calls for reconciliation reasonably offer when human and Indigenous rights violations continue to occur on an all-too-frequent basis in Canada and elsewhere (Anaya 2014)? To address the great imbalance in the relationship between Indigenous and non-Indigenous peoples in Canada, the TRC called for a journey of reconciliation to be undertaken. However, limiting the discussion of reconciliation to relations between peoples is short-sighted, as is solely relying on a state-sponsored conception of reconciliation that Indigenous peoples have challenged. As Green argues in Chapter 14, reconciliation in this context falls short of providing policy and legal and practical mechanisms for achieving justice that will actually enable and support Indigenous peoples' goals and aspirations. Although justice inquiries and commissions have rightly focused on Indigenous people's lived reality of oppression, dispossession, and violence, there is more to the story of what an Indigenous conception of reconciliation may be. Elder Reg Crowshoe explains:

> Reconciliation requires talking, but our conversations must be broader than Canada's conventional approaches. Reconciliation between Aboriginal and non-Aboriginal Canadians, from an Aboriginal perspective, also *requires reconciliation with the natural world. If human beings resolve problems between themselves but continue to destroy the natural world, then reconciliation remains incomplete.*
>
> This is a perspective that we as Commissioners have repeatedly heard: that reconciliation will never occur unless *we are also reconciled with the earth.* Mi'kmaq and other Indigenous laws stress that humans must journey through life in conversation and negotiation with all creation. Reciprocity and mutual respect help sustain our survival. (TRC 2015; italics mine)

Indigenous conceptions of reconciliation extend beyond relationships between peoples. Returning these broader relationships to a balanced state may also help bring about reconciliation and healing in human society and with other orders of beings central to Indigenous world view and relationships (McGregor 2018). Indigenous conceptions of reconciliation are supported by the architecture of Indigenous legal orders, knowledges, and systems of justice. As noted above, Indigenous peoples cannot rely on colonial systems to deliver justice to people and the natural world. Indigenous environmental principles may also inform Indigenous conceptions of reconciliation that can provide guidance for reconciling humanity's relationships with the Earth.

The TRC recognized this reality and put forth an explicit principle specifically advocating for the revitalization of Indigenous legal orders, laws, protocols, oral histories, and connections to the land as essential for achieving reconciliation (TRC 2015).

Moving Forward: Nation-to-Nation Relationships

Much remains to be achieved in terms of the overall impact of Indigenous peoples' involvement in environmental governance in Canada. Self-government agreements and comprehensive land claim processes (modern-day treaty-making) offer important opportunities to some Indigenous peoples and provide some reason for optimism in this area. There are numerous examples of successfully implemented Indigenous environmental governance frameworks across Canada, including those developed by members of the Sechelt and West Bank First Nations in British Columbia (Wyatt, Fortier, and Hebert 2009). The comprehensive land claim process also offers opportunities for collaboration and co-management of institutionalized environmental initiatives. For example, the Mackenzie Valley Resource Management Act (1998) established land and water co-management boards that implemented rigorous environmental assessment processes informed by TK guidelines. It is also important to recognize that there are critiques of these processes as well, as they continue to limit the full expression of Indigenous sovereignty and autonomy.

In 2008, the Chiefs of Ontario, in *Water Declaration of Anishinabek, Mushkegowuk and Onkwehonwe in Ontario*, called on interested parties (governments, ENGOs, academic institutions, and others) to contribute to *First Nations-led* environmental governance discussions. This approach, which honours the unique status of Indigenous peoples and their ability to establish and maintain environmental partnerships, represents a departure from the Western paradigm that expects First Nations to become involved in *state-led* environmental governance. As Indigenous peoples and their many supporters demanded in the Canada-wide Idle No More protests that began in late 2012, it is time for all environmental decisions impacting Indigenous peoples in this country to be developed in the context of nation-to-nation relationships (RCAP 1996).

Central to this environmental discussion is the need to recognize that Indigenous peoples have always developed and drawn upon their own intellectual and legal traditions to adapt to changing environmental conditions and to develop or renew nation-to-nation relationships with other peoples and "all our relations." And this recognition is increasingly apparent. Over the past two decades of policy consultation, collaborative research, and inclusive grassroots activity in Canada there has been growing support for alternative models of environmental governance that embrace different and equally valuable ways of knowing, including recognizing the living Earth as an entity with agency and rights. Certainly, barriers and challenges persist, just as colonialism does, but Indigenous peoples and their supporters can work in many ways towards honouring and remaining accountable to "all our relations" by giving life to Indigenous ways of knowing through the development of nation-to-nation relationships that honour Indigenous nationhood, sovereignty, and self-determination.

Discussion Questions

1. The list of environmental principles in this chapter is not exhaustive. Describe other environmental principles or teachings you are familiar with that can be added to those included here. Describe stories you have heard that convey environmental messages.

2. Compare and contrast the two common definitions of "environment" that shape how the concept of "environment" is understood in Canada. What do you see as the main similarities and differences between the Indigenous and Euro-Canadian perspectives?

3. Participants of Idle No More and other environmental movements and protests view their actions as a way to protect the environment, raise awareness of environmental

problems, or express Aboriginal and treaty rights. Discuss any recent environmental protests you have read or heard about in the news or online in terms of the main issue, who was involved, how environmental concerns were expressed and ethics invoked in the conflicts, whether or not the issue was resolved, and whether you think such protests and actions are effective in achieving environmental protection.

4.   What challenges or barriers exist for successfully incorporating traditional ecological knowledge (TEK) into environmental governance, and what kinds of opportunities are there for the recognition of TEK in environmental legislation in Canada?

5.   Comprehensive land claims, self-government agreements, and recent court decisions that call for the recognition of Aboriginal rights and title all offer opportunities for increased Indigenous control of lands and resources (or environment) in Canada. What are the limitations to these processes? Why do these limitations exist? Describe other opportunities that exist that can lead to greater co-operation and coexistence on environmental matters.

Recommended Reading

Bellrichard, Chantelle, and Michelle Ghoussoub. 2019. "14 Arrested as RCMP Break Gate at Gidimt'en Camp Checkpoint Set Up to Stop Pipeline Company Access." *CBC News*, 7 Jan. https://www.cbc.ca/news/indigenous/rcmp-injunction-gidimten-checkpoint-bc-1.4968391.

Crowshoe, C. 2005. *Sacred Ways of Life: Traditional Knowledge.* Prepared for the National Aboriginal Health Association. Ottawa. http://www.naho.ca/firstnations/english/documents/FNC-TraditionalknowledgeToolkit-Eng.pdf.

Haudenosaunee Environmental Task Force. 1999. *The Words That Come Before All Else: Environmental Philosophies of the Haudensaunee.* Akwesasne, NY: Native North American Travelling College.

Kermoal, Nathalie J., and Isabel Alamirano-Jimenez. 2016. *Living on the Land: Indigenous Women's Understanding of Place.* Edmonton: Athabasca University Press.

Kimmerer, R. 2013. *Braiding Sweetgrass: Indigenous Wisdom, Scientific Knowledge, and the Teachings of Plants.* Minneapolis: Milkweed Editions.

Menzies, C., ed. 2006. *Traditional Ecological Knowledge and Natural Resource Management.* Lincoln: University of Nebraska Press.

Royal Commission on Aboriginal Peoples (RCAP). 1996. "Lands and Resources." In *Report of the Royal Commission on Aboriginal Peoples,* vol. 2, *Restructuring the Relationship,* 421–685. Ottawa: Minister of Supply and Services Canada, Canada Communication Group.

Whyte, Kyle. 2011. "The Recognition Dimensions of Environmental Justice in Indian Country." *Environmental Justice* 4, no. 4: 199–205.

Additional Resources

Indigenous Climate Action. n.d. https://www.indigenousclimateaction.com/.

Indigenous Environmental Justice. n.d. http://iejproject.info.yorku.ca/.

Indigenous Environmental Network. n.d. http://www.ienearth.org/.

Environmental Noxiousness Racial Inequalities & Community Health Project. n.d. https://www.enrichproject.org/.

Notes

1. The Haudenosaunee, for example, acknowledge all aspects of the environment in their Thanksgiving Address, including (but not limited to) Mother Earth, the Moon, the Sun, the Thunderers, and Creation as well as the Creator (HETF 1999).

2. While the early colonization of the Americas was largely European in nature, the emergence of globalization now means that non-Western peoples, powers, and interests have become part of the "settlement and resource development problem" (and potential solution) for Indigenous peoples in Canada.

12 Learning from Indigenous Knowledge in Education

Jan Hare and Sara Florence Davidson

> *Put simply, each and every learning experience that affirms Indigenous knowledge systems enhances the quality of life for Aboriginal people.*
>
> —Hare 2011

Introduction

The educational landscape for Indigenous children and families in what is currently known as Canada has undergone many changes since Europeans first settled in our country. But no matter how the educational landscape has been transformed, the transmission and continuity of Indigenous knowledges have been the foundation for learning that Indigenous families, communities, and nations have always maintained for their children. Indigenous knowledges are deeply rooted within Indigenous lands and places that we all occupy. It has been the knowledge systems, cultural traditions and values, and ancestral languages that have ensured the survival of Indigenous people since time immemorial and that enrich the depth and breadth of the social, intellectual, and cultural diversity in Canada. In fact, the histories and knowledges of Indigenous peoples are integral to the local and national identities of all who make their home in Canada.

Indigenous knowledges are the sources of strength Indigenous children and youth draw upon as they navigate educational challenges, whether they attend schools on-reserve or in rural or urban communities. Indigenous families and communities are well aware that navigating the educational terrain of community-controlled, public, and independent schooling requires their children to experience Western forms of knowledge, which are valued within the curriculum and practices of schools. But they have always asserted that educational approaches should never be to the exclusion of Indigenous knowledge systems. In addition, Indigenous perspectives on learning do not see Indigenous and Western knowledge traditions in opposition to one another (Battiste 2002). Rather, Indigenous peoples' ability to thrive is a testament to the ways they can accommodate and choose from changing traditions, including Western educational approaches.

We know that future generations of Indigenous children will walk in "two worlds" and need to be armed with a strong sense of who they are as Indigenous people, contributing to their families and communities while ensuring our participation in the social, economic, and political fabric of Canadian society. This chapter describes the role of Indigenous knowledge in education, examining how Canadian educational policies and practices have moved from the denigration of Indigenous knowledges in learning institutions to finding spaces where the integration of Indigenous knowledges as a foundation for learning is having a positive impact on the educational outcomes of Indigenous children and youth. Equally important are the new learning opportunities that Indigenous knowledges and Indigenous approaches to education provide for all learners from early childhood, Kindergarten through to Grade 12, and post-secondary education.

Many Indigenous children and youth do not experience the same success with schooling as their non-Indigenous counterparts. For example, though graduation rates may show slight improvements, Statistics Canada (2018) indicates that among First Nations young adults (ages 20 to 24 years) living off-reserve 75 per cent completed high school as of 2016, yet only 46 per cent of those living on-reserve graduated. Among non-Indigenous youth, high school completion rates are noticeably higher, with 92 per cent having a high school certificate. The most common post-secondary education qualification for Indigenous learners aged 25 to 64 years is college. Despite educational gains being observed among First Nations, Inuit, and Métis, employment rates have not increased for Indigenous peoples.

Too often, Indigenous learners and their families bear the blame for their failure to achieve success in educational systems that do little to recognize the systematic and valued forms of learning in their cultures, values, languages, and ways of knowing. The education of Indigenous people must therefore be understood within the larger colonial enterprise that has long sought to use educational institutions as a primary means of eliminating the "Indian problem" in this country. Indigenous education also must be viewed in the context of the systemic barriers and inequalities inherent in the current education system that marginalize Indigenous knowledge systems and result in significant challenges to the educational success of Indigenous children and youth. The historical legacy and contemporary realities of schooling for Indigenous peoples must be understood by all Canadians if we hope to attain equality and mutual respect for all learners in our schools today, as well as strengthen relations between Indigenous peoples and the rest of Canada.

Long-standing local, national, and international policy statements convincingly argue that improved educational outcomes for Indigenous learners are critical to enhancing more general social, health, and economic indicators for Indigenous peoples in Canada. Indigenous peoples have always attended to the education of their children and youth, as observed in treaty documents across Canada. *Indian Control of Indian Education* (NIB 1972), the final *Report of the Royal Commission on Aboriginal Peoples* (RCAP 1996), the Truth and Reconciliation Commission of Canada's final report (2015), and the United Nations Declaration on the Rights of Indigenous Peoples (United Nations 2007) all affirm that education is the means by which Indigenous peoples in Canada will strengthen their identities, families, communities, and economies, and that they have the right to an education that reflects the cultures, histories, traditions, languages, and aspirations of their peoples. Along with asserting that Indigenous people will find greater meaning and relevance in educational opportunities through the inclusion of Indigenous knowledge in curricula, they note the many ways that paying respectful attention to Indigenous knowledge will benefit Canada's ability to address a wide variety of economic, environmental, social, and educational issues we confront as a society.

An increasing sense of urgency for creative and focused dialogue aimed at change in the educational system is required. The Indigenous population in this country continues to grow steadily, and half of the 1.4 million people who identify as First Nations, Inuit, or Métis are under 25 years of age. Moreover, Indigenous youth ages 16–24 now represent the fastest-growing segment not only of the Indigenous population but of the Canadian population overall (Statistics Canada and Council of Ministers of Education 2006). The urgent need for fully collaborative and creative dialogue in education in Canada is partly based on the recognition that the growing number of Indigenous youth in this country who will require the necessary knowledge and skills to navigate a future as change agents for Indigenous communities (Shirley 2017). The following discussion, however, is much more than a call for open dialogue about the need to effect positive educational change on behalf of Indigenous peoples in Canada. Our goal is that more people come to understand the colonial legacies of educational institutions that will contribute to creating a better future.

The Role of Indigenous Knowledge in Traditional Education

Indigenous knowledge represents the local and culturally specific knowledge of a people that is dynamic, adapting over time and place (Battiste 2005). The knowledges of Indigenous peoples are derived from their ways of living, knowing, and being in this world. Indigenous knowledge emerges from the values, beliefs, and practices associated with their world views (Barnhardt and Kawagley 2005). Mi'kmaw scholar Marie Battiste (2005, 8) tells us that "Indigenous peoples have their own methods for classifying and transmitting knowledge, just as they have Indigenous ways of deriving a livelihood from their environment. Information, insight, and techniques are passed down and improved from one generation to another."

Indigenous knowledge is intimately connected to land (Barnhardt and Kawagley 2005; Battiste 2002; Cajete 2000), where meaning and identity are constructed through landscapes, territory, and relationships with place and the natural world (Hare 2005). Living, learning, and land come together as land is both the context and process for relations and understanding (Simpson 2014). The natural world is the source of Indigenous peoples' livelihood, laws, governance, kinship systems, language, and culture. Since time immemorial, the sea mammals and caribou have provided food, clothing, shelter, and tools among the Inuit; the maple sugar harvest has formed social relations and economies among the Anishinaabe; and the abundance of salmon and strength of cedar on the west coast have supported practical and spiritual aspects of life among the Coast Salish and other peoples. Young people learned how to live in balance and relationship with their environment. The land connects them to both physical and metaphysical worlds (Ermine 2000).

Processes that are intergenerational, experiential, and tied to narrative and relational ways ensure the continuity and relevance of Indigenous knowledge systems. Indigenous scholars Barnhardt and Kawagley (2005, 10) tell us that traditional education practices:

> were carefully constructed around observing natural processes, adapting modes of survival, obtaining sustenance from the plant and animal world, and using

natural materials to make their tools and implements. All of this was made understandable through demonstration and observation accompanied by thoughtful stories in which the lessons were embedded.

The emphasis on learning by watching, listening, and then doing is underscored by many Indigenous Elders reflecting on their childhoods. In recalling her Kwakwaka'wakw childhood on the northwest coast of British Columbia, Agnes Alfred (2004, 83–5) recounts that "I watched my grandmother in her daily activities, whether cooking, preparing fish, digging roots or clams, weaving baskets or making rope. . . . I also followed my grandmother around when she was stripping bark off the trees so I would know how to do it myself." And at the eastern extreme of the continent, in Labrador, Innu Elder Elizabeth Penashue shares her parents' hands-on approach to learning: "When I was old enough as a little girl my mother encouraged me to work, cleaning beaver and other animals. My mother would perform and the children would sit around and watch, so that they can learn" (Kulchyski, McCaskill, and Newhouse 1999, 200).

Storytelling has always provided Indigenous children with valuable teachings about how things came to be and how to live in this world in a "good way." Mary Lou Andrew, in an interview with Stó:lō scholar Jo-ann Archibald (2008, 73), explains:

> Stories were told when children were being taught how to sew, how to do laundry . . . in my childhood, my grandmother, my grandfather, always had

Elder Siipa Isullatak teaches children how to sew at the Nakasuk Elementary School in Iqaluit, Nunavut.

stories . . . [when] walking through the fields or if you went to gather fruit or food, or just going from point A to point B, there was a story to be told. . . . You got not only the history about the place, the land; you were taught [other] lessons. . . . You got social studies . . . sometimes even science was thrown in, when you had to deal with herbs and medicines. You learned the importance of why you do something.

The teachings inherent in the living earth are also evident in Indigenous peoples' Creation stories, which often direct Indigenous peoples how to live in the natural world. For instance, Anishinaabe children learn that they came to the world by being lowered from above after a union of Mother Earth's four elements, wind, air, fire, and water. When the Earth was flooded, it was Nanaboozho and other animals floating on a log that searched below the waters for any sign of Earth. It was Muskrat who was successful in the animals' attempts to bring up the dirt from the depths below. And it is Turtle who bears the weight of Earth, which expands on the turtle's shell to form what we know today as Turtle Island or, more familiar to non-Indigenous people, North America. It is through the amusing, and sometimes serious, antics of the trickster that Indigenous children learn important life lessons. Known as Raven or Coyote among First Nations communities in British Columbia, Glooskap among the Mi'kmaq, Nanaboozho to the Anishinaabe, Wesakechak in Cree oral traditions, or identified as a shape-shifter within specific language traditions, this character provides us with new understandings of the world by taking on many transformations.

Ancestral languages are intimately connected to the world views of Indigenous peoples (Battiste 2000). As the very means by which the oral content of Indigenous knowledge is contained and transmitted, ancestral languages may convey cultural values, shape thought and identity, and describe relationships to people and place. Odawa Elder Liza Mosher explains the visceral connection to the thought and feelings that ancestral languages provide:

Native language is very important because our teachings are in the language. You miss out on the meaning when you talk about it in English. . . . What I understand is when I hear the teachings in the Lodge, how beautiful and sacred it is when it reaches people in the language I can't even describe how it feels. But when you talk about it in English, it is not the same, you don't have that feeling as you have in the language. (Quoted in Kulchyski, McCaskill, and Newhouse 1999, 160)

The languages of Indigenous peoples express their distinct relationship with land, as Deborah McGregor notes in Chapter 11 (see Task Force on Aboriginal Languages and Culture 2005). Place names, land-based experiences, custodial responsibilities to landscapes, and traditional territories and identity all are given expression and meaning through ancestral languages. Moreover, the transmission of language from one generation to another ensures the continuity of Indigenous knowledge.

Living and learning have always been interwoven for Indigenous peoples. Family and community were responsible for making sure that children learned the necessary skills and knowledge to ensure their survival. Elders and other traditional people in the community such as traditional healers, two-spirited and medicine people, and knowledge carriers also had specific roles and have always been important sources of Indigenous knowledge. For example, Elders are revered for their role as holders of traditional knowledge and for the responsibility they carry for sharing that knowledge. Elders are leaders among their people who help guide, teach, and care for children and families. Traditional healers took a holistic approach to helping the mind, body, and spirit. They drew on the natural world of plants and medicines, as well as on the guidance of prayer and ceremony and the wisdom of the Elders to provide healing. Extended family has always been highly valued, and it was not unusual for children to live with grandparents, aunties, and cousins who shared responsibilities to care for children.

Indigenous knowledge and pedagogies have always been at the heart of educational approaches. Children acquire knowledge and skills through looking, listening, and experiential learning (Miller 1996). They come to understand who they are and their place in this world through the stories inscribed in landscape and other narrative texts in their lives (Hare 2005). Learning takes place in meaningful contexts such as on the land, in specific places, or within celebration and ceremony. Family and community members are teachers and caregivers to children, and ancestral languages are the mode of communication for transmitting our knowledge through the generations. The many sources of Indigenous knowledge not only prepare children for a sustainable lifestyle, they also serve to enrich families, communities, and nations. For thousands of years and prior to contact with European colonizers, strong vibrant nations gave rise to proud and prosperous children and families who thrived on Indigenous ways of knowing and being in the world. As is evident in the following sections, centuries of injustices and trauma experienced by Indigenous peoples are linked to historical and contemporary forms of colonialism.

Colonizing Indigenous Knowledge in Education

Missionaries were the first outsiders to take on the task of providing a formal education system for Indigenous peoples, with the primary goal of civilizing "Indians" to Christian and settler ways. Schooling options offered by missionaries included day and boarding schools, early integration experiments, and schooling for alliances (Hare 2003). Missionaries in New France set up day schools and boarding schools where Indigenous children could attend daily or live for a certain length of time. These schools were established as early as the 1600s, with the first known boarding school set up by the Recollects in 1620 (Miller 1996). The Jesuits followed shortly thereafter, and residential schools eventually became the norm across Canada as settlement expanded westward. Most of these early schooling arrangements allowed the people to carry on with their seasonal living and maintain their cultural practices and traditions. Initially, missionaries gained knowledge of ancestral languages in the locales where they established their missions to Indigenous peoples, who, for the most part, accepted missionaries for their own purposes in their changing world. These purposes included developing literacy skills through Bible reading and aligning with specific missionaries, who sometimes served as conduits to government officials and traders (Hare and Barman 2007). Development of these and other new skills demonstrates Indigenous peoples' ability to learn from others and to accommodate them within their own traditions.

After Confederation, when Indigenous peoples came to be viewed as a threat to the plans of the government of Canada, they were construed as a problem and a hindrance to the formation of the Canadian state and the settlement of a new European-founded nation (Hare and Barman 2000). The government deemed the assimilation of Indigenous people into the settler society as a necessary means of gaining access to their land and resources that would benefit settlers and newcomers. Assimilation was also seen as a way of ridding themselves of the "Indian problem." Government officials believed that if Indigenous people gave up their seasonal lifestyle and "lost" their cultural practices, values, and languages, they could be persuaded to take up sedentary pursuits among white settlers in towns and villages and on farms. As historian John Milloy (1999, 4–5) notes in his comprehensive review of the residential school system in Canada, "Aboriginal knowledge and skills were neither necessary nor desirable in a land that was to be dominated by European industry and, therefore, by Europeans and their culture."

Since European newcomers deemed the original inhabitants to be inferior (Dickason 1984), they assumed that these people needed to be assimilated through strict indoctrination into Christian ways in the most expedient and aggressive manner. Day and boarding schools had proven to be ineffective means of assimilation because they allowed children to remain with their families, clans, and villages. This kept Indigenous knowledges intact and gave Indigenous people choices about their children's schooling, including whether or not they would even allow them to take part.

The government soon recognized that to "do away with the tribal system and assimilate the Indian people in all respects with the inhabitants of the Dominion" (Sir John A. Macdonald, cited in Milloy 1999, 6), it was necessary to remove Indigenous children and youth from their families. This, officials determined, would help prevent the intergenerational transmission of Indigenous knowledge. Motivated by Indian policy in the United States that saw Native American children confined to segregated residential institutions, Canada soon adopted a similar approach based on the recommendations put forward by Nicholas Davin (1879) in his report to the government. By 1880, residential schools had become the model of schooling for Indigenous children and youth across Canada, and the government decided that Indigenous people would be required by law to send their children to these schools. As Métis Elder Grace Zoldy describes: "We never said anything 'cause we thought it was normal. We thought it was normal in the white system. We didn't know they were coming here to use us and abuse us in any way possible. We didn't know that. Our parents didn't know that" (Logan 2012, 82).

The number of residential schools in Canada exceeded 80 by the 1930s (Dickason and Newbigging 2015, 238), and at one time there were nearly 140 schools in operation. There is now widespread agreement, thanks in large part to the many stories told by residential school survivors and others to Canada's Truth and Reconciliation Commission (TRC 2015), that the entire history of residential schools has left a painful legacy that belongs to all Canadians. It is a shared past that has produced very different outcomes for Indigenous and non-Indigenous peoples as a result of the policies and practices that were the foundation of this totalizing and brutal system.

From the beginning, the government gave responsibility for "civilizing" Indigenous children and youth to various Christian denominations and ecclesiastical traditions. Government and religious representatives were convinced that full transformation of the Indian child called for indoctrination into Christianity alongside a basic education. Institutional routines included giving children a number associated with their Christian name, having children wear school uniforms and follow strict rules that governed all behaviour inside as well as outside of the classroom, a rigorous program of prayer, and a combination of labour that was decisively gendered and very rudimentary in-class learning. Recalling her early mornings at Kamloops Indian Residential School in the 1930s, Sophie shared that:

> We marched from there down to the chapel and we spent over an hour in the chapel every morning, every blessed morning. And there they interrogated us on what it was all about being an Indian. . . . He [the priest] would get so carried away; he was punching away at the old altar rail . . . to hammer it into our heads that we were not to think or act or speak like an Indian. And that we would go to hell and burn for eternity if we did not listen to their way of teaching. (Quoted in Haig-Brown 1988, 59)

Although manual labour was not viewed as a necessary part of the educational curriculum, school administrators deemed it necessary because of the minimal funding the government provided to run the schools. Children were needed to help with the daily operation of schools as well as to provide paid services for businesses and individuals in neighbouring towns, with payment generally going directly to the school. Children and youth would attend classes for part of the day and provide labour for the school in another portion of the day.[1] Clara Campbell, who attended the St Mary's Mission located on Stó:lō territory in British Columbia, recalls this half-day system: "I think we maybe only had two hours of school in the morning. We didn't have much school. The bigger girls sort of were working. They did two or three hours of work, and then in the afternoon they had two or three out of school. That's the way it was when I was there" (quoted in Glavin 2002, 30).

There is widespread agreement in personal accounts as well as in comprehensive reviews of residential schooling in Canada (AFN 1994; Furniss 1995; Glavin 2002; Grant 2004; Haig-Brown 1988; Ing 1991; Jaine 1993; Knockwood 1992; Miller 1996; Milloy 1999; Nuu-chah-nulth Tribal Council 1996; Secwepemc Cultural Education Society 2000; TRC 2015) that the most destructive feature of residential schools was the denigration of Indigenous knowledges that were embedded within ancestral languages, traditional cultural practices, and ways of living. Upon their arrival at school, Indigenous children were immediately forbidden to speak their ancestral languages and were expected to take up English, or French in Quebec. The fact that children only spoke an Indigenous language upon their arrival at school made it extremely difficult for them to learn in the classroom and to adjust to the expectations of teachers and administrators. A member of the Nuu-chah-nulth Nation, Ambrose Maquina, recalls just how difficult it was when he came to Old Christie Residential School (at what is now Tofino, BC): "We ended up in a school room. I didn't know what A.B.C. was. I never spoke English. I didn't understand English . . . I couldn't even speak English . . . I felt really lost! Yeah, really, really, lost" (quoted in Nuu-chah-nulth Tribal Council 1996, 45).

What stands out most for survivors of residential schools was the abuse they experienced as punishment whenever they were caught speaking their languages. Children were hit, strapped, whipped, and beaten by teachers and administrators who refused to accept their languages as valid. In her memoir of her time at Shubenacadie Residential School in Nova Scotia, Isabelle Knockwood (1992, 98) observed, "when little children first arrived at school we would see bruises on their throats and cheeks that told us they had been caught speaking Mi'kmaw." One Indigenous woman's unsettling recollection reveals the extent of the punishment:

> Today I understand quite a few words in my language. But every time I try and talk it, my tongue hurts. I didn't know why. I ran into another woman who went to residential school with me and we were talking about it. She asked me if I remembered how they would stick a needle in our tongue if we got caught talking our language. . . . Maybe that's why my tongue hurts whenever I try to talk my language. (Quoted in AFN 1994, 25)

The widespread prohibition against speaking one's ancestral language was devastating. As noted previously, ancestral languages are at the very heart of Indigenous peoples' culture and are the primary means by which Indigenous knowledge is expressed, cultivated, and learned. The loss of Indigenous languages by the majority of students who attended these institutions was inevitable, and it continues to have devastating consequences in the lives of Indigenous individuals, families, and communities throughout Canada. Knockwood (1992, 99) explains: "The punishment of speaking Mi'kmaw began on our first day at school, but the punishment has continued all our lives as we try to piece together who we are and what the world means to us with a language many of us had to re-learn as adults."

Expressions of Indigenous knowledge in the form of social practices, cultural traditions, and values also suffered irreparable damage as a result of assimilation policies and practices of residential schools. Outward appearance was altered by way of dress and grooming. Girls had their hair cut to "respectable" lengths, and boys had their heads shorn, which ignored the fact that many young Indigenous children had been raised to understand the sacredness and the status associated with how their hair was kept. For example, among the Anishinaabe, a braid in the hair was a symbol of strength and unity whereby mind, body, and spirit, represented in the three strands of the braid, are woven together. In other words, Indigenous children had their pride and dignity taken away when their hair was cut. The consequences for those who attempted to maintain aspects of their culture were the same as for speaking the language. Recalling her time at Kamloops Indian Residential School in the interior of British Columbia, one woman explained just what could happen if children attempted to maintain any of their traditional ways:

> We were not allowed to speak our language; we weren't allowed to dance, sing because they told us it was evil. It was evil for us to practice any of our cultural ways. . . . Some of the girls would get some Indian food . . . they'd take it away from us and just to be mean they'd destroy it right in front of us. (Quoted in Haig-Brown 1988, 58)

The forced separation of children and youth from families and members of their communities also prevented the passing on of Indigenous knowledge from one generation to another. Whereas parents, Elders, extended family, and community members shared the collective responsibility of helping children make sense of their world and how to live in it, residential schools prevented family and community involvement in the schools and ultimately in their children's lives during the formative years into young adulthood. The schools provided an environment devoid of family interactions as children were separated from their siblings. The result of this was that many children never returned to their families after attending a residential school. The former National Chief of the Assembly of First Nations, Phil Fontaine, attended the Fort Alexander Residential School north of Winnipeg. He describes how even his most basic emotional needs were not met in the 10 years he attended: "At home I learned certain things about love and how it was expressed, but that was cast aside when I went to residential school. There, I was completely cut off from my parents and I lost a lot. I lost my sense of family. I didn't develop the kind of love one should experience in a family" (Jaine 1993, 53).

Remembering his time with his family, another residential school survivor shared that "I learned my language from my dad, I learned about the medicine, I learned about the land, some of the old stories" (quoted in Secwepemc Cultural Education Society 2000, 167). The connections to family and community were intentionally severed by law so that children and youth could be under the complete control of government and church. By preventing Indigenous children and youth from maintaining the traditional ways of their people, the government, through school administrators, ensured that they would be unable to return to them after they left school.

There is clear evidence that Indigenous families and communities have suffered greatly from the disparaging of Indigenous knowledge at these institutions. In fact, the forms of physical abuse, torture, and deaths suffered by Indigenous children at these schools meet the United Nations definition of genocide, which includes "causing serious bodily harm or [harm to] mental health" with intent "to destroy, in whole or part, a national, ethnical, racial, or religious group" (United Nations 2010, 2). Our traditional approaches to living and learning were eroded as the policies and practices of these schools emphasized preparing children and youth for agricultural, industrial, and domestic pursuits patterned on Euro-Canadian ways and denying the importance of land-based relationships, cultural and language continuity, and learning. Banning practices such as ceremonies, singing, smudging, and drumming meant that children were unable to carry their meaning forward to future generations. The emotional and spiritual toll on children and their families from being punished whenever they attempted to express Indigenous knowledge has left their identities in a fragile state. As one Indigenous survivor of the Kamloops Indian Residential School shared:

They took away my belongings, they took away everything from me. Everything that's important to me, mother, father, culture. . . . And they put what they wanted in us, made us ashamed of who we are. Even right to this day, it still affects me. Like I really want to get in to Indian things and I just can't because of them telling us it was of the devil. Every time I try, something blocks me. I can't, because I am afraid. (Quoted in Secwepemc Cultural Education Society 2000, 29)

The Intergenerational Legacy of Residential Schooling

What cannot go untold is the fact that the abuse that children and youth suffered at these institutions resulted in intergenerational trauma for individuals, families, and communities. The personal recollections of those who attended these schools reveal dehumanizing experiences marked by isolation, hunger, humiliation, hypocrisy, shame, torture, and fear, all carried out through spiritual, emotional, physical, and mental abuse (Hare 2007). Residential school survivors have revealed that sexual abuse was rampant in these institutions. The abusive practices of many adults who ran these schools also turned many of the youth into aggressors against their fellow students. The tragic results of this legacy have spilled back into Indigenous families and communities and into Canadian society generally.

Recent court proceedings, in which many former students brought criminal charges against school administrators and teachers, provided an opportunity for school survivors to share their experiences and for healing to begin. Following the public disclosure in the 1980s of abuse against former students, churches began to publicly apologize for their role in the schools. The Royal Commission on Aboriginal Peoples (1996) called for a public inquiry to investigate and document the totally devastating impact of residential schools. The federal government responded, first in 1998 when the Indian Affairs minister, Jane Stewart, issued an apology. As residential school survivors continued to seek redress through the courts, the government and churches eventually signed a settlement agreement that promised to provide compensation to residential school survivors. Part of this process involved Prime Minister Stephen Harper making a formal apology on behalf of the government in the House of Commons in June 2008. The prime minister's statement, and those of other party leaders, expressed profound regret for past actions of the government and was met with responses from the leaders of national Indigenous organizations.[2] Along with the apology the government announced a healing fund to support community initiatives that would provide aid to residential school survivors and their families. The Assembly of First Nations assisted survivors throughout the compensation process. A key component of the Indian Residential Schools Settlement Agreement was the establishment of the Truth and Reconciliation Commission of Canada (TRC), whose mandate was to document and witness survivor testimonies with the goal of creating a complete historical record of the system and its legacy, and to promote education and awareness among all Canadians about the residential school system and its impacts.

The TRC, which delivered a final report in 2015, bridged truth-telling with education as 6,000 witnesses shared their experiences in public and private forums. Seven national events took place across Canada, allowing many Canadians to engage with the process. This was because, "Without truth, justice is not served, healing cannot happen, and there can be no genuine reconciliation between Aboriginal and non-Aboriginal peoples in Canada" (TRC 2015, 12). There is concern that current approaches to reconciliation have outpaced an emphasis on truth-telling, putting at risk the very goals and intentions that underlie reconciliation (Justice 2018). All Canadians need to learn much more about Indigenous–settler history, including residential schooling, told from the perspectives of Indigenous peoples if reconciliation is to be a transformative framework for relations in this country.

Reconciliation as a framework for changing Indigenous–settler relations is seen as necessary to closing the gap in significant social, economic, and educational disparities that exist between Indigenous and non-Indigenous peoples (AFN 2015). Other advocates underscore the personal and collective healing needed to redress past injustices (Reconciliation Canada n.d.). The 94 "Calls to Action" of the TRC provide policy directives for government, education, and religious institutions. For example, post-secondary institutions have mobilized approaches that include strategic plans, symbolic representations on campuses, Indigenous faculty hires, symposiums and workshops, Indigenous community engagement initiatives, new programs, and enhancing curriculum, including required coursework that incorporates Indigenous perspectives, content, and pedagogies (Universities Canada 2016).

Approaches to reconciliation have also been criticized for focusing on residential schools, rather than on the policies and practices that continue to contribute to ongoing colonialism (Corntassel and Chah-win-is 2009). Others take issue with the disconnect between reconciliation, decolonization, and Indigenous land rights (Alfred 2017; Coulthard 2014). By attending exclusively to relationship-building, settler Canadians fail to understand their own complicity in destructive histories and problematic power structures (McCoun 2016). Instead, they remain invested in their own innocence, rather than grappling with settler privilege that comes from occupation of Indigenous lands (Scully 2015). Indigenous and ally scholars have long asserted that for reconciliation to be sustainable and advance Indigenous rights and priorities, the United Nations Declaration of the Rights of Indigenous Peoples (UNDRIP) must be used to guide Indigenous–settler relations. UNDRIP recognizes that "Indigenous peoples have the right to maintain, control, protect and develop their cultural heritage, traditional knowledge, and traditional cultural expressions" (United Nations 2007, 11).

Creating Space for Indigenous Knowledge in Education Today

Residential schools began to fade from the Canadian educational landscape in the early 1950s, which is when educational policy started to promote Indigenous children attending schools alongside non-Indigenous students. Increasing pressure came from Indigenous political groups and communities for more educational options for Indigenous children, including providing schools under government control on reserves as well as opportunities to attend public schools off-reserve. Nonetheless, every schooling option failed to incorporate Indigenous knowledge into curriculum and teaching approaches as schools still relied on provincial curricula, which did not reflect the histories, experiences, or perspectives of Indigenous people. Families and communities remained on the margins of their children's education, since on-reserve schools continued to be governed by policies set out by the Department of Indian Affairs. Moreover, provincial school boards did not consider the participation of Indigenous parents and Elders as necessary or valuable. As a result, early efforts to integrate Indigenous children with their non-Indigenous peers failed to enhance Indigenous student success. This was evidenced in a high incidence of school-leaving, low parental participation, streaming of Indigenous children and youth into special education, and age–grade lags.

Despite attempts to provide a wider range of educational opportunities for Indigenous students, efforts to assimilate Indigenous peoples through federal government policies continued throughout the 1960s. Then, in 1969, the federal government attempted to do away with the Indian Act by passing responsibility for Indigenous affairs to provincial governments through its infamous White Paper. In a varied set of political responses exemplified in the Indian Chiefs of Alberta's 1970 Red Paper and the Union of British Columbia Indian Chiefs' Brown Paper, Aboriginal groups overwhelmingly rejected the proposed policy on the grounds that it would see their political and legal rights to self-determination relegated to the status of other Canadians. A clear response came from the National Indian Brotherhood in a policy focused on education for self-determination and fostering a positive Indigenous identity. Their document, *Indian Control of Indian Education*, remains a landmark in Indigenous education in Canada. It proposed that Indigenous peoples had the right to determine how best to meet their educational goals. While providing a vision for the future of Indigenous education in this country, the policy document was highly critical of the lack of educational facilities for Indigenous students, the poor quality of teacher training, and the limited way school curricula included Indigenous perspectives, pedagogies, and histories. In effect, it insisted that Indigenous knowledge must be at the core of all learning experiences for Indigenous children and youth.

Today, Indigenous people across Canada are increasingly asserting that the responsibility rests with all Canadians to create space for Indigenous knowledge in formal learning settings. They note that if education in Canada is to benefit all students, this will require all Canadians opening their minds as well as their hearts to the different ways that knowledge is constructed, shared, and valued. This vision was articulated in the national Accord on Indigenous Education (Archibald et al. 2010) launched by the Association of Canadian Deans of Education. The Accord recognizes that Indigenous ways of knowing should flourish at all educational levels and that engaging Indigenous world views and ways of knowing will benefit all learners in Canada. In other words, the Accord asserts that Indigenous knowledge systems should be central to education policy, curriculum, and pedagogy, and that will be of benefit to all Canadians.

The TRC "Calls to Action" also make explicit the role of Indigenous knowledge in teaching and learning—for all learners—from early childhood through post-secondary education. As a response, undergraduate students at the University of Winnipeg and Lakehead University take a course on Indigenous knowledge as part of their program requirements. Many professional programs, including nursing, law, education, and social work, also now require course instruction emphasizing the legacy and impact of residential schooling and the importance of developing cross-cultural competencies. In December 2014, Colleges and Institutes Canada announced the launch of its Indigenous Education Protocol for Colleges and Institutes. Developed by its Indigenous Education Committee, the document outlines a number of principles that signing institutions agree to adopt, including: ensuring that Indigenous knowledge and education are respected and given proper priority; increasing Indigenous content and approaches to learning; and building understanding and relationships among Indigenous and non-Indigenous peoples (Colleges and Institutes Canada 2014). More recent innovations by post-secondary institutions to implement the "Calls to Action" include a complement of massive open online courses (MOOCs), which are free courses delivered in a multimodal format through different platforms that are available to anyone with access to the Internet. Courses include "Reconciliation through Indigenous Education" offered by the Faculty of Education at the University of British Columbia, "Aboriginal Worldviews and Education" through the University of Toronto, and "Indigenous Canada" from the University of Alberta. These developments are part of an Indigenization movement aimed at systemic change of post-secondary institutions. Such transformation requires collaboration with Indigenous peoples and communities and long-term and sustainable commitments by higher education systems. Otherwise, these efforts are limited in their potential and relegate Indigenous contributions to a cultural category rather than a challenge to the colonial character of the academy (Widdowson 2016).

TRC "Call to Action" 63 advises "developing and implementing Kindergarten to Grade Twelve curriculum and learning resources on Aboriginal peoples in Canadian history, and the history and legacy of residential school" (TRC 2015, 7). While there has been a long history of education on Indigenous–settler treaties in provinces such as Saskatchewan and Manitoba, other provinces such as Nova Scotia and Ontario are beginning to make changes to integrate treaty education into all parts of the curriculum. British Columbia has implemented a new curriculum for all public school students that draws from Indigenous perspectives, histories, and world views framed through the lens of the First Peoples Principles of Learning. This lens conveys that learning is embedded in history, memory, and story and recognizes the foundational role of Indigenous knowledges. Such an approach is likened to the central place Inuit Qaujimajatuqangit—loosely, Inuit traditional knowledge, including beliefs, values, and skills—has attained within the curriculum and education system of Nunavut (Nunavut Department of Education 2007). It is clear that there is widespread and growing support for the idea that such curriculum reform will contribute to the success of Indigenous learners, as well as build the knowledge of other learners in ways that will enable them to engage in respectful relations with Indigenous people.

Efforts that support Indigenous knowledge being central to learning experiences are not new in education. Programs and initiatives have been designed and implemented by Indigenous peoples that continue to make a significant impact on teaching and learning. One of the most promising initiatives for Indigenous children is Aboriginal Head Start (AHS),[3] a nationally funded early childhood education intervention program begun in 1995 that enables on-reserve and urban Aboriginal communities to design and deliver pre-educational programming for their children. AHS now operates in over 450 Indigenous communities and organizations across Canada. The program takes a holistic approach to helping families prepare young Indigenous children (up to six years of age) for schooling by nurturing their emotional, social, cognitive, and spiritual development. Family and community work together to help realize the operating principles of the program, which include family involvement, health promotion, nutrition, social support, culture and language, and school readiness. A Public Health Agency of Canada (2012) evaluation of the urban and northern communities program of AHS found that children participating in the program experienced significant gains in their use of language as well as in their motor skills and in academic development overall as compared to non-participating Indigenous children. Moreover, a comparison of Indigenous and non-Indigenous children found that the scores for the two groups were similar by the end of the school year (Public Health Agency of Canada 2012). In their analysis of literature examining early childhood education for Indigenous children, Preston and colleagues (2012) found that Indigenous pedagogies were one of five features of effective Indigenous early childhood learning environments. This evidences the need to focus increased resources and efforts on training Indigenous educators in culturally grounded ways of knowing and learning, such as those outlined earlier in this chapter.

Several post-secondary institutions across Canada have been offering Indigenous teacher education programs for years. For example, the Native Indian Teacher Education Program at the University of British Columbia has integrated traditional Indigenous values in a way that has prepared graduates to teach in public, band-operated, and independent schools for over 45 years. Furthermore, the program has always provided opportunities for students to start their program in field centres located in rural areas, thus allowing them to remain closely connected to their communities (Teacher Education Office n.d.). It has graduated over 400 Indigenous teachers and equipped them to bring Indigenous perspectives and world views to classrooms. Since 2000, preparing Indigenous language teachers has been a priority of the Canadian Indigenous Languages and Literacy Development Institute at the University of Alberta. Their programming brings together faculties of Education, Arts, and Native Studies to support courses in Indigenous languages and knowledge systems, immersion teaching, theatre to teach language, school- and community-based language policy, and curriculum development (Blair, Pelly, and Starr 2018). A more recent model of Indigenous language teacher education at the University of Victoria focuses on assisting learners to revitalize language in their own communities by building their own language proficiency as they move towards a certificate and then diploma in language fluency. This laddered approach leads to professional teacher certification for Indigenous language speakers (McIvor et al. 2018).

Given the current state of traditional language loss among Indigenous peoples, language revitalization is perhaps the most urgent realm of Indigenous education today and also has the greatest potential to advance Indigenous education goals. Hermes (2007) asserts that Indigenous language immersion programs offer the greatest promise in Indigenous language revitalization, while others describe them as the most effective means of ensuring the intergenerational transmission of Indigenous knowledge (McCarty 2003; Reyhner et al. 2003). Languages are intimately connected to world view and relevant to land and identity (Battiste 2013). In their research with Mi'kmaw language programs, Usborne and colleagues (2011) determined that Indigenous language immersion programs not only supported the learning of the Mi'kmaw language, but that students enrolled in such programs also demonstrated as much success in English-language proficiency as students in classrooms where the instruction was primarily in English. Across Canada, immersion language programming is taking hold slowly as communities struggle with loss of language speakers and communities and governments offer piecemeal support for language revitalization initiatives. There are, however, some hopeful signs of success. Immersion programs exist from preschool to Grade 3 in Onion Lake, Saskatchewan, and Kahnawake, Quebec. The Adams Lake Indian Band in British Columbia hosts a "language nest" for preschool as well as a full language immersion program from Kindergarten to Grade 7 in its community school (McIvor 2009). Efforts to meaningfully integrate Indigenous knowledges to improve educational experiences for Indigenous children and youth have resulted in some promising programs; however, there is still much systemic change needed to further support the advancement of such initiatives.

The Way Ahead

Once the foundation of the learning experience of Indigenous children and youth, the sharing of Indigenous knowledge was severely disrupted by assimilationist schooling policies and practices that aimed to rid Indigenous peoples of their identities. For well over a century, residential schools were the primary means by which governmental and religious bodies attempted to systematically eradicate languages, cultures, and values from the lives of Indigenous children. In short, they sought to alter completely the way Indigenous children and youth came to understand and live within their world. The legacies of residential schooling are still very evident and will undoubtedly persist into the future, and as a result Indigenous learners continue to face many challenges and barriers in the educational system. It is a colonial history that all Canadians share, and as such we must address the legacy of this past through shared responsibilities towards reconciliation.

The educational initiatives discussed in this chapter demonstrate the role of Indigenous knowledges and approaches in education curricula, pedagogies, and policies at all levels of education, as well as in community settings. Evidently, Indigenous students increasingly are able to experience meaningful educational success when teaching and learning attends to Indigenous knowledge systems. Further, the benefits for all students to engage with Indigenous people and perspectives within education must be realized, especially as we seek more socially just, equitable, and sustainable ways of living in relationship to one another and to the land. Learning from the knowledge systems and world views of Indigenous peoples who have long-standing relationships to the lands we call Canada can challenge our own assumptions and expand our own learning experiences. This is important for reconciliation between Indigenous peoples and the rest of Canada, which requires knowledge of Indigenous–settler histories and attending to Indigenous voices and priorities. Likewise, when Indigenous knowledges shape the structures and processes of our educational institutions we are able to address the intergenerational legacies of racism and colonialism and better educate both Indigenous and non-Indigenous learners (Widdowson 2016). As Barnhardt and Kawagley (2005) note, "Our challenge now is to devise a system of education for all people that respects the epistemological and pedagogical foundations provided by both Indigenous and Western cultural traditions."

Discussion Questions

1. How do Indigenous approaches to education relate to current practices and policies you observe in early childhood, Kindergarten to Grade 12, or post-secondary education today?

2. Compare Indigenous peoples' sources of knowledge and the kinds of knowledge they value with the sources and kinds of knowledge that you learned to value in school, within your own family system, or community. How are they similar? How are they different?

3. What have you learned about Indigenous knowledge and the history of Indigenous peoples in schooling? How do you think your experience of school might have been different if Indigenous knowledge and approaches to learning had been an integral part of your education?

4. How do you see yourself participating in reconciliation processes that ask you to consider how you have been affected by or benefited from colonial policies and practices directed at Indigenous peoples?

5. What might the future of education in Canada look like if Indigenous peoples' vision of education is embraced by the rest of Canada?

Recommended Reading

Battiste, Marie. 2013. *Decolonizing Education: Nourishing the Learning Spirit*. Saskatoon: Purich Publishing.

Bouvier, R., M. Battiste, and J. Laughlin. 2016. "Centering Indigenous Intellectual Traditions on Holistic Lifelong Learning." In *Indigenous Perspectives on Education for Well-Being*, edited by F. Deer and T. Falkenberg, 21-40. Winnipeg: ESWB Press, University of Winnipeg. https://www.eswb-press.org/uploads/1/2/8/9/12899389/indigeneous_perspectives_2016.pdf.

Canadian Association of University Teachers (CAUT). 2017. *Guide to Acknowledging First Peoples & Traditional Territory*. Ottawa: CAUT. https://www.caut.ca/sites/default/files/caut-guide-to-acknowledging-first-peoples-and-traditional-territory-2017-09.pdf.

Castellano, M., L. Brant, L. Davis, and L. Lahache. 2001. *Aboriginal Education: Fulfilling the Promise*. Vancouver: University of British Columbia Press.

Government of Saskatchewan. 2013. *Learning Resources Evaluation Guidelines*. Saskatoon. http://publications.gov.sk.ca/documents/11/40280-learning-resource-evaluation-guidelines.pdf.

Kirkness, Verna J. 2013. *Creating Space: My Life and Work in Indigenous Education*. Winnipeg: University of Manitoba Press.

Miller, J.R. 1996. *Shingwauk's Vision: A History of Native Residential Schools*. Toronto: University of Toronto Press.

Additional Resources

Legacy of Hope Foundation. n.d. "Where Are the Children?" http://wherearethechildren.ca/en/timeline/.

Native-Land.ca. n.d. "Our Home on Native Land." https://native-land.ca.

National Film Board. 2019. "Indigenous Cinema." https://www.nfb.ca/indigenous-cinema/?&film_lang=en&sort=year:desc,title&year=1917..2018.

National Centre for the Collaboration in Indigenous Education. https://www.nccie.ca.

National Centre for Truth and Reconciliation. http://www.trc.ca

Project of Heart. http://projectofheart.ca.

Notes

1. This practice was the origin of the "half-day" schooling system.

2. For complete texts of the apologies of Prime Minister Harper and other party leaders, as well as the responses of Indigenous leaders, see http://www.ourcommons.ca/DocumentViewer/en/39-2/house/sitting-110/hansard.

3. For information on Aboriginal Head Start, see www.hc-sc.gc.ca/fniah-spnia/famil/develop/ahsor-papa_intro-eng.php.

13 Moosehide Tanning and Wellness in the North

Mandee McDonald

When I was 16 years old, I was invited to an Indigenous women's sewing circle. I accepted the invitation. Most of the ladies there were beading, but they didn't have much extra supplies. I didn't have any beads, and I didn't know how to bead. When my mom got home from work that night, I told her that I went to the sewing group, but I didn't have any beads. She walked to her bedroom, opened her closet, and pulled out an old black leather bag. She said, "This is all I have from our culture to pass on to you," and gave me the bag. It was full of beads in glass jars, in old pill bottles, and wrapped in cloths. To be honest, I already knew what was in the bag because, as a child, I used to pull all the containers out and stare at the beads inside. I'd roll the jars around on the floor and wish I knew what to do with them. Some of my grandmother's patterns were in the bag too, so I used one to bead my first flower, and I gave it to my mom. It's framed on the wall in her house. My grandmother's beads inspired me to learn to bead and sew, which led to my interest in tanning hides, which led me on a path to a totally different life than I would otherwise be living.

It is a good life.

When I envision myself in the future, there's a family with me, and they're dressed in moose and caribou hide that I tanned.

Introduction

I started learning to tan hides with the support of my friend and hide-tanning mentor Melaw Nakehk'o, a Dehcho Dene/Dënesųłiné artist from Łı́ı́dlı̨ı̨ Kų́é First Nation, almost 10 years ago. Since then, a resurgence of hide tanning has been steadily growing in the North, led by Indigenous women. The impacts of this resurgence have been and continue to be amazing to experience and witness. For myself, tanning hides has been a source of strength, grounding, sobriety, and community. It's been the genesis of many positive, healthy intergenerational relationships with people older and younger than me. As hide tanners, we have initiated new and strengthened existing relationships with hunters and harvesters who provide us with skilfully skinned hides. I've witnessed the sense of cultural pride and community belonging that Indigenous people feel when they're learning to work a hide for the first time, and this can be applied to learning other land-based and cultural practices, but hide tanning is the focus of this chapter as that is my experience to describe and share.

Danya Erasmus

A child's hand on muskox hide.

Self-Location

Hide tanning has brought a sense of purpose, meaning, connection, and identity to my life as a Maskîgow-iskwew living on Dene territory. I live in Sòmba K'é, Denendeh (Yellow-knife, Northwest Territories), on the traditional territories of the Yellowknives Dene First Nation, in the Akaitcho Region of Treaty 8 territory. My great-grandmother was the last woman in my family to tan hides. We are Maskîkowak (Swampy Cree People or People of the Great Swamp Land) from the Treaty 5 adhesion territory in northern Manitoba. My Maskîkow grandparents William Joseph McDonald and Maria McDonald (born Spence) were born near York Factory, Manitoba. My mom, aunties, uncles, brother, and I were all born at Mántéwisipihk (Churchill, Manitoba). My paternal grandfather, Joseph Compayre, has Spanish ancestry, and my paternal grandmother, Mary Compayre (born Olsen) has Icelandic ancestry. They were both born near Tuelon, Manitoba, and my dad, Lorne Compayre, like the rest of my immediate family, was also born in Mántéwisipihk, i.e., Fort Churchill.

Omantewi Sipiy (Churchill River) means River of Strangers in Ininímowin (Swampy Cree language). This was its name because many different people of different nations fre-quented the river and area, and still do to this day.[1] The traditional Ininímowin name for the area around Churchill is Mántéwisipihk, meaning at the River of Strangers. Sayisi Dene territory is to the west of Mántéwisipihk. Maskîkow territory is further south, in-cluding the James Bay Lowlands, and Inuit territory is to the north. The town of Churchill was built around a Hudson Bay Company (HBC) Trading Post, which brought Maskîkowak workers from York Factory when the HBC shut down its operations in 1957.[2] York Factory obtained reserve status in 1989.

Where Mántéwisipihk, at the River of Strangers, once referred to a site where people came to access bounty before colonization, it began to take on a more distressing implication later on as a site of forced or coerced displacement. In 1956, the Sayisi Dene were forcefully relocated from their home at Duck Lake to a camp on the outskirts of Churchill called Dene Village. It was a difficult journey under oppressive circumstances, and many of them perished. Some Sayisi Dene returned to their territory at Tadoule Lake in 1973, and some remained in Churchill.[3] My family lived on a hill near Dene Village. My mom remembers the sound of the Dene drums. Churchill was also the site of the Churchill Vocational Centre, a residential school founded in 1967 that held Inuit youth from Nunavut (part of the Northwest Territories at the time), and Nunatsiavut (part of northern Quebec). Today, though Churchill's population is less than 800 people, it is very diverse with a majority Indigenous population (primarily Inuit, Dene, and Cree), and is accessible by air or rail.

My mother left Mántéwisipihk with my younger brother and I when I was nine years old. When people ask me why we left, I usually share the standard sterilized answers that many would, and do, when they don't want to share personal and painful details about their lives with well-meaning acquaintances or total strangers. I tell them we left for better jobs, or better education, or better access to services, cheaper groceries, or so we could date people that weren't our cousins, all of which is partially true. When I write about hide tanning in Denendeh as a Maskîkow transplant, I think of people with similar experiences, who are dispossessed of their traditional territories, Elders, cultural knowledge holders, and extended families due to gendered, sexualized systemic violence. I tend to identify with Indigenous people who have a desire to engage in self-determination, decolonization, or cultural resurgence, but who are confused about how to relate to the predominant Indigenous international decolonial rhetoric that appears to value, above all else, the experiences of Indigenous peoples reconnecting experientially to their *own* specific geographically defined homelands, when many of us may not be able to or necessarily want to return to those spaces. Hide tanning has provided me with some understanding about how to start having these discussions and how to think about international Indigenous cultural resurgence and mobility.[4] Based on what I know about my family's history, which is limited, I feel that the practice of mobility is a part of my people's tradition, though I don't feel particularly confident at this point in asserting that claim. It's something I feel is true and hope to investigate further.

I've been living in Sòmba K'é for the past 20 years, and I've been fortunate to find fulfilling work planning and managing land-based and Indigenous cultural programs led by and for Indigenous peoples in Denendeh. Organizing and co-ordinating hide-tanning initiatives has been a part of my job over the past few years, but I am far from a hide-tanning expert. I am grateful for the guidance and work of many knowledgeable Elders,[5] hide-tanning masters,[6] and comrades,[7] bush-proficient friends, collaborators, and innovators[8] who ensure the delivery of meaningful and valuable programming.

Method

This chapter is a collection of reflections, observations, interviews, and stories about land-based education, with a specific focus on hide tanning as an approach for instilling, developing, and affirming Indigenous leadership skills and capacity in my communities and kinship networks. I invoke my own work with Dene Nahjo, an Indigenous innovation collective I co-founded[9] based out of Sòmba K'é, Denendeh, as well as the experiences of fellow hide tanners Stephanie Poole and Cheyanna Fraser. Indigenous leadership skills and capacity are informed by Indigenous values, which are learned, affirmed, and practised through cultural teachings, languages, and relationship to land. My hope is that the stories and perspectives I share here might be useful for understanding, applying, and nuancing some of the high-level theoretical work available in the field of Indigenous studies, cultural resurgence, and Indigenous land-based education today.

While acknowledging that Indigenous nations are distinct from one another, and that pan-Indigenous generalizations can be and often are problematic, I still opt to use the word "Indigenous" when talking about urban Indigenous experiences or referring to multicultural Indigenous groups, because the people in these spaces tend to come from many different Indigenous nations. If an Ojibway person is learning from Ojibway Elders on Ojibway territory, then I understand why their process or method would be identified specifically as Ojibway. I often opt to use the term "Indigenous" for lack of a better or more appropriate term to identify a multicultural Indigenous group. If a teaching, person, or group identifies itself by a specific name I will use that name.

Land-Based Education

When I use the term "land-based education" I define it simply as a process of learning from the land, informed by Indigenous cultural values and teachings such as respect and reciprocity. I've held this simple definition in my mind for a few years, though extensive literature is available on place-based education, environmental education, land-based education, Indigenous education, and recently, land education (Tuck, McKenzie, and McCoy 2014). Land-based education can include fostering and maintaining a relationship directly from the land, learning Indigenous languages or songs that come from the land, and/or participating in ceremonies that come from the land. All of our practices and knowledge are informed by a relationship to land in one way or another, so engaging with any of these is a form of ongoing land-based learning. "Land-based education" is a term I use to describe an approach for relearning how to think Maskîkow. It's an approach for becoming Dene Nahjo, which means a good Dene person, or a good person according to Dene values.[10] It's a smart person, good in the bush, quick, kind, patient, good for the community, good to have around. It's the kind of person I want to be. Land-based learning can and does happen in urban environments. As Dallas Hunt explains in Chapter 6 of this volume, urban is not the opposite of land. I generally use the term "urban" to refer to a space, place, or experience that includes things characteristic of urban centres like pavement, high concentrations of people, vehicle traffic, and many layers of regulatory policies.

Some of my closest friends are my hide-tanning mentors and comrades. At certain times of the year, the majority of my time spent socializing outside of my paid work hours and self-care time (which I spend completely alone sewing) involves tanning hides, or planning to tan hides, with my friends. Working on hides is done in relation to the people working around and with me, the animal itself, the hunter who harvested it, and all the natural materials that had to be gathered in order to tan it. Gratitude is an important part of this relational web, as the respect we are taught to demonstrate by practising certain protocols is driven by gratitude for all the things that make it possible to tan hides together. This includes gratitude for the ancestors who protected and passed on this knowledge to us, the children we then pass the knowledge on to, the space to work, the materials, the animals, the water, the favourable weather, our health, and each other. It is in recognition of the interconnected nature of knowledge production, and my gratitude towards these relations, that I shift the focus of the chapter to the words and experiences of two of my hide-tanning friends: Stephanie Poole and Cheyanna Fraser.

The Łútsël K'é Women's Group has organized the Łútsël K'é Hide Tanning Camp annually since 2014. Coincidentally, this was the same year that Dene Nahjo organized our first hide-tanning camp and toolmaking workshop. One of the lead organizers for the Łútsël K'é Hide Tanning Camp, my friend and hide-tanning comrade, Stephanie Poole, agreed to let me interview her about the camp this year. Stephanie and I met through our passion for hide tanning during Dene Nahjo's 2014 toolmaking workshop, where I managed to produce several beautiful tools, of which only one remains functional.

Interview with Stephanie Poole

Mandee: Stephanie, would you please introduce yourself how you like to identify—how you like to be known.

Stephanie: My name is Stephanie Poole and my family name is Nįjá Gahdële. Nįjá means the one that came back, and Gahdële is my great-grandfather's name. My mother is Florence Catholique, and I think my father is Frank McDonald. My grandmother is Madeline Catholique and my late grandfather is Jonas Catholique. I live here in the community of Łútsël K'é with my family, and I'm a member of Łútsël K'é Dene First Nation.

M: Mahsi. Could you tell us where we are right now?

S: Right now we're at hide camp. [Laughs.] Łútsël K'é Hide Tanning Camp. This is our fifth year at hide camp. We are on the eastern shore of where Łútsël K'é is located at the outflow of the Stark River, and this area is where Elders, when they were younger, and other ancestors used to camp along this side of the point here in the spring time. I really enjoy bringing a big camp—it's growing every year—back to this place in the spring time.

M: You're one of the organizers of this camp, right?

S: Yes. I'm a member of Łútsël K'é Women's Group. We mostly get together Thursday evenings and help each other with different projects like sewing projects and different kinds of things. We just sort of get together and have a snack and something to drink. Sometimes we buy a moosehide for the women in the community to use, so women who don't tan hides can have something to sew with, and different kinds of fabrics and beads and the different things you need to make stuff like canvas—everything (laughs).

When you do a lot of sewing or beading you need hide to make projects. Since we like to tan hides together, and we think it's fun to tan hides with lots of different people—plus we work during the days so we don't have a lot of free time for tanning hides—we thought it would be fun just to carve out this space the first week of June where that's all we do, just tan hides together and invite everyone. Everyone's welcome. It's turning out to be better and better every year.

M: And how has the camp changed or how has it been getting better?

S: Well, the first year we were in a different location a little further down where the fire break is. It's a little more steep and rocky there, and the Elders didn't really like it because they couldn't walk around easily so we moved up this way a little further, and we've been building tent frames, platforms, just to make it easier to set up the camp. That way you can get started on your hides right away, and you don't have to keep breaking so much poles every year. Some people like sleeping on the ground, so we try to make spaces for that too. There's always been a lot of other things that go on like the country foods and the dry fish and all the ducks and geese and things like that, and children of all ages. I think it's just gotten bigger and bigger, and it's been really interesting to see where all the visitors come from. We don't charge people to come for a couple different reasons. One of them is that it's really expensive to get here to Łútsël K'é, and so if people really want to come they're going to have to sacrifice, like take time off from work and pay to fly here with all their supplies, freight, and everything they need. It's pretty expensive already, so we didn't really want to charge them a fee. We appreciate the effort to get here and spend time with us. One of the other reasons is that we don't want to feel like we're selling something, and we don't want participants to feel like they're buying something so that they can take our culture and misappropriate it, and use it however they want to use it. We want to build that respectful relationship, honour the treaty, welcome people into our territory, teach them about our way of life, and sort of Indigenize them rather than them colonize us. That's kind of the approach for hide camp.

M: Was that an approach that kind of just happened or was that something explicit—was there a conversation and decision to try and do that?

S: It's sort of in the way that we're raised. It kind of comes naturally, and from our collective experiences with colonization I suppose. As one of the organizers, it's important for me to make sure that it's a comfortable space for me.

M: Have you learned any big major lessons over the years organizing this camp?

S: It's important to have good camp workers. It's important to have a solid group of Elders—hide tanners. If you're lucky to have Elders like that we really appreciate them, and the camp workers; the people that get our wood; the cook. Lunch was something that we didn't do in the beginning. Only after the camp started getting bigger were we able to fundraise more, so we started adding that in. We really appreciate them, and try to find good solid workers to help us at hide camp. We've been really lucky.

It's important to have the support of the community also. Our community is really supportive of hide camp. People look forward to it. They ask about it year-round. You see more hunters who are bringing back hides and things, and starting to make tools again. You see more people in the community working on hides. It's been really beneficial for Łútsël K'é as well. That's something that I really appreciate about hide camp too.

M: That was kind of what my next question was going to be—what do you think the impact of the camp has been, not just on the community, but on anything or anyone?

S: We've noticed, too, that more hide camps are coming up in different communities and we really think that's cool. We always want to go to everyone's hide camp. We always want to learn about how other people do their hides and stuff like that. In our community more people are working on hides. More people are interested. More people are bringing back hides and bones. More people are making tools. More people are making art and beautiful things for their families, and sort of bolstering that economy. Some people sell their stuff. I really enjoy that too. Trying to build a sustainable economy and community is important to me. What I always love is the youth because they're so full of hope and promise, so having them be familiar with hide tanning and with all the things that go on at Hide Camp and all the smells and everything and the protocols and the stories. When they get older it will just be something that's natural to them. It will be easy as something to come back to as

Danya Erasmus

Sadeya Hayden Scott tanning a moosehide during the 2018 urban hide tanning camp.

adults. Today I was really impressed with Rainah. She's our niece and she's really outgoing. In spring carnival she enters every competition. She helps us start seeds when we were planting seeds for the garden, and she was here today fleshing a hide. It makes me really happy to see kids want to be a part of that and enjoying themselves. Little ancestors running around.

M: Those were my main questions about the camp. Is there anything you want to ask me as a part of the interview?

S: Are you going to come back next year? Can you come back?

M: I'd love to come back.

S: Please come back.

M: Thank you for that. Is there anyone else I should acknowledge?

S: Hanna and Mary Rose Casaway, Saniz Catholique, the regular Łútsël K'é Women's Group. They all give us input. Granny [Madeline Catholique] and Aunty Madeline. Celine Marlowe gives us a lot of support even though she couldn't be here this year. The community also is really supportive of Hide Camp. Like Mary Rose said, people just show up and bring food and set nets. We don't ask them to do that. We don't pay them to do that. They just do that because they want to be at camp, too, and it's a part of our culture to welcome visitors and share what we have with them. People like to sort of show you around the east arm, and want you to come back. Want you to enjoy yourself while you're here, so that's really nice too.

M: Thanks so much for all your work, and your women's group.

Interview with Cheyanna Fraser

Cheyanna Fraser is another hide-tanning comrade who agreed to an interview for this chapter. Cheyanna and I met in 2017 at Dene Nahjo's Urban Hide Tanning Camp in Sòmba K'é.

Mandee: Could you please introduce yourself?

Cheyanna: My name is Cheyanna Fraser. I'm from Yellowknife, NWT—born and raised. My mom is from Inuvik, and my dad is from Fort Smith. I'm 23 years old, and this is my second year ever working on hides. I'm Gwich'in.

M: Could you talk a little bit about where we are right now and how you ended up here?

C: So we're in Łútsël K'é. I think I learned about this camp from Dene Nahjo at their Urban Hide Tanning Camp last year. That's the first time I ever worked on my caribou hide. It's the first one my cousin hunted and shot, so I was proud to be working on it. I did not finish my hide then, so I brought it here. When I found out about this camp, I decided that I was going to do anything I could to come here. It didn't matter if I couldn't afford it or whatever. I was just going to come here and see how it all was. It's a small community. We're all helping each other and cooking with each other.

M: When did you first start working on hides?

C: September 2017 was the first time I ever tried to work on a hide. I knew it was a lot of work but I didn't realize just how much. It's almost like birth. You think you're ready. You think you know what it's going to be like, but there's no way that anybody could warn you how intense it actually is.

M: Has it discouraged you from wanting to keep going?

C: No. Even though it's hard work it's definitely worth it.

M: What made you want to start working with hides?

C: Since I was young I've always been into sewing and jigging and anything cultural. I was always around our culture, but there wasn't really anybody that knew how to tan hides in my family, because of the oppression and everything. When there was an opportunity to learn to tan hides, I jumped right into it. Anytime there's an opportunity to learn anything related to my culture, I'm always right in there. I've always been like that since I was a little kid.

M: Did you have tools already that you got from somewhere?

C: Yes. My mom gave me these awesome tools that her grandma gave to her, which I was able to use like a bone scraper and this one [shows me the tools]. One of the tools is just for the drying and softening process. The other one is a dull metal one for softening. My dad bought me another tool from Dave Giroux, who was selling tools at the Urban Hide Camp. That was really helpful because they were really sharp and worked good to scrape my hides.

M: How did it feel to use your gramma's tools?

C: It's definitely an honour because I never got to meet her and my mom always speaks so nicely of her. She misses her. I've always had this sense of my ancestors always watching me and being around me. My grampa died when I was five, but anytime I get scared all I can think of is like, well, why am I scared? I always have someone right there with me. I always have protection. So when I was using my gramma's tools, it was just like she was right there with me.

M: Are there any other skills or teachings or lessons you're learning that are a part of this experience that's not just necessarily how to scrape a hide?

C: There are all kinds of lessons like learning how to provide for yourself. You don't want to sleep on the cold ground. You have to learn how to go get spruce boughs. You have to keep your fire going all night. You can't just turn on a furnace and expect to be warm.

You have to work for that type of stuff. You learn how to come together as a community, as an actual community and help each other out. No one gets hungry here. If you're hungry someone will help you or you cook for yourself. If you do cook for yourself usually you cook for your friends. Somebody's doing the dishes. Someone's getting the wood. It's a big family almost.

Is there scissors? [I pass her the scissors.] Thank you.

M: What are we doing now?

C: Right now we are patching up your hide before the final smoke, and working together to get it done because earlier we were working together on my hide to get the brain paste on and into the smoker again.

M: Who prompted us to put the brains on and all that?

C: An Elder named Madeline. She's the pro hide tanner, and she inspects everyone's hides. When we thought that we could just dry out the hide, she said no, you should put the brain paste on and put it in the smoker.

M: What are your biggest take-aways from this experience at the Łútsël K'é Hide Tanning Camp?

C: I didn't go straight for the hides this time around. I tried to relax, spend time with the Elders, and listen to stories. At the Urban Hide Camp, I was so obsessed with finishing my hides, and I almost made myself sick. I cried at the end because I was so disappointed that I didn't get my hide done. My first hide. Usually nobody gets their first hide done their first time trying it. This time around I was way more relaxed and not worried about getting it done right now. I got to know the community. Got to know the Elders and the land. I went for walks by myself in the bush.

M: Do your parents have any thoughts about you learning to tan hides?

C: My parents are very proud. My parents are just happy that I'm able to come out here and experience this type of thing. My mom originally wanted to come to this camp, but she was busy with work. She wants me to teach her how to tan hides. After this we're going to get set up at my cabin, and I'm sure she'll come out to that. They fully support this, and they're very happy that I'm learning.

On-the-Land Programming

From what I've learned about on-the-land programming in Denendeh,[11] different Indigenous land-based initiatives tend to share similar goals, but with distinctions. The goals of community hunts tend to be to provide food for the community while teaching subsistence skills. Paddling programs teach paddling skills. Hide-tanning camps teach hide-tanning skills. On a deeper level, those programs are fostering a relationship between the program participants, the land, their culture, and their communities. Participants are learning to be on the land respectfully, according to the teachings and protocols of mentors and teachers who are usually Indigenous knowledge holders and land users. With enough practice, those teachings permeate into all realms of life. The outcomes that these types of programs have on community capacity (including health, wellness, and leadership skills) are immense, and they are of major evaluative interest right now to many people, including those working in the field of Indigenous health, reconciliation, as well as philanthropists and foundations that want to support reconciliation and partner with Indigenous groups. Documenting and evaluating the impacts and outcomes of Indigenous-led land-based programming are important in that this information influences the distribution and allocation of resources required to deliver these services, though most people who are passionate about the land and land-based education are already experientially aware of the positive impacts associated with it. We don't require a peer-reviewed research article to understand this, but the people who control the resources, to which we need access, might.

In a 2014 report I wrote on land-based education, I noted that many people romanticize land-based education, which I still believe to be true. I read a lot of work that argued reconnecting to land, cultural teachings, and values was how Indigenous peoples were going to liberate themselves from colonization. It sounded romantic and easy to me, but I have experienced many logistical, legislative, psychological, and interpersonal challenges in the past seven years working in land-based program management. I've learned that the process for reconnecting to land and culture is different for everyone, and my experience of figuring this out for myself was and continues to be challenging at every turn, though nonetheless rewarding. This is especially challenging for urban Indigenous people as we navigate our rights to relate to someone else's traditional territory, how to relate to land covered in cities, and how to have a long-distance relationship with our own ancestral storied landscapes.

When I first started doing land-based education as my job, I didn't think there was a wrong way to do it as long as everyone had enough food, didn't freeze, and didn't seriously cut or burn themselves. Minor physical injuries were perfectly acceptable. I thought that whatever issues or challenges a person was experiencing, the land could just fix you right up if you let it. Somehow, "the land heals all" became a mantra I repeated in my mind, and also saw and heard everywhere. It wasn't until a year or so later that the mental, emotional, and even legislative challenges that accompanied land-based programming became clear to me. The more intensive the program (the longer duration of time spent on the land with a group as a part of a scheduled program), the more challenging it is for both program staff and participants. The mental and emotional challenges are generally only discussed privately during debriefing meetings, or anecdotally among close colleagues who work on the ground delivering land-based programs and providing support to program participants or students, while the legislative or institutional challenges are more frequently and publicly addressed. It's important to address all of these challenges more openly so practitioners can exchange knowledge and best practices for delivering quality and effective land-based education.

Obstacles and Opportunities

Melaw Nakehk'o invited me to Sambaa K'e (formerly Trout Lake) in 2012 to tan hides with a group of women as a part of the Golo-Dheh Project,[12] an initiative she organized to travel across the Dehcho Region learning moosehide-tanning techniques from different Dehcho Elders.[13] Our teachers in Sambaa K'e were Maggie Jumbo and Helen Tutcho. That was the summer Bill C-38 became law, which was one of the catalysts for the Idle No More movement (see Kino-nda-niimi Collective 2014). On 4 June 2012, a demonstration was taking place in Yellowknife to protest the bill. We decided to issue a statement from Sambaa K'e, in solidarity with those opposing Bill C-38, called "Moosehide Tanners Against Fascism." We wrote:

> We stand in solidarity on June 4 with the countless numbers of peoples across
> Canada opposing Bill C-38. This proposed bill will have direct consequences

Lesley Johnson and Exhea Nakehk'o

Moosehide tanners against fascism.

for those of us actively engaged in moosehide tanning, something that has been traditionally practiced by Indigenous peoples from time immemorial. We consider this proposal a direct attack on Indigenous peoples' constitutionally protected rights, physical, mental, emotional, and spiritual well-being, not only to those who continue to practice moosehide tanning, but to all peoples, Indigenous and non-Indigenous, who derive spiritual and physical sustenance from the land, water, and air.[14]

This was the first time I experienced cultural resurgence and political activism as the same thing. It was the first time I felt like I understood decolonial praxis, theory and practice together, because we were tanning hides and, at the same time, were critically engaged in efforts to assert Indigenous livelihood in the face of ongoing colonial control at a more public political level. These are the types of experiences I'm working to facilitate for others.

Urban hide tanning has been an extremely interesting initiative to be a part of, and also a surprisingly generative site of understanding for what Indigenous resurgence could look like in an urban environment. Dene Nahjo[15] fosters Indigenous leadership values and skills through cultural resurgence initiatives. Hide tanning is one of our streams of programming, and we have organized four urban hide-tanning camps in downtown Sòmba K'é to date. The camps are two weeks long, and somewhat complex to co-ordinate as there are many moving parts to manage. There are elementary and high school tours of the camps twice a day, plus scheduled tours for the general public. People who want to

Danya Erasmus

A hide drying in the tent by the stove.

learn hide tanning can participate by either bringing their own hide to work on, or learn by working on the community hides provided by Dene Nahjo. Hide-tanning mentors, including Dene masters and young experienced hide tanners, provide guidance to hide-tanning learners while also leading demonstrations. Each year, about 2,000 people visit the camp, and each year a handful of hide-tanning learners engage intensely throughout the duration of camp.

The main goal of the Urban Hide Tanning Camp is to create an accessible Indigenous-led community space for Indigenous people in Yellowknife to engage in hide tanning together, whether they want to come and watch the demonstrations, learn to tan hides, or just hang out and drink tea in a space where they feel safe. Another goal is to provide mentorship for Indigenous people who want to learn to tan hides. These two goals are the driving force behind my involvement in the project. Creating an inclusive space for non-Indigenous people to learn about Dene culture and Indigenous perspectives on cultural resurgence and colonization is also one of Dene Nahjo's stated goals, which it meets by organizing panels or presentations on these topics and addressing them as a part of camp tours. Last but not least, by providing an opportunity where people can try hide-tanning techniques, they begin to understand experientially how much work is involved in producing a beautifully tanned hide, and hopefully that will lead people to respect the fair cost of artwork made from tanned hide. The camp has been questioned for being a site of cultural tourism, a critique we anticipated and have taken seriously. While some of the projects we organized are for Indigenous people exclusively, the Urban Hide Tanning Camp is meant to be as inclusive a space as possible for everyone. We wouldn't hold an Indigenous-only initiative in the middle of downtown Yellowknife where we would have to constantly police people's participation and identities. The Urban Hide Camp is an example of what an inclusive, but Indigenous-led, space can look and feel like.

In 2018, Dene Nahjo was invited to lead an Urban Hide Tanning Residency at the Banff Centre, an upscale art educational institution that I associated with privilege and wealth since I first heard about it. I had a brief conversation with a colleague leading up to this residency about whether it makes more sense to focus our energies on negotiating for inclusion in urban, institutionalized spaces or to focus on working in the bush, where we can engage in our practices freely and unfettered by regulatory hurdles, tourists, and the lack of accessible natural materials. When I went to the Banff Centre for a site visit in preparation for the residency, I met with several staff members and Parks Canada staff to let them know what we needed and what we were going to do. It was an interesting experience; while everyone I spoke to was kind and supportive of the residency, I was struck by the many layers of colonial imposition through which I had to negotiate a bypass. This is typical of land-based programming and/or engaging in land-based practices in urban, institutionalized areas, whether you're on a university campus or municipal property, or in a national park. First, there is often the layer of concrete, sidewalks, and asphalt to work around. This is a significant condition to overcome because the water we use for the hides needs to be taken care of in a specific way, which we have to modify in an urban space covered in cement. Then there are institutional policies around food, communications, and safety that don't necessarily align with some aspects of our practice, or that seem pointless or irrelevant. On top of that, municipal laws regulate fire and smoke, provincial laws restrict the export of animal parts from territory to province, and Parks Canada regulations control harvesting, managing animal attractants, and disposing of animal parts. Working to organize the Banff Centre initiative, I spent most of the day addressing policies like these before I met with a local Stoney Nakoda Elder to discuss the project. In a bush or community setting, you're more likely to spend days with local Elders and knowledge holders with little to no interference from or expectation to engage with other authorities to figure out how to run a program. Despite the regulatory hoops, Dene Nahjo's hide-tanning residency at the Banff Centre was wonderful. There were many amazing Indigenous applicants from across Turtle Island, which is indicative of the widespread resurgence of this particular practice.

The urban hide-tanning camps I've been a part of are sites of Indigenous international (see Simpson 2017) and intergenerational knowledge exchange. That's one of the most compelling things about them. This is also true for non-urban community hide-tanning camps, but it is especially true for urban ones because many of the Indigenous residents of urban centres typically come from elsewhere, and they're drawn together by things like sewing circles, singing/drumming groups, and cultural projects or programs. Urban hide-tanning participants typically include a group of diverse Indigenous people sharing their knowledge, whether that knowledge comes from watching a relative tan hides as a child, or a hunter who knows a good way to skin a moose, or hide tanners showing off their tools and explaining how to make them. Though this type of Indigenous international knowledge exchange is incredibly enriching, it can also be challenging.

The psychological and interpersonal challenges that arise in land-based programs are more challenging than the logistical or legislative challenges. Conflict mediation is a skill I had to learn through experience when group dynamics became difficult or dysfunctional because, at times, the group wasn't able to function to meet its stated goals because of conflicts. Conflicts arise between participants, between children, between children and adults, between participants and site staff, between Elders, between Elders and students, and so on. The most challenging situation for me is when conflict or disagreement arises between Elders from different nations. I still don't know the most ethical way to share my experiences with this, so I do not do that here. What do you do when two wise and respected Elders disagree on a course of action or method? Such disagreements could be anything from how to address someone's problematic behaviour in camp, to how thin to scrape a hide, and include matters related to gender, religion, or spirituality. Early on in my career I would defer to the most local Elder of the host territory for the program, but I don't actually believe that that is always the best approach.

Land-based education poses some other challenges. From a Canadian legal perspective, land-based programs are supposed to meet the industry standards for outdoor guiding. This means that staff must be certified in wilderness first aid, certified to run any motorized equipment such as boats or chainsaws, certified in predator defence, and have a possession and acquisition licence if they're operating firearms. Also, children must be under constant supervision, and a detailed emergency response plan must be in place. There are industry standards around food preparation, food storage, and how to manage human waste. If participants are paddling on moving water they need to demonstrate a certain level of paddling proficiency, and there must be a high ratio of certified paddling staff to non-certified program participants. If the program includes hunting, hunting permits need to be acquired and reporting has to be submitted afterwards. This is not usually the case for community-led hunts, but for educational institutions and private businesses it is usually a requirement.

The issue raised by having to abide by Canadian industry standards is that they do not acknowledge the expertise and experience of our own Indigenous knowledge holders and land-based practitioners. Asking an Elder, who travelled a certain river for an entire life on boat, to acquire a boat operator's licence by taking an online test was one of the funniest (because we already had established a great rapport) and most insightful things I had to do. We discussed it openly, and decided together that he wasn't going to take the test. I've been asked many times why we, as in the organizations I've worked for to deliver land-based programming, don't do away with those colonial standards for taking people out on the land and defer to our own land-based experts instead. What it comes down to for me is that there are land users and knowledge holders I would trust not only with my life, but also with the lives of the participants in a program for which I'm responsible. If I'm confident that the staff on my program are qualified to take people out on the land safely according to Dene/Maskîkow/Nêhiyaw cultural standards, then I feel comfortable forgoing the industry standard requirements. However, I'm only going to feel that confident with people I've developed relationships with over many years, spent time on the land with, and have seen handle difficult and potentially dangerous situations. I don't expect all Indigenous land-based practitioners, knowledge holders, or Elders to know what to do in every possible situation on the land, so I wouldn't put them in a situation where they would have to be responsible for any dangers that could arise unless they agreed to that responsibility ahead of time. If someone died or was seriously injured on a program for which I was responsible, and I was questioned in court, I would stand by my decision to hire land users who weren't certified according to Western guiding standards. If we are not going to impose colonial standards for outdoor guiding on our own land-based programs, we need to take the time and have the respect to develop relationships with the people we expect to be responsible for people's safety on the land. While there is an empowering element to doing this work of developing culturally informed practices for land-based programming, it also requires the long-term commitment and attention of a team of people, including program managers, administrators, instructors, safety staff, and child-care providers. In other words, Western certification serves to verify a standard of proficiency in the absence of relationship, while Indigenous methods rely on trust and observation over time.

It's not just people's physical safety that should be kept in mind on the land, but also their emotional and mental well-being. Being on the land is often like a cleanse that expels unwanted stuff from your mind and body. Similar to the way in which a physical cleanse sometimes makes people feel sicker before they feel better, being on the land often brings up memories of traumatic experiences, including intergenerational trauma, for Indigenous people. Supporting participants through this process requires a tremendous amount of thought and care. This is another challenging aspect of land-based education, whether a project is just a few days long in an urban centre, or several weeks out on the land. One of the draws of land-based programs for Indigenous people is accessing an experience and learning opportunity that they otherwise have limited or no access to. Even while being grateful for learning a practice for the first time, when it's something your ancestors practised consistently and mastered, this can bring up feelings of anger and shame. Being on the land requires physical work, as well as collaboration with a small community of people that one may not have ever met before and who may have never spent a significant amount of time on the land. Spending time on the land with friends or family is different from a structured land-based program with learning goals and schedules. The participants on these programs don't have access to the coping mechanisms they would back home, whether that's access to friends to talk to, the Internet, or substances like sugar or alcohol. They're outside of their comfort zone, forced to interact every day with people they just met, and they might be cold, sore, or hungry for whatever they regularly eat back home. For people with pre-existing trauma loads, this added discomfort may trigger some unexpected feelings or memories. Acknowledging that this will be a part of the program experience beforehand is as important as having tools or systems in place to support people on the land when emotional/mental/spiritual challenges arise. This is especially the case for supporting program staff who are responsible for the well-being of participants.

Conclusion

When I'm engaging in land-based activities personally or when I'm organizing land-based initiatives for other people, I do so with specific goals and intention in mind. I engage in land-based practices to maintain and deepen my relationship to land, my friends, colleagues, and the Elders I work with. Ultimately, I'm doing this in an effort to reprogram my brain, to expel what I've come to identify as internalized colonial values like jealousy, individualism, competitiveness, consumerism, and self-loathing, and replace them with what I identify as Maskîgow, Nêhiyaw, and Dene values like respect, reciprocity, patience, creativity, kindness, and genuine care for the well-being and learning of the people around me. In my mind, this is part of becoming Dene Nahjo, a good and competent person according to Dene values. When I organize land-based initiatives like hide-tanning camps, my goal is to facilitate a space where participants can engage with all aspects of the processes and considerations involved in the specific practice of focus, whether hide tanning, harvesting, or building. By doing this, I feel that participants can (if they're open to it) experientially learn and internalize those values of respect and reciprocity for the land, animals, water, and our communities, which are foundational to the good and effective leadership that we need.

Discussion Questions

1. What are some of the opportunities land-based practices like hide tanning bring about in the contemporary world? How might they strengthen relationships between Indigenous peoples or between Indigenous and non-Indigenous peoples?

2. What are some of the challenges of land-based programming identified by the author?

3. What implications does increased urbanization have on Indigenous land-based practices like hide tanning?

4. Implicit in this chapter is that there are not enough resources available for Indigenous land-based programming, even though it leads to positive health outcomes. Why do you think that is? How could the value of land-based programming be proven within a Western framework?

Additional Resources

Dene Nahjo. https://www.denenahjo.com/.
Nakehk'o, Melaw. "I swim when the ice has melted and make a fire when it's cold." https://melawnakehko.wordpress.com/2012/05/02/a-dene-mamas-journey/.
Reclaiming Urban Spaces, Adze Studios (2018). https://vimeo.com/273550231.
Revolution Moosehide, a film by Lesley Johnson and Melaw Nakehk'o (2019).

Notes

1. I learned this from Ken Paupanakis, an In-inímowin instructor at the University of Manitoba.
2. HBC Heritage: http://www.hbcheritage.ca/places/forts-posts/york-factory.
3. Sayisi Dene First Nation Relocation Settlement Trust: http://sdfntrust.ca/history/.
4. Thanks to Dr Gina Starblanket for helping me to think this through. For an exploration of questions of land and mobility, see Starblanket and Stark (2018). Also see the discussion on mobility and Indigenous freedom in Borrows (2016).
5. Ethel Lamothe, Paul Andrew, Stephen Kakfwi, Jim Antoine, Celine Antoine, Alice Vittrekwa, Ernest Vittrekwa, Paul Mackenzie.
6. Judy Lafferty, Lucy Ann Yakelaya, Bertha Francis, Celine Marlowe.
7. Melaw Nakehk'o, Tania Larsson, Stephanie Poole, Cheyanna Fraser, Angela Code, Meagan Wohlberg.
8. Kyla Kakfwi-Scott, Nina Larsson, Heather Nakehk'o, Amos Scott, Deneze Nakehk'o, Eugene Boulanger, Daniel T'seleie, Kristen Tanche, Lesley Johnson.

9. The rest of the Dene Nahjo Co-Founders include Kyla Kakfwi-Scott, Amos Scott, Nina Larsson, Tania Larsson, Heather Nakehk'o, Deneze Nakehk'o, Melaw Nakehk'o, Eugene Boulanger, Daniel T'seleie, with a special mention to our Program Coordinator Danya Erasmus. This is my interpretation of Dene Nahjo after hearing many stories and explanations from different Dene Elders.

10. There are many OTL programs in Denendeh. For more information on many of them, see the NWT On The Land Collaborative website: http://www.nwtontheland.ca/.

11. Melaw Nakehk'o blog, at https://melawnakehko.wordpress.com/2012/05/02/a-dene-mamas-journey/.

12. To learn more about this story, see the forthcoming film *Revolution Moosehide* directed by Lesley Johnson.

13. Unpublished, June 2012.

14. Dene Nahjo's vision is *Land, Language, Culture. Forever.*

14 Enacting Reconciliation

Joyce Green

Reconciliation calls upon us all to confront our past and commit to charting a brighter, more inclusive future. We must acknowledge that centuries of colonial practices have denied the inherent rights of Indigenous Peoples. . . . We have listened and learned and we will work together to take concrete action to build a better future and a new relationship.

—The Rt. Hon. Justin Trudeau, Prime Minister of Canada

"When I use a word," Humpty Dumpty said, in rather a scornful tone, "it means just what I choose it to mean—neither more nor less."

—Lewis Carroll, *Through the Looking-Glass*, 1871

Introduction: The Formation of the TRC

Following an apology to those affected by Canada's residential school policy by Prime Minister Stephen Harper, the government of Canada established the Truth and Reconciliation Commission (TRC) in 2008 to consider the effects of residential schools for Indian students and their descendants. In 2015 the TRC, using a victim-centred approach (James 2012), concluded its painstaking and pain-filled exposition of the misery inflicted by the Canadian policy of enforced residential schooling of Indian[1] children. It is important to note that the Commission's terms of reference did not include consideration of the many day schools deployed for the same objectives as the residential schools, nor did they permit consideration of or compensation to the many Métis and non-status Indian students who were the subjects of the same kinds of abuses and deprivations as were status Indian students. The Commission heard the testimony of many who attended the residential schools, which had been subcontracted by the state to various Christian denominations, and produced its final report, *Honouring the Past, Reconciling for the Future*, an Executive Summary, and its "Calls to Action" so that all Canadians may know the truth. All of these components are available online.

At its core, the residential school policy was part of the Canadian government's drive to eliminate Indigenous legal and cultural particularity and its potential to impede the expansion of the colonial state. The TRC Summary opens thusly:

> For over a century, the central goals of Canada's Aboriginal policy were to elim-inate Aboriginal governments; ignore Aboriginal rights; terminate the Treaties; and, through a process of assimilation, cause Aboriginal peoples to cease to exist as distinct legal, social, cultural, religious, and racial entities in Canada. The es-tablishment and operation of residential schools were a central element of this policy, which can best be described as "cultural genocide." (TRC 2015, 7)

The residential school program actually wasn't much of an education program at all. Through a nationwide collection of day schools, trade and training schools, and residential schools (only the last were the subject of the TRC's study), Indigenous children (primarily status Indian children, but also many non-status and Métis children) were subjected to a hostile process of psycho-social transformation that rendered them psychologically fra-gile and often unable to competently fit into their home communities or into the dominant settler society. The students were being prepared, not for further education or taking on leadership roles in society nor for beneficial activity in any economy, but for partial ab-sorption into the racist settler society, for erasure as culturally distinct persons. Of course, complete assimilation is not possible in a racially organized society such as Canada, so the survivors of residential schools found themselves nonetheless stigmatized as "native" in settler society, which understood that to infer all kinds of deficiencies. At the same time, the residential school process left many unable to relate to family and community or to maintain cultural connections.

As noted by Hare and Davidson in Chapter 12 and by Anderson and Ball in Chap-ter 9, Indigenous education continues to be deeply problematic. Non-Indigenous schools and universities remain primarily bastions of white settler culture and knowledge (Kuokkanen 2007; Smith 1999; Wadsworth 2014) despite the presence of Indigenous stu-dents. Thus, these institutions fail *all* of their students by presenting racist curricula and colonial mythologies as the Truth, the canon to be absorbed and regurgitated. On-reserve in-school education is woefully underfunded by the federal government, which spends thousands of dollars less per student in reserve schools than provinces do in the public school system.

The TRC conducted its hearings across the country and documented the conse-quences of the residential school policy in the suffering of those who survived it, and in the accounts of descendants of survivors who are also impacted by the policy. In the exe-cution of this policy over about a century, across the country, students were *uneducated* and undereducated while being tormented in ways that violate fundamental human rights protected by international law to which Canada is signatory. The effect of the torment and the objectives of the schools meet the definition of genocide at international law. Many students died because of it. The torment for many of those children is not over—will never be over—and its consequences are experienced intergenerationally in families and com-munities. The residential school policy was a toxic gift that keeps on giving. How does a state perpetrator reconcile this in a contemporary relationship with those who have sur-vived, though not unscathed, such destructive assaults by state policy for so long?

Truth and reconciliation were in the title of the Commission, but that could not create reconciliation, which really needs to be initiated and implemented by those who have either enacted or benefited from the abusive policy, not from those who have endured it. In this chapter I take up the problematics of truth and reconciliation in the conditions of colonialism, which is not only historic but contemporary; it is both philosophical and structural. I then proceed to the possibility of reconciliation.

Canada is a settler state, conceived over and against Indigenous sovereignties. It was designed for settler populations. And thus, while most settler Canadians have never personally committed an act of explicit racism against an Indigenous person, they have benefited from the structures and the consequences of colonialism. This is what we call "privilege," and it includes the comfort of not knowing about these things. Eroding this collective convenient amnesia requires truth-telling, heard broadly and responded to by citizens as well as by political elites.

Since the state's inception Canadians have not taken responsibility for knowing their Indigenous neighbours, or for knowing what their governments were doing to their neighbours in the state's collective democratic name. Because of the differential power relations consequent to this history and the politics implicit in a challenge to the status quo, there has been little appetite within the privileged cadre of citizens to grapple with the subject. Fundamentally, there is little consideration by Canadians of the architecture of colonialism, the *enabling conditions* that produced and executed the impugned policy animating the residential schools. We return to this subject below. Nor is there evident appreciation by the political and corporate classes or by citizens generally of the range and duration of forms of colonial oppression with which Project Canada is maintained.

The TRC's evidence is the *truth* part of its process: Canadian democratic governments initiated and sustained genocide[2] and human rights abuses against children. The residential school policy was not for the benefit of "Indians" but of settlers: it was intended to de-Indianize the youngest generations so that there would be "no Indians and no Indian problem," in the crystal-clear words of Duncan Campbell Scott, the deputy superintendent of Indian Affairs from 1913 to 1932 (Titley 1986). It involved "inhumane and racist medical treatment, deaths and surreptitious burials, the failure of authorities to take even a minimally acceptable interest in student welfare, and above all, about command responsibility, policy roles and decision making . . . right up to past prime ministers and federal Cabinets" (James 2012, 22).

And for all this documented misery, the residential schools program was merely one of many policies and practices and legislative initiatives that constructed the architecture of colonial occupation and dispossession of Indigenous peoples. This corpus of colonialism, with its democratic imprimatur, is "what makes human rights violations so atrocious, namely, that they were collectively organized by the state and justified in the name of a people" (Schaap 2008, 253).

Colonialism Then and Now

Significantly, while colonialism is too often framed as a historic matter, it continues unabated, now in the form of resource extraction and related activities at the behest and under the protection of the state and without due regard for the fundamental right of "free, prior and informed consent" of Indigenous peoples and their rights at constitutional and international law (UNDRIP; Benjamin 2014; Joffe 2014). These violations affect Indigenous rights to "land and resources, food security, environment and climate change, free trade, essential services and children's rights" (Joffe 2014, 217). To this we must add the violation of Indigenous women's rights, perpetually an oversight in political theory and policy (but see also Brodsky 2014; Kuokkanen 2014; Eberts 2014, 2017). In the process, Canada has consistently violated its obligations at domestic and international law (Joffe 2014).

Contemporary Canadian colonialism includes the failure of the state to grapple with returning at least some measure of its stolen lands to Indigenous nations. It includes the continued bungling of legislative changes to the Indian Act membership provisions (Brodsky 2014) and the protracted and largely unproductive roll-out of the National Inquiry on Missing and Murdered Indigenous Women and Girls (MMIWG). The final report of this inquiry is, however, considered to be useful. It includes the federal Trudeau Liberal government's Orwellian-titled "Recognition of Rights Framework" initiative of 2018, which both failed to recognize rights and was framed to limit them (a final version has not been released and, indeed, the initiative may be shelved by the government).[3] It includes the stratospheric numbers of incarcerated Indigenous people and Indigenous children in state care, and the statistically dramatic differences in the life and health outcomes between settler Canadians and Indigenous people—and in the perpetual budgetary and policy indifference to these phenomena by Canada. No Canadian government has turned away from colonial assumptions and towards reconciliation, despite the occasional rhetoric of nation-to-nation relationships and turning new pages. In sum, in matters of colonial practice, *plus ça change, plus c'est la même chose*. This, too, tarnishes the reconciliatory moment produced by the TRC and the alleged commitment of the federal government to it.

Recognition, Remorse, Restitution, Reconciliation

Truth is a necessary but insufficient condition for reconciliation. Reconciliation requires changes in power relationships, institutions, and specific and continuing actions, not simply the telling of truth. Thus it is important to understand the processes and the implications of the relationship between truth and reconciliation. I hope to make it clear that decolonization *and* Indigenization of the state are aspects of the same libratory process and that both are essential components of reconciliation. Moreover, decolonization implies the elimination of settler or white privilege, a challenge to the logics of capitalism, a privileging of Indigenous epistemologies, of the integrity of the environment and of Indigenous peoples' ancient relationship with their lands, and a commitment to a mutual future shaped more by Indigenous cosmologies and polities than by colonial ones.

There also needs to be space in any discussion of truth and reconciliation for consideration of the role that educators at universities have played as apologists for colonialism—and the possibility that they can remediate their sins with better teaching, better research that attends to colonialism, and acts of reconciliation. This process is generally referred to as Indigenization of the university (see Kuokkanen 2007; Smith 1999). Universities are the "privileged center of meaning-making" whose work has sustained colonialism (Justice 2004, 101), and those who inhabit the ivory towers do much to shape the thinking of emerging elites and contribute to the ongoing structural replication of colonial privilege.

Truth-telling in a reconciliatory process is meaningless if the truth is not heard by those who have benefited from or inflicted the damage—that is, by those who enjoy what, for shorthand, we'll call white settler privilege—and for those who have laid their truths bare, the exercise is unsatisfying without some positive consequence that can produce a measure of change. As Jeremy Patzer (2014, 167) notes, there is a problem of "promoting pre-emptive reconciliation while eliding underlying issues, the greatest of which is colonial dispossession and the struggle for decolonization and self-determination." It's the truth of that little land-theft matter that needs recognition and restitution if reconciliation is to be meaningful for Indigenous peoples.

There is danger of an assumption by Canadians that the TRC effectively reconciled us all; that by virtue of the residential school survivors having *told* their truths, reconciliation is attained as we all just "get over it" "going forward." But between truth and reconciliation there must be *recognition* of what happened *in our collective name*: recognition of the damage done by the democratic state to those who have been oppressed by definition since occupation by the state and its chosen people; recognition of the illegal and immoral nature of this continuing state of affairs; and recognition of the requirement for remediation of all of these things by those who have obtained all the goodies the state has to offer, at the expense of those who have been stripped of virtually all of their sovereignty, autonomy, cultural corpus, languages, children, Elders, health, wealth, and opportunities.

In other words, recognition of the harm done to Indigenous peoples in and through the colonial project that is Canada requires some thoughtful engagement with history and with public policy. It requires empathy, for without empathy one cannot recognize the awful consequences borne by colonized people. It requires humility, as we begin to learn that we don't know what we don't know, and that our civil and political order is less meritocratic than it is a system of white male privilege. It requires commitment, as we determine to learn the often uncomfortable facts of our fraught relationship and the especially discomforting facts of the maintenance of white privilege. It requires political resolution to transform this unhappy state of affairs, which also entails a will on the part of beneficiaries of this system to back away from their privilege in the interests of justice. It requires a commitment to reconciliation, a state of future peace. And it requires confronting that land-theft matter with "massive restitution, including land, financial transfers, and other forms of assistance to compensate for past and continuing injustices" against Indigenous people (Alfred, cited in Coulthard 2014, 122). Unless and until the colonial state returns at least some of the land, negotiates shared jurisdiction over resources and tax room, and makes other amends, there will be no reconciliation.

As with truth-telling, recognition is a necessary though insufficient condition for reconciliation. To be clear, the kind of recognition being discussed here is not the liberal theoretical concept of seeing and tolerating others. Rather, it involves understanding the relationship between self and others who are radically different because of political processes in which we are all situated, though not identically.

The *reconciliation* part of truth and reconciliation is far less clear. Reconciliation is a state of relational peace achieved by processes and practices intended to convey contrition, accountability, empathy, and commitment to transformation from a damaged to a better relationship, and it must be accepted by those who have been injured by those practices and processes. It can also be a mutual commitment to maintaining peace through agreed-upon processes defining requisite responsibilities, as in the oral versions of the "numbered" treaties and in the Treaty of Niagara. For the Native Women's Association of Canada, "reconciliation is a relational process meant to restore dignity, respect and equality in the aftermath of human rights violations" (NWAC 2010, 29–30). While the need for reconciliation is premised on past as well as present relational evils, it must be oriented towards a reconciled future (Chambers and Blood 2009, 266).

Reconciliation, according to the TRC, requires "awareness of the past, acknowledgement of the harm that has been inflicted, atonement for the causes, and action to change the behaviour" (2015, 6), and it also requires "real social, political, and economic change" (2015, 238). Further, the TRC recommends the United Nations Declaration on the Rights of Indigenous Peoples (UNDRIP) as the "framework for reconciliation in Canada" in which "Canada's political and legal systems, educational and religious institutions, the corporate sector and civil society [could] function in ways that are consistent with the [UNDRIP principles]" (2015, 20). And the Native Women's Association of Canada reminds us to gender the reconciliatory project thusly: "Truth telling and reconciliation must represent a reparative process that promotes restoration of Indigenous women's dignity, safety, authority and agency" (NWAC 2010, 1).

Yet, reconciliation where such grievous harms have been inflicted on so many for so long may not be conceivable as an end state, but rather as a process of recognizing, addressing, and unwinding the multifarious ways in which the harms functioned and continue to function.[4] While the TRC specifically addresses the legacy of the residential schools, the entire project of the colonial settler state has been genocidal. Canada is in need of both truth-telling and the transformative changes that would enable reconciliation into the future.

Reconciliation is often understood as akin to the Christian theological conceptions of repentance, penance, and absolution. This understanding also focuses on the proposition of a final state of relational peace achieved in fairly quick order by an act of apology and contrition—and, of course, a commitment to go forth and sin no more. Unfortunately, this view of reconciliation frames it as a one-time event that releases liabilities for the continuing effects of the matter for which reconciliation is to be obtained, from the perpetrators of those matters. This formula is transactional in its character. A more useful model is the Indigenous model of perpetually renewed political and social relationships through formalized enactments.

The Canadian apology issued by Prime Minister Harper on 8 June 2008, in which he asked for forgiveness from Indigenous peoples for the harms of the residential schools (Aboriginal and Northern Affairs Canada 2008; Miller 2015), was to have begun the process of reconciliation. Thereafter, however, nothing more was said or done by that government to *enact* reconciliation. The subsequent Trudeau government spoke more convincingly of reconciliation and renewed relationships, but as of the date of this writing its inability or unwillingness to move beyond liberal inclusion and equality objectives has resulted in the government failing to recognize that Indigenous rights, title, and jurisdiction place obligations *on Canada* that precede the priorities of the expansionist capitalist economy of the state.

It appears that the state and the settler public assumed that the initial apology for the residential school harms and the striking of the TRC produced reconciliation without the intervening steps of reflection, remorse, restitution, and renewed relationship, and really, without most Canadians and our elite political institutions having grappled with the truth. And reconciliation, surely, cannot be framed as a transaction, of forgiveness *in return for* an apology. Indeed, reconciliation must recognize the impossibility of any final resolution (Schaap 2008, 259).

Enacting Reconciliation

The TRC did not primarily frame truth or reconciliation as structural and cultural processes. As Coburn (2016) argues, it "sidestepped reconciliation between two solitudes by making it about individuals and their individual experiences, not about nations or communities and the state." If the deliberate structural political *dis*organization of Indigenous peoples is ignored, the state can continue to assert its sovereignty as unproblematic. Yet colonial occupation and Indigenous dispossession are the foundation of the matters that now need "reconciling."

Enacting reconciliation requires Canadians to explore the path not to a renewed but rather to a new relationship with Indigenous peoples, a path marked by historic and contemporary oppression, by relations of dominance and subordination, but with the potential for a transformed and equitable future. The relationship is not fundamentally between individual Canadians and individual Indigenous people (although individuals may grapple with reconciliation), but between Indigenous nations and communities and the settler state. Canada is a federal state with sovereignty divided between provincial and federal orders, and both have appropriated Indigenous lands and sovereignties. Reconciliation, then, must be a collective political commitment made by both provincial and federal governments, not simply multiple individual acts of empathy and regret. And commitment must be manifested by changes to power and economic relations and by return of stolen land. Indeed, failure to grasp this essentially renders the theft of Indigenous lands historic and without contemporary significance or consequence (see also Coulthard 2014, 125). Unless and until the colonial state returns at least some of the land, negotiates shared jurisdiction over resources and tax room, and makes other amends, there will be no reconciliation.

In the spirit of reconciliation, Canada needs to confront its historic and contemporary colonial practices, and move towards a future that is acceptable to and imagined with Indigenous people, and that accommodates all of us in an as-yet to be imagined post-colonial framework. This alternative future depends on a "willingness to reconcile [that] should be understood as providing a political context in terms of which justice can be staged . . . (including via) redistribution, reparations, criminal trials, apologies, indigenous rights, constitutional recognition, etc." (Schaap 2008, 257). And the state, the perpetrator of the violence of colonialism, should take the lead on building Canadians' commitment to and initiating the processes to ensure this happens.

The path to reconciliation must wend its way through the quagmire of unequal power relations, of settler denial and resistance, to transformation and potential for a better relationship in the future. It is a new path because it is in all respects moving in a different direction than the old path of colonial domination, management, and definition of Indigenous peoples, which was a sideshow to the main event of colonial political and territorial expansion. The old path, approved by successive Canadian governments and citizens (and taught uncritically in many university courses as the ineluctable advance of progress), was assimilative. Indigenous peoples were to be subjects and eventually citizen Canadians with equal individual rights, but not with collective Indigenous rights that preceded the state and constituted claims against the state. Thus, particularly myopic iterations of Canadian liberalism (and I mean this as the ideological and theoretical liberalism, not in the partisan sense) proposed a form of equality that erased Indigenous rights and particularities, and, fundamentally, erased the genocidal violence and relational rupture produced by colonial occupation. Indeed, "'equality' has been both a stalking horse for assimilation and an unrealized state relative to the measures of quality of life of settler society" (Green 2014, 27).

Ignorance, Myth, and Memory

Colonialism is the process through which the residential school policy was developed and executed. Thus there is limited value in focusing on the residential schools without considering the structuring environment of colonialism. Nor can reconciliation be obtained for the genocidal effects of the residential schools outside of the context of colonialism, a historic and continuing set of structures and processes that implicates Project Canada and its citizens. Yet most Canadians view colonialism as a historic rather than a contemporary phenomenon—and few appreciate the profound differentials in power and life outcomes depending where one is situated in the colonial relationship. As Alfred writes, "the complete ignorance of Canadian society about the facts of their relationship with Indigenous peoples and the wilful denial of historical reality by Canadians detracts from the possibility of any meaningful discussion on true reconciliation" (2009, 181 cited in Patzer 2014, 180). And denial is useful, for it shields the "power asymmetries [that] . . . militate against appropriate responsibility taking in the settler society" (James 2012, 15).

There is a popular mythical history central to Canadian political culture about the emergence and development of the Canadian state (see, e.g., Thobani 2007; Green 1995, 2014), yet there is little popular or scholarly work on Canada as an exercise of colonialism. The mythical history produces the patriotic self-congratulatory puffery devoid of any recognition of colonialism evident in events such as the organized celebrations in 2017 of Canada's 150th anniversary of the 1867 Confederation. Canada has what Tricia Logan (2014, 149) calls a "memory block" about its violent assault on and removal and dispossession of Indigenous people in the course of building the not-so-peaceable dominion. Indeed, former prime minister Harper displayed that memory block when, days after making his apology for the residential schools, he volunteered to the media at a meeting of the G20 in Pittsburgh that Canada has "no history of colonialism" (cited in Comack 2014, 60; Green 2014, 28).

Canadian colonialism was directed at objectives and relied on practices that can only be described as genocidal. The TRC wrote that "Residential schooling was always more than simply an educational program: it was an integral part of a conscious policy of cultural genocide" (2015, 57; see also Logan 2014, 151). As Cynthia Chambers and Narcisse Blood (2009, 257) put it, "Epidemic and famine can sound innocuous, as if there were no perpetrators, as if the near decimation of a people is the inevitable result of natural events, perhaps even fated." Yet these consequences to "Indian" policies were known, executed, and justified by state agents and bureaucracies (Daschuk 2013; Savage 2012; Titley 1986).

And colonialism has been gendered; thus, its effects are experienced differently by men and women, and reconciliation itself must be gendered. The Native Women's Association of Canada (NWAC) writes that "The ongoing violation of Indigenous women through systemic subjugation, marginalization and violence is a legacy of colonialism in Canada" (2010, 1). The NWAC notes that Indigenous women have also been subjected to intergenerational "gendered injustices of marginalization, dispossession and violence within their own communities as well as in the larger Canadian society" as a consequence of colonialism and the residential school experience (2010, 30). The truth of this is evident in the numbers of missing and murdered Indigenous women.[5]

The residential school policy was part of the toolkit of Canadian colonialism. The purpose of residential schools—enforced deculturation and then assimilation into the settler state's preferred social paradigm—was intended to de-Indianize the country. Other policies in that toolkit included starvation via elimination of the bison (Daschuk 2013; Savage 2012), treaty-making, reserves as concentration camps to control the "natives," military and police control of Indians, military dispersal of the Métis, and mechanisms to divest Indigenous communities of their lands. Indigenous peoples—"Indians" in the nomenclature of the day[6]—were considered unfit for citizenship and were "intolerable as impediments to colonial settlement, expansion, and capitalist and agricultural development" (Green and Burton 2015). All of this enabled the execution of the signal 1878 National Policy of Prime Minister Sir John A. Macdonald's government, a policy designed to secure an economic framework for the new state while populating its territories with settlers chosen from approved racial and cultural communities (Green 1995).

Colonies become settler states precisely through these processes. Settler states emerge from colonial enterprises that establish permanent settlements, which are intended to become both the focus and the enactment of a politico-cultural project of the founding colonial entity. To execute this project, Indigenous populations must be contained or eliminated. After all, it is not their labour but their land that is necessary for the settler state (Green 1995; Veracini 2010, 9). And this is a continuing project (Snelgrove, Dhamoon, and Corntassel 2014, 21), which is, in the words of Coulthard, "*territorially acquisitive in perpetuity*" (2014, 125; emphasis in original).

The impulse to eliminate or assimilate "the other" is common to settler states confronting the inconvenient fact of Indigenous nations. Colonialism is predicated on profitability—it is, after all, an economic and political venture. Profitability increases with the amount of land and resources stolen. The political value of the colonized territory corresponds to its place in the economic and political universe of the colonizer. The foundational myths of settlement inevitably frame *progress* as a process emerging from the settlement of wildness; the imposition of order over disorder; the virtues of the colonial civilizations against the uncivilized state of Indigenous peoples; and the religious justifications inherent in a muscular and xenophobic conception of Christianity. Several of these myths have been theorized and disseminated by prominent intellectuals, further implicating the academy in colonialism. These are the key elements of the process of colonialism in Canada, now celebrated in cultural and political myths that unify settler populations while alienating Indigenous ones.

As an example of mythmaking concretized in power relations, consider my home community, Cranbrook, British Columbia, named by one Colonel Baker after his English home—or ʔa·kiskaq̓łiʔit in Ktunaxa, meaning "where two creeks meet"—where the "locals" celebrate Sam Steele Days every summer, named after one of the earliest military oppressors of the Ktunaxa. The practice of naming is imbued with the politics of domination. I look out my window at ʔakinmi—a mountain with an ancient Ktunaxa story explaining its origins—yet the settler community calls it "Mount Baker," after that same transplanted Englishman who obtained thousands of hectares of unceded Ktunaxa territory and who has been venerated ever after, with streets, businesses, and high schools (attended by Ktunaxa students as well as "locals") named after him in Cranbrook and Nelson, also in Ktunaxa territory. And in this way we all come to know who counts and who is in control. Every settler community in the country can provide similar examples, for all are squatted on Indigenous territory yet were created by and for anybody but Indigenous people.

"Erasure is an elegant method of revising history," writes Logan, adding that "Omissions in national history become omissions in national identity" (2014, 149). At their core, these settler myths celebrate an unbroken practice of genocide and oppression, which today is manifest in the continued corporate predation on Indigenous lands and resources, the denial of the incidents of fundamental human rights in Canada to Indigenous people, and the unrelenting obsession of the state and its elites with absorbing Indigenous particularity into the dominant body politic and obtaining "certainty" for government-supported capitalist activity on Indigenous lands.

The governments of Canada and several provinces are participating in land claim and treaty implementation processes, but negotiations, particularly in British Columbia, are not going well. Despite nearly three decades of negotiations, BC has signed only four treaties, all of which are problematic on measures of retention (or rather, loss) of traditional territory and self-determination. This is because present-day negotiations for land claims are functionally land surrenders, as their objective is to make Indigenous territories available for capitalist development (Coulthard 2014, 125).

As an example of this from my home territory, consider the case of Jumbo Glacier/ Jumbo municipality/future year-round ski hill[7] on the glacier—or, Qat'muk, the sacred home of the Grizzly Bear Spirit, on unceded Ktunaxa territory. The particulars of this case make for fascinating reading. There is no municipality at the glacier, yet the former Liberal

In 2017, the Supreme Court of Canada ruled to allow the development of Qat'muk, home to the Grizzly Bear Spirit and a core territory of the Ktunaxa Nation, which strongly opposed the decision.

government of BC created the municipality of Jumbo,[8] appointed a few stooges as mayor and council—who represent no citizens as no one is there—and has funded them to do nothing more than show the flag for BC's occupation of the land, in the process of working with the developer to create the ski resort. The Ktunaxa Nation opposes the development and wishes Qat'muk to remain as it is, for the Grizzly Bear Spirit.[9] Many "locals" support the Ktunaxa on this. Bumper stickers can be seen everywhere in the area reading "Keep Jumbo Wild"—but also "Pave Jumbo" and "I'm Going to Ski the Shit Out of Jumbo."

The case, *Ktunaxa Nation v. British Columbia (Forests, Lands and Natural Resource Operations)*, in which the Ktunaxa Nation argued that development would infringe the Ktunaxa Charter right of religious freedom, was heard by the Supreme Court of Canada in 2017. It didn't go well. The Court held that:

> the Ktunaxa are not seeking protection for the freedom to believe in Grizzly Bear Spirit or to pursue practices related to it. Rather, they seek to protect the presence of Grizzly Bear Spirit itself and the subjective spiritual meaning they derive from it. . . . The state's duty under s. 2(a) is not to protect the object of beliefs or the spiritual focal point of worship, such as Grizzly Bear Spirit. Rather, the state's duty is to protect everyone's freedom to hold such beliefs and to manifest them in worship and practice or by teaching and dissemination. (SCC 2017)

And since the Ktunaxa are allowed to believe what they want, the fact of the impact of development on the object of their belief is of no interest to the court. The inability of the Court to appreciate the indivisibility of the belief systems of the Ktunaxa (including the Grizzly Bear Spirit) from their territorial context (Qat'muk, the glacier and environs) demonstrates a colossal impediment to the conditions for reconciliation. It also demonstrates the Court's, and arguably Canada's, inability to grasp the indivisibility of Indigenous peoples' lands from their identities, their cultures, their spirituality, and their viable existences.

Reconciliation: Really?

Beware of settler-state governments rushing to claim reconciliation without going through the difficult processes that lead to reconciliation. That way lies erasure of the colonial past, denial of the settler-state present, and an uncertain future framed by the enormous pressure of the investment of colonial practices in ensuring colonial interests. Coulthard (2014, 108) warns that in settler-colonial contexts, state approaches to reconciliation consign the abuses of settler colonization to the dustbins of history and divorce settler-colonial interests from the imperatives of reconciliation. In other words, Coulthard reminds us that language can be co-opted to legitimate new forms of oppression or incorporation into the settler state. Similarly, James (2012, 17) warns that "discourses of therapy, healing and forgiveness" can elide "colonial dispossession and governance." We must correct the prevalent view of colonialism and Indigenous rights abuses as *only* historical: they continue in contemporary forms. Still, Canadians' awareness of our colonial relationship is beginning. Politically and economically significant acknowledgement must follow if Coulthard's and James's fears are not to be realized. Atonement and remediating action, however, are far from certain at this juncture.

Nor can the variety of "self-government" initiatives be considered sufficient for reconciliation. Self-government, a perennial and restrictive policy variously framed by past Liberal, Progressive Conservative, and Conservative federal governments, is generally a formula for Indigenous self-administration of policies and programs established, funded, and evaluated by the bureaucratic wing for Indigenous pacification: the Department of Crown–Indigenous Relations and Northern Affairs (formerly known as Indian Affairs and subsequent variants). Indian Act band councils are only the most ubiquitous and perpetual form of that genre.

Sovereignty and self-determination, far more robust forms of political autonomy, are claimed as rights by many Indigenous leaders, scholars, and organizations. Their enactment requires the co-operation of the occupying settler state, including by making jurisdictional and constitutional space for another non-subordinate order of government: that is, it requires restructuring of the federal order and obliging federal and provincial orders of government to respect the (hopefully) newly recognized Indigenous political entities. Self-determination is animated theoretically by "resurgence": "an intellectual, social, political, and artistic movement geared toward the self-reflective revitalization" of Indigenous traditional values, principles, and cultural practices that enable a "contemporary political and economic reality" (Alfred and Simpson, cited in Coulthard 2014, 156–7; see also Starblanket 2017). The 1996 Royal Commission on Aboriginal Peoples (RCAP) proposed self-determination as the foundation for a new relationship between Indigenous peoples and Canada. The UNDRIP lists self-determination as a fundamental right of Indigenous peoples. The TRC cites the UN Special Rapporteur on Indigenous Peoples, James Anaya, who called self-determination an "animating force" for reconciliation (TRC 2015, 241).

Is Canada at a historic juncture where reconciliation can be contemplated? Few settler Canadians have heard the truth of the residential school survivors, much less embraced its implications. Moreover, the residential school phenomenon was only one of a number of colonial violations of Indigenous peoples' fundamental rights, and thus, while the TRC can point to processes of recognition and responsibility, it cannot function to include all of these other injuries sustained at the behest of colonial power. Reconciliatory turns in other states have sometimes relied on stepping back from claiming reparations from the oppressor in return for recognition, apology, and transformation. However, some scholars suggest that reconciliation should imply "a political context in terms of which justice can be staged . . . (including via) redistribution, reparations, criminal trials, apologies, indigenous rights, constitutional recognition, etc." (Schaap 2008, 257). Who decides on the acceptability of a reconciliatory initiative, and on what constitutes a transformative reconciliatory opportunity? Indigenous peoples must make this determination. The adequacy of reconciliatory action for colonialism is not the state's decision to make: if the initiatives are not acceptable to Indigenous peoples, reconciliation cannot occur.

Indigenous self-determination will unsettle the settler. It "requires a dismantling of other, related forms of domination" (Snelgrove et al. 2014, 21). Coulthard (2014, 14) lists these as including "capitalism, patriarchy, White supremacy, and the totalizing character of state power . . . [which forms] the constellation of power relations that sustain colonial patterns of behavior [sic], structures, and relationships." The symbiotic relationship between the state and the elite corporate class implies that corporate ambitions and expectations of profitability will be affected by practices of reconciliation. Take, for example, the legal requirement that governments and corporate agents must "consult" with Indigenous peoples prior to enacting "developments" on their territories. This is more robustly framed as the right to "free, prior and informed consent" (FPIC) articulated in the United Nations Declaration on the Rights of Indigenous Peoples (see also Benjamin 2014). As in any relational transaction, consultation and consent include the possibility of withholding consent: "no" is an option.

The TRC suggests that reconciliation requires "Aboriginal peoples' right to self-determination within, and in partnership with, a viable Canadian sovereignty" (TRC 2015, 238). That certainly is a pragmatic objective, but not everyone is willing to accept that Canada is the necessary framework for the exercise of Indigenous self-determination. Indeed, it may be the other way around. Canada, a settler state initiated by colonialism, needs to be legitimated as a post-colonial state by Indigenous reconciliation, political protocols, treaties, Indigenization of state institutions, and right relationships enacted into the future. We should beware of calls for reconciliation framed as inclusion in the status quo and in a liberal group hug. Neither political inclusion nor personal friendships are prerequisites for reconciliation, and, as Schaap (2008, 255) writes, "Reconciliation as nation-building may be viewed as assimilative since it seeks to overcome the state's crisis of legitimacy by *incorporating* the colonized into the political community as free and equal citizens rather than recognizing their right *not* to reconcile." This is a variation on the rights-denying, assimilative objectives and practices of every Canadian government since 1867. Put another way, Indigenous political and social assimilation into the Canadian status quo cannot be prerequisites for the amends and relational possibilities inherent in reconciliation for state oppression and genocide.

Decolonization is possible if reconciliation is enacted well. All important political projects emerge from imagination, take shape from collaboration and struggle, and are animated by action over time and against the status quo. Decolonization requires imagination, collaboration, solidarity, and replacement of the settler-state status quo with a concrete set of acceptable liberatory alternatives. And only then can we anticipate the possibility of Right Relationship—a state that is constantly negotiated, beneficial to all, and is the manifestation of reconciliation involving "a restructuring of the fundamental relationship between Indigenous nations and Canada" (Coulthard 2014, 168). As the TRC put it, reconciliation "is not a one-time event [but] . . . a multi-generational journey that involves all Canadians" (TRC 2015, 262). The model exists in treaty frameworks, which envisioned ongoing adaptable relationships with the capacity to carry us all into a positive future. This model has never yet been recognized or animated by Canada.

The status quo is patently divorced from Canada's putative political values of an inclusive democracy, accountable representative government, respect for fundamental human rights, a just rule of law, respect for minority rights, fair dealing on the part of the state, and an equitable citizenship producing benefits and emancipation for all. Reconciliation with those who have endured colonialism will produce systemic change to remediate the systemic evils produced by colonialism. Will Canada accept responsibility for educating its citizens about the truth of its colonial relationship with Indigenous peoples? Will settler Canadians accept responsibility for knowing the truth and for turning away from this colonial relationship and its unearned privileges? Will settler Canadians trust an Indigenized state for their futures? Canadians should grasp this opportunity for reconciliation. We can all do better than the settler-state status quo. And until we have the preconditions for reconciliation, the truth will not make us free of the reality of colonialism—not historically, and not now, across Canada, in Indigenous communities and everywhere else as well.

Discussion Questions

1. Can you both conceptualize and define colonialism? Reconciliation? White privilege? Structural racism? If not, re-read, consult recommended readings, and revisit the discussion.

2. Consider how Canada was constructed—by whom and for whom, and at whose expense.

3. Consider how privilege and mythmaking construct a comfortable racism in otherwise pleasant people.

4. Consider where you fit on the scale of relative social and political privilege, and how your skin colour marks you into that scale.

5. Discuss how these factors shape relationships, politics, and possibility in Canada.

Recommended Reading

Coulthard, Glen. 2014. "The Politics of Recognition in Colonial Contexts." In Coulthard, *Red Skins, White Masks: Rejecting the Colonial Politics of Recognition*, 25–49. Minneapolis: University of Minnesota Press.

Green, Joyce. 2017. "The Impossibility of Citizenship Liberation for Indigenous People." In *Citizenship in a Transnational Perspective: Australia, Canada, and New Zealand*, edited by Jatinder Mann. New York: Palgrave Macmillan, Politics of Citizenship and Migration Series.

———— and Mike Burton. 2016. "Twelve Steps to Post-Colonial Reconciliation." *Wrongs to Rights: How Churches Can Engage the United Nations Declaration on the Rights of Indigenous Peoples*, edited by Steve Heinrichs, 154–7. Winnipeg: Mennonite Church of Canada. (Earlier versions published in *Canadian Dimension* http://canadiandimension.com/articles/5705/ and rabble.ca.

LaRocque, Emma. 2017. "My Hometown, Northern Canada, South Africa." In *Making Space for Indigenous Feminism*, 2nd edn, edited by Joyce Green. Halifax: Fernwood Publishing.

Savage, Candace. 2012. *A Geography of Blood: Unearthing Memory from a Prairie Landscape*. Vancouver: Greystone Books.

Notes

1. The Canadian nomenclature for Indigenous peoples is historically complicated and fluid. Initially, Indigenous peoples were categorized as Indians, Inuit, and Métis, with the first being identified by "status" requirements under the Indian Act and the second later being identified by disc numbers. Métis were ignored for public policy purposes and some scholars and propagandists insist(ed) that the Métis are not an authentic Indigenous people. In Canada's federal structure, the federal government has sole jurisdiction over "Indians and lands reserved for Indians" in section 91(24) of the Constitution Act, 1867, formerly called the British North America Act. The Supreme Court found that Inuit ("Eskimos," as they were then called by settler society) were Indians for the purposes of the Constitution, and more recently has found that Métis are also Indian for those purposes. Thus, the 1867 term, "Indians," was a crude colonial label for Indigenous peoples, and legislation and policy initiatives of Canada were designed to limit and eliminate the populations under consideration. The Constitution Act, 1982, and its Charter of Rights and Freedoms recognize "Indians, Inuit, and Métis" as holding protected rights. The term "Indigenous" is largely replacing "Aboriginal," as the former is most commonly used around the world by Indigenous

peoples to refer to themselves in their colonized contexts and is used by the United Nations Declaration on the Rights of Indigenous People, which Canada has adopted. In this chapter I use the terms as they were used for specific policies and legislation, and the term "Indigenous" to refer to present-day communities of Indigenous peoples.

2. The Convention on the Prevention and Punishment of the Crime of Genocide defines genocide as "any of the following acts committed with intent to destroy, in whole or in part, a national, ethnical [sic], racial or religious group, as such:

> Killing members of the group;
> Causing serious bodily or mental harm to members of the group;
> Deliberately inflicting on the group conditions of life calculated to bring about its physical destruction in whole or in part;
> Imposing measures intended to prevent births within the group;
> Forcibly transferring children of the group to another group."

3. The Framework ignores constitutional rights under s. 35 in favour of a "recognition framework," which also both ignores land title matters and constitutional, treaty, and international legal rights of Indigenous peoples. See Green and Starblanket (2018), as well as the federal government's Engagement page at https://www.rcaanc-cirnac.gc.ca/eng/1522086494578/1539960373711 and its initial public statement on the framework at https://pm.gc.ca/eng/news/2018/02/14/government-canada-create-recognition-and-implementation-rights-framework.

4. I am indebted to Matt James for his discussion of the distinctions between the concepts of reconciliatory processes and absolute reconciliation.

5. A more complete discussion of this may be found in Amnesty International (2004, 2009) and in Mary Eberts's work showing how Indigenous women have always been framed as sexually licentious and morally depraved, constructed by colonial mythologies as a population of prey (Eberts 2014, 2017).

6. As the Supreme Court of Canada ruled in *Daniels* v. Canada (Indian Affairs and Northern Development) (SCC 2016)

7. http://jumboglacierresort.com/about/.

8. http://www.jgmrm.ca/.

9. The Ktunaxa Nation declaration may be read in full at http://www.ktunaxa.org/who-we-are/qatmuk-declaration/.

Imagining New Futures

A Concluding Dialogue

Gina Starblanket and David Long

David (speaking to Gina): I think it is remarkable that *Visions of the Heart* is in its fifth edition, for when I approached Olive Dickason with an invitation to co-edit the first edition of this collection back in 1993, my simple hope was that it would challenge as well as contribute positively to the understanding of our readers and in relations between Indigenous and other peoples in Canada. Throughout the years, Olive and I agreed that the essential purpose of each edition was to invite readers into a scholarly dialogue that was based on respectful listening, careful observation, and the open and honest exchange of perspectives, ideas, and analyses.

When Oxford University Press approached me about putting together a fifth edition of *Visions of the Heart*, I anticipated that it would be very different from the previous four. I was eager to work with a new co-editor, for I recognized that this person would bring a unique perspective as well as different scholarly interests and colleagues to the "*Visions* project." I was looking forward to seeing how such a new co-editor's involvement would affect not only our list of contributors and what each of them would write about, but also how we would work together and what we would come to understand as the purpose of the new collection. It was after I heard you giving a radio interview in which you shared your perspective on the National Inquiry into Missing and Murdered Indigenous Women and Girls that I decided to contact you about co-editing the fifth edition. Despite the brevity of the interview, I appreciated your forthrightness and I resonated with your comments about the need to acknowledge and address the many ways that the violence of colonialism was being made public in and through the Inquiry. Even though I was not overly familiar with your writing, I was hopeful that you would be open to collaborating with me on the fifth edition of this collection. And so our relationship began.

Gina (speaking to David): I know that you and I share a certain degree of faith in the transformative potential of cross-cultural dialogue and education, but I remember telling you when you first reached out that at the current moment, I had concerns about any project that sought to ask Indigenous people to share our "visions" or "hopes" for the future. What would be the purpose of such a project? Why had you approached me to be part of it? I realize that you have trusted me (and for no apparent reason) since early in our relationship. I can't say that I felt the same way; in fact, I started from a place of quite significant uncertainty about you and this project. Only about halfway through did I start to realize that I could trust you to be supportive of my vision and ideas on just about every turn this book has taken.

It's not that I was unaware of the pressing need to strengthen dialogue and understanding around matters of concern to Indigenous peoples, but more so that I wasn't sure if this was the right time. For hundreds of years Indigenous peoples have been trying to talk to non-Indigenous peoples and governments, to explain our rights and responsibilities, our laws and our governance, our desires and aspirations about the future. What would be the point of reiterating this yet again in a book of readings, particularly at a time when Indigenous peoples are starting to look for means of pursuing our visions of freedom that aren't dependent on buy-in from the rest of Canada. Indeed, many Indigenous people are taking much-needed time away from engaging with mainstream systems to rebuild, reconstitute, renew, learn, unlearn, organize, teach, mobilize, and grow.

Given that the emphasis on reconciliation in the last edition of this book, I very much questioned whether this would be the right project for me. I certainly believe that there is a need for students to begin to think critically about Indigenous and non-Indigenous relations at an early stage in their learning. And I also think that it's important to educate people about matters that lay beyond the so-called "Indigenous issues" in Canada. But as in any relationship that has been so deeply damaged and marked by conflict, it becomes difficult to talk to one another when the talks themselves continue to take place within a repressive dynamic, when they are dictated by one party's terms, by one party's conceptions of what is good, what is right, what is real, and, indeed, what is possible. I felt there was simply too much work to be done in order for Indigenous and non-Indigenous peoples to be able to talk to one another in a healthy and generative way, and one that isn't voyeuristic, objectifying, appropriative, assimilative, or in one way or another expecting "education in Indigenous issues" to stand in for more material forms of change.

For instance, the last edition began with the statement "all acts of justice are acts of reconciliation." This is the sort of framing that concerned me, not because of my disinterest in engaging in yet another critique of reconciliation as it has been taken up by the Truth and Reconciliation Commission (TRC) in Canada, for despite the many excellent critiques in this area, much work remains to be done. My concern was around the justice part. As I would go on to tell you, justice was, in my view, a prerequisite to any conversation about reconciliation. This would involve talking about land theft, genocide, settler privilege, and the illegitimacy of the Canadian state. It would involve a willingness to take these up not as historic phenomena but as a crucial part of Canada's present and, evidently, its foreseeable future. But it would also involve more than education; justice would necessitate structural forms of change, including the return of land and a reconfiguration of federal and provincial claims to jurisdiction. These are conditions that increasingly appear to be impossibilities, as proposed measures of change are always situated within the existing parameters of the Canadian state.

If justice gives way to reconciliation, then in my mind we should seriously consider forgetting about reconciliation because the justice being offered by Canada will never come close to the levels of change desired by many Indigenous peoples. More realistically, we should eschew both of these imperatives, as it has become increasingly clear that political efforts to renew or heal the relationship will always be contained by dominant logics and ideologies. Indigenous peoples are simply too often expected to find some negotiated measure of justice within terms that are dictated by Canada and the provinces, which, in and of itself, is a project that perpetuates the subordination of our laws, governance, world views, forms of relationality, social norms, and so on. For me, the questions of "what form of justice, on whose terms, and what visions of justice are precluded in the process" always seem paramount to these sorts of conversations.

David: I too understand justice in very concrete, relational terms. I also agree that without redress there can be no justice, and that without justice there can be no reconciliation. I appreciate your questions of what justice may look like and whose interests and visions it may or may not serve, for they also suggest that redress can take many forms and reconciliation can follow many different paths. At the time of writing the introduction to the fourth edition I was involved in a support group for street-involved, mostly Indigenous men in downtown Edmonton. Being a member of the group challenged and invited me to think and feel in a very different way about justice and reconciliation from what I had experienced in my involvement with the TRC hearings. It wasn't just that all participants in our men's groups listened respectfully as everyone took turns sharing our stories of hope; it was that we all understood that we each had something unique and valuable to give to one another. I'm not suggesting here that my experience of justice and reconciliation in the context of this men's group precludes the many expressions of justice you describe above and that are discussed in detail throughout this collection. Indeed, my intent is quite the opposite, as was my purpose in introducing the fourth edition with the statement "all acts of justice are acts of reconciliation," for it has always been my view that reconciliation in relations between Indigenous and settler peoples requires justice in our relations, not that it precludes or gives way to it. Put another way, it is only when the actions of settlers and leaders of a settler-colonial state are just that reconciliation in relations involving Indigenous and settler peoples will follow.

While some contributors to the fourth edition expressed hope that the TRC would help relations between Indigenous and settler peoples in Canada move forward in a good way, all contributors agreed with Susan Dion's view that the process of reconciliation in Canada is deeply complicated, and that research, writing, discussions, and initiatives must do much more than shed light on some of the horrors that Indigenous people experienced in the past and the resulting challenges many of them experience in the present. Specifically, they recognized the importance of inviting as well as challenging settlers to understand their complicity in the ongoing colonial project and to accept responsibility for how they respond in their present, everyday lives. I also appreciate the clarity with which Joyce Green articulates in her concluding chapter that meaningful efforts to reconcile require not only a fundamental change in how colonizers see ourselves and the cultural and structural conditions that contribute to both our place in Canada and our relations with Indigenous people, but also that reconciliation requires an openness on our part to supporting material redress in our relations. I also think—given the complexity of Indigenous–settler relations and the inherently violent nature and consequence of colonialism—that we must understand the importance of stepping back from a relationship in order to honour another person's or another people's right to address the challenges they face as they see fit. At the same time, we need to listen respectfully and carefully when they are willing to share their thoughts and experiences, work with others to dismantle the colonial structures in our everyday lives, and honour the need to acknowledge as well as return stolen lands; and countless other "everyday acts of justice" may each in their own way contribute to transformative change in our relations.

The concern you expressed about how justice and reconciliation seemed to be approached in the fourth edition reminded me of the uneasiness that many of the contributors expressed in their chapters about the way reconciliation was being framed and played out in many circles in Canada. It was not simply that they were concerned about the lack of agreement about the meaning of reconciliation or that the TRC hearings and the many reconciliation-focused initiatives it was engendering seemed to be overly preoccupied with providing public platforms for Indigenous witnesses as victims/survivors to give account of the damage that Indian residential schools had wrought in their lives and communities. While all contributors agreed that it was essential for Canadians to face up to the ugliness of the "Indian residential school chapter" in Canada's colonial history, their unease had more to do with the fact that Canada's approach to reconciliation was not only leaving the colonial past and present largely intact and without meaningful redress, but also that it was failing in many ways to build upon the wisdom and strengths of Indigenous traditions and teachings, to honour Indigenous peoples' agency, and to acknowledge the significance and ascendency of Indigenous resurgence.

Gina: And this concern over Canada's unwillingness or inability to address the foundational structure of the unjust relationship between Indigenous and non-Indigenous peoples is definitely one that we continue to see reflected in the fifth edition, even though we have shifted the frame to questions of relationship. Indeed, many of the chapters highlight the ways in which dominant discourses overlook the ongoing and very real forms of violence, hierarchy, and oppression that continue to structure Indigenous–state relations and that many Indigenous peoples continue to suffer from.

I think it's important to remember that in enacting critiques of the challenges that came before us and that remain in the present, our contributors are presenting us with their visions of the future. That is, their critiques are ultimately grounded in the desire for a better present and future, one where Indigenous peoples can work towards stronger relations on our own terms, rather than terms defined by others who think that they have our best interests at heart. By refusing to accept the ways in which colonialism continues to structure our lives, we are also envisioning an alternative that we are continually finding new ways to work towards.

Too often in academia, we are constrained by the foundations, standards, and debates surrounding the ways that questions have predominantly been taken up in our disciplines or fields. We become stuck in seemingly endless quibbles over particular terms or referents, and in doing so we sometimes overlook the need to step back and think about whether the overarching frames are themselves still adequate. By foregrounding Indigenous peoples' many complex conceptions of freedom in our relationship with one another and the worlds we live in, our contributors unsettle colonial terms, organizing logics, and social and political landscapes, and so continually work to advance the range of the discourse rather than reinforcing its existing parameters.

Gina and David: Although this edition of *Visions of the Heart* invited/challenged us to listen to each other and learn from our differences, we agreed from the outset that the voices of this generation of Indigenous activists, artists, and scholars have a crucial intervention to make in the discourse on Indigenous and non-Indigenous relations in Canada. This process of working towards a better future outside of dominant frames, of collapsing tired tropes of Indigeneity, inclusion, and change, and of reframing the questions themselves is incredibly transformative. This is why we think it important that students realize at an early stage of their learning that the ways they are engaging with "Indigenous issues" are themselves political, rather than learning about this in graduate school or later on in their learning. The more that we continue to bring new voices and visions to the fore, and juxtapose them with the ways that matters of concern to Indigenous peoples have been represented and that solutions have been proposed in the past, we incrementally broaden our capacity to think and talk about these questions. In so doing, we invite new understandings of the present and more hopeful visions of the future for us all.

Glossary

Glossaries are comprised of definitions of terms specified by the author(s) of a given text. It is therefore important to recognize that each definition contained in this (or any other) glossary reflects the particular perspective and focus of its contributors, and that definitions of many terms often change over time as they are informed by new experiences, attitudes, and understandings. It is also important to note that the following definitions were arrived at through dialogue among various contributors to this as well as previous editions of *Visions of the Heart* and that, in the end, the definitions that follow are those that appealed most to the majority of discussants.

Aboriginal Peoples Survey (APS) National survey by Statistics Canada of First Nations people living off reserve, Métis, and Inuit throughout Canada. The purpose of the survey is to identity the needs of Indigenous people and focus on issues such as health, language, employment, income, education, housing, and mobility. The fifth cycle of the survey was conducted in 2017.

Assembly of First Nations (AFN) National organization established in 1982 to represent the perspectives and interests of status Indians in Canada. Successor to the National Indian Brotherhood.

Assimilation Process through which a dominant group seeks to undermine the cultural distinctiveness of a subordinate group by subjecting them to the rules, values, and norms of the dominant group and then by absorbing the "de-cultured" minority into the mainstream.

Bill C-31 Parliamentary Act to Amend the Indian Act passed in 1985 that brought the Indian Act into line with the provisions of the Canadian Charter of Rights and Freedoms. The three principles that guided the amendments were: the removal of sex discrimination; restoring Indian status and membership to women; and increasing the control Indian bands have over their own affairs.

Blood quantum A highly contentious, racializing concept referring to the "measure or degree" of one's Indigenous ancestry.

Capitalism A mode of production defined by the search for profit. Because exchange happens on the market—retrospectively and outside of social control—producers are compelled to drive down the costs of production. This occurs through increasing the exploitation of labourers and the "free" or cheap expropriation of labour and land.

Charter of Rights and Freedoms The Charter adopted when the Canadian Constitution Act, 1982, terminated the United Kingdom's imperial rule over Canada. The Charter protects certain fundamental rights and freedoms of Canadian citizens such as equality before the law.

Collage A metaphorical and arts-based Indigenous research methodology that brings together a number of different pieces—images, stories, poetry, and analysis—in order to understand Indigenous politics.

Colonization The establishment, exploitation, maintenance, acquisition, and expansion of colonies in one territory by a political power from another territory.

Comprehensive land claims Negotiation process wherein Indigenous peoples are asked to cede their land rights, title, and jurisdiction to the Crown in exchange for revenue-sharing from development projects, select degrees of authority, and clarification and certainty surrounding their rights.

Co-optation Process through which socially, organizationally, and/or politically marginalized people come to support the perspectives of those who have power and control over them.

Cultural competence The ability to communicate effectively with individuals from other cultures. Also entails one's attitude towards and knowledge and awareness of different cultural practices and beliefs.

Cultural genocide Destruction of a people's cultural ways and means, often through colonial policies, legislation, and practices.

Cyclical thinking An understanding of the world that envisions all parts of Creation as flowing in a cycle.

Decolonization Process of restructuring relations between Indigenous and colonizing peoples, often through efforts to establish Indigenous social, political, and economic authority and jurisdiction free from colonial interference or control.

Department of Indian Affairs and Northern Development (DIAND) Federal government department established in 1966. Also referred to as Department of Indian Affairs (DIA), Department of Indian and Northern Affairs (DINA), and Indian and Northern Affairs Canada (INAC).

Environmental injustice issues Resource development initiatives that negatively impact Indigenous peoples' lands and communities.

Environmental racism The deliberate or intentional siting of hazardous waste sites, landfills, incinerators, and polluting industries in communities inhabited by minority or marginalized populations. Peoples and communities subject to this type of racism are often impoverished, marginalized, and excluded from dominant society in a variety of ways.

Ethic of reciprocal visiting A theory and set of culturally informed principles designed to inform how individuals move through complex worlds in a good way. Such an ethic also includes an appreciation for the space and time needed for negotiation, and the opportunity for correction.

Ethnocentrism The view that a people's cultural and institutional ways are superior to those of other peoples.

Families of the heart Name of an emerging kinship model developed by Marlene Brant-Castellano in and through which Indigenous adults are finding their way "home" by knitting together connections in an urban environment with Indigenous people who come from diverse nations.

First Nation reserve Land, the legal title to which is vested in the Crown, that has been set apart for the use and benefit of a First Nation and that is subject to the terms of the Indian Act.

Global cultural pathology Set of perspectives, attitudes, and actions that are contributing to the destruction of the Earth's ecology.

Grounded normativity A term that, as described by Leanne Simpson (Chapter 3), involves "ethical frameworks generated by place-based practices and associated knowledges." Simpson adds that grounded normativity "is the base of Indigenous political systems, economy, and nationhood" and that it "creates process-centred modes of living."

Guswenteh (also two-row wampum) The wampum depicts two solid blue or purple parallel lines separated by a row of white space. The blue/purple lines symbolize two nations, separate and distinct, engaged in a relationship of mutual friendship and non-interference. The spaces between the rows are and can be places of conversation, dialogue, debate, discussion, sharing, listening, and learning.

Hawthorn Report Two-volume parliamentary report of 1966–7 that laid the foundation for modern Indian policy by rejecting the idea of assimilation and suggesting that Indians ought to be "citizens plus" by virtue of promises made to them and from the simple fact that they once used and occupied lands to which others came to gain enormous wealth in which the original inhabitants shared little.

Hegemonic masculinity A specific, culturally idealized strategy for the subordination of women that is presented and maintained as "natural." It represents a loosely defined and at times contradictory set of cultural values associated with "being a man" that includes courage, inner direction, certain forms of aggression, autonomy, mastery, technological skill, group solidarity, and adventurous spirit, as well as toughness in mind and body.

Hegemony Ideological as well as political processes and structures through which one class or a people achieve domination over others.

Heteronormativity Perspective based on the assumption that heterosexuality is the only normal and natural expression of sexuality.

Holism The perspective that the inner and outer states of existence are profoundly connected and that the purpose of all of life is harmony and balance between all aspects and dimensions of reality.

Idle No More Indigenous political movement initiated in 2012 that based its position and actions on Indigenous conceptions of responsibility for water and the natural environment.

Indian Acts (1876, 1951) Bodies of federal legislation that specify who, legally, is an Indian, what Indian peoples are entitled to under the government's legal obligation, who can qualify for enfranchisement, what can be done with Indian lands and resources, and how Indian peoples are to be governed (through Indian agents and elected band councils).

Indian control of Indian education Policy initiated by the National Indian Brotherhood in 1972 that sought to shift control of First Nation education into the hands of First Nation people, including increasing the involvement of Indigenous parents in the education of their children.

Indian Registry A list of all people registered according to the Indian Act. The register carries information about the name, date of birth, gender, marital status, and place of residence (on- or off-reserve) of all registered people.

Indigeneity Indigenous identity, encompassing one's sense of belonging and one's ancestral and ongoing relationships to creation.

Indigenization Process through which colonial laws, policies, and organizational practices are reformulated according to Indigenous peoples' perspectives and interests.

Indigenous Original occupant of a specified territory or land, often defined by shared language, cultures, spirituality, and ancestry; distinct from racial or cultural minorities. Indigenous people remain a fundamentally autonomous and self-determining political community that continues to possess distinct political relationships with the colonizers, together with the rights and entitlements that flow from their unique status. Legal categories for Indigenous people in Canada include registered or status Indians, Métis, Inuit, and non-status Indians. However, many Indigenous people in Canada prefer to identify themselves by their cultural community of origin (e.g., Gwich'in, Cree, Métis, Nisga'a).

Indigenous cultural revitalization The renewal of Indigenous spirituality and cultural traditions in a wide variety of modern social and political contexts.

Indigenous knowledge The local and culturally specific knowledge of a people that is dynamic, adapting over time and place. The knowledges of Indigenous peoples are derived from their ways of living, knowing, and being in this world.

Indigenous masculinities Innes and Anderson define this term as "the ways in which Indigenous men, and those who assert Indigenous masculine identities, perform their identities, why and how they perform them and the consequences to them and others because of their attachment to those identities." (Robert Alexander Innes and Kim Anderson, *Indigenous Men and Masculinities: Legacies, Identities, Regeneration* [Winnipeg: University of Manitoba Press, 2015], 4.)

Indigenous research methodology The broad range of ethics, methods, and practices that guide ways of conducting research with or relating to Indigenous peoples; a way of conducting research that flows from an Indigenous world view or way of knowing.

Indigenous rights (also Aboriginal Peoples' rights) Rights held by Indigenous peoples by virtue of their status as the original occupants of a given territory.

Indigenous self-government The governing powers that may be exercised by an Indigenous nation. Self-government occurs along a spectrum, and can represent anything from a delegated, negotiated set of administrative powers exercised by an Indigenous community, to the ability of a First Nation to enact its own political freedom and autonomy in a non-hierarchical relationship with provincial and federal political authorities.

Indigenous sovereignty The independence and autonomy that an Indigenous Nation exercises relative to other nations; the ability to assert rights and responsibilities in relation to a territory.

Intergenerational trauma The transmission of historical oppression and its negative consequences on people's health and well-being across generations.

Intersectionality The interconnected nature of social categorizations such as race, class, and gender as they apply to a given individual or group, regarded as creating overlapping and interdependent systems of discrimination or disadvantage.

Inuit Indigenous people from Inuit Nunangat, i.e., the Canadian Arctic regions of Nunatsiavut (northern Labrador), Nunavik (Arctic Quebec), Nunavut (formerly the eastern portion of the Northwest Territories), and Inuvialuit (northwestern NWT). The term "Inuit Nunangat" is a Canadian Inuit term that includes land, water, and ice. The Inuit, one of Canada's three constitutionally recognized Indigenous groups, consider the land, water, and ice of their homeland to be integral to their way of life.

Inuit Qaujimajatuqangit A body of knowledge and unique cultural insights of the Inuit into the workings of nature, humans, and animals.

Kimberly Declaration Declaration of 2002 from the International Indigenous Peoples Summit on Sustainable Development that affirmed previous Indigenous environmental declarations and clearly articulated the relationships between Indigenous peoples' right to self-determination and sustainability.

Kinship A complex system of laws and customs that govern how people organize themselves and relate to each other and to the universe, prescribing their roles and responsibilities in all their relations.

Land-based education A process of learning from the land, informed by Indigenous cultural values and teachings such as respect and reciprocity. Land-based education includes fostering and maintaining a relationship directly from the land, learning Indigenous languages or songs that come from the land, and/or participating in ceremonies that come from the land.

Land claims Process of negotiating agreements that specify the rights of occupation in relation to a particular territory, as well as arrangements among governments, private enterprises, and Indigenous peoples to control the resources available on lands or other places designated sacred by Indigenous groups.

Land dispossession The theft or unauthorized removal of land from those who exercise rights and responsibilities towards it.

Marginality Personal experiences and social designation of those with subordinate social, economic, and political status.

Métis An Indigenous people primarily of the Northwest Plains, possessing a history, language, politics, and culture rooted to their territories. One of Canada's three constitutionally recognized Indigenous peoples, they are part of kinship networks connecting them to other Indigenous nations. Métis communities define themselves as people who have historic Métis ancestry and are accepted by the Métis Nation. This term is sometimes simplified to refer to those with mixed European and Indigenous heritage.

Modern treaties Process initiated by the government of Canada that uses land claim settlements and self-government agreements to negotiate renewed legal and political relationships with Indigenous peoples in places where governing arrangements have not been negotiated through other means, for example, through historic treaties.

National Indian Brotherhood (NIB) National organization established in 1968 by Indigenous people to represent the perspectives and interests of status Indians; became the Assembly of First Nations in 1982.

Native Council of Canada (NCC) National organization established in 1968 by Indigenous people to represent the perspectives and interests of the Métis and non-status Indians; reorganized as the Congress of Aboriginal Peoples in 1993 after formation of the Métis National Council ten years earlier.

Native Women's Association of Canada (NWAC) National organization established in 1973 by Indigenous women to represent the perspectives and interests of non-status Indian, status Indian, Métis, and Inuit women.

Natural law As described by Elder Cecile King, a code of conduct, a set of lessons derived from the Law of the Orders. Natural law pertains to the relationships among human beings as well as the awesome responsibilities of coexistence with members of the other orders. It includes acceptance of the way things are (nature and environment),

whether we fully understand them or not, and that we are to relate to all things in a respectful manner.

Netukulimk The use of the natural bounty provided by the Creator for the self-support and well-being of the individual and the community. Netukulimk is achieving adequate standards of community nutrition and economic well-being without jeopardizing the integrity, diversity, or productivity of our environment.

Non-status Indians Individuals who identify as Indigenous and who have Indigenous ancestry but who are not eligible for registration under the Indian Act because their ancestors had their status removed or were never registered initially.

Numbered treaties Legal, political, and spiritual agreements entered into by representatives of the Crown, Indigenous peoples, and the Creator, which outline the conditions of the formal relationship between the sovereign peoples designated in the document. Eleven numbered treaties were negotiated between Indigenous peoples and settlers from 1871 to 1921. Indigenous people understand the numbered treaties as frameworks for sharing the land, while the Canadian government understands them as land surrenders.

Nunavut A northern territory in Canada, established as a separate political jurisdiction in 1999, that stretches from Hudson Bay to the northernmost parts of Ellesmere Island. Under the terms of the Nunavut Land Claims Agreement of 1993, which is the largest land claim settlement in Canadian history, the Inuit of Nunavut negotiated recognition of their title to approximately 350,000 km^2 of land in a territory of about 1.9 million km^2. The government of Nunavut, while public, is de facto an Inuit consensus-based government since more than 85 per cent of the population is Inuit.

Origin or creation stories Stories that inform us of our relationships with the natural world and guide our conduct within it. They outline our duties as humans to ensure Creation continues and lay out principles (often implicitly) for how humans are to coexist with non-human relatives and beings. Indigenous origin stories point to the centrality of spirituality in how humans should conduct themselves respectfully in relation to the natural world.

Paternalism A male-centric ideology that allows people to hold authority and decision-making power over other people. Paternalistic policies such as the Indian Act have historically and continue to endow the Canadian government with authority over many areas of Indigenous peoples' lives in Canada.

Patriarchy A social system marked by the supremacy of the father, the reckoning of descent and inheritance according to male lineage, and the dependent legal status of wives and children.

Politics of recognition According to Glen Coulthard, this encompasses the "expansive range of recognition-based models of liberal pluralism that seek to reconcile Indigenous claims to nationhood with Crown sovereignty via the accommodation of Indigenous identities in some form of renewed relationship with the Canadian state. Although these models tend to vary in both theory and practice, most involve the delegation of land, capital and political power from the state to Indigenous communities through land claims, economic development initiatives, and self-government processes." (Glen Coulthard, "Subjects of Empire: Indigenous Peoples and the Politics of Recognition in Canada," *Contemporary Political Theory* 6 [2007], 438.)

Post-colonialism Deconstructing analysis and critique of the social ideas, policies, everyday practices, and administrative structures that perpetuate the subordination of Indigenous and other marginalized peoples.

Project Canada Term coined by Joyce Green, who describes it as "the state constructed from the colonies by colonial and then settler elites, evolving but firmly grounded on the original and continuing appropriation of Indigenous land and resources, and built on racist and sexist practices." (Joyce Green, "Canaries in the Mines of Citizenship: Indian Women in Canada," *Canadian Journal of Political Science* 34, no. 4 [2001], 716.)

Racism Assumption that psycho-cultural traits and capacities are determined by biological race, coupled with the belief in the inherent superiority of a particular race and the right of its people to have domination over others.

Reconciliation According to Canada's Truth and Reconciliation Commission, reconciliation in Canada is an ongoing process of establishing and maintaining a mutually respectful relationship between Indigenous and settler peoples through awareness of the past, acknowledgement of the harm that has been inflicted through colonization, atonement for the causes, and actions that bring about positive change in social conditions and behaviours.

Redfacing The act of performing Indigeneity (whether or not an actor is Indigenous).

Red Paper Name given to the 1970 paper by the Indian Chiefs of Alberta, *Citizens Plus*, which articulated their political vision of the nature of the Indian–Canada relationship as rooted in the numbered treaties.

Residential schools A nation-wide system of government-sponsored, church-run schools intended to facilitate the assimilation of Indigenous children and their partial absorption into the racist settler society, for erasure as culturally distinct persons. Residential schools were in operation in Canada from1880 to 1996.

Resurgence A theoretical, intellectual, and activist movement geared towards the regeneration and re-establishment of Indigenous nations, that is, the efforts of Indigenous peoples to ground their movements in relationships to place and in the legal and political theories, ideas, ethics, and norms embodied in these relations. This movement emphasizes Indigenous peoples' ground-up efforts not just to respond to these struggles but to reframe them on their own terms.

Self-determination The right of a people to freely determine their political status and freely pursue their economic, social, and cultural development. (*United Nations Declaration on the Rights of Indigenous Peoples* [2007], 6.)

Self-government Authority of a group to create and maintain the organizational structures necessary for administering various aspects of community life, including a limited degree of social and political policies and programs.

Settler colonialism A form of colonialism where settler collectives permanently occupy Indigenous lands, seek to replace the original population, and assert the sovereignty and jurisdiction of the settler state over Indigenous peoples and their territories.

State A set of politically dominant institutions that has a monopoly over the legitimate use of violence and that is formally comprised of the legislature, executive, central and local administration, judiciary, police, and armed forces.

Status Indians First Nation individuals whose Indian ancestry is formally recognized by the federal government.

Systemic racism Policies and practices in social, economic, and political structures that place minority racial and ethnic groups at a disadvantage and result in disparities in relation to wealth, income, criminal justice, education, employment, housing, health care, and political power.

Territorial acknowledgements Public acknowledgements that use words to give thought and form to Indigenous territoriality, initially done by Indigenous academics, activists, and their allies to unsettle preconceived notions of what a settler relationship to land means, and to point out what most people give no thought to: the land under their feet is the territory of Indigenous peoples. There is now a territorial acknowledgement at the beginning of many different public events including hockey games, university and other public meetings, school days, major TV broadcasts, and concerts as well as festivals.

Toxic masculinities Narrow and repressive cultural ideals that define and measure manhood in relation to violence, sex, status, and aggression.

Tradition World views, customs, values, and beliefs passed on intergenerationally. Anderson and Ball (Chapter 9) use "tradition" to signify Indigenous ways of living relationally with creation and in light of the wisdom of their ancestors.

Traditional knowledge (TK) Knowledge that arises from Indigenous peoples' cultures, traditions, and long-standing experiences of living in shared spaces; can be derived from teachings drawn out from the living Earth, from stories, observations, and interactions with localized contexts.

Treaty mythologies Constructions of treaties that centre Western understandings while invisibilizing Indigenous peoples' understanding of treaties. Treaty mythologies include representations of treaties as transactions of Indigenous land and political authority in exchange for a fixed set of rights and the protection of the Crown.

Truth and Reconciliation Commission of Canada (TRC) A component of the Indian Residential Schools Settlement Agreement established to inform all Canadians about what happened in Indian residential schools. The TRC was given a five-year mandate to document the truth of survivors, families, communities, and anyone personally affected by the residential school experience, including First Nations, Inuit, and Métis former Indian residential school students, their families, communities, the churches, former school employees, government, and other Canadians. The TRC presented its final report in 2015.

Umbrella Final Agreement (UFA) Agreement reached in 1988 (finalized in 1990) between the Council for Yukon Indians (now named the Council of Yukon First Nations), the Yukon territorial government, and the government of Canada. The UFA is a framework outlining the general provisions that inform each individual First Nation's final agreement with the government of Canada on a range of topics including taxation, enrolment, water management, fish and wildlife, land-use planning, and implementation.

Urban Indigeneity Refers to the identity or experiences of Indigenous people who are situated in urban centres, including but not limited to cities, towns, and municipal and regional hubs. Often contrasted with rural, remote, or reserve populations.

Wahkootowin A word defined as "the act of being related to each other" in Nancy LeClaire and George Cardinal, *Alberta Elders' Cree Dictionary* (Edmonton: University of Alberta Press, 1998). It speaks to a world view in which everything is understood to be interrelated: humans, animals, plants, the land, and the spirit world, and implies a fundamental sense of accountability and responsibility towards other living beings within these networks of relation.

White Paper The 1969 *Statement of the Government of Canada on Indian Policy* that rejected the Hawthorn–Tremblay report's notion of "citizens plus" and was designed to phase out federal responsibilities towards First Nation people and to eventually remove the special status of "Indian" peoples in Canada.

White supremacist capitalist patriarchy The interlocking racialized, economic, and gendered systems of domination in Western capitalist societies that simultaneously and at all times privilege/empower white heterosexual males and marginalize/disempower people with different/other social characteristics.

Wisdom The ability to think and act in a true, right, and lasting way based on a holistic understanding of one's knowledge, experience, understanding, common sense, and insight.

World view The basic outlook on humanity and the world that pervades a culture so thoroughly that it becomes a culture's concept of reality—what is good, what is important, what is sacred, what is real. The fundamental beliefs, values, and behaviours of a culture stem directly from its world view.

References

Introduction

Canada. 2018. "Principles Respecting the Government of Canada's Relationship with Indigenous Peoples." http://www.justice.gc.ca/eng/csj-sjc/principles-principes.html.

Clibbon, Jennifer. 2013. "Native Voices on the Pressure to Fix Canada's Oldest Relationship." *CBC News*, 10 Jan. https://www.cbc.ca/news/canada/native-voices-on-the-pressure-to-fix-canada-s-oldest-relationship-1.1323980.

Cardinal, Harold. 1969. *The Unjust Society: The Tragedy of Canada's Indians*. Edmonton: Hurtig.

Environics Institute. 2016. *Canadian Public Opinion on Aboriginal Peoples, Final Report*. 30 June. https://www.environicsinstitute.org/projects/project-details/public-opinion-about-aboriginal-issues-in-canada-2016.

Snelgrove, C., R.K. Dhamoon, and Jeff Corntassel. 2014. "Unsettling Settler Colonialism: The Discourse and Politics of Settlers, and Solidarity with Indigenous Nations." *Decolonization: Indigeneity, Education & Society* 3, no. 2.

Veracini, Lorenzo. 2011. "Introduction: Settler Colonial Studies." *Settler Colonial Studies* 1, no. 1: 1–12.

Vimalassery, Manu, Juliana Hu Pegues, and Alyosha Goldstein. 2016. "Introduction: On Colonial Unknowing." *Theory & Event* 19, no. 4.

Wolfe, Patrick. 1999. *Settler Colonialism and the Transformation of Anthropology*. London: Bloomsbury.

Young, Alex Trimble. 2017. "A Response to 'On Colonial Unknowing.'" *Theory & Event* 20, no. 4.

Chapter 1

Arnot, D. 1997. Treaty No. 6 Elders' Forum. LaRonge: Federation of Saskatchewan Indian Nations. 27–8 Nov.

Asch, Michael. 2014. *On Being Here To Stay: Treaties and Aboriginal Rights in Canada*. Toronto: University of Toronto Press.

Boldt, Menno. 1993. *Surviving as Indians: The Challenge of Self-Government*. Toronto: University of Toronto Press.

Borrows, John. 2002. *Recovering Canada: The Resurgence of Indigenous Law*. Toronto: University of Toronto Press.

Canada, Parliament, *House of Commons Debates*, 2nd Session, 21st Parliament, 21 June 1950, 3393.

Canada, Indian and Northern Affairs. 2013. "The Numbered Treaties (1871–1921)." https://www.aadnc-aandc.gc.ca/eng/1360948213124/1360948312708.

Cardinal, H. 1969. *The Unjust Society: The Tragedy of Canada's Indians*. Edmonton: Hurtig.

——— and W. Hildebrandt. 2000. *Treaty Elders of Saskatchewan: Our Dream Is That Our Peoples Will One Day Be Clearly Recognized as Nations*. Calgary: University of Calgary Press.

Carr-Stewart, S. 2001. "A Treaty Right to Education." *Canadian Journal of Education* 26, no. 2: 125–43.

Carter, S. 1999. *Aboriginal People and Colonizers of Western Canada to 1900*. Toronto: University of Toronto Press.

Coulthard, Glen. 2010. "Place against Empire: Understanding Indigenous Anti-Colonialism." *Affinities: A Journal of Radical Theory, Culture, and Action* 4, no. 2.

Craft, A. 2016. *Breathing Life into the Stone Fort Treaty: An Anishinabe Understanding of Treaty One*. Saskatoon, SK: Purich Publishing.

Dawson, S.J. 1868. *Report on the Line of Route between Lake Superior and the Red River Settlement*. Ottawa.

Dickason, Olive Patricia, and William Newbigging. 2010. *A Concise History of Canada's First Nations*, 2nd edn. Toronto: Oxford University Press.

Goeman, M. 2017. "Ongoing Storms and Struggles: Gendered Violence and Resource Exploitation." In *Critically Sovereign: Indigenous Gender, Sexuality, and Feminist Studies*, edited by Joanne Barker. Durham, NC: Duke University Press.

Green, J. 1995. "Towards a Détente with History: Confronting Canada's Colonial Legacy." *International Journal of Canadian Studies* 12, no. 25.

———. 2004. "Equality Quest: It's Time to Undermine the Institutional and Cultural Foundations That Support Inequality." *Briarpatch*, Nov. https://briarpatchmagazine.com/articles/view/equality-quest-its-time-to-undermine-the-institutional-and-cultural-foundat.

Henderson, James Youngblood. 2002. "Sui Generis and Treaty Citizenship." *Citizenship Studies* 6, no. 4.

Hildebrandt, W., D.F. Rider, and S. Carter. 1996. *True Spirit and Original Intent of Treaty 7*. Montreal and Kingston: McGill-Queen's University Press.

Hunt, D. 2016. "Nikîkîwân: Contesting Settler Colonial Archives through Indigenous Oral History." *Canadian Literature* 230: 25–42.

Kovach, M. 2013. "Treaties, Truths and Transgressive Pedagogies: Re-Imagining Indigenous Presence in the Classroom." *Socialist Studies* 9, no. 1.

Ladner, K. 2003. "Treaty Federalism: An Indigenous Vision of Canadian Federalisms." In *New Trends in Canadian Federalism*, edited by François Rocher and Miriam Smith, 167–94. Peterborough, ON: Broadview Press.

Little Bear, Leroy. 1986. "Aboriginal Rights and the Canadian 'Grundnorm.'" In *Arduous Journey: Canadian*

Indians and Decolonization, edited by J. Rick Ponting, 243–59. Toronto: McClelland & Stewart.

McNeil, K. 2001. "Extinguishment of Aboriginal Title in Canada: Treaties, Legislation, and Judicial Discretion." *Ottawa Law Review* 33: 301.

Miller, J.R. 2009. *Compact, Contract, Covenant: The Evolution of Indian Treaty-Making*. Toronto: University of Toronto Press.

Milloy, J.S. 2009. "Tipahamatoowin or Treaty 4? Speculations on Alternate Texts." *Native Studies Review* 18, no. 1.

Morris, A. 1880. *The Treaties of Canada with the Indians of Manitoba and the North-West Territories: Including the Negotiations On Which They Were Based, and Other Information Relating Thereto*. Toronto: Belfords, Clarke.

Musqua, D. 1997. Treaty No. 4 Elders' Forum. Federation of Saskatchewan Indian Nations: Nekaneet, SK.

Oakes G. 1997. Interview by Harold Cardinal, translation by Albert Angus. Treaty No. 4 Elders' Forum. Federation of Saskatchewan Indian Nations: Wapiimoostoosis Reserve, Lebret, SK.

Wapiimoostoosis Reserve, Lebret, SK, transcript, 76.

Re Paulette et al. and Registrar of Titles (No. 2), 1973 CanLII 1298 (NWT SC).

Royal Commission on Aboriginal Peoples. 1996. *Report of the Royal Commission on Aboriginal Peoples*. Ottawa: Minister of Supply and Services.

Royal Proclamation, 1763, R.S.C., 1985, App. II, No. 1.

Simpson, Leanne. 2008. "Looking after Gdoo-naaganinaa: Precolonial Nishnaabeg Diplomatic and Treaty Relationships." *Wicazo Sa Review* 23, no. 2: 29–42.

——. 2017. *As We Have Always Done: Indigenous Freedom through Radical Resistance*. Minneapolis: University of Minnesota Press.

Stark, Heidi K. 2010. "Respect, Responsibility, and Renewal: The Foundations of Anishinaabe Treaty Making with the United States and Canada." *American Indian Culture and Research Journal* 34, no. 2: 145–64.

——. 2016. "Criminal Empire: The Making of the Savage in a Lawless Land." *Theory & Event* 19, no. 4.

——. 2017. "Changing the Treaty Question: Remedying the Right(s) Relationship." In *The Right Relationship: Reimagining the Implementation of Historical Treaties*, edited by J. Borrows and M. Coyle. Toronto: University of Toronto Press.

Taylor, J.L. 1985. *Treaty Research Report: Treaty Four (1874)*. Ottawa: Treaties and Historical Research Centre, Indian and Northern Affairs Canada.

Tobias, J. L. 1986. *The Origins of the Treaty Rights Movement in Saskatchewan*. Regina SK: Canadian Plains Research Centre, University of Regina.

Tully, J. 2000. "The Struggles of Indigenous Peoples for and of Freedom." In *Political Theory and the Rights of Indigenous Peoples*, edited by Duncan Ivison, Paul Patton, and Will Sanders, 36–59. Cambridge: Cambridge University Press.

Venne, S. 1998. "Understanding Treaty 6: An Indigenous Perspective." In *Aboriginal and Treaty Rights in Canada*, edited by Michael Asch, 173-207. Vancouver: University of British Columbia Press.

Williams, Robert A. 1999. *Linking Arms Together: American Indian Treaty Visions of Law and Peace, 1600–1800*. New York: Routledge.

Wolfe, Patrick. 2006. "Settler Colonialism and the Elimination of the Native." *Journal of Genocide Research* 8, no. 4: 387–409.

Chapter 2

Abele, Frances, and Katherine A.H. Graham. 2011. "Federal Urban Aboriginal Policy: The Challenge of Viewing the Stars in the Urban Night Sky." In *Urban Aboriginal Policy Making in Canada Municipalities*, edited by Evelyn J. Peters, 33–52. Montreal and Kingston: McGill-Queen's University Press.

Ajzenstat, Janet, Paul Romney, Ian Gentles, and Williams Gairdner, eds. 2003. *Canada's Founding Debates*. Toronto: University of Toronto Press.

Alfred, Taiaiake. 2005. *Wasase: Indigenous Pathways of Action and Freedom*. Peterborough, ON: Broadview Press.

Andersen, Chris. 2011. "I'm Métis: What's Your Excuse? On the Optics of Misrecognition of Métis in Canada." *Federation for the Humanities and Social Sciences: Equity Matters*, 22 Feb. http://www.ideas-idees.ca/blog/im-metis-whats-your-excuse-optics-and-misrecognition-metis-canada.

Battell-Lowman, Emma, and Adam J. Barker. 2015. *Settler Identity and Colonialism in 21st Century Canada*. Halifax: Fernwood Publishing.

Belanger, Yale D. 2006. "Seeking a Seat at the Table: A Brief History of Indian Political Organizing in Canada, 1870–1951." PhD diss., Trent University.

——. 2017. "The Road to Reconciliation? Premier Gordon Campbell and BC Aboriginal Policy." In *The Campbell Revolution: Power, Politics, and Policy in British Columbia*, edited by J.R. Lacharite and Tracy Summerville. Montreal and Kingston: McGill-Queen's University Press.

—— and David R. Newhouse. 2004. "Emerging from the Shadows: The Pursuit of Aboriginal Self-Government to Promote Aboriginal Well-being." *Canadian Journal of Native Studies* 24, no. 1: 129–222.

—— and ——. 2008. "Reconciling Solitudes: A Critical Analysis of the Self-Government Ideal." In *Aboriginal Self-Government in Canada: Current Trends and Issues*, 3rd edn, edited by Yale D. Belanger. Saskatoon, SK: Purich Publishing.

Bellegarde, Perry. 2015. "Address to the Special Chiefs Assembly, National Chief Perry Bellegarde." 8 Dec. https://www.afn.ca/uploads/files/2015_usb_documents/15-12-08_nc_speech_to_sca.pdf.

Berdahl, Loleen, Ryan Walker, Erin Lashta, David Newhouse, and Yale Belanger. 2017. "Public Attitudes towards Indigeneity in Canadian Prairie Urbanism." *Canadian Geographer* 61, no. 2: 212–23.

Borrows, John. 1997. "Wampum at Niagara: The Royal Proclamation, Canadian Legal History, and Self-Government." In *Aboriginal and Treaty Rights in Canada: Essays on Law, Equality, and Respect for Difference*, edited by Michael Asch, 155–72. Vancouver: University of British Columbia Press.

———. 2002. *Recovering Canada: The Resurgence of Indigenous Law.* Toronto: University of Toronto Press.

———. 2017. "Canada's Colonial Constitution." In *The Right Relationship: Reimagining the Implementation of Historical Treaties,* edited by John Borrows and Michael Coyle, 17–38. Toronto: University of Toronto Press.

Canada. 1961. *The Report of the Joint Parliamentary-Senate Committee Hearings on Indian Affairs in Canada.* Ottawa: Queen's Printer.

———. 1969. Statement of the Government of Canada on Indian Policy. Cat. no. R32-2469. Ottawa: Queen's Printer.

———. 1995. "The Government of Canada's Approach to Implementation of the Inherent Right to the Negotiation of Aboriginal Self-Government." https://www.aadnc-aandc.gc.ca/eng/1100100031843/1100100031844.

———. 1997. *Gathering Strength: Canada's Aboriginal Action Plan.* Ottawa: Minister of Public Works and Government Services Canada.

———. 2008. House of Commons Debates 142, no. 110, 2nd Session, 39th Parliament (11 June), pp. 6849–57. Ottawa: Queen's Printer.

CBC. 2017. "Indigenous Leaders Give Trudeau Government Failing Grade on Delivering Promises." *The Current.* 25 Jan. https://exhibits.library.utoronto.ca/items/show/2430.

Coates, Ken Coates. 2015. *#IdleNoMore: And the Remaking of Canada.* Regina, SK: University of Regina Press.

Council for Yukon Indians (CYI). 1973. *Together Today for Our Children Tomorrow: A Statement of Grievances and an Approach to Settlement by the Yukon Indian People.* Whitehorse, YT: CYI.

Dockstator, Mark S. 1993. "Toward an Understanding of Aboriginal Self-Government: A Proposed Theoretical Model and Illustrative Factual Analysis." PhD diss., York University.

Dyck, Noel. 1991. *"What Is the Indian Problem": Tutelage and Resistance in Canadian Indian Adminis tration.* St John's, NL: Institute of Social and Economic Research.

Elliott, Michael. 2018. "Indigenous Resurgence: The Drive for Renewed Engagement and Reciprocity in the Turn Away from the State." *Canadian Journal of Political Science* 51, no. 1: 61–81.

Environics Institute. 2016. *Canadian Public Opinion on Aboriginal Peoples, Final Report.* 30 June. https://www.environicsinstitute.org/projects/project-details/public-opinion-about-aboriginal-issues-in-canada-2016.

Federation of Saskatchewan Indians. 1977. *Indian Government.* Saskatoon, SK.

Foster, Hamar. 2008. *Let Right Be Done: Aboriginal Title, the Calder Case, and the Future of Indigenous Rights.* Vancouver: University of British Columbia Press.

Gaudry, Adam. 2013. "The Métis-ization of Canada: The Process of Claiming Louis Riel, Métissage and the Métis People as Canada's Mythical Origin." *Aboriginal Policy Studies* 2 no. 2: 64–87.

Goikas, John. 1995. "The Indian Act: Evolution, Overview and Options for Amendment and Transition." Paper produced for the Royal Commission on Aboriginal Peoples. http://www.bac-lac.gc.ca/eng/discover/aboriginal-heritage/royal-commission-aboriginal-peoples/Pages/item.aspx?IdNumber=232.

Graham, Katherine, Carolyn Dittburner, and Frances Abele. 1996. "Soliloquy and Dialogue: The Evolution of Public Policy Discourse on Aboriginal Issues since the Hawthorn Report." In *For Seven Generations: An Information Legacy of the Royal Commission on Aboriginal Peoples*, CD-ROM. Ottawa: Canada Publications Group.

———, ———, ———. 1996. "Summaries of Reports by Federal Bodies and Aboriginal Organizations." In *For Seven Generations: An Information Legacy of the Royal Commission on Aboriginal Peoples*, CD-ROM. Ottawa: Canada Publications Group.

Hawthorn, H.B., ed. 1966. *A Survey of the Contemporary Indians of Canada: A Report on Economic, Political, Educational Needs and Policies,* vol. 1. H.A.C. Cairns, S.M. Jamieson, and K. Lysyk, principal authors. Ottawa: Indian Affairs Branch.

Henderson, James [Sákéj] Youngblood. 1994. "Implementing the Treaty Order." In *Continuing Poundmaker's and Riel's Quest: Presentations Made at a Conference on Aboriginal Peoples and Justice,* edited by Richard Gosse, James [Sákéj] Youngblood Henderson, and Roger Carter , 52–62. Saskatoon, SK: Purich Publishing.

———. 1997. *The Mi'kmaw Concordat.* Halifax: Fernwood.

———. 2008. *Indigenous Diplomacy and the Rights of Peoples: Achieving UN Recognition* Saskatoon, SK: Purich Publishing.

Indian Chiefs of Alberta. 1970. Citizens Plus: A Presentation by the Indian Chiefs of Alberta to Right Honourable P.E. Trudeau, Prime Minister, and the Government of Canada. Edmonton: Indian Association of Alberta.

Kernerman, Gerald. 2005. *Multicultural Nationalism: Civilizing Difference, Constituting Community.* Vancouver: University of British Columbia Press.

Kino-nda-niimi Collective. 2014. *The Winter We Danced: Voices from the Past, the Future, and the Idle No More Movement*. Winnipeg: APR Books.

Ladner, Kiera L. 2001. "Negotiated Inferiority: The Royal Commission on Aboriginal Peoples' Vision of a Renewed Relationship." *American Review of Canadian Studies* 31, nos 1–2: 241–64.

Leslie, John. 1978. *The Historical Development of the Indian Act*. Ottawa: Treaties and Historical Research Centre, Indian and Northern Affairs.

Liberal Party of Canada, Aboriginal Peoples' Commission. 2014. Policy Resolution 21. https://www.liberal.ca/policy-resolutions/21-acknowledging-order-move-resolution-officially-reject-1969-white-paper/.

Maaka, Roger, and Augie Fleras. 2005. *The Politics of Indigeneity: Challenging the State in Canada and Aotearoa New Zealand*. Dunedin, NZ: Otago University Press.

McAdam, Sylvia. 2015. *Nationhood Interrupted: Revitalizing nêhiyaw Legal Systems*. Saskatoon, SK: Purich Publishing.

Macklem, Patrick. 2001. *Indigenous Difference and the Constitution of Canada*. Toronto: University of Toronto Press.

Manitoba Indian Brotherhood. 1971. *Wahbung: Our Tomorrows*. Winnipeg: Manitoba Indian Brotherhood.

Mercredi, Ovide, and Mary Ellen Turpel. 1993. *In The Rapids: Navigating the Future of First Nations*. Toronto: Penguin Books.

Miller, J.R. 2017. *Residential Schools and Reconciliation: Canada Confronts Its History*. Toronto: University of Toronto Press.

Milloy, J.S. 1992. *A Historical Overview of Indian–Government Relations, 1755–1940*. Ottawa: Indian and Northern Affairs.

Murray, James. 2018. "Chiefs Oppose Canada's Efforts to Impact Treaty Nations' Self Determination." *Net News Ledger*, 8 Dec.

Newhouse, David. R., and Yale D. Belanger. 2010. "Beyond the 'Indian Problem': Aboriginal Peoples and the Transformation of Canada." In *The Oxford Handbook of Canadian Politics*, edited by John Courtney and David Smith, 339–61. Toronto: Oxford University Press.

Office of the Treaty Commission (OTC). 2007. Treaty Implementation: Fulfilling the Covenant Office of the Treaty Commissioner. Saskatoon, SK: OTC.

Papillon, Martin. 2009. "Towards Postcolonial Federalism? The Challenges of Aboriginal Self-Determination in the Canadian Context." In *Contemporary Canadian Federalism: Foundations, Traditions, Institutions*, edited by Alain-G. Gagnon, 405–27. Toronto: University of Toronto Press.

Penner, Keith. 1983. *Report of the Special Committee on Indian Self-Government*. Ottawa: Ministry of Supply and Services.

Regan, Paulette. 2010. *Unsettling the Settler Within: Indian Residential Schools, Truth Telling, and Reconciliation in Canada*. Vancouver: University of British Columbia Press.

Royal Commission on Aboriginal Peoples (RCAP). 1996. *Report*, vol. 1. Ottawa: Minister of Supply and Services Canada.

Saul, John Ralston. 2008. *A Fair Country: Telling Truths about Canada*. Toronto: Viking Canada.

Saul, John Ralston. 2014. *The Comeback: How Aboriginals Are Reclaiming Power and Influence*. Toronto: Random House Canada.

Second Joint General Assembly of the Indian Brotherhood of the Northwest Territories. 1975. *Declaration of Dene Nationhood*. Fort Simpson, NWT, 19 July.

Shrubb, Rebecca. 2014. "'Canada Has No History of Colonialism': Historical Amnesia: The Erasure of Indigenous Peoples from Canada's History." MA thesis, University of Victoria.

Slowey, Gabrielle. 2007. "Federalism and First Nations: In Search of Space." In *Constructing Tomorrow's Federalism: New Perspectives on Canadian Governance*, edited by Ian Peach, 157–70. Winnipeg: University of Manitoba Press.

Smith, Charlie. 2018. "Trudeau's Undisclosed Plan for Indigenous Self-Government Sets Stage for Election of Next National Chief." *The Georgia Straight*, 21 Jan.

Stewart, Jane. 1998. *Address by the Honourable Jane Stewart Minister of Indian Affairs and Northern Development on the occasion of the unveiling of Gathering Strength — Canada's Aboriginal Action Plan*. 7 January 1998. https://www.aadnc-aandc.gc.ca/eng/1100100015725/1100100015726 Last accessed 9 November 2018.

Tobias, John. 1976. "Protection, Civilization, Assimilation: An Outline History of Canada's Indian Policy." *Western Journal of Anthropology* 6, no. 2: 13–30.

Trudeau, Justin. 2015. "Prime Minister Justin Trudeau Delivers a Speech to the Assembly of First Nations Special Chiefs Assembly." https://pm.gc.ca/eng/news/2015/12/08/prime-minister-justin-trudeau-delivers-speech-assembly-first-nations-special-chiefs.

Truth and Reconciliation Commission of Canada (TRC). 2015. *Honouring the Truth, Reconciling for the Future: Summary of the Final Report of the Truth and Reconciliation Commission of Canada*. Ottawa: Government of Canada. http://www.trc.ca/assets/pdf/Honouring_the_Truth_Reconciling_for_the_Future_July_23_2015.pdf.

Tully, James. 1995. *Strange Multiplicity: Constitutionalism in an Age of Diversity*. Cambridge: Cambridge University Press.

Turner, Dale. 2006. *This Is Not a Peace Pipe: Towards a Critical Indigenous Philosophy*. Toronto: University of Toronto Press.

Williams, Robert A. 1992. *The American Indian in Western Legal Thought: The Discourses of Conquest.* New York: Oxford University Press.

———. 1997. *Linking Arms Together: American Indian Treaty Visions of Law and Peace 1600–1800.* Oxford: Oxford University Press.

Wolfe, Patrick. 2006. "Settler Colonialism and the Elimination of the Native." *Journal of Genocide Research* 8, no. 4: 387–409.

Chapter 3

Benton-Banai, Eddie. 1988. *The Mishonmis Book: The Voice of the Ojibway.* Hayward, WI: Indian Country Communications.

Coulthard, Glen. 2014. *Red Skin, White Masks: Rejecting the Colonial Politics of Recognition.* Minneapolis: University of Minnesota Press.

Geniusz, Wendy Makoons. 2000. *Our Knowledge Is Not Primitive: Decolonizing Botanical Anishinaabe Teachings.* Syracuse, NY: Syracuse University Press.

Johnson, Jessica Marie. 2016. "We Need Your Freedom: An Interview with Alexis Pauline Gumbs." *Black Perspectives*, 13 Dec. https://www.aaihs.org/we-need-your-freedom-an-interview-with-alexis-pauline-gumbs/.

Roberts, Neil. 2015. *Freedom as Marronage.* Chicago: University of Chicago Press.

Simpson, Audra. 2014. *Mohawk Interruptus: Political Life across the Borders of Settler States.* Durham, NC: Duke University Press.

Simpson, Leanne. 2011. *Dancing on Our Turtle's Back: Stories of Nishnaabeg Re-creation, Resurgence, and a New Emergence.* Winnipeg: ARP Books.

———. 2013. *Islands of Decolonial Love: Stories and Songs.* Winnipeg: ARP Books.

Yellowbird, Michael. 2015. "Decolonizing the Mind: Healing through Neurodecolonization and Mindfulness." Lecture, Portland State University, Portland, Oregon, 24 Jan.

Chapter 4

Barman, Jean. 1997–8. "Taming Aboriginal Sexuality: Gender, Power, and Race in British Columbia, 1850–1900." *BC Studies* no. 115/116 (Autumn/Winter): 237–66.

Benaway, Gwen. 2018. "Rihanna's Lingerie Line Brings Up a Complicated Discussion about Language." *Flare*, 25 Apr. https://www.flare.com/fashion/rihanna-savage-fenty-lingerie/.

Berg, Kristian, et al. 1993. *Dakota Conflict,* 1 videocassette (VHS). St Paul, MN: KTCA/Video.

Blee, Lisa. 2014. *Framing Chief Leschi: Narratives and the Politics of Historical Justice.* First Peoples: New Directions in Indigenous Studies. Chapel Hill: University of North Carolina Press.

Carter, Sarah. 1993. *Lost Harvests: Prairie Indian Reserve Farmers and Government Policy.* Montreal and Kingston: McGill-Queen's University Press.

———. 2005. "Creating 'Semi-Widows' and 'Supernumerary Wives': Prohibiting Polygamy in Prairie Canada's Aboriginal Communities to 1900." In *Contact Zones: Aboriginal and Settler Women in Canada's Colonial Past,* edited by Myra Rutherdale and Katie Pickles, 131–59. Vancouver: University of British Columbia Press.

Casselman, Amy L. 2016. *Injustice in Indian Country: Jurisdiction, American Law, and Sexual Violence against Native Women. Critical Indigenous and American Indian Studies,* vol.1, edited by A. Jolivette. New York: Peter Lang Publishing.

CBC News. 2015. "Miss Universe Canada's Totem Pole Dress Shocks First Nations People." 22 Dec. https://www.cbc.ca/news/canada/toronto/totem-pole-dress-1.3376366.

———. 2016. "Dsquared2 Apologizes to Indigenous Peoples for '.dsquaw' collection." 26 Feb. https://www.cbc.ca/news/canada/north/dsquared2-dsquaw-apology-letter-1.3466472.

Celescoop. 2014. "Pharrell Williams Receives Backlash over Elle Native American Headdress Cover." June. http://celescoop.com/2014/06/pharrell-williams-recieves-backlash-over-elle-native-american-headdress-cover/.

Chomsky, Carol. 1990. "The United States–Dakota War Trials: A Study in Military Injustice." *Stanford Law Review* 43, no. 1: 13–95.

Cothran, Boyd. 2014. *Remembering the Modoc War: Redemptive Violence and the Making of American Innocence.* First Peoples: New Directions in Indigenous Studies. Chapel Hill: University of North Carolina Press.

Deer, Sarah. 2015. *The Beginning and End of Rape: Confronting Sexual Violence in Native America.* Minneapolis: University of Minnesota Press.

Dhillon, Jaskiran K. 2015. "Indigenous Girls and the Violence of Settler Colonial Policing." *Decolonization: Indigeneity, Education and Society* 4, no. 2: 1–31.

Fay, Amelia. 2014. "Big Men, Big Women, or Both? Examining the Coastal Trading System of the Eighteenth-Century Labrador Inuit." In *History and Renewal of Labrador's Inuit-Métis,* edited by John C. Kennedy, 75–93. St John's: ISER Books.

Francis, Margot. 2012. *Creative Subversions: Whiteness, Indigeneity, and the National Imaginary.* Vancouver: University of British Columbia Press.

Garoutte, Eve. 2003. *Real Indians: Identity and the Survival of Native America.* Berkeley: University of California Press.

Gavigan, Shelley A.M. 2012. *Hunger, Horses, and Government Men: Criminal Law on the Aboriginal Plains,*

1870–1905. Vancouver: University of British Columbia Press.

Harring, Sidney L. 1994. *Crow Dog's Case: American Indian Sovereignty, Tribal Law, and United States Law in the Nineteenth Century*. Cambridge Studies in North American Indian History. Cambridge: Cambridge University Press.

———. 1998. *White Man's Law: Native People in Nineteenth-Century Canadian Jurisprudence*. Osgoode Society for Canadian Legal History. Toronto: University of Toronto Press.

Houston, James. 1989. *Running West*. Toronto: McClelland & Stewart.

Hunt, Sarah E. July 2010. "Colonial Roots, Contemporary Risk Factors: A Cautionary Exploration of the Domestic Trafficking of Aboriginal Women and Girls in British Columbia, Canada." *Alliance News*, 27–31.

———. 2014. "Witnessing the Colonialscape: Lighting the Intimate Fires of Indigenous Legal Pluralism." PhD diss., Simon Fraser University.

Kaplan, Amy. 2002. *The Anarchy of Empire in the Making of U.S. Culture*. Cambridge, MA: Harvard University Press, 25.

Keene, Adrienne. 2010. "Ke$ha, the Headdress, and a Trend That Won't Go Away." *Native Appropriations*, 18 Mar. http://nativeappropriations.com/2010/03/keha-the-headdress-and-a-trend-that-wont-go-away.html.

———. 2011a. "Oh (Miss) Canada." *Native Appropriations*, 12 Sept. https://nativeappropriations.com/2011/09/oh-miss-canada.html.

———. 2011b. "Halloween Costume Shopping: A Sampling of the Racism for Sale." *Native Appropriations*, 27 Oct. https://nativeappropriations.com/2011/10/halloween-costume-shopping-a-sampling-of-the-racism-for-sale.html.

———. 2013. "The Paul Frank x Native Designers Collaboration Is Here!" *Native Appropriations*, 18 June. http://nativeappropriations.com/2013/06/the-paul-frank-x-native-designers-collaboration-is-here.html.

Lynskey, Dorian. 2014. "This Means War: Why the Fashion Headdress Must Be Stopped." *The Guardian*, 30 July. https://www.theguardian.com/fashion/2014/jul/30/why-the-fashion-headdress-must-be-stopped.

McClintock, Anne. 1995. *Imperial Leather: Race, Gender, and Sexuality in the Colonial Contest*. New York: Routledge.

Million, Dian. 2013. *Therapeutic Nations: Healing in the Age of Indigenous Human Rights*. Tucson: University of Arizona Press.

Nasser, Shanifa. 2017. "Toronto Gallery Cancels Show after Concerns Artist 'Bastardizes' Indigenous Art." *CBC News*, 28 Apr. https://www.cbc.ca/news/canada/toronto/toronto-gallery-indigenous-art-cancels-amandapl-1.4091529.

Palmater, Pamela D. 2011. *Beyond Blood: Rethinking Indigenous Identity*. Saskatoon, SK: Purich Publishing.

Piatote, Beth H. 2013. *Domestic Subjects: Gender, Citizenship, and Law in Native American Literature*. The Henry Roe Cloud Series on American Indians and Modernity. New Haven, CT: Yale University Press.

Perry, Adele. 2005. "Metropolitcan Knowledge, Colonial Practice, and Indigenous Womanhood: Missions in Nineteenth-Century British Columbia." In *Contact Zones: Aboriginal and Settler Women in Canada's Colonial Past*, edited by Myra Rutherdale and Katie Pickles, 109–30. Vancouver: University of British Columbia Press.

Razack, Sherene. 2002. "Gendered Racial Violence and Spatialized Justice: The Murder of Pamela George." In *Race, Space and the Law: Unmapping a White Settler Society*, edited by Sherene Razack, 121–56. Toronto: Between the Lines.

———. 2015. *Dying from Improvement: Inquests and Inquiries into Indigenous Deaths in Custody*. Toronto: University of Toronto Press.

Riley, Angela R., and Kristen A. Carpenter. 2016. "Owning Red: A Theory of Indian (Cultural) Appropriation." *Texas Law Review* 94.

Smith, Keith D. 2009. *Liberalism, Surveillances and Resistance: Indigenous Communities in Western Canada, 1877–1927*. Edmonton: Athabasca University Press.

Stark, Heidi. 2016. "Criminal Empire: The Making of the Savage in a Lawless Land." *Theory and Event* 19, no. 4 (Oct.).

Trimble, Ken. 2018. "Supreme Court Will Hear Appeal of New-Trial Decision in Cindy Gladue Case." *CTV News*, 8 Mar. https://www.ctvnews.ca/canada/supreme-court-will-hear-appeal-of-new-trial-decision-in-cindy-gladue-case-1.3834282.

Voyles, Traci Brynne. 2015. *Wastelanding: Legacies of Uranium Mining in Navajo Country*. Minneapolis: University of Minnesota Press.

Walker, Taté. 2015. "How to Support Your Young, Indigenous Daughter in Fighting Hypersexualization." *Everyday Feminism*, 9 Mar. https://everydayfeminism.com/2015/03/supporting-indigenous-daughter/.

Chapter 5

Alfred, Taiaiake. 2001. "Deconstructing the British Columbia Treaty Process." *Balayi: Culture, Law, and Colonialism* 3: 37–66.

———. 2005. *Wasáse: Indigenous Pathways of Action and Freedom*. Toronto: University of Toronto Press.

Allen, Chadwick. 2012. *Trans-Indigenous: Methodologies for Global Native Literary Studies*. Minneapolis: University of Minnesota Press.

Coulthard, Glen Sean. 2014. *Red Skin, White Masks: Rejecting the Colonial Politics of Recognition*. Minneapolis: University of Minnesota Press.

Council for Yukon Indians. 1973. *Together Today for Our Children Tomorrow: A Statement of Grievances and an Approach to Settlement.* Whitehorse, YT: Council for Yukon Indians.

Davis, Donna. 2008. "Collage Inquiry: Creative and Particular Applications." *Learning Landscapes* 2, no. 1: 245–65.

Canada. 2015. "Comprehensive Claims." 13 July. https://www.aadnc-aandc.gc.ca/eng/1100100030577/1100100030578.

Government of Canada, Council for Yukon Indians, and Government of the Yukon. 1993. *Umbrella Final Agreement.* http://www.eco.gov.yk.ca/pdf/umbrellafinalagreement.pdf.

Simpson, Audra. 2014. *Mohawk Interruptus: Political Life across the Borders of Settler States.* Durham, NC: Duke University Press.

Simpson, Leanne. 2011. *Dancing on Our Turtle's Back: Stories of Nishnaabeg Re-creation, Resurgence and a New Emergence.* Winnipeg: ARP Books.

———. 2017. *As We Have Always Done: Indigenous Freedom through Radical Resistance.* Minneapolis: University of Minnesota Press.

Tully, James. 2001. "Reconsidering the B.C. Treaty Process." In *Speaking Truth to Power: A Treaty Forum,* 3–17. Ottawa: Law Commission of Canada.

Chapter 6

Barman, Jean. 2007. "Erasing Indigenous Indigeneity in Vancouver." *BC Studies* no. 155: 3–30.

Brooks, Lisa. 2008. *The Common Pot: The Recovery of Native Space in the Northeast.* Minneapolis: University of Minnesota Press.

Daschuk, James. 2013. *Clearing the Plains: Disease, Politics of Starvation, and the Loss of Aboriginal Life.* Regina, SK: University of Regina Press.

Grande, Sandy. 2003. "Whitestream Feminism and the Colonialist Project: A Review of Contemporary Feminist Pedagogy and Praxis." *Educational Theory* 53, no. 3: 329–46.

Harjo, Joy. 1990. "Deer Dancer." In Harjo, *In Mad Love and War.* Middletown, CT: Wesleyan University Press.

Johnson, Jay T. 2013. "Dancing into Place: The Role of the Powwow within Urban Indigenous Communities." In *Indigenous in the City: Contemporary Identities and Cultural Innovation,* edited by Evelyn Peters and Chris Andersen, 216–30. Vancouver: University of British Columbia Press.

King, Thomas. 2003. *The Truth about Stories.* Toronto: House of Anansi.

Krotz, Larry. 1980. *Urban Indians: The Strangers in Canada's Cities.* Edmonton: Hurtig.

Lawrence, Bonita. 2004. *"Real" Indians and Others: Mixed-Blood Urban Native Peoples and Indigenous Nationhood.* Lincoln: University of Nebraska Press.

Lincoln, Kenneth. 1985. *Native American Renaissance.* Berkeley: University of California Press.

McNickle, D'Arcy. 1978. *The Surrounded.* Albuquerque: University of New Mexico Press. Originally published 1936.

Momaday, N. Scott. 1968. *House Made of Dawn.* New York: Perennial, 1989.

Newhouse, David, and Evelyn Peters, eds. 2003. *Not Strangers in These Parts: Urban Aboriginal Peoples.* Toronto: Policy Research Initiative.

Peters, Evelyn J. 1998. "Subversive Spaces: First Nations Women and the City." *Environment and Planning D: Society and Space* 16, no. 6: 665–85.

——— and Chris Andersen, eds. 2013. *Indigenous in the City: Contemporary Identities and Cultural Innovation.* Vancouver: University of British Columbia Press.

Ramirez, Renya K. 2007. *Native Hubs: Culture, Community, and Belonging in Silicon Valley and Beyond.* Durham, NC: Duke University Press.

Silko, Leslie Marmon. 1977. *Ceremony.* New York: Penguin.

Simpson, Leanne Betasamosake. 2011. *Dancing on Our Turtle's Back: Stories of Nishnaabeg Re-creation, Resurgence and a New Emergence.* Winnipeg: ARP Books.

———. 2014. "Land as Pedagogy: Nishnaabeg Intelligence and Rebellious Transformation." *Decolonization: Indigeneity, Education & Society* 3, no. 3: 1–25.

———. 2017. "Plight." In Simpson, *This Accident of Being Lost: Songs and Stories,* 5–8. Toronto: House of Anansi.

Snipp, Matthew C. 2013. "American Indians and Alaska Natives in Urban Environments." In *Indigenous in the City: Contemporary Identities and Cultural Innovation,* edited by Evelyn Peters and Chris Andersen 173–92. Vancouver: University of British Columbia Press.

Tuck, Eve. 2009. "Suspending Damage: A Letter to Communities." *Harvard Educational Review* 79, no. 3: 409–28.

Van Camp, Richard. 2002. "Sky Burial." In Van Camp, *Angel Wing Splash Pattern.* Wiarton, ON: Kegedonce. 37–47.

Wagamese, Richard. 1994. *Keeper'n Me.* Toronto: Anchor Canada.

Warrior, Robert. 1995. *Tribal Secrets: Recovering American Indian Intellectual Traditions.* Minneapolis: University of Minnesota Press.

Wiget, Andrew. 1985. *Handbook of Native American Literature.* New York: Twayne Publishers.

Womack, Craig S. 1999. *Red on Red: Native American Literary Separatism.* Minneapolis: University of Minnesota Press.

———, Daniel Heath Justice, and Christopher B. Teuton, eds. 2008. *Reasoning Together: The Native Critics Collective.* Norman: University of Oklahoma Press.

Woodsworth, James S. 1909. *Strangers within Our Gates; Or Coming Canadians.* Toronto: Methodist Mission Rooms, 1909.

Chapter 7

Adams, H. 1975. *Prison of Grass: Canada from the Native Point of View.* Toronto: New Press.

Andersen, Chris. 2010. "Mixed Ancestry or Metis?" In *Indigenous Identity and Resistance: Researching the Diversity of Knowledge*, edited by B. Hokowhitu, N. Kermoal, C. Andersen, A. Petersen, M. Reilly, I. Altamirano-Jimenez, and P. Rewi, 23–36. Dunedin, NZ: Otago University Press.

——. 2014. *"Métis": Race, Recognition, and the Struggle for Indigenous Peoplehood.* Vancouver: University of British Columbia Press.

Anderson, Kim. 2011. *Life Stages and Native Women: Memory, Teachings, and Story Medicine.* Winnipeg: University of Manitoba Press.

Brown, Jennifer S.H. 2007. *Strangers in Blood: Fur Trade Company Families in Indian Country.* Vancouver: University of British Columbia Press. Originally published 1980.

Calgary Herald. 1885, 16 Apr., p. 2, col. 2.

Campbell, M. 2007. "We Need to Return to the Principles of Wahkotowin." *Eagle Feather News* 10, no. 1: 5. eaglefeathernews.com.

Cassese, A. 2005. *International Law*, 2nd edn. Oxford: Oxford University Press. http://www.loc.gov/catdir/toc/ecip0422/2004020238.html.

Belcourt, Christi. 2018. The Earth Is My Government. 51" x 72" acrylic on canvas [tweet, 16 Mar.]. https://twitter.com/christibelcourt/status/974531021751267329.

Dempsey, Hugh A. 1972. *Crowfoot: Chief of the Blackfeet.* Edmonton: Hurtig.

——. 1995. *Red Crow: Warrior Chief*, 2nd edn. Saskatoon, SK: Fifth House.

——. 2015. *The Great Blackfoot Treaties.* Victoria, BC: Heritage House.

Devine, H. 2010. "The Alberta Disadvantage: Métis Issues and the Public Discourse in Wild Rose Country." *London Journal of Canadian Studies* 26: 26–62.

Ens, Gerhard. 1996. *Homeland to Hinterland: The Changing Worlds of the Red River Metis in the Nineteenth Century.* Toronto: University of Toronto Press.

Gaudry, A. 2013. "The Métis-ization of Canada: The Process of Claiming Louis Riel, Métissage." *Aboriginal Policy Studies* 2, no. 2: 64–87.

——. 2014. "Kaa-tipeyimishoyaahk—'We Are Those Who Own Ourselves': A Political History of Metis Self-Determination in the North-West, 1830–1870." PhD diss., University of Victoria.

—— and D. Leroux. 2017. "White Settler Revisionism and Making Métis Everywhere: The Evocation of Métissage in Quebec and Nova Scotia." *Critical Ethnic Studies* 3, no. 1: 116–42. doi:10.5749/jcritethnstud.3.1.0116.

Goeman, Mishuana. 2015. "Land as Life: Unsettling the Logics of Containment." In *Native Studies Keywords*, edited by S. Teves, A. Smith, and M. Rajeja. Tucson: University of Arizona Press.

HBC Archives, Alexander Morris Fonds, P5284.8.

Hogue, M. 2015. *Métis and the Medicine Line : Creating a Border and Dividing a People.* Chapel Hill: University of North Carolina Press.

Hogue, T. 2017. "Walking Softly with Christi Belcourt." *Canadian Art*, 21 June. https://canadianart.ca/features/walking-softly-with-christi-belcourt/.

Hildebrandt, W., D. First Rider, and S. Carter. 1996. *The True Spirit and Original Intent of Treaty 7.* Montreal and Kingston: McGill-Queen's University Press.

Innes, Robert A. 2013. *Elder Brother and the Law of the People: Contemporary Kinship and Cowessess First Nation.* Winnipeg: University of Manitoba Press.

Lutz, Hartmut. 1991. *Contemporary Challenges: Conversations with Canadian Native Authors.* Saskatoon, SK: Fifth House.

Macdougall, B. 2010. *One of the Family: Métis Culture in Nineteenth-Century Northwestern Saskatchewan.* Vancouver: University of British Columbia Press.

Mount Royal University. 2016. "Indigenous Strategic Plan 2016–2021." http://mtroyal.ca/IndigenousMountRoyal/indigenous-strategic-plan/index.htm.

Nixon, L. 2017. "This Work Is Not for You." *Canadian Art.* https://canadianart.ca/essays/summer-2017-editors-note-lindsay-nixon/.

Nor'Wester. 1862, Jan., p. 1 col. 2.

Potskin, B. 2005. "Brent Potskin Interview—Part 2." Gabriel Dumont Institute. Back to Batoche virtual exhibit. http://www.virtualmuseum.ca/sgc-cms/expositions-exhibitions/batoche/html/resources/videos.php.

Quick, S. 2017. "Red River Jigging: 'Traditional,' 'Contemporary,' and in Unexpected Places." *Canadian Folk Music* 39, nos 2/3. http://www.canfolkmusic.ca/index.php/cfmb/article/viewFile/731/716.

Simpson, L. 2017. *As We Have Always Done : Indigenous Freedom through Radical Resistance.* Minneapolis: University of Minnesota Press.

Teillet, J. 2008. "Understanding the Historic and Contemporary Métis of the Northwest." *Canadian Issues* (Fall): 36–9.

Thistle, J. 2016. "Listening to History: Correcting the Toronto Metis Land Acknowledgement." ActiveHistory.org. http://activehistory.ca/2016/12/listening-to-history-correcting-the-toronto-metis-land-acknowledgement/.

University of Calgary. 2017. "ii' taa'poh'to'p (a place to rejuvenate and re-energize during a journey): Together in a Good Way: A Journey of Transformation and Renewal." https://www.ucalgary.ca/indigenous-strategy/.

Vowel, Chelsea. 2016. "Beyond Territorial Acknowledgements." âpihtawikosisân. http://apihtawikosisan.com/2016/09/beyond-territorial-acknowledgments/.

Wilson, A. 2015. "Our Coming In Stories: Cree Identity, Body Sovereignty and Gender Self-Determination." *Journal of Global Indigeneity* 1, no. 1. https://ro.uow.edu.au/jgi/vol1/iss1/4.

Wolfe, Patrick. 2006. "Settler Colonialism and the Elimination of the Native." *Journal of Genocide Research* 8, no. 4: 387–409.

Chapter 8

Aleiss, Angela. 1991. "'The Vanishing American': Hollywood's Compromise to Indian Reform." *Journal of American Studies* 25, no. 3: 467–72.

———. 1995. "Native Americans: The Surprising Silents." *Cineaste* 21, no. 3: 34–5.

———. 2005. *Making the White Man's Indian: Native Americans and Hollywood Movies*. Westport, CT: Praeger.

Allen, Chadwick. 1999. "Blood (and) Memory." *American Literature: A Journal of Literary History, Criticism and Bibliography* 71, no. 1: 92–116.

———. 2002. *Blood Narrative: Indigenous Identity in American Indian and Maori Literary and Activist Texts*. Durham, NC: Duke University Press.

Anderson, Kim. 2016. *Recognition of Being: Reconstructing Native Womanhood*, 2nd edn. Toronto: Women's Press.

———et al. 2015. "To Arrive Speaking: Voice from the Bidwewidam Indigenous Masculinities Project." In *Indigenous Men and Masculinities: Legacies, Identities, Regeneration*, edited by Kim Anderson and Robert Alexander Innes, 283–308. Winnipeg: University of Manitoba.

Arvin, Maile, Eve Tuck, and Angie Morrill. 2013. "Decolonizing Feminism: Challenging Connections between Settler Colonialism and Heteropatriarchy." *Feminist Formations* 25, no. 1: 8–34.

Bataille, Gretchen M., and Charles L.P. Silet. 1980. *The Pretend Indians: Images of Native Americans in the Movies*. Ames: Iowa State University Press.

———, eds. 1986. *Images of American Indians on Film: An Annotated Bibliography*. New York: Garland Publishing.

Bayers, Peter L. 2016. "Spirituality and the Reclamation of Lakota Masculinity in Chris Eyre's *Skins* (2002)." *American Indian Quarterly* 40, no. 3: 191–215.

Bird, S. Elizabeth, ed. 1996. *Dressing in Feathers: The Construction of the Indian in American Popular Culture*. Boulder, CO: Westview Press.

Boyd, Julia. 2015. "An Examination of Native Americans in Film and the Rise of Native Filmmakers." *Elon Journal of Undergraduate Research in Communications* 6, no. 1 (Spring): 105–13.

Buscombe, Edward. 2006. *"Injuns!" Native Americans in the Movies*. London: Reaktion Books.

Casebier, Allan. 1991. *Film and Phenomenology: Towards a Realist Theory of Cinematic Representation*. Cambridge: Cambridge University Press.

Colorado School of Public Health. 2017. "Healthy Natives Initiative. Northwest New Mexico Fighting Back." Aurora, CO: Centers for American Indian and Alaska Native Health. Colorado School of Public Health, University of Colorado.

Connell, R.W., and James W. Messerschmidt. 2005. "Hegemonic Masculinity: Rethinking the Concept." *Gender Society* 19, no. 6.

Cooms, Jessica. 2006. "Calendar Featuring Navajo Women Hot Seller. Modest Poses May Help Launch Careers for Some." *Arizona Republic*, 12 Oct.

Cummings, Denise K., ed. 2011. *Visualities: Perspectives on Contemporary American Indian Film and Art*. East Lansing: Michigan State University Press.

Denetdale, Jennifer Nez. 2007. *Reclaiming Diné History: The Legacies of Chief Manuelito and Juanita*. Tucson: University of Arizona Press.

———. 2008. "Carving Navajo National Boundaries: Patriotism, Tradition, and the Diné Marriage Act of 2005." *American Quarterly* 60, no. 2: 289–94.

———. 2014. "The Value of Oral History on the Path to Diné/Navajo Sovereignty." In *Diné Perspectives: Revitalizing and Reclaiming Navajo Thought*, edited by Lloyd Lee. Tucson: University of Arizona Press.

———. 2015. "'Drunktown's Finest' Papers Over Border Town Violence and Bigotry." *Indian Country Media Network*, Jan.

Diamond, Neil. 2010. *Reel Injun: On the Trail of the Hollywood Indian*. National Film Board of Canada.

Dowell, Kristin. 2006. "Indigenous Media Gone Global: Strengthening Indigenous Identity On- and Offscreen at the First Nations/First Features Film Showcase." *American Anthropologist* 108, no. 2: 376–84.

Driskill, Qwo-Li, Chris Finley, Brian Joseph Gilley, and Scott Lauria Morgensen, eds. 2011. *Queer Indigenous Studies: Critical Interventions in Theory, Politics and Literature*. Tucson: University of Arizona Press.

Drunktown's Finest. 2014. Directed by Sydney Freeland. Indion Entertainment Group.

Edwards, Jason Morgan. 2014. "Breaking Good: Jeremiah Bitsui's Road to Sundance, via 'Drunktown.'"*Indian Country Today*, 17 Jan.

Flowers, Rachel. 2015. "Refusal to Forgive: Indigenous Women's Love and Rage." *Decolonization: Indigeneity, Education & Society* 4, no. 2: 32–49.

Frisbie, Charlotte Johnson. 1967. *Kinaaldá: A Study of the Navaho Girl's Puberty Ceremony*. Middletown, CT: Wesleyan University Press.

Gatewood, Tara. 2014. "Shifting Views with Drunktown's Finest." *Native Peoples Magazine*, Mar./Apr.

Graver, David. 2015. "'Drunktown's Finest' Director Sydney Freeland on Growing Up Navajo and Trans." *Vice Media*, 23 Feb.

Green, Joyce, ed. 2007. *Making Space for Indigenous Feminisms*. Winnipeg: Fernwood Publishing.

Hearne, Joanna. 2012. *Native Recognition: Indigenous Cinema and the Western.* Albany: State University of New York Press.

Hilger, Michael. 1995. *From Savage to Nobleman: Images of Native Americans in Film.* London: Scarecrow Press.

Hokowhitu, Brendan. 2007. "The Death of Koro Paka: Traditional Māori Patriarchy." *Contemporary Pacific* 20, no. 1: 115–41.

———. 2015. "Taxonomies of Indigeneity: Indigenous Heterosexual Patriarchal Masculinity." In *Indigenous Men and Masculinities: Legacies, Identities, Regeneration*, edited by Kim Anderson and Robert Alexander Innes, 80–98. Winnipeg: University of Manitoba Press.

hooks, bell. 1996. *Reel to Real. Race, Sex and Class at the Movies.* New York: Routledge, 1996.

Howe, LeAnne, and Harvey Markowitz, eds. 2013. *Seeing Red: Hollywood's Pixeled Skins: American Indians and Film.* East Lansing: Michigan State University Press.

Innes, Robert Alexander. 2015. "Moose on the Loose: Indigenous Men, Violence, and the Colonial Excuse." *Aboriginal Policy Studies* 4, no. 1.

———and Kim Anderson. 2015. *Indigenous Men and Masculinities: Legacies, Identities, Regeneration.* Winnipeg: University of Manitoba Press.

Jolly, Margaret, guest ed. 2008. Special Issue of *Contemporary Pacific: Re-membering Oceanic Masculinities* 20, no.2.

Kermoal, Nathalie, and Isabel Altamirano-Jiménez, eds. 2016. *Living on the Land: Indigenous Women's Understanding of Place.* Edmonton: Athabasca University Press.

Kilpatrick, Jacquelyn. 1999. *Celluloid Indians: Native Americans and Film.* Lincoln: University of Nebraska Press.

Lee, Lloyd. 2013. *Diné Masculinities: Conceptualizations and Reflections.* Createspace Independent Publishing Platform.

Leuthold, Steven. 1998. *Indigenous Aesthetics: Native Art, Media, and Identity.* Austin: University of Texas Press.

Lewis, Randolph. 2010. "The New Navajo Cinema: Cinema and Nation in the Indigenous Southwest." *Velvet Light Trap* 66: 50–7.

McDavid, Jodi. 2014. "Drunktown's Finest." dir. Sydney Freeland. *Journal of Religion & Film* 18, no. 1: Article 18.

McKegney, Sam. 2012. "Warriors, Healers, Lovers, and Leaders: Colonial Impositions on Indigenous Male Roles and Responsibilities." In *Canadian Perspectives on Men and Masculinities: An Interdisciplinary Reader*, edited by Jason A. Laker 241–68. Toronto: Oxford University Press.

———. 2014. *Masculindians: Conversations about Indigenous Manhood.* Winnipeg: University of Manitoba Press.

Marsh, Charity. 2011. "'Keepin' It Real'? Masculinity, Indigeneity, and Media Representations of Gangsta Rap in Regina." In *Making It Like a Man: Canadian Masculinities in Practice*, edited by Christine Ramsey. Waterloo, ON: Wilfrid Laurier University Press.

Marubbio, M. Elise. 2006. *Killing the Indian Maiden: Images of Native American Women in Film.* Lexington: University Press of Kentucky.

———and Eric L. Buffalohead. 2012. *Native Americans on Film: Conversations, Teaching, and Theory.* Lexington: University Press of Kentucky.

Mithlo, Nancy. 2011. "Blood Memory and the Arts: Indigenous Genealogies and Imagined Truths." *American Indian Culture and Research Journal* 35, no. 4: 103–18.

Momaday, N. Scott. 1968. *House Made of Dawn.* New York: Harper & Row.

———. 1976. *The Names: A Memoir.* Tucson: University of Arizona Press.

Morgensen, Scott L. 2015. "Cutting to the Roots of Colonial Masculinity." In *Indigenous Men and Masculinities: Legacies, Identities, Regeneration*, edited by Robert Alexander Innes and Kim Anderson, 38–61. Winnipeg: University of Manitoba.

Pavlik, Steve, M. Elise Marubbio, and Tom Holm, eds. 2017. *Native Apparitions: Critical Perspectives on Hollywood's Indians.* Tucson: University of Arizona Press.

Peterson, Leighton C. 2011. "'Reel Navajo': The Linguistic Creation of Indigenous Screen Memories." *American Indian Culture and Research Journal* 35, no. 2: 111–34.

Raheja, Michelle. 2010. *Reservation Reelism: Redfacing, Visual Sovereignty, and Representations of Native Americans in Film.* Lincoln: University of Nebraska Press.

Rollins, Peter C. 1998. *Hollywood's Indian: The Portrayal of the Native American in Film.* Lexington: University Press of Kentucky.

Schweninger, Lee. 2013. *Imagic Moments: Indigenous North American Film.* Athens: University of Georgia Press.

Silversmith, Shondiin. 2013. "A Question of Human Rights: Is It Time to Repeal the Diné Marriage Act?" *Navajo Times Online*, 4 July. https://www.navajotimes.com/news/2013/0713/070413marriage.php.

Simpson, Audra. 2016. "The State Is a Man: Theresa Spence, Loretta Saunders and the Gender of Settler Sovereignty." *Theory & Event* 19, no. 4.

Singer, Beverly. 2001. *Wiping the War Paint off the Lens: Native American Film and Video.* Minneapolis: University of Minnesota Press.

Smith, Andrea. 2006. "Heteropatriarchy and the Three Pillars of Settler Colonialism." In *The Color of Violence: The INCITE! Anthology*, edited by Andrea

Smith, Beth E. Richie, Julia Sudbury, and Janelle White, 66–73. Boston: South End Press.

Solis, Jose. 2014. "An Interview with 'Drunktown's Finest' Writer/Director Sydney Freeland." *Stage Buddy Online.*

Soliz, Cristine. 2008. "*The Searchers* and Navajos: John Ford's Retake on the Hollywood Indian." *Wičazo Ša Review* 23, no. 1: 73–95.

Sujsik, Mark. 2015. "Drunktown's Finest." *RogerEbert .com,* 20 Feb.

Suzack, Cheryl, Shari M. Hundorf, Jeanne Perrault, and Jean Barman, eds. 2010. *Indigenous Women and Feminism: Politics, Activism, Culture.* Vancouver: University of British Columbia Press.

Tatonetti, Lisa. 2015. "'Tales of Burning Love': Female Indigenous Masculinity in Contemporary Native Literature." In *Indigenous Men and Masculinities: Legacies, Identities, Regeneration,* edited by Robert Alexander Innes and Kim Anderson, 130–44. Winnipeg: University of Manitoba Press.

Tengan, Ty P. Káwika. 2008. *Native Men Remade: Gender and Nation in Contemporary Hawaii.* Durham, NC: Duke University Press.

———. 2014. "The Return of Ku? Re-membering Hawaiian Masculinity, Warriorhood, and Nations." In *Performing Indigeneity: Global Histories and Contemporary Experiences,* edited by Laura R. Graham and H. Glenn Penny. Lincoln: University of Nebraska Press.

Toledo-Benalli, Eulynda. 2003. "Kinaaldá: Diné Women Knowledge." PhD diss., University of New Mexico.

Tuyuc, Genesis. 2015. "In NYC, Native American Students Celebrate Indigenous Films, Filmmakers." *Indian Country Media Network Online,* 30 Nov.

Watchman, Casey. 2018. Personal communication, text messages, 16 Sept.

Wissot, Lauren. 2014. "Director Sydney Freeland Discusses *Drunktown's Finest.*" *Filmmaker Magazine online,* 23 Jan.

Werito, Vincent. 2014. "Understanding Hózhǫ́ to Achieve Critical Consciousness: A Contemporary Diné Interpretation of the Philosophical Principles of Hózhǫ́." In *Diné Perspectives: Revitalizing and Reclaiming Navajo Thought,* edited by Lloyd Lee, 25–38. Tucson: University of Arizona Press.

Wright, Andrea. 2016. "'I thought I was like you, but I'm not': Identity, Masculinity and Make-Believe in Taika Waititi's *Boy* (2010)." *Journal of New Zealand & Pacific Studies* 4, no. 2 (Dec.): 153–68.

Zolbrod, Paul. 1987. *Diné Bahane': The Navajo Creation Story.* Albuquerque: University of New Mexico Press.

Chapter 9

Aboriginal Healing Foundation. 2006. *Final Report of the Aboriginal Healing Foundation, vol. 3, Promising Healing Practices in Aboriginal Communities.* Ottawa: Aboriginal Healing Foundation.

Adoption Council of Canada. 2009. "Canada's Waiting Children." www.adoption.ca.

Akee, R., and D. Feir. 2018. "Estimating Institutionalization and Homelessness for Status First Nations in Canada: A Method and Implication." University of Victoria, Department of Economics Discussion Paper.

Allen, S., and K. Daly. 2007. *The Effects of Father Involvement: A Summary of the Research Evidence.* Research review for the Public Health Agency of Canada Population Health Fund Project: Fathers Involvement. Ottawa: Fathers Involvement Initiative.

———, ———, and J. Ball. 2012. "Fathers Make a Difference in Their Children's Lives: A Review of the Research Evidence." In *Father Involvement in Canada: Diversity, Renewal, and Transformation,* edited by Jessica Ball and Kerry Daly. Vancouver: University of British Columbia Press.

Amadahy, Z., and B. Lawrence. 2009. "Indigenous People and Black People in Canada: Settlers or Allies." In *Breaching the Colonial Contract: Anti-Colonialism in the US and Canada,* edited by A. Kempf, 105–36. New York: Springer.

Anaya, James, United Nations Special Rapporteur on the Rights of Indigenous Peoples. 2013. "Statement upon Conclusion of the Visit to Canada." United Nations, 15 Oct. http://unsr.jamesanaya.org/statements/statement-upon-conclusion-of-the-visit-to-canada.

Anderson, Karen. 1991. *Chain Her by One Foot: The Subjugation of Native Women in Seventeenth-Century New France.* New York: Routledge.

Anderson, Kim. 2007. "Giving Life to the People: An Indigenous Ideology of Motherhood." In *Maternal Theory: Essential Readings,* edited by A. O'Reilly, 761–81. Toronto: Demeter Press.

———. 2011. *Life Stages and Native Women: Memory, Teachings and Story Medicine.* Winnipeg: University of Manitoba Press.

———. 2016. *A Recognition of Being: Reconstructing Native Womanhood,* 2nd edn. Toronto: Canadian Scholars' Press.

———, Robert Alexander Innes, and John Swift. 2012. "Indigenous Masculinities: Carrying the Bones of Our Ancestors." In *Canadian Men and Masculinities: Historical and Contemporary Perspectives,* edited by Christopher Greig and Wayne Martino, 266–84. Toronto: Canadian Scholars' Press.

———, Maria Campbell, and Christi Belcourt. 2018. *Keetsahnak: Our Missing and Murdered Indigenous Sisters.* Edmonton: University of Alberta Press.

Arnott, J. 2006. "Dances with Cougar: Learning from Traditional Skills Parenting Programs." In *Until Our Hearts Are on the Ground: Aboriginal Mothering, Oppression, Resistance and Rebirth,* edited by

D.M. Harvard-Lavell and J. Corbiere Lavell, 94–104. Toronto: Demeter Press.

Assembly of First Nations (AFN). n.d. "Fact Sheet: The Reality for First Nations in Canada." www.afn.ca/article.asp?id=764.

——. 1988. *Tradition and Education: Towards a Vision of Our Future*. Ottawa: AFN.

——. 2006a. *Leadership Action Plan on First Nations Child Welfare*. Ottawa: AFN.

——. 2006b. *Royal Commission on Aboriginal Peoples at Ten Years: A Report Card*. Ottawa: AFN.

——. 2013. *Annual Report, 2012–2013*. http://www.afn.ca/uploads/files/afn_annual_report_2012-13_en_final.pdf.

Atleo, E.R. 2004. *Tsawalk: A Nuu-chah-nulth Worldview*. Vancouver: University of British Columbia Press.

Bala, N., et al. 2004. *Canadian Child Welfare Law: Children, Families and the State*. Toronto: Thompson.

Ball, J. 2005. "Early Childhood Care and Development Programs as Hook and Hub for Intersectoral Service Delivery in Indigenous Communities." *Journal of Indigenous Health* 1: 36–49.

——. 2006. "Developmental Monitoring, Screening and Assessment of Indigenous Young Children: Findings of a Community–University Research Partnership." Paper presented at the Indigenous Supported Child Care Conference, Vancouver, Nov.

——. 2008. "Promoting Equity and Dignity for Aboriginal Children in Canada." *IRPP Choices* 14, 7: 1–30.

——. 2009. "Centring Community Services around Early Childhood Care and Development: Promising Practices in Indigenous Communities Canada." *Child Health and Education* 1, 4: 183–206.

——. 2010. "Indigenous Fathers Reconstituting Circles of Care." *American Journal of Community Psychology*, special issue on "Men, Masculinity, Wellness, Health and Social Justice–Community-Based Approaches." doi 10.1007/s10464- 009-9293-1.

——. 2012. Lifeline: Creating Community Service Hubs for Aboriginal Children and Families. Victoria, BC: University of Victoria. www.ecdip.org/mediaresources.

——. 2014. "Improving the Reach of Early Childhood Education for First Nations, Inuit and Métis Children." *Moving Child Care Forward*. www.movingchildcareforward.ca.

——and R.T. George. 2007. "Policies and Practices Affecting Aboriginal Fathers' Involvement with Their Children." In *Aboriginal Policy Research: Moving Forward, Making a Difference*, vol. 3, edited by J.P. White, S. Wingert, D. Beavon, and P. Maxim, 123–44. Toronto: Thompson.

——and K. Moselle. 2007. *Fathers' Contributions to Children's Well-Being*. Research review for the Public Health Agency of Canada Population Health Fund Project: Fathers' Involvement. Ottawa: Fathers' Involvement Initiative.

Bennett, M., and C. Blackstock. 1992. *A Literature Review and Annotated Bibliography Focusing on Aspects of Aboriginal Child Welfare in Canada*. Winnipeg: First Nations Child and Family Caring Society.

Blackstock, C. 2016. "The Complainant: The Canadian Human Rights Case on First Nations Child Welfare." *McGill Law Journal* 62, no. 2: 285–328.

——et al. 2005. *Wen:de: We Are Coming to the Light of Day*. Ottawa: First Nations Child and Family Caring Society of Canada. www.cwrp.ca/sites/default/files/publications/en/ WendeReport.pdf.

——et al. 2006. *Reconciliation in Child Welfare: Touchstones of Hope for Indigenous Children, Youth, and Families*. Ottawa: First Nations Child and Family Caring Society of Canada.

——, with M. Bennett. 2003. *National Children's Alliance: Policy Paper on Aboriginal Children*. Ottawa: First Nations Child and Family Caring Society of Canada.

——, D. Bruyere, and E. Moreau. 2005. "Many Hands, One Dream: Principles for a New Perspective on the Health of First Nations, Inuit and Métis Children and Youth." www.manyhandsonedream.ca.

Brave Heart, M.Y.H. 1998. "The Return to the Sacred Path: Healing the Historic Trauma and Historical Unresolved Grief Response among the Lakota through a Psychoeducational Group Intervention." *Smith College Studies in Social Work* 68, no. 3: 288–305.

Brittain, M., and C. Blackstock. 2015. *First Nations Child Poverty*. Ottawa: First Nations Child and Family Caring Society of Canada.

Brown, J.S.H. 1980. *Strangers in Blood: Fur Trade Company Families in Indian Country*. Vancouver: University of British Columbia Press.

Bourgeois, Robyn. 2018. "Generations of Genocide: The Historical and Sociological Context of Missing and Murdered Indigenous Women and Girls." In *Keetsahnak: Our Missing and Murdered Indigenous Sisters*, edited by Kim Anderson, Maria Campbell, and Christi Belcourt, 65–87. Edmonton: University of Alberta Press.

Cabrera, N. 2016. "Why Do Fathers Matter for Children's Development?" In *Gender and Couple Relationships*, edited by Susan M. McHale, Valerie King, Jennifer Van Hook, and Alan Booth, 161–8. National Symposium on Family Issues Book Series, vol. 6. New York: Springer.

Campbell, Maria. 2008. Personal communication (summer).

Canada Council on Learning. 2007. *State of Learning in Canada: No Time for Complacency*. Report on Learning in Canada 2007. Ottawa: Canada Council on Learning.

Canadian Institute for Health Information (CIHI). 2004. "Aboriginal Peoples' Health." In *Improving the Health of Canadians*, edited by CIHI, 73–102. Ottawa: CIHI.

———. 2013. "Treatment of Preventable Dental Cavities in Preschoolers: A Focus on Day Surgery under General Anesthesia." https://secure.cihi.ca/free_products/ Dental_Caries_Report_en_web.pdf.

Canadian Incidence Study of Reported Child Abuse and Neglect—First Nations Component. 2008. http:// cwrp.ca/fn-cis-2008.

Canadian Institute of Child Health. 2000. *The Health of Canada's Children*, 3rd edn. Ottawa: Canadian Institute of Child Health.

Carter, S. 1997. *Capturing Women: The Manipulation of Cultural Imagery in Canada's Prairie West*. Montreal and Kingston: McGill-Queen's University Press.

Castellano, M. Brant. 2002. *Indigenous Family Trends: Extended Families, Nuclear Families, Families of the Heart*. Ottawa: Vanier Institute of the Family. www .vifamily.ca/library/cft/Indigenous.html.

Claes, R., and D. Clifton. 1998. *Needs and Expectations for Redress of Victims of Abuse at Residential Schools*. Ottawa: Law Commission of Canada.

Congress of Aboriginal Peoples (CAP). 2015. Miykiwan Toolkit for Aboriginal Families Living Off-Reserve. Ottawa: CAP.

Cooke, M., D. Beavon, and M. McHardy. 2004. "Measuring the Well-Being of Aboriginal People: An Application of the United Nations Human Development Index to Registered Indians in Canada, 1981–2001." In *Aboriginal Policy Research: Setting the Agenda for Change*, vol. 1, edited by J.P. White, P. Maxim, and D. Beavon, 47–70. Toronto: Thompson.

de Finney, S. 2015. "Playing Indian and Other Settler Stories: Disrupting Western Narratives of Indigenous Girlhood." *Continuum: Journal of Media and Cultural Studies* 29, no. 2: 169–81.

deLeeuw, S., J. Fiske, and M. Greenwood. 2002. *Rural, Remote and North of 51: Service Provision and Substance Abuse-Related Special Needs in British Columbia's Hinterlands*. Prince George, BC: University of Northern British Columbia Task Force on Substance Abuse.

Deer, S. 2009. "Decolonizing Rape Law: A Native Feminist Synthesis of Safety and Sovereignty." *Wičazo Ša Review* (Fall): 149–67. https://turtletalk.files.wordpress .com/2009/10/deer-decolonizing -rape-law.pdf.

Di Tomasso, L., S. de Finney, S., and K. Grzybowski. 2015. "Honouring Our Caretaking Traditions: A Review of Custom Adoptions." *First Peoples Child & Family Review* 10, no. 1: 19–38.

Dion Stout, M., and G. Kipling. 2003. *Aboriginal People, Resilience and the Residential School Legacy*. Ottawa: Aboriginal Healing Foundation.

Dickason, O.P., with D.T. McNab. 2009. *Canada's First Nations: A History of Founding Peoples*, 4th edn. Toronto: Oxford University Press.

Driskill, Quo-Li, Chris Finley, Brian Joseph Gilley, Scott Lauria Morgensen, eds. 2011. *Queer Indigenous Studies: Critical Interventions in Theory, Politics and Literature*. Tucson: University of Arizona Press, 2011.

Duran, E. 1990. *Transforming the Soul Wound: A Theoretical/Clinical Approach to American Indian Psychology*. Delhi, India: Archana.

Emmerich, L. 1991. "'Right in the Midst of My Own People': Native American Women and the Field Matron Program." *American Indian Quarterly* 15, no. 2: 201–16.

Farris-Manning, C., and M. Zandstra. 2003. "Children in Care in Canada: A Summary of Current Issues and Trends with Recommendations for Future Research." Ottawa: Child Welfare League of Canada. www.cecw-cepb.ca/publications/574.

First Nations and Inuit Regional Health Survey National Steering Committee. 1999. *First Nations and Inuit Regional Health Survey: National Report 1999*. First Nations and Inuit Regional Health Survey National Steering Committee.

First Nations Centre. 2005. "First Nations Regional Longitudinal Health Survey (RHS) 2002/03: Results for Adults, Youth and Children Living in First Nations Communities." www.naho.ca/firstnations/english/ regional_health.php.

First Nations Child and Family Caring Society of Canada. 2005. "A Chance to Make a Difference for This Generation of First Nations Children and Young People: The UNCRC and the Lived Experience of First Nations Children in the Child Welfare System of Canada." Submission to the Standing Senate Committee on Human Rights, 7 Feb.

First Nations Information Governance Centre. 2012. First Nations Regional Health Survey (RHS), 2008/10. *National Report on Adults, Youth and Children Living in First Nations Communities*, Sept. http://www.fnigc .ca/sites/default/files/docs/first_nations_regional_ health_survey_rhs_2008-10__national_report.pdf.

Fournier, S., and E. Crey. 1997. *Stolen from Our Embrace: The Abduction of First Nations Children and the Restoration of Indigenous Communities*. Vancouver: Douglas & McIntyre.

Garner, R., E. Guimond, and S. Senécal. 2013. "The Socio-Economic Characteristics of First Nation Teen Mothers." *International Indigenous Policy Journal* 4, no. 1. https://ir.lib.uwo.ca/iipj/vol4/iss1/9.

Gionet, L., and S. Roshanafshar. 2013. "Select Health Indicators of First Nations People Living Off Reserve, Métis and Inuit." Jan. Catalogue no.82-624-X. http:// www.statcan.gc.ca/pub/82-624-x/2013001/article/ 11763-eng.pdf.

Greenwood, M. 2006. "Children Are a Gift to Us: Aboriginal-Specific Early Childhood Programs and Services in Canada." *Canadian Journal of Native Education* 29, no. 1: 12–28. www.accel-capea.ca/pdf/FinalGreenwood.pdf.

Guimond, E., and N. Robitaille. 2008. "When Teenage Girls Have Children: Trends and Consequences." *Horizons* 10, no. 1: 49–51.

Hall, Rebecca. 2016. "Caring Labours as Decolonizing Resistance." *Studies in Social Justice* 10, no. 2: 220–37.

Health Canada. 2003. *A Statistical Profile on the Health of First Nations in Canada*. Ottawa: Health Canada, First Nations Inuit Health Branch.

———. 2005. "First Nations Comparable Health Indicators." www.hc-sc.gc.ca.

Hunter, Justine. 2018. "Defending the Indigenous Newborns of B.C." Globe and Mail. 9 Mar. https://www.theglobeandmail.com/news/british-columbia/defending-the-indigenous-newborns-of-british-columbia/article38268621/.

Indian and Northern Affairs Canada. 2008. "Early Childhood Development: Programs and Initiatives." www.ainc-inac.gc.ca/hb/sp/ecd/index-eng.asp.

——— and Canada Mortgage and Housing Corporation. 2007. *Aboriginal Demography: Population, Household and Family Projections, 2001–2026*. Ottawa: Indian and Northern Affairs Canada and Canada Mortgage and Housing Corporation.

Inukshuk, Rhoda. 2007. Personal communication (winter).

Innes, Robert Alexander, and Kim Anderson, eds. 2015. *Indigenous Men and Masculinities: Identities, Legacies, Regeneration*. Winnipeg: University of Manitoba Press.

——— 2018. "The Moose in the Room: Indigenous Men and Violence against Women." In *Keetsahnak: Our Missing and Murdered Indigenous Sisters*, edited by K. Anderson, M. Campbell, and C. Belcourt, 175–91. Edmonton, University of Alberta Press.

Jacobs, Margaret. 2007. "Working on the Domestic Frontier: American Indian Domestic Servants in White Women's Households in the San Francisco Bay Area, 1920–1940." *Frontiers: A Journal of Women's Studies* 27, nos. 1–2: 165–99.

———. 2011. *White Mother to a Dark Race: Settler Colonialism, Maternalism and the Removal of Indigenous Children in the American West and Australia*. Lincoln: University of Nebraska Press.

John, E. 2003. Presentation to the Aboriginal Leadership Forum on Early Childhood Development, University of British Columbia, Vancouver, 10–11 Mar.

Lavell-Harvard, D.M., and J. Corbiere Lavell, eds. 2006. *Until Our Hearts Are on the Ground: Aboriginal Mothering, Oppression, Resistance and Rebirth*. Toronto: Demeter.

LeClaire, N., and G. Cardinal. 1998. *Alberta Elders' Cree Dictionary*, edited by E. Waugh. Edmonton: University of Alberta Press.

Link, B.G., and J. Phelan. 1995. "Social Conditions and Fundamental Causes of Disease." *Journal of Health and Social Behaviour* 35: 80–94.

Loppie Reading, C., and F. Wien. 2009. *Health Inequalities, Social Determinants and Life Course Health Issues among Aboriginal Peoples in Canada*. Prince George, BC: National Collaborating Centre for Indigenous Health.

Longman, Nikita. 2018. "End Forced Sterilization of Indigenous Women in Canada." *Washington Post*, 4 Dec.

Macdonald, D., and D. Wilson. 2013. *Poverty or Prosperity: Indigenous Children in Canada*. Ottawa: Canadian Centre for Policy Alternatives, Save the Children Canada. www.policyaltneratives.ca.

Macdougall, Brenda. 2010. *One of the Family: Metis Culture in Nineteenth-Century Northwestern Saskatchewan*. Vancouver: University of British Columbia Press.

McDonald, R.J., and P. Ladd. 2000. *First Nations Child and Family Services Joint National Policy Review: Final Report*. Ottawa: Assembly of First Nations, First Nations Child and Family Service Agency Representatives, and Department of Indian Affairs and Northern Development.

Mashford-Pringle, A. 2012. "Early Learning for Aboriginal Children: Past, Present and Future and an Exploration of the Aboriginal Head Start Urban and Northern Communities Program in Ontario." *First Peoples Child and Family Review* 7, no. 1: 127–40.

Maxwell, Krista. 2014. "Historicizing Historical Trauma Theory: Troubling the Trans-generational Transmission Paradigm." *Transcultural Psychiatry* 51, no. 3: 407–35.

———. 2017. "Settler-Humanitarianism: Healing the Indigenous Child-Victim." *Comparative Studies in Society and History* 59, no. 4: 974–1007.

McKenzie, H., C. Vance, A. Browne, and L. Day. 2016. "Disrupting the Continuities among Residential Schools, the Sixties Scoop, and Child Welfare: An Analysis of Colonial and Neocolonial Discourses." *International Indigenous Policy Journal* 7, no. 2: 1–24.

Miller, J.R. 1996. *Shingwauk's Vision: A History of Native Residential Schools*. Toronto: University of Toronto Press.

Million, Dian. 2013. *Therapeutic Nations: Healing in an Age of Indigenous Human Rights*. Tuscon: University of Arizona Press.

Minister of Indian Affairs and Northern Development. 1997. *Gathering Strength: Canada's Indigenous Action Plan*. Ottawa.

Minister of Public Works and Government Services. 2002. *Aboriginal Head Start in Urban and Northern Communities: Program and Participants 2001*. Ottawa: Minister of Public Works and Government Services.

Mussell, W.J. 2005. *Warrior-Caregivers: Understanding the Challenges and Healing of First Nations Men*. Ottawa: Indigenous Healing Foundation.

Morphy, F. 2007. "Uncontained Subjects: Population and Household in Remote Aboriginal Australia." *Family Matters* 73: 23–31.

National Collaborating Centre for Aboriginal Health. 2016. *Family Is the Focus: Proceedings Summary*. Prince George, BC. https://www.ccnsa-nccah.ca/495/Family_is_the_Focus_-_Proceedings_summary.nccah?id=155.

———. 2017. Indigenous Children and the Child Welfare System in Canada. Prince George, BC. https://www.ccnsa-nccah.ca/docs/health/FS-ChildWelfare Canada-EN.pdf.

National Council of Welfare. 2007. *First Nations, Métis and Inuit Children and Youth: Time to Act*. Ottawa: National Council of Welfare Reports, vol. 127.

National Inquiry on Missing and Murdered Indigenous Women and Girls. 2017. *Interim Report: Our Women and Girls Are Sacred*. Ottawa: Government of Canada.

Native Council of Canada. 1990. *Native Child Care: The Circle of Care*. Ottawa: Native Council of Canada.

Native Women's Association of Canada. 2012. *Good Relations: Supporting Aboriginal Women and Families Who Have Experienced Violence*. Ottawa.

Newhouse, D., and E. Peters, eds. 2003. *Not Strangers in These Parts: Urban Aboriginal Peoples*. Ottawa: Indian and Northern Affairs Canada.

Norris, M.J., and S. Clatworthy. 2006. "Aboriginal Mobility and Migration in Canada: Factors, Policy Implications and Responses." Paper presented at the Second Aboriginal Policy Research Conference, Ottawa, Mar.

Office of the Correctional Investigator. 2013. "Backgrounder: Aboriginal Offenders—A Critical Situation." http://www.oci-bec.gc.ca/cnt/rpt/oth-aut/oth-aut20121022info-eng.aspx.

Office of the Prime Minister of Canada. 2008. "Prime Minister Offers Full Apology on Behalf of Canadians for the Indian Residential Schools." Press release, 11 June. http://pm.gc.ca/eng/media/asp?id2149.

Ontario Federation of Indian Friendship Centres. 2002. "Aboriginal Approaches to Fetal Alcohol Syndrome/Effects."

———. 2014. "Akwe:go Wholistic Longitudinal Study (AWLS): Phase I Baseline Report." Toronto: OFIFC (www.ofifc.org).

Palkovitz, Robert. 2002. "Involved Fathering and Child Development: Advancing Our Understanding of Good Fathering." In *Handbook of Father Involvement: Multidisciplinary Perspectives*, edited by C.S.

Tamis-LeMonda and N. Cabrera, 119–40. New York: Routledge.

Palmater, Pam. 2018. "Indigenous Rights Are Not Conditional on Public Opinion." *Maclean's*, 8 June.

Peers, L., and J.S.H. Brown. 2000. "There is No End to Relationship among the Indians: Ojibwa Families and Kinship in Historical Perspective." *History of the Family* 4, no. 4: 529–55.

Perry, A. 2005. "Metropolitan Knowledge, Colonial Practice, and Indigenous Womanhood: Missions in Nineteenth-Century British Columbia." In *Contact Zones: Aboriginal and Settler Women in Canada's Colonial Past*, edited by K. Pickles and M. Rutherdale, 109–30. Vancouver: University of British Columbia Press.

Preston, J. 2014. "Early Childhood Education and Care for Aboriginal Children in Canada." *Moving Child Care Forward*. www.movingchildcareforward.ca.

———, M. Cottrell, T. Pelletier, and J.V. Pearce. 2012. "Aboriginal Early Childhood Education in Canada: Issues in Context." *Journal of Early Childhood Research* 10, no. 1: 3–18.

Public Health Agency of Canada. 2012. The Impact of the Aboriginal Head Start in Urban and Northern Communities (AHSUNC) on School Readiness Skills: Technical Report. Ottawa.

——— and Canadian Institute for Health Information. 2011. *Obesity in Canada: A Joint Report from the Public Health Agency of Canada and the Canadian Institute for Health Information*. https://secure.cihi.ca/free_products/Obesity_in_canada_2011_en.pdf.

Quinless, J.M. 2013. "First Nations Teenaged Female Lone Parent Families in Canada: Recognizing Family Diversity and the Importance of Networks of Care." *International Indigenous Policy Journal* 4, no. 1. https://ir.lib.uwo.ca/iipj/vol4/iss1/12 DOI: 10.18584/iipj.2013.4.1.12.

Ralstin-Lewis, D. Marie. 2005. "The Continuing Struggle against Genocide: Indian Women and Reproductive Rights." *Wíčazo Ša Review* 20, no. 1: 71–95.

Red Horse, J. 1997. "Traditional American Indian Family Systems." *Family Systems and Health* 15, no. 3: 243–50.

Richmond, C. 2009. "Explaining the Paradox of Health and Social Support among Aboriginal Canadians." *Canadian Issues* (Winter): 65–71.

——— and N.A. Ross. 2008. "Social Support, Material Circumstance and Health Behaviour: Influences on Health in First Nation and Inuit Communities of Canada." *Social Science and Medicine* 67: 1423–33.

——— and C. Cook. 2016. "Creating Conditions for Canadian Aboriginal Health Equity: The Promise of Healthy Public policy." *Public Health Reviews* 37, no. 2: 1–16.

Royal Canadian Mounted Police (RCMP). 2014. *Missing and Murdered Indigenous Women: A National*

Operational Overview. Ottawa: Her Majesty the Queen in Right of Canada.

Royal Commission on Aboriginal Peoples (RCAP). 1996. *Report of the Royal Commission on Aboriginal Peoples*. Ottawa: Canada Communication Group.

Rutherdale, M. 2002. *Women and the White Man's God: Gender and Face in the Canadian Mission Field*. Vancouver: University of British Columbia Press.

Salee, D., with D. Newhouse and C. Levesque. 2006. "Quality of Life of Aboriginal people in Canada: An Analysis of Current Research." *IRPP Choices* 12, no. 6: 1–38.

Sinclair, R. 2016. "The Indigenous Child Removal System in Canada: An Examination of Legal Decision-Making and Racial Bias." *First Peoples Child & Family Review* 11, no. 2: 8–18.

Sinha, V., N. Trocmé, B. Fallon, B. MacLaurin, E. Fast, S. Prokop, et al. 2011. *Kiskisik Awasisak: Remember the Children. Understanding the Overrepresentation of First Nations Children in the Child Welfare System*. Ottawa: Assembly of First Nations. http://cwrp.ca/sites/default/files/publications/en/FNCIS-2008_March2012_RevisedFinal.pdf.

Smylie, J., and P. Adomako. 2009. *Indigenous Children's Health Report: Health Assessment in Action*. Toronto: Centre for Research on Inner City Health. www.crich.ca.

Statistics Canada. 2001. *A Portrait of Aboriginal Children Living in Non-Reserve Areas: Results from the 2001 Aboriginal Peoples Survey*. Catalogue no. 89-597-XIe. Ottawa: Statistics Canada.

———. 2003. *Aboriginal Peoples of Canada: Highlight Tables, 2001 Census*. Ottawa: Statistics Canada.

———. 2006. "Census of Population 2006." www.statcan.gc.ca.

———. 2009. "Selected Findings from 2006 Aboriginal Children's Survey. First Nations People, Métis in Canada, Inuit in Canada." *Canadian Social Trends*, special issue. Catalogue no. 11-008. Ottawa: Statistics Canada.

———. 2011a. *Population Projections by Aboriginal Identity in Canada, 2006–2031*. Catalogue no. 91-552-X. http://www.statcan.gc.ca/pub/91-552-x/ 91-552-x2011001-eng.pdf.

———. 2011b. *The Educational Attainment of Aboriginal Peoples in Canada*. Catalogue no. 99-012-X2011003. http://www12. statcan.gc.ca/nhs-enm/2011/as-sa/99-012-x/99-012-x2011003_3-eng.pdf.

———. 2013. *Aboriginal Peoples in Canada: First Nations People, Métis and Inuit. National Household Survey, 2011*. www12.statcan.gc.ca/nhs-enm/2011/ as-sa/99-011-x/99-011-x2011001-eng.pdf.

———. 2016. "Aboriginal Population Profile, 2016 Census." Ottawa: Statistics Canada. https://www12.statcan.gc.ca/census-recensement/2016/dp-pd/abpopprof/details/page.cfm?Lang=E&Geo1=PR&Code1=01&

Data=Count&SearchText=Canada&SearchType=Begins&B1=All&SEX_ID=1&AGE_ID=2&RESGEO_ID=1.

———. 2017a. "Adult Correctional Statistics in Canada, 2015/2016." (J. Reitano, author). Ottawa: Statistics Canada. https://www150.statcan.gc.ca/n1/pub/85-002-x/2017001/article/14700-eng.htm.

———. 2017b. Aboriginal Head Start in Urban and Northern Communities: Closing the Gap in Health and Education Outcomes for Indigenous Children in Canada. Ottawa. https://www.canada.ca/content/dam/hc-sc/documents/services/publications/healthy-living/aboriginal-head-start/closing-the-gap-fact-sheet-en.pdf.

Stote, Karen. 2015. *An Act of Genocide: Colonization and the Sterilization of Aboriginal Women*. Halifax: Fernwood.

Stremlau, R. 2005. "To Domesticate and Civilize Wild Indians: Allotment and the Campaign to Reform Indian Families, 1875–1887." *Journal of Family History* 30, no. 3: 265–86.

Tait Neufeld, H., and J. Cidro. 2017. *Indigenous Experiences of Pregnancy and Birth*. Toronto: Demeter Press.

Tam, B.Y., L.C. Findlay, and D. Kohen. 2017. "Indigenous Families: Who Do You Call Family?" *Journal of Family Studies* 23, no. 3: 243–59.

Tjepkema, Michael, and Russell Wilkins. 2011. "Remaining Life Expectancy at Age 25 and Probability of Survival to Age 75, by Socio-economic Status and Indigenous Ancestry." *Health Reports* 22, no. 4. Ottawa: Statistics Canada Catalogue no. 82-003-X. http://www.statcan.gc.ca/pub/82-003-x/2011004/article/11560-eng.pdf.

Torpy, Sally J. 2000. "Native American Women and Coerced Sterilization on the Trail of Tears in the 1970s." *American Indian Culture and Research Journal* 24, no. 2: 1–22.

Trocme, N., et al. 2005. *The Experience of First Nations Children Coming into Contact with the Child Welfare System in Canada: The Canadian Incidence Study on Reported Child Abuse and Neglect*. Ottawa: First Nations Child and Family Caring Society.

———et al. 2006. *Mesnmimk Wasatek—Catching a Drop of Light. Understanding the Overrepresentation of First Nations Children in Canada's Child Welfare System*. CIS-2003. http://www.fsin.com/healthandsocial/childportal/images/mesnmimk%20wasatek%20Catching%20a%20Drop%20of%20Light.pdf.

Truth and Reconciliation Commission of Canada (TRC). 2012. *Canada, Aboriginal Peoples and Residential Schools: They Came for the Children*. Ottawa: Government of Canada.

———. 2015. Honouring the Truth, Reconciling for the Future. Final Report. http://www.trc.ca/websites/trcinstitution/File/2015/Honouring_the_Truth_Reconciling_for_the_Future_July_23_2015.pdf.

UNICEF Canada. 2009. *Canadian Supplement to the State of the World's Children 2009: Aboriginal Children's Health: Leaving No Child Behind.* Toronto: UNICEF Canada.

——. 2017. "Ten Years and Four Rulings Later, First Nations Children Still Waiting for Equity." Blog post by Mary Bernstein, 21 June. https://www.unicef.ca/en/category/tags/national-aboriginal-day.

Van Kirk, S. 1980. *Many Tender Ties: Women in Fur-Trade Society in Western Canada, 1670–1870.* Winnipeg: Watson and Dwyer.

Volo, J.M., and D.D. Volo. 2007. *Family Life in Native America.* Westport, CT: Greenwood.

Weitzman, M. 2003. "Low Income and Its Impact on Psychosocial Child Development." In *Encyclopedia on Early Childhood Development,* 1–8. Montreal: Centre of Excellence for Early Childhood Development.

Wemigwans, J., prod. and dir. 2002. *Seven Fires* (feature video). Available from V-tape.org, Toronto.

Wesley-Esquimaux, C.C., and M. Smolewski. 2003. *Historic Trauma and Aboriginal Healing.* Ottawa: Aboriginal Healing Foundation Research Series.

Chapter 10

Aboriginal Justice Implementation Commission. 1999. *Report of the Aboriginal Justice Inquiry of Manitoba.*

Ahluwalia, Seema. 2009. *Supporting Aboriginal Literacy: A Guide for Decolonizing Curricula.* Surrey: Kwantlen Polytechnic University.

Alfred. Taiaiake. 1992. "The People." In *Words That Come Before All Else: Environmental Philosophies of the Haudenosaunee,* edited by Haudenosaunee Environmental Task Force, 8–14. Native North American Travelling College.

——. 2005. *Wasáse: Indigenous Pathways of Action and Freedom.* Toronto: University of Toronto Press.

—— and Jeff Corntassel. 2005. "Being Indigenous: Resurgences against Contemporary Colonialism." *Government and Opposition* 40, 4.

Amnesty International. 2004. *Stolen Sisters: A Human Rights Response to Discrimination and Violence against Indigenous Women in Canada.* Ottawa: Amnesty International.

——. 2013. "Invasive Surveillance of Human Rights Defender Cindy Blackstock." http://www.amnesty.ca/news/news-updates/ invasive-surveillance-of-human-rights-defender-cindy-blackstock.

Anderson, Kim. 2016. *A Recognition of Being: Reconstructing Native Womanhood,* 2nd edn. Toronto: Women's Press.

Ansloos, Jeffrey Paul. 2017. *The Medicine of Peace: Indigenous Youth Decolonizing Healing and Resisting Violence.* Black Point, NS: Fernwood.

Borrows, John. 1997. "Wampum at Niagara: The Royal Proclamation, Canadian Legal History, and Self-Government." In *Aboriginal Treaty Rights in Canada,* edited by Michael Asch, 155–72. Vancouver: University of British Columbia Press.

Boyce, Jillian. 2016. "Victimization of Aboriginal people in Canada, 2014." *Juristat,* 1–44. http://www.statcan.gc.ca/pub/85-002-x/2016001/article/14631-eng.pdf.

Campbell, Colin S., John Cater, and Nahanni Pollard. 2017. *Canadian Policing.* Toronto: Oxford University Press.

Canadian Bar Association Committee on Imprisonment and Release. 1988. *Locking Up Natives in Canada.* Ottawa: Canadian Bar Association.

Cannon, Martin J., and Lina Sunseri. 2011. "Conclusion." In *Racism, Colonialism, and Indigeneity in Canada,* edited by Martin J. Cannon and Lina Sunseri, 263–72. Toronto: Oxford University Press.

Cohen, Stanley. 1985. *Visions of Social Control.* Cambridge: Polity Press.

Comack, Elizabeth. 2012a. *Racialized Policing: Aboriginal People's Encounters with the Police.* Black Point, NS: Fernwood.

Comack, Elizabeth. 2012b. "Reproducing Order: The Policing of Aboriginal Peoples." *Canadian Dimension* 63, no. 3 (May/June). https://canadiandimension.com/articles/view/reproducing-order.

Correctional Services Canada. 2016. "Correctional Service Canada Healing Lodges." http://csc-scc.gc.ca/aboriginal/002003-2000-eng.shtml.

Cummins, Bryan D., and John L. Steckley. 2003. *Aboriginal Policing: A Canadian Perspective.* Toronto: Prentice-Hall.

Dhillon, Jaskiran. 2017. *Prairie Rising: Indigenous Youth, Decolonization, and the Politics of Intervention.* Toronto: University of Toronto Press.

Environics Institute. 2010. *Urban Aboriginal Peoples Study: Main Report.* Toronto: Environics Institute.

Erasmus, Georges. 1996. "Address for the Launch of the *Report of the Royal Commission on Aboriginal Peoples.*" http://www.aadnc-aandc.gc.ca/eng/1100100014639/ 1100100014640.

Fennig, Tamie Helena. 2002. "Sentencing Aboriginal Offenders: Section 718.2(e) of the Criminal Code of Canada and Aboriginal Over-Representation in Canadian Prisons." Master's thesis, Simon Fraser University.

Fleming, Thomas, Subhas Ramcharan, Ken Dowler, and Willem de Lint. 2008. *The Canadian Criminal Justice System,* 2nd edn. Toronto: Pearson Prentice-Hall.

Garland, David. 2001. *The Culture of Control: Crime and Disorder in Contemporary Society.* Chicago: University of Chicago Press.

Gehl, Lynn. 2011. "Indigenous Knowledge, Symbolic Literacy and the 1764 Treaty at Niagara." Federation for the Humanities and Social Sciences. http://www.ideas-idees.ca/blog/indigenous-knowledge-symbolic-literacy-and-1764-treaty-niagara.

Green, Joyce. 2006. "From Stonechild to Social Cohesion: Anti-Racist Challenges for Saskatchewan." *Canadian Journal of Political Science* 39, no. 3: 507–27.

Gunn Allen, Paula. 1992. *The Sacred Hoop: Recovering the Feminine in American Indian Traditions*. Boston: Beacon Press.

Hansen, John G. 2012. "Countering Imperial Justice: The Implications of a Cree Response to Crime." *Indigenous Policy Journal* 23, no. 1: 1–16.

Heckbert, Doug, and Douglas Turkington. 2001. *Turning Points: A Study of the Factors Related to the Successful Reintegration of Aboriginal Offenders*. Ottawa: Correctional Service of Canada.

Hickman, Alexander T., Chief Justice, Associate Chief Justice Lawrence A. Poitras, and the Honourable Mr. Gregory T. Evans, QC. 1989. *Royal Commission on the Donald Marshall, Jr., Prosecution* (Province of Nova Scotia).

Hildebrandt, Walter. 2008. *Views from Fort Battleford: Constructed Visions of an Anglo-Canadian West*. Regina, SK: Canadian Plains Research Centre, University of Regina.

Hunt, Sarah. 2015. "Representing Colonial Violence: Trafficking, Sex Work, and the Violence of Law." *Atlantis* 37.2, no. 1: 25–39.

Irinici, Angelina. 2018. "Complaint Filed against Saskatoon Police Accuses Officers of Conducting a 'Starlight Tour.'" *CTV News*, 24 Apr. https://saskatoon.ctvnews.ca/complaint-filed-against-saskatoon-police-accuses-officers-of-conducting-a-starlight-tour-1.3900740.

Jacobs, Beverley. 2014. "There Has Been a War against Indigenous Women Since Colonization: Former NWAC President." *APTN News*, 23 Sept. http://aptnnews.ca/2014/09/23/war-indigenous-women-since-colonization-former-nwac-president/.

Johnson, Sandy, and Dan Budnik. 1994. *The Book of Elders: The Life Stories & Wisdom of Great American Indians*. New York: HarperCollins.

Jolly, S. 1983. *Warehousing Indians: Fact Sheet on the Disproportionate Imprisonment of Native People in Ontario*. Toronto: Ontario Native Council on Justice.

Kelling, George L., Tony Pate, Duane Dieckman, and Charles E. Brown. 1974. *The Kansas City Preventative Patrol Experiment: A Summary Report*. Washington, DC: Police Foundation.

Kennedy, Mark. 2014. "Stephen Harper Blasted for Remarks on Missing and Murdered Aboriginal Women." *Ottawa Citizen*, 23 Aug. https://ottawacitizen.com/news/national/stephen-harper-blasted-for-remarks-on-missing-and-murdered-aboriginal-women.

LaRocque, Emma. 2002. "Re-examining Culturally Appropriate Models in Criminal Justice Applications." In *Aboriginal and Treaty Rights in Canada*, edited by Michael Asch, 75–96. Vancouver: University of British Columbia Press.

Lavell-Harvard, D. Memee, and Jennifer Brant. 2016. "Introduction: Forever Loved." In *Forever Loved: Exposing the Crisis of Missing and Murdered Indigenous Women and Girls in Canada*, edited by D. Memee Lavell-Harvard and Jennifer Brant, 1–13. Bradford, ON: Demeter Press.

Law Reform Commission of Canada. 1991. *Aboriginal Peoples and Criminal Justice: Report on Aboriginal Peoples and Criminal Justice*. Ottawa: Law Reform Commission of Canada.

Lawrence, Bonita. 2002. "Rewriting Histories of the Land: Colonization and Indigenous Resistance in Canada." In *Race, Space, and the Law. Unmapping a White Settler Society*, edited by Sherene H. Razack, 21–46. Toronto: Between the Lines.

Ling, Justin. 2013. "Snooping Idle No More: When Native Protestors Were Talking Last Year, CSIS Was Paying Close Attention." *Maclean's*. http://www.macleans.ca/news/canada/the-spooks-werent-idle-either.

MacLean, Cameron. 2018. "Jury Finds Raymond Cormier Not Guilty in Death of Tina Fontaine." *CBC News*, 22 Feb. https://cbc.ca/news/canada/manitoba/raymond-cormier-trial-verdict-tina-fontaine-1.4542319.

Martel, Joane, Renée Brassard, and Mylène Jaccoud. 2011. "When Two Worlds Collide: Aboriginal Risk Management in Canadian Corrections." *British Journal of Criminology* 51: 235–55.

Martens, Kathleen. 2018. "National MMIWG Inquiry 'Speeding towards Failure,' Says Latest Lawyer to Resign." *APTN News*, 3 July. http://aptnnews.ca/2018/07/03/national-mmiwg-inquiry-speeding-towards-failure-says-latest-lawyer-to-resign/.

Melnyk, George. 2007/2008. "The Imagined City: Toward a Theory of Urbanity in Canadian Cinema." *Cineaction* 73/74: 20–7.

Monchalin, Lisa. 2016. *The Colonial Problem: An Indigenous Perspective on Crime and Injustice in Canada*. Toronto: University of Toronto Press.

Monchalin, Lisa, and Olga Marques. 2014. "'Canada under Attack from Within': Problematizing 'the Natives,' Governing Borders and the Social Injustice of the Akwesasne Border Dispute." *American Indian Culture and Research Journal* 38, no. 4: 57–84.

Monture, Patricia. 2007. "Race and Erasing: Law and Gender in White Settler Societies." In *Race and Racism in 21st Century Canada*, edited by Sean P. Hier and B. Singh Bolaria, 197–216. Peterborough, ON: Broadview Press.

———. 2011. "The Need for Radical Change in the Canadian Criminal Justice System: Applying a Human Rights Framework." In *Visions of the Heart: Canadian Aboriginal Issues*, 3rd edn, edited by David Long and Olive Patricia Dickason. Toronto: Oxford University Press.

Morito, Bruce. 1999. "The Rule of Law and Aboriginal Rights: The Case of the Chippewas of Nawash." *Canadian Journal of Native Studies* 19, no. 2: 263–88.

Muller, Kathryn V. 2007. "The Two 'Mystery' Belts of Grand River: A Biography of the Two Row Wampum and the Friendship Belt." *American Indian Quarterly* 31, no. 1: 129–64.

Mulligan, Leah, Marsha Axford, and André Solecki. 2016. *Homicide in Canada, 2015.* Ottawa: Canadian Centre for Justice Statistics.

National Inquiry into Missing and Murdered Indigenous Women and Girls. 2018. "National Inquiry into Missing and Murdered Indigenous Women and Girls Remains Independent and Impartial." 4 July. http://mmiwg-ffada.ca/wp-content/uploads/2018/07/National-Inqury-independent-and-impartial.pdf.

Native Women's Association of Canada. 2010. *What Their Stories Tell Us: Research Findings from the Sisters in Spirit Initiative.* Ohsweken, ON: Native Women's Association of Canada.

Nettelbeck, Amanda, and Russell Smandych. 2010. "Policing Indigenous Peoples on Two Colonial Frontiers: Australia's Mounted Police and Canada's North-West Mounted Police." *Australian and New Zealand Journal of Criminology*, 43, no. 2: 356–75.

Neugebauer, Robynne. 1999. "First Nations People and Law Enforcement: Community Perspectives on Police Response." In *Interrogating Social Justice: Politics, Culture and Identity*, edited by Marilyn Corsianos and Kelly Amanda Train, 247–69. Toronto: Canadian Scholars' Press.

NoiseCat, Julian Brave. 2018. "I Am Colten Boushie. Canada Is the All-White Jury That Acquitted His Killer." *The Guardian*, 28 Feb. https://theguardian.com/commentisfree/2018/feb/28/colten-boushie-canada-all-white-jury-acquitted.

Office of the Correctional Investigator. 2012. *Spirit Matters: Aboriginal People and the Corrections and Conditional Release Act.* Ottawa: Office of the Correctional Investigator.

———. 2016. *Annual Report of the Office of the Correctional Investigator 2015–2016.* Ottawa: Her Majesty the Queen in Right of Canada.

———. 2017. *Annual Report of the Office of the Correctional Investigator 2016–2017.* Ottawa: Her Majesty the Queen in Right of Canada.

Palmater, Pamela. 2018. "Why Canada Should Stand Trial for Tina Fontaine's Murder." *Now Toronto*, 25 Feb. https://nowtoronto.com/news/why-canada-should-stand-trial-for-tina-fontaine-murder/.

Paul, Daniel N. 2006. *We Were Not the Savages: Collision between European and Native American Civilizations*, 3rd edn. Black Point, NS: Fernwood.

Pearce, Maryanne. 2013. "An Awkward Silence: Missing and Murdered Vulnerable Women and the Canadian Justice System." PhD diss., University of Ottawa.

Poisson, Jayme. 2018. "Toronto Protestors Demand Justice for Tina Fontaine and Other Indigenous Girls." *Toronto Star*, 3 Mar. https://www.thestar.com/news/gta/2018/03/03/toronto-protesters-demand-justice-for-tina-fontaine-and-other-indigenous-girls.html.

Public Safety Canada. 2017. *Corrections and Conditional Release Statistical Overview: 2016 Annual Report.* Ottawa: Public Works and Government Services Canada

Razack, Sherene. 1994. "What Is to Be Gained by Looking White People in the Eye? Culture, Race, and Gender in Cases of Sexual Violence." *Signs*, 19, no. 4: 894–923.

———. 2015. *Dying from Improvement. Inquests and Inquiries into Indigenous Deaths in Custody.* Toronto: University of Toronto Press.

Reiman, Jeffrey, and Paul Leighton. 2017. *The Rich Get Richer and the Poor Get Prison: Ideology, Class, and Criminal Justice*, 11th edn. New York: Routledge.

Riel-Johns, Jessica. 2016. "Understanding Violence against Indigenous Women and Girls in Canada." In *Forever Loved: Exposing the Crisis of Missing and Murdered Indigenous Women and Girls in Canada*, edited by D. Memee Lavell-Harvard and Jennifer Brant, 34–46. Bradford, ON: Demeter Press.

Royal Canadian Mounted Police (RCMP). 2014. *Missing and Murdered Aboriginal Women: A National Operational Overview.* Ottawa: Her Majesty the Queen in Right of Canada.

Royal Commission on Aboriginal Peoples (RCAP). 1995. *Bridging the Cultural Divide: A Report on Aboriginal People and Criminal Justice in Canada.* Ottawa: Minister of Supply and Services Canada.

Savard, Rémi. 2003. "Les peuples américains et le système judiciaire canadien: Spéléologie d'un trou de mémoire." *Revue Canadienne Droit et Société* 17, no. 2: 123–48.

Simpson, Leanne. 2011. *Dancing on Our Turtle's Back: Stories of Nishnaabeg Re-Creation, Resurgence and a New Emergence.* Winnipeg: ARP Books.

Solicitor General Canada. 1975. *Native Peoples and Justice: Reports on the National Conference and the Federal–Provincial Conference on Native Peoples and the Criminal Justice System, both held in Edmonton, Feb. 3–5, 1975.* Ottawa: Ministry of the Solicitor General, Communication Division.

Solomon, Arthur. 1994. *Eating Bitterness: A Vision beyond the Prison Walls*, edited by C. Kneen and M. Posluns. Toronto: NC Press.

Stark, Heidi Kiiwetinepinesiik. 2016. "Criminal Empire: The Making of the Savage in a Lawless Land." *Theory and Event*, 19, no. 4.

Steckley, John L., and Bryan D. Cummins. 2008. *Full Circle: Canada's First Nations.* Toronto: Pearson Prentice-Hall.

Steinmetz, Kevin F., Brian P. Schaefer, and Howard Henderson. 2017. "Wicked Overseers: American Policing and Colonialism." *Sociology of Race and Ethnicity* 3, no. 1: 68–81.

Story, Rod, and Tolga R. Yalkin. 2013. *Expenditure Analysis of Criminal Justice in Canada.* Ottawa: Office of the Parliamentary Budget Officer.

Tasker, John Paul. 2016. "Confusion Reigns over Number of Missing, Murdered Indigenous Women." *CBC News*, 16 Feb. http://www.cbc.ca/news/politics/ mmiw-4000-hajdu-1.3450237.

Truth and Reconciliation Commission (TRC) of Canada. 2015. *Honouring the Truth, Reconciling for the Future: Summary of the Final Report of the Truth and Reconciliation Commission of Canada.* http://www .myrobust.com/websites/trcinstitution/File/Reports/ Executive_Summary_English_Web.pdf.

Turner, K.B., David Giacopassi, and Margaret Vandiver. 2006. "Ignoring the Past: Coverage of Slavery and Slave Patrols in Criminal Justice Texts." *Journal of Criminal Justice Education* 17, no. 1: 181–95.

Waller, Irvin. 2008. *Less Law, More Order: The Truth about Reducing Crime.* Ancaster, ON: Manor House.

———. 2014. *Smarter Crime Control: A Guide to a Safe Future for Citizens, Communities and Politicians.* Lanham, MD: Rowman & Littlefield.

Wilson, Waziyatawin Angela, and Michael Yellow Bird. 2012. "Introduction: Decolonizing Our Minds and Actions." In *For Indigenous Eyes Only: A Decolonization Handbook,* edited by Waziyatawin Angela Wilson and Michael Yellow Bird, 1–14. Santa Fe, NM: School of American Research Press.

Williams, Robert A. Jr. 1986. "The Algebra of Federal Indian Law: The Hard Trail of Decolonizing and Americanizing the White Man's Jurisprudence." *Wisconsin Law Review*: 219–99.

Wozniak, Kevin H. 2014. "American Public Opinion about Prisons." *Criminal Justice Review* 39, no. 3: 305–24.

Yeung, Lien, and Roshini Nair. 2017. "National Inquiry into Missing and Murdered Indigenous Women and Girls Announces Fall Hearings." *CBC News*, 6 July. http://www.cbc.ca/news/canada/british-columbia/ mmiwg-announcement-1.4192573.

Chapter 11

Anaya, J. 2014. *Report of the Special Rapporteur on the Rights of Indigenous Peoples, James Anaya, on the Situation of Indigenous Peoples in Canada.* Advance unedited version. New York: United Nations Human Rights Council. http://unsr.jamesanaya.org/docs/ countries/ 2014-report-canada-a-hrc-27-52-add-2-en- auversion.pdf.

Agyeman, J., R. Haluza-Delay, C. Peter, and P. O'Riley, eds. 2009. *Speaking for Ourselves: Constructions of Environmental Justice in Canada.* Vancouver: University of British Columbia Press.

Assembly of First Nations (AFN). 1993. "Environment." In Reclaiming Our Nationhood, Strengthening Our Heritage, 39–50. Report to the Royal Commission on Aboriginal Peoples. Ottawa: AFN.

———. 2010. *First Nations Ethics Guide on Research and Aboriginal Traditional Knowledge.* Ottawa: AFN.

Atleo, R. 2004. *Tsawalk: A Nuu-chah-nulth Worldview.* Vancouver: University of British Columbia Press.

Bannister, K., and P. Hardison. 2006. "Mobilizing Traditional Knowledge and Expertise for Decision-Making on Biodiversity." Case study conducted in the framework of the consultative process towards an International Mechanism of Scientific Expertise on Biodiversity (IMoSEB). German Federal Agency for Nature. Conservation. http://www.polisproject.org/node/167.

Bellrichard, Chantelle, and Michelle Ghoussoub. 2019. "14 Arrested as RCMP Break Gate at Gidimt'en Camp Checkpoint Set Up to Stop Pipeline Company Access." *CBC News*, 7 Jan. https://www.cbc.ca/news/indigenous/ rcmp-injunction-gidimten-checkpoint-bc-1.4968391.

Benton-Banai, E. 1988. *The Mishomis Book: The Voice of the Ojibway.* Hayward, WI: Indian Country Communications.

Berneshawi, S. 1997. "Resource Management and the Mi'kmaq Nation." *Canadian Journal of Native Studies* 1: 115–48.

Bocking, S. 2005. "Scientists and Evolving Perceptions of Indigenous Knowledge in Northern Canada." In *Walking a Tightrope: Aboriginal Peoples and Their Representation,* edited by U. Lischke and D. McNab , 215–48. Waterloo, ON: Wilfrid Laurier University Press.

Borrows, J. 2005. *Crown Occupations of Land: A History and Comparison.* Prepared for the Ipperwash Inquiry. Toronto: Office of the Attorney General, Government of Ontario. http://www.attorneygeneral.jus.gov.on.ca/ inquiries/ipperwash/policy_part/research/index.htm.

———. 2010. *Canada's Indigenous Constitution.* Toronto: University of Toronto Press.

———. 2016. *Freedom and Indigenous Constitutionalism.* Toronto: University of Toronto Press.

Bowie, R. 2013. "Indigenous Self-Governance and the Deployment of Knowledge in Collaborative Environmental Management in Canada." *Journal of Canadian Studies* 47, no. 1: 91–256.

Butler, C. 2006. "Historicizing Indigenous Knowledge: Practical and Political Issues." In *Traditional Ecological Knowledge and Natural Resource Management,* edited by C. Menzies, 107–26. Lincoln: University of Nebraska Press.

Canadian Environmental Protection Act. SC 1999. c. 33, s. 3.

Chiefs of Ontario. 2008. *Water Declaration of Anishinabek, Mushkegowuk and Onkwehonwe in Ontario.* Toronto: Chiefs of Ontario. www.coo.org.

Centre for Indigenous Environmental Resources (CIER). 2005. *Environmental Issues Report.* Winnipeg: CIER.

http://www.cier.ca/information-and-resources/
publications-and-products.

Clarkson, L., V. Morrrissette, and G. Regallet. 1992. *Our
Responsibility to the Seventh Generation: Indigenous
Peoples and Sustainable Development*. Winnipeg:
International Institute for Sustainable Development.

Collins, L, D. McGregor, S. Allen, C. Murray, and C.
Metcalfe. 2017. "Source Water Protection Planning
for Ontario First Nations Communities: Case Studies
Identifying Challenges and Outcomes." *Water* 9: 550.
doi:10.3390/w9070550.

Craft, A. 2014. *Anishinaabe Nibi Inaakonigewin
Report: Reflecting the Water Laws Research
Gathering*. Winnipeg: University of Manitoba
Human Rights Research and the Public
Interest Law Centre. http://static1.squarespace
.com/static/54ade7ebe4b07588aa079c94/t/
54ec082ee4b01dbc251c6069/1424754734413/
Anissinaabe-Water-Law.pdf.

Dhillon, C., and M. Young. 2010. "Environmental
Racism and First Nations: A Call for Socially Just
Public Policy Development." *Canadian Journal
of Humanities and Social Science* 1, no. 1: 25–39.
http://cjhss.org/_cjhss/pubData/v_1/i_1/ contents-
Frame.php.

Doyle-Bedwell, P., and F. Cohen. 2001. "Aboriginal People
in Canada: Their Role in Shaping Environmental
Trends in the Twenty First Century." In *Governing
the Environment: Persistent Challenges, Uncertain
Innovations*, edited by E. Parson, 169–206. Toronto:
University of Toronto Press.

Dumont, J. 2006. *Indigenous Intelligence*. Sudbury, ON:
University of Sudbury.

Edgar, L., and J. Graham. 2008. *Environmental Protection:
Challenges and Prospects for First Nations under the
First Nations Land Management Act*. Ottawa: Institute
on Governance. http://iog.ca/sites/iog/files/2008_fn_
land_mgt_act.pdf.

Government of Canada. 2011. "Aboriginal Consultation
and Accommodation: Updated Guidelines for Federal
Officials to Fulfill the Duty to Consult. Ottawa: Minister of Department of Aboriginal Affairs and Northern Development Canada.

Haudenosaunee Environmental Task Force (HETF).
1999. *Words That Come Before All Else: Environmental Philosophies of the Haudenosaunee*. Cornwall
Island, ON: Native North American Travelling
College.

Higgins, C. 1998. "The Role of Traditional Ecological
Knowledge in Managing for Biodiversity." *Forestry
Chronicle* 7, no. 3: 323–6.

Houde, N. 2007. "The Six Faces of Traditional Ecological
Knowledge: Challenges and Opportunities for Canadian Co-Management Arrangements." *Ecology and
Society* 12, no. 2: 34. http://www.ecologyandsociety
.org/vol12/iss2/art34/.

Indigenous Circle of Experts (ICE). 2018. *We Rise Together:
Achieving Pathway to Canada Target 1 through the
Creation of Indigenous Protected and Conserved Areas
in the Spirit and Practice of Reconciliation*. Mar. http://
publications.gc.ca/collections/collection_2018/pc/
R62-548-2018-eng.pdf.

Jacobs, B. 2010. "Environmental Racism on Indigenous
Lands and Territories." http://www.cpsa-acsp.ca/
papers-2010/ Jacobs.pdf.

Johnston, B. 1976. *Ojibway Heritage*. Toronto: McClelland
& Stewart.

Johnston, D. 2006. *Respecting and Protecting the Sacred*.
Research paper, prepared for the Ipperwash Inquiry.
Toronto: Ministry of the Attorney General. http://
www.attorneygeneral.jus.gov.on.ca/inquiries/
ipperwash/policy_part/research/pdf/Johnston_
Respecting-and-Protecting-the-Sacred.pdf.

King, C. 2013. *Balancing Two Worlds: Jean-Baptiste As-
siginak and the Odawa Nation 1768–1866*. Saskatoon,
SK: Cecil King.

LaDuke, W. 1994. "Traditional Ecological Knowledge and
Environmental Futures." *Colorado Journal of International Environmental Law and Policy*: 126–48.

———. 1999. *All Our Relations: Native Struggles for Land
and Life*. Cambridge, MA: South End Press.

Linden, S. 2007. *Report of the Ipperwash Inquiry: Volume
4: Executive Summary*. Toronto: Office of the Attorney
General. http://www.attorneygeneral.jus.gov.on.ca/
inquiries/ipperwash/ index.html.

Lyons, O. 1980. "An Iroquois Perspective." In *American
Indian Environments: Ecological Issues in Native
American History*, edited by C. Vecsey and R. Ven-
ables, 171–4. Syracuse, NY: Syracuse University Press.

McDermott, L., and P. Wilson. 2010. "Ginawaydaganuk:
Algonquin Law on Access and Benefit Sharing." *Policy
Matters* 17: 205–14.

McDonald, M., L. Arragutainaq, and Z. Novalinga. 1997.
*Voices from the Bay: Traditional Ecological Know-
ledge of Inuit and Cree in the Hudson Bay Bioregion*.
Ottawa: Canadian Arctic Resources Committee and
Environmental Committee of the Municipality of
Sanikiluaq.

Mandamin, J. 2003. "Mother Earth Walk: Lake Superior." http://www.mother earthwaterwalk.com/
aboutus.html.

Métis National Council (MNC). 2011. *Métis Traditional
Knowledge*. Ottawa: Métis National Environment Committee. http://www.Métisnation.ca/
wp-content/ uploads/2011/05/Métis-Traditional-
Knowledge.pdf.

Métis Nation of Ontario (MNO). 2012. *Special Impacts
Report: Lands, Resources and Consultations*. Ottawa:

Métis Nation of Ontario. http://www.Métisnation.org/media/354499/ special_impacts_report-screen.pdf.

Menzies, C. 2006. *Traditional Ecological Knowledge and Natural Resource Management*. Lincoln: University of Nebraska Press.

Natcher, D., and S. Davis. 2007. "Rethinking Devolution: Challenges for Aboriginal Resource Management in the Yukon Territory." *Society and Natural Resources* 20, no. 3: 271–9.

O'Connor, D. 2002. "First Nations." Chapter 15 in: *Part Two. Report of the Walkerton Inquiry: A Strategy for Safe Drinking Water*, 485–97. Toronto: Queen's Printer for Ontario.

Oxford On-Line Dictionary."Environment." http://www.oxforddictionaries.com/definition/english/environment.

Qikiqtani Inuit Association. 2007. "Inuit Qaujimajatuqangit." http://www.qia.ca/i18n/english/iq.shtm.

Richmond, C.A.M. 2015. "The Relatedness of People, Land, and Health." In *Determinants of Indigenous People's Health in Canada: Beyond the Social*, 2nd edn, edited by M. Greenwood, S. de Leeuw, and M.M. Lindsay, 47–63. Toronto: Canadian Scholars' Press.

Royal Commission on Aboriginal Peoples (RCAP). 1996. *People to People, Nation to Nation: Highlights from the Report of the Royal Commission on Aboriginal Peoples*. Ottawa: Minister of Supply and Services.

Sable, T., G. Howell, D. Wilson, and P. Penashue. 2006. "The Ashkui Project: Linking Western Science and Environmental Knowledge in Creating a Sustainable Environment." In *Local Science vs. Global Science: Approaches to Indigenous Knowledges in International Development*, edited by P. Sillitoe, 109–27. Oxford, NY: Berghahn Books.

Settee, P. 2000. "The Issue of Biodiversity, Intellectual Property Rights, and Indigenous Rights." In *Expressions in Canadian Native Studies*, edited by R. Laliberte, P. Settee, J. Waldram, R. Innes, B. Macdougall, L. McBain, and F. Barron. Saskatoon, SK: University of Saskatchewan Extension Press.

Spak, S. 2005. "The Position of Indigenous Knowledge in Canadian Co-management Organizations." *Anthropologica* 47, no. 2: 233–46.

Stevenson, M. 2006. "The Possibility of Difference: Rethinking Co-management." *Human Organization* 65, no. 2: 167–80.

Teillet, J. 2005. *The Role of the Natural Resources Regulatory Regime in Aboriginal Rights Disputes in Ontario*. Toronto: Ipperwash Inquiry, Office of the Attorney General.

Truth and Reconciliation Commission of Canada (TRC). 2015. *What We Have Learned: Principles of Truth and Reconciliation*. Winnipeg: TRC. http://www.trc.ca/assets/pdf/Principles%20of%20Truth%20and%20Reconciliation.pdf.

Unamak'ki Institute of Natural Resources. 2011. "Mi'kmaq Sustainable Resources." http://www.uinr.ca.

Victor, W. 2007. "Indigenous Justice: Clearing Space and Place for Indigenous Epistemologies." Research paper. Victoria, BC: First Nations Centre for Governance.

Walken, A. 2007. "The Land Is Dry: Indigenous Peoples, Water, and Environmental Justice." In *Eau Canada: The Future of Canada's Water*, edited by K. Bakker, 303–20. Vancouver: University of British Columbia Press.

White, G. 2006. "Cultures in Collision: Traditional Knowledge and Euro-Canadian Governance Processes in Northern Land-Claim Boards." *Arctic* 59, no. 4: 401–14.

Whyte, K. 2017. "Indigenous Climate Change Studies: Indigenizing Futures, Decolonizing the Anthropocene." *English Language Notes* 55, nos 1–2: 153–62.

Williams, P. 1999. "Creation." In *Words That Come Before All Else: Environmental Philosophies of the Haudenosaunee*, edited by Haudenosaunee Environmental Task Force, 1–7. Cornwall Island, ON: Native North American Travelling College.

Wyatt, S., J. Fortier, and M. Hebert. 2009. "Multiple Forms of Engagement: Classifying Aboriginal Roles in Contemporary Canadian Forestry." In *Changing the Culture of Forestry in Canada: Building Effective Institutions for Aboriginal Engagement in Sustainable Forest Management*, edited by M. Stevenson and D. Natcher, 163–80. Edmonton: CCI Press and Sustainable Forest Management Network.

Chapter 12

Alfred, A. 2004. *Paddling to Where I Stand*. Edited by M.J. Reid; translated by D. Sewid-Smith. Toronto: University of Toronto Press.

Alfred, T. 2017. "It's All about the Land." In *Whose Land Is It Anyway? A Manual for Decolonization*, edited by P. McFarlane and N. Schabus, 10–13. Vancouver: Federation of Post-Secondary Educators of British Columbia.

Archibald, J. 2008. *Indigenous Storywork: Educating the Heart, Mind, Body, and Spirit*. Vancouver: University of British Columbia Press.

———, J. Lundy, C. Reynolds, and L. Williams. 2010. *Accord on Indigenous Education*. Association of Canadian Deans of Education.

Assembly of First Nations (AFN). 1994. *Breaking the Silence: An Interpretive Study of Residential School Impact and Healing as Illustrated by the Stories of First Nations Individuals*. Ottawa: AFN.

———. 2015. "2015 Federal Election Priorities for First Nations and Canada: Closing the Gap." https://www.afn.ca/uploads/files/closing-the-gap.pdf.

Barnhardt, R., and A.O. Kawagley. 2005. "Indigenous Knowledge Systems and Alaska Native Ways of

Knowing." *Anthropology and Education Quarterly* 36, no. 1: 8–23.

Battiste, M. 2000. *Reclaiming Indigenous Voice and Vision*. Vancouver: University of British Columbia Press.

———. 2002. *Indigenous Knowledge and Pedagogy in First Nations Education: A Literature Review with Recommendations*. Ottawa: National Working Group on Education, Indian Affairs and Northern Development Canada.

———. 2005. "Indigenous Knowledge: Foundations for First Nations." *World Indigenous Nations Higher Education Consortium Journal*. www.win-hec.org/docs/pdfs/Journal/Marie%20Battiste %copy.pdf.

———. 2013. *Decolonizing Education: Nourishing the Learning Spirit*. Saskatoon, SK: Purich Publishing.

Blair, H., L. Pelly, and R. Starr. 2018. "Connecting Indigenous Languages and Policy, Programs, and Practices." In *Promising Practices in Indigenous Teacher Education*, edited by P. Whitinui, M. Rodriguez de France, and O. McIvor, 119–30. Singapore: Springer.

Cajete, G. 2000. *Look to the Mountain: An Ecology of Indigenous Education*. Durango, CO: Kivaki Press.

Canadian Association of University Teachers (CAUT). 2017. *Guide to Acknowledging First Peoples and Traditional Territory*. Ottawa: CAUT. https://www.caut.ca/sites/default/files/caut-guide-to-acknowledging-first-peoples-and-traditional-territory-2017-09.pdf.

Colleges and Institutes Canada. 2014. "Indigenous Protocol for Colleges and Institutes." http://www.collegesinstitutes.ca/the-issues/indigenous-learners/approaches-and-exemplary-practices-to-guide-implementation/.

Corntassel, J., and T. Chah-win-is. 2009. "Indigenous Storytelling, Truth-Telling, and Community Approaches to Reconciliation." *English Studies in Canada* 35, no. 1: 137–59.

Davin, N.F. 1879. *Report on Industrial Schools for Indians and Half-Breeds*. Ottawa.

Dickason, O.P. 1984. *The Myth of the Savage and the Beginnings of French Colonialism in the Americas*. Edmonton: University of Alberta Press.

——— and W. Newbigging. 2015. *A Concise History of Canada's First Nations*, 3rd edn. Toronto: Oxford University Press.

Ermine, W. 2000. "Aboriginal Epistemology: In *First Nation Education in Canada: The Circle Unfolds*, edited by M. Battiste and J. Barman, 101–11. Vancouver: University of British Columbia Press.

Furniss, E. 1995. *Victims of Benevolence: The Dark Legacy of Williams Lake Residential School*. Vancouver: Arsenal Pulp Press.

Glavin, T. 2002. *Among God's Own: The Enduring Legacy of St. Mary's Mission*. Vancouver: New Star Books.

Grant, A. 2004. *Finding My Talk: How Fourteen Women Reclaimed Their Lives after Residential School*. Calgary: Fifth House.

Haig-Brown, C. 1988. *Resistance and Renewal: Surviving the Indian Residential School*. Vancouver: Tillicum Library.

Hare, J. 2003. "September 11 and Its Aftermath: A Roundtable. Is the Bingo Palace Burning?" *Journal of Women in Culture and Society* 29, no. 2: 589–91.

———. 2005. "To Know Papers: Aboriginal Perspectives on Literacy." In *Portraits of Literacy across Families, Communities and Schools: Tensions and Intersections*, edited by J. Anderson, M. Kendrick, T. Rogers, and S. Smythe, 243–63. Mahwah, NJ: Lawrence Erlbaum.

———. 2007. "Aboriginal Education Policy in Canada: Building Capacity for Change and Control." In *Multicultural Education Policies in Canada and the United States*, edited by R. Joshee and L. Johnson, 51–68. Seattle: University of Washington Press/University of British Columbia Press.

———. 2011. "Learning from Indigenous Knowledge in Education." In *Visions of the Heart: Canadian Aboriginal Issues*, 3rd edn, edited by D. Long and O.P. Dickason, 90–112. Toronto: Oxford University Press.

——— and J. Barman. 2000. "Aboriginal Education: Is There a Way Ahead?" In *Visions of the Heart: Canadian Aboriginal Issues*, 2nd edn, edited by D. Long and O.P. Dickason, 331–59. Toronto: Harcourt Brace.

——— and ———. 2007. *Good Intentions Gone Awry: Emma Crosby and the Methodist Mission on the Northwest Coast*. Vancouver: University of British Columbia Press.

Harper, S. 2008. "Prime Minister Stephen Harper's Statement of Apology." http://www.cbc.ca/news/canada/prime-minister-stephen-harper-s-statement-of-apology-1.734250.

Hermes, M. 2007. "Moving toward the Language: Reflections on Teaching in an Indigenous Immersion School." *Journal of American Indian Education* 46, no. 3: 54–71.

Indian Chiefs of Alberta. 1970. *Citizens Plus*. Edmonton: Indian Association of Alberta.

Ing, N.R. 1991. "The Effects of Residential Schools on Native Child-rearing Practices." *Canadian Journal of Native Education* 18: 65–118.

Jaine, L., ed. 1993. *Residential Schools: The Stolen Years*. Saskatoon, SK: University Extension Press, University of Saskatchewan.

Justice, Daniel Heath. 2018. *Why Indigenous Literatures Matter*. Waterloo, ON: Wilfrid Laurier University Press.

Knockwood, I. 1992. *Out of the Depths: The Experiences of the Mi'kmaw Children of the Indian Residential School at Shubenacadie, Nova Scotia*. Lockeport, NS: Roseway.

Kulchyski, P., D. McCaskill, and D. Newhouse, eds. 1999. *In the Words of Elders: Aboriginal Cultures in Transition.* Toronto: University of Toronto Press.

Logan, T. 2012. "A Métis Perspective on Truth and Reconciliation: Reflections of a Métis Researcher." http://speakingmytruth.ca/downloads/AHFvol1/06_Logan.pdf.

McCarty, T. 2003. "Revitalising Indigenous Languages in Homogenising Times." *Comparative Education* 39, no. 2: 147–63.

McIvor, O. 2009. "Strategies for Indigenous Language Revitalization and Maintenance." http://literacyencyclopedia.ca/ index.php?fa=items.show&topicId=265.

———, T. Rosborough, C. McGregor, and A. Marinakis. 2018. "Lighting a Fire: Community-Based Delivery of a University Indigenous-Language Teacher Education Program." In *Promising Practices in Indigenous Teacher Education,* edited by P. Whitinui, M. Rodriguez de France, and O. McIvor, 189–203. Singapore: Springer.

Macoun, A. 2016. "Colonising White Innocence: Complicity and Critical Encounters." In *The Limits of Settler Colonial Reconciliation,* edited by S. Maddison, T. Clark, and R. de Costa, 85-102. Singapore: Springer.

Miller, J.R. 1996. *Shingwauk's Vision: A History of Native Residential Schools.* Toronto: University of Toronto Press.

Milloy, J.S. 1999. *A National Crime: The Canadian Government and the Residential School System, 1879–1986.* Winnipeg: University of Manitoba Press.

National Indian Brotherhood (NIB). 1972. *Indian Control of Indian Education.* Ottawa: NIB.

Nunavut Department of Education. 2007. *Inuit Qaujimajatuqangit: Education Framework for Nunavut Curriculum.* Iqaluit, NU: Nunavut Department of Education, Curriculum and School Services Division.

Nuu-chah-nulth Tribal Council. 1996. *Indian Residential Schools: The Nuu-chah-nulth Experience: Report of the Nuu-chah-nulth Tribal Council Indian Residential School Study, 1992–1994.* Port Alberni, BC: Nuu-chah-nulth Tribal Council.

Preston, J.P., M. Cottrell, T. Pelletier, and J.V. Pearce. 2012. "Aboriginal Early Childhood Education in Canada: Issues of Context." *Journal of Early Childhood Research* 10, no. 3: 3–18.

Public Health Agency of Canada. 2012. "Evaluation of the Aboriginal Headstart in Northern Communities Program at the Public Health Agency of Canada." http://www.phac-aspc.gc.ca/about_apropos/evaluation/reports-rapports/2011-2012/ahsunc-papacun/index-eng.php#toc.

Reconciliation Canada. n.d. "Our Story." http://reconciliationcanada.ca/about/history-and-background/our-story/.

Royal Commission on Aboriginal Peoples (RCAP). 1996. *Report of the Royal Commission on Aboriginal Peoples,* vol. 1, *Looking Forward, Looking Back.* Ottawa: Minister of Supply and Services Canada.

Reyhner, J., O. Trujilio, R. Carrasco, and L. Lockard, eds. 2003. *Nurturing Native Languages.* Flagstaff, AZ: Northern Arizona University.

Scully, A. 2015. "Unsettling Place-Based Education: Whiteness and Land in Indigenous Education in Canadian Teacher Education." *Canadian Journal of Native Education* 38, no. 1: 80–100.

Secwepemc Cultural Education Society. 2000. *Behind Closed Doors. Stories from the Kamloops Indian Residential School.* Kamloops, BC: Secwepemc Cultural Education Society.

Shirley, V.J. 2017. "Indigenous Social Justice Pedagogy: Teaching into the Risks and Cultivating the Heart." *Critical Questions in Education* 8, no. 2: 163–77.

Simpson, L.B. 2014. "Land as Pedagogy: Nishnaabeg Intelligence and Rebellious Transformation." *Decolonization: Indigeneity, Education, & Society* 3, no. 3: 1–25.

Statistics Canada. 2018. *First Nations People, Métis, and Inuit in Canada: Diverse and Growing Populations.* Ottawa: Minister of Industry. https://www150.statcan.gc.ca/n1/en/pub/89-659-x/89-659-x2018001-eng.pdf?st=3wPYGNXs.

——— and Council of Ministers of Education. 2006. *Education Indicators in Canada: Report of the Pan-Canadian Education Indicators Program 1999.* Ottawa: Statistics Canada.

Task Force on Aboriginal Languages and Cultures. 2005. *Towards a New Beginning: A Foundational Report for a Strategy to Revitalize First Nation, Inuit, and Métis Languages and Cultures.* Ottawa: Canadian Heritage, Aboriginal Affairs.

Teacher Education Office, University of British Columbia. n.d. "NITEP—The Indigenous Teacher Education Program." http://teach.educ.ubc.ca/bachelor-of-education-program/nitep.

Truth and Reconciliation Commission of Canada (TRC). 2015. *The Survivors Speak: A Report of the Truth and Reconciliation Commission of Canada.* Winnipeg: TRC. http://www.trc.ca/assets/pdf/Survivors_Speak_English_Web.pdf.

United Nations. 2007. *United Nations Declaration on the Rights of Indigenous Peoples.* http://www.un.org/esa/socdev/unpfii/documents/DRIPS_en.pdf.

———. 2010. *Office of the Special Adviser on the Prevention of Genocide.* http://www.un.org/ar/preventgenocide/adviser/pdf/osapg_booklet_eng.pdf.

Universities Canada. 2016. "Resources on Canada's Universities and Reconciliation." Oct.

Usborne, E., J. Peck, D. Smith, and D. Taylor. 2011. "Learning through an Aboriginal Language: The Impact on Students' English and Aboriginal Language Skills." *Canadian Journal of Education* 34, no. 4: 200–15.

Widdowson, F. 2016. "Indigenizing the University and Political Science: Exploring the Implications for the Discipline." Paper presented at the annual meeting of the Canadian Political Science Association, University of Calgary, May. https://cpsa-acsp.ca/documents/conference/2016/Widdowson.pdf.

Chapter 13

Borrows, John. 2016. *Freedom and Indigenous Constitutionalism.* Toronto: University of Toronto Press.

HBC Heritage. 2016. "York Factory." http://www.hbcheritage.ca/places/forts-posts/york-factory.

Kino-nda-niimi Collective. 2014. *The Winter We Danced: Voices from the Past, the Future, and the Idle No More Movement.* Winnipeg: ARP Books.

Sayisi Dene First Nation Relocation Settlement Trust. n.d. "Sayisi Dene First Nation History." http://sdfntrust.ca/history/.

Simpson, Leanne. 2017. *As We Have Always Done: Indigenous Freedom through Radical Resistance.* Minneapolis: University of Minnesota Press.

Starblanket, Gina, and Heidi K. Stark. 2018. "Towards a Relational Paradigm—Four Points for Consideration: Knowledge, Gender, Land, and Modernity." In *Resurgence and Reconciliation: Indigenous–Settler Relations and Earth Teachings,* edited by Michael Asch, John Borrows, and James Tully, 175–208. Toronto: University of Toronto Press.

Tuck, Eve, Marcia McKenzie, and Kate McCoy. 2014. "Land Education: Rethinking Pedagogies of Place from Indigenous, Post-Colonial, and Decolonizing Perspectives on Place and Environmental Education Research." *Environmental Education Research* 20, no. 1: 1–23.

Chapter 14

Amnesty International. 2004. *Stolen Sisters.* https://www.amnesty.ca/sites/amnesty/files/amr200032004enstolensisters.pdf.

———. 2009. *No More Stolen Sisters: The Need for a Comprehensive Response to Discrimination and Violence against Indigenous Women in Canada.* Sept.

———. 2014. "Violence against Indigenous Women and Girls in Canada: A Summary of Amnesty International's Concerns and Calls to Action." Feb. https://www.amnesty.ca/sites/amnesty/files/iwfa_submission_amnesty_international_february_2014_-_final.

Armstrong, Jane. 2016. "Supreme Court to Hear Ktunaxa Nation Opposition to Jumbo Ski Resort." *CBC News,* 17 Mar. http://www.cbc.ca/news/canada/british-columbia/jumbo-ktunaxa-nation-supreme-court-of-canada-1.3495494.

Benjamin, Craig. 2014. "Free, Prior and Informed Consent: Defending Indigenous Rights in the Global Rush for Resources." In *Indivisible: Indigenous Human Rights,* edited by J. Green, 168–93. Halifax: Fernwood.

Borrows, John. 2016. "Legislation and Indigenous Self-Determination in Canada and the United States." In *From Recognition to Reconciliation: Essays on the Constitutional Entrenchment of Aboriginal and Treaty Rights,* edited by Patrick Macklem and Douglas Sanderson, 474–505. Toronto: University of Toronto Press.

Brodsky, Gwen. 2014. "McIvor v. Canada: Legislated Patriarchy Meets Aboriginal Women's Equality Rights." In *Indivisible: Indigenous Human Rights,* edited by J. Green, 100–25. Halifax: Fernwood.

Castellano, Marlene Brandt, Linda Archibald, and Mike DeGagne. 2008. "Conclusion: The Journey." In *From Truth to Reconciliation: Transforming the Legacy of Residential Schools,* edited by Marlene Brandt Castellano, Linda Archibald, and Mike DeGagne, 403–10. Ottawa: Aboriginal Healing Foundation.

Chambers, Cynthia M., and Narcisse J. Blood. 2009. "Love Thy Neighbour: Repatriating Precarious Blackfoot Sites." *International Journal of Canadian Studies* 39–40: 253–79.

Coburn, Veldon. 2016. Private conversation, 26 Sept.

Comack, Elizabeth. 2014. "Colonialism Past and Present: Indigenous Human Rights and Canadian Policing." In *Indivisible: Indigenous Human Rights,* edited by J. Green, 60–82. Halifax: Fernwood.

Coulthard, Glen Sean. 2014. *Red Skin, White Masks: Rejecting the Colonial Politics of Recognition.* Minneapolis: University of Minnesota Press.

Daschuk, James. 2013. *Clearing the Plains: Disease, Politics of Starvation, and the Loss of Aboriginal Life.* Regina, SK: University of Regina Press.

Eberts, Mary. 2014. "Victoria's Secret: How to Make a Population of Prey." In *Indivisible: Indigenous Human Rights,* edited by J. Green, 126–43. Halifax: Fernwood.

———. 2017. "Being an Indigenous Woman Is a 'High-Risk Lifestyle'." In *Making Space for Indigenous Feminism,* 2nd edn, edited by J. Green, 69–102. Halifax: Fernwood.

Green, Joyce. 1995. "Towards a Detente with History: Confronting Canada's Colonial Legacy." *International Journal of Canadian Studies* 12 (Fall): 85–105.

———. 2014. "From Colonialism to Reconciliation through Indigenous Human Rights." In *Indivisible: Indigenous Human Rights,* edited by J. Green, 18–42. Halifax: Fernwood.

——— and Michael Burton. 2013. "A Twelve-Step Program for a Post-Colonial Future." *Canadian Dimension* (Dec.).

——— and Gina Starblanket. 2018. "Recognition of Rights Framework Risks Terminating Rights for Indigenous Peoples." *Regina Leader-Post,* 7 Aug. https://leaderpost.com/opinion/columnists/recognition-of-rights-framework-risks-terminating-rights-for-indigenous-people.

Grey, Sam, and Alison James. 2016. "Truth, Reconciliation, and 'Double Settler Denial': Gendering the Canada–South Africa Analogy." *Human Rights Review* 17: 303–28.

James, Matt. 2012. "A Carnival of Truth? Knowledge, Ignorance and the Canadian Truth and Reconciliation Commission." *International Journal of Transitional Justice* 6, no. 2: 182–204.

Joffe, Paul. 2014. "Undermining Indigenous Peoples' Security and Human Rights: Strategies of the Canadian Government." In *Indivisible: Indigenous Human Rights*, edited by J. Green, 217–43. Halifax: Fernwood.

Justice, Daniel Heath. 2004. "Seeing (and Reading) Red: Indian Outlaws in the Ivory Tower." In *Indigenizing the Academy: Transforming Scholarship and Empowering Communities*, edited by Devon Abbott Mihesuah and Angela Cavender Wilson, 100–23. Lincoln: University of Nebraska Press.

Kirkup, Kristy. 2015. "Inquiry into Missing and Murdered Aboriginal Women to Begin within Two Weeks: Minister." *Global News*, 10 Nov. http://globalnews.ca/news/2329813/inquiry-into-missing-and-murdered-aboriginal-women-to-begin-within-two-weeks-minister/.

Ktunaxa Nation v. British Columbia (Forests, Lands and Natural Resource Operations). 2015 BCCA 352: http://www.canlii.org/en/bc/bcca/doc/2015/2015bcca352/2015bcca352.pdf; 2017 SCC (2 SCR 386): https://scc-csc.lexum.com/scc-csc/scc-csc/en/item/16816/index.do.

Ktunaxa Nation Council and Kathryn Teneese, on their own behalf and on behalf of all citizens of the Ktunaxa Nation v. Minister of Forests, Lands and Natural Resource Operations et al. Supreme Court of Canada 2017. http://www.scc-csc.ca/case-dossier/info/sum-som-eng.aspx?cas=36664.

Kuokkanen, Rauna. 2007. *Reshaping the University.* Vancouver: University of British Columbia Press.

Logan, Tricia E. 2014. "Memory, Erasure, and National Myth." In *Colonial Genocide in Indigenous North America*, edited by Andrew Woolford, Jeff Benvenuto, and Alexander Laban Hinton, 149–65. Durham, NC: Duke University Press

MacDonald, David B. 2014. "Genocide in the Indian Residential Schools." In *Colonial Genocide in Indigenous North America*, edited by Andrew Woolford, Jeff Benvenuto, and Alexander Laban Hinton, 306–24. Durham, NC: Duke University Press.

Mandel, Charles. 2015. "Justice Minister Jody Wilson-Raybould's Big Plans for Canadian Law." *National Observer*, 10 Nov. http://www.nationalobserver.com/2015/11/10/news/jody-wilson-rayboulds-steady-rise-top-job-justice.

Native Women's Association of Canada (NWAC). 2010. "Culturally Relevant Gender Based Models of Reconciliation." Ottawa: NWAC.

Patzer, Jeremy. 2014. "Residential School Harm and Colonial Dispossession: What's the Connection?" In *Colonial Genocide in Indigenous North America*, edited by Andrew Woolford, Jeff Benvenuto, and Alexander Laban Hinton, 168–85. Durham, NC: Duke University Press.

Royal Commission on Aboriginal Peoples. 1996. *Gathering Strength*. Ottawa: Government of Canada.

Savage, Candace. 2012. *A Geography of Blood: Unearthing Memory from a Prairie Landscape*. Vancouver: Greystone Books and the David Suzuki Foundation.

Schaap, Andrew. 2006. "Agonism in Divided Societies." *Philosophy & Social Criticism* 32, no. 2: 255–77.

———. 2008. "Reconciliation as Ideology and Politics." *Constellations* 15, no. 2: 249–64.

Smith, Linda Tuhiwai. 1999. *Decolonizing Methodologies: Research and Indigenous Peoples*. Dunedin, NZ: Otago University Press.

Snelgrove, Corey, Rita Kaur Dhamoon, and Jeff Corntassel. 2014. "Unsettling Settler Colonialism: The Discourse and Politics of Settlers, and Solidarity with Indigenous Nations." *Decolonization: Indigeneity, Education & Society* 3, no. 2: 1–32.

Starblanket, Gina. 2017. "Being Indigenous Feminists: Resurgences against Contemporary Patriarchy." In *Making Space for Indigenous Feminism*, 2nd edn, edited by J. Green. Halifax: Fernwood.

Stewart-Harawira, Makere. 2013. *The New Imperial Order: Indigenous Responses to Globalization*. London: Zed Books.

Supreme Court of Canada. *Daniels v. Canada (Indian Affairs and Northern Development)*. 2016. https://scc-csc.lexum.com/scc-csc/scc-csc/en/item/15858/index.do.

Thobani, Sunera. 2007. *Exalted Subjects: Studies in the Making of Race and Nation in Canada*. Toronto: University of Toronto Press.

Titley, Brian. 1986. *A Narrow Vision: Duncan Campbell Scott and the Administration of Indian Affairs in Canada*. Vancouver: University of British Columbia Press.

Trudeau, Justin. 2018. "Government of Canada to Create Recognition and Implementation of Rights Framework." https://pm.gc.ca/eng/news/2018/02/14/government-canada-create-recognition-and-implementation-rights-framework.

Truth and Reconciliation Commission of Canada (TRC). 2015. *Honouring the Truth, Reconciling for the Future: Summary of the Final Report of the Truth and Reconciliation Commission of Canada*. Ottawa: Government of Canada. http://www.trc.ca/assets/pdf/Honouring_the_Truth_Reconciling_for_the_Future_July_23_2015.pdf.

Veracini, Lorenzo. 2010. *Settler Colonialism: A Theoretical Overview.* London: Palgrave Macmillan.

Wadsworth, Nancy D. 2014. "Unsettling Lessons: Teaching Indigenous Politics and Settler Colonialism in Political Science." *PS: Political Science and Politics* 47, no. 3: 692–7.

Woolford, Andrew, Jeff Benvenuto, and Alexander Laban Hinton. 2014. "Introduction." In *Colonial Genocide in Indigenous North America*, edited by Andrew Woolford, Jeff Benvenuto, and Alexander Laban Hinton, 1–25. Durham, NC: Duke University Press.

Index